Meanwhile, Next Door to the Good Life

By Jean Hay Bright

Copyright 2003, Jean Hay Bright.

All rights reserved. No part of this book may be reproduced or transmitted in any form or by any means, electronic or mechanical, including photocopying, recording, or by any information storage and retrieval system, without permission in writing from the publisher, except for the inclusion of brief quotations in a review.

Cover design by Chameleon Illustration, Inc.
Cover illustration by Samantha C. S. Jones,
    Front cover photo by Jean Hay Bright
    Back cover photo by David N. Walsh

Printed in the United States of America
by King Printing, Lowell, Massachusetts

First printing September 2003

Library of Congress Control Number: 2003092457

ISBN 0-9720924-1-2

Other books by the author

Proud to Be a Card-Carrying, Flag-Waving, Patriotic
    American Liberal   (1996) ISBN 0-9657759-0-9

A Tale of Dirty Tricks So Bizarre:
    Susan Collins v. Public Record   (2002) ISBN 0-9720924-0-4

BrightBerry Press
**4262 Kennebec Road
Dixmont, Maine, USA 04932
(207) 234-4225
www.brightberrypress.com**

Meanwhile, Next Door to the Good Life

By Jean Hay Bright

BrightBerry Press
Dixmont, Maine, USA

To Mom
Olga Alice (Bodnar) Hay
also known as
Mrs. Joseph C. Hay Jr.

who prompted my letters —
and who saved them
and gave them back to me

Acknowledgements

I thank the Good Life Center in Harborside, Maine, for granting permission to use excerpts from books written by Helen and Scott Nearing, including, but not limited to:

Living the Good Life   *Continuing the Good Life*
Loving and Leaving the Good Life   *Making of a Radical*
Simple Food for the Good Life   *Our Home Made of Stone*

I further thank the Good Life Center for granting permission to use excerpts from the various records, papers and letters of Helen and Scott Nearing, whether located at Forest Farm in Harborside, Maine, at the Thoreau Institute in Concord, Massachusetts, or at the University of Vermont in Burlington. I would specifically like to thank the University of Vermont for allowing access to letters written by Helen and Scott Nearing to their old friends Hank and Ada Mayer. Those letters, spanning four decades, were donated by the Mayers to the University of Vermont and can be found in its Special Collections, Bailey Howe Library division, in Burlington, Vermont.

I also thank the ***Bangor Daily News, Penobscot Bay Press (Weekly Packet), the Ellsworth American, Yankee Magazine, Maine Times, Boston Globe, The New York Times,*** and ***Mother Earth News*** for granting permission for us to reprint various articles or portions of articles from those publications.

I was unable to locate Jackie Breen or to source the newspaper clipping found among Helen's papers with the penciled date of August 30, 1983. We also attempted, but were unable, to get permission to reprint the 1941 feature on Helen Knothe Nearing written by Clementine Paddleford that appeared in the ***New York Herald*** because that publication is now defunct. I would like to think both authors would approve of our resurrecting their stories here.

Thanks too, to the woman I knew as Susie Coleman (who has since remarried) for allowing me to reprint her poem about Heidi. And likewise to Sara Christy for the text of her poem about Stan.

Invaluable to the completion of this book were the details and perspectives provided by the many knowledgeable "locals" in and around the Brooksville area. They graced me with their comments, their memories, and their wisdom. Many thanks, individually and collectively.

No list of acknowledgements would be complete without mentioning the help provided by Greg Joly of Jamaica, Vermont. A fellow member of the Board of Stewards of the Good Life Center, for the last several years, at every opportunity, Greg has dug through Nearing papers in piles of files and stacks of boxes, in whatever archive or location he could find them, trying to understand how that pair lived their complicated lives. In the process, he has become a recognized authority on both Helen and Scott, particularly in their early years. A play he wrote in 2002 based on their letters to each other, titled "A Love Greater than 70 Bushels of Baked Potatoes," has been well received, and he tells me a book is in the works.

Some time ago Greg read an early draft of this book, and offered several helpful suggestions. Since then, when he has chanced upon a gem in his document searches, he has kindly passed them on to me. I have tried to acknowledge those contributions (and there are many) as they appear in this book.

Lastly, I thank David Bright, editor and truth-seeker, my partner and husband, for his patience and continued encouragement over the many years that it took me to finally put this book together.

Other books by the author

Proud to Be a Card-Carrying, Flag-Waving, Patriotic American Liberal
   (1996) ISBN 0-9657759-0-9

*A Tale of Dirty Tricks So Bizarre:
Susan Collins v. Public Record*
   (2002) ISBN 0-9720924-0-4

Table of Contents

	Acknowledgments	vi
	Foreword	x
1	Stan	1
2	The First Time	6
3	Getting Ready	24
4	Transients and Transplants	33
5	The CIA and a Real Jewish Princess	45
6	Feet First	64
7	Building a Life	71
8	Setting Up	81
9	The Invasion of People Who Take Aim	103
10	Energy Highs and Lows	107
11	We're NBC News and We're Here to Make You Famous	111
12	The Calm Before	115
13	Having Your Baby	117
14	Loaves and Fishes	127
15	We Have Seen the Enemy and They Are Part of Us	138
16	Canning Lids, the Achilles Heel	156
17	The Nukes and Me	161
18	On the Record	169
19	Chicken Entrails and Other Private Parts	178
20	Cracks in the Façade	188
21	More News and Letters	203
22	Heidi	211
23	And the World Came Tumbling After	220
24	In and Out of Focus	223
25	Shopping Around	232
26	Missed Demeanors	240
27	Winter, Spring of 1978	245
28	The Summer of 1978	250
29	First Divorce in the Family	260
30	And They Lived … After	264
31	Going, Going	267
32	The In-Between Time	292
33	The Rest of Stan's Story	300
34	And the Time Came	306
35	Good Life Economics 101	327
	Afterword	353
	List of Family Photos	362
	Index	363

Foreword

In one of my two brief stints as the token liberal on the local right-wing radio talk show in Bangor, Maine, a caller raised the issue of truth.
I said I tell the truth as I see it.
The caller took umbrage at my arrogance.
"The truth as *you* see it?" he asked derisively.
"Yes," I replied, "I can only tell the truth as I see it. I have no other perspective. And you can only tell the truth as you see it. Where we differ in what we see as the truth is where the discussion begins."

It was impossible to hide in the woods of Harborside, Maine, during the 1970s. Impossible, that is, if your humble cabin and 25-acre homestead had the neighbors we had back then. On one side were back-to-the-land gurus Helen and Scott Nearing, authors of **Living the Good Life**. On the other side was the young Eliot Coleman, who would later write the highly-popular books, **The New Organic Grower** and **Four Season Harvest**.

I recognized, almost from the very beginning that I should at some point write about what it was like to live on Cape Rosier, in the village of Harborside, in those years.

This memoir was pieced together over the course of three decades. As much as possible I used material contemporary to the time — my own letters to my mother, random notes to myself, and personal journal entries.

To broaden the story, I dug into public records, newspaper stories, town birth records from another century, and hand-written deeds recorded in Vermont town offices. I read personal letters from Helen and Scott, that had been carefully saved in publicly-available archives.

To fill in remaining gaps, I sought out knowledgeable locals, who graced me with their comments, their memories, and their wisdom.

Bridging all these and woven intricately through them, of course, were my own personal memories of that time of my life decades ago.

The result is this story of one woman's personal homesteading experience in the 1970s, and the ramifications that followed.

Jean Hay Bright
September 2003

Sketch by Samantha C. S. Jones

Carved plaque located in the southwest corner
of the main room at Forest Farm, Harborside, Maine

The emblem is that of the Theosophical Society
The quote is attributed to Helena Petrovna Blavatsky (1831-1891)

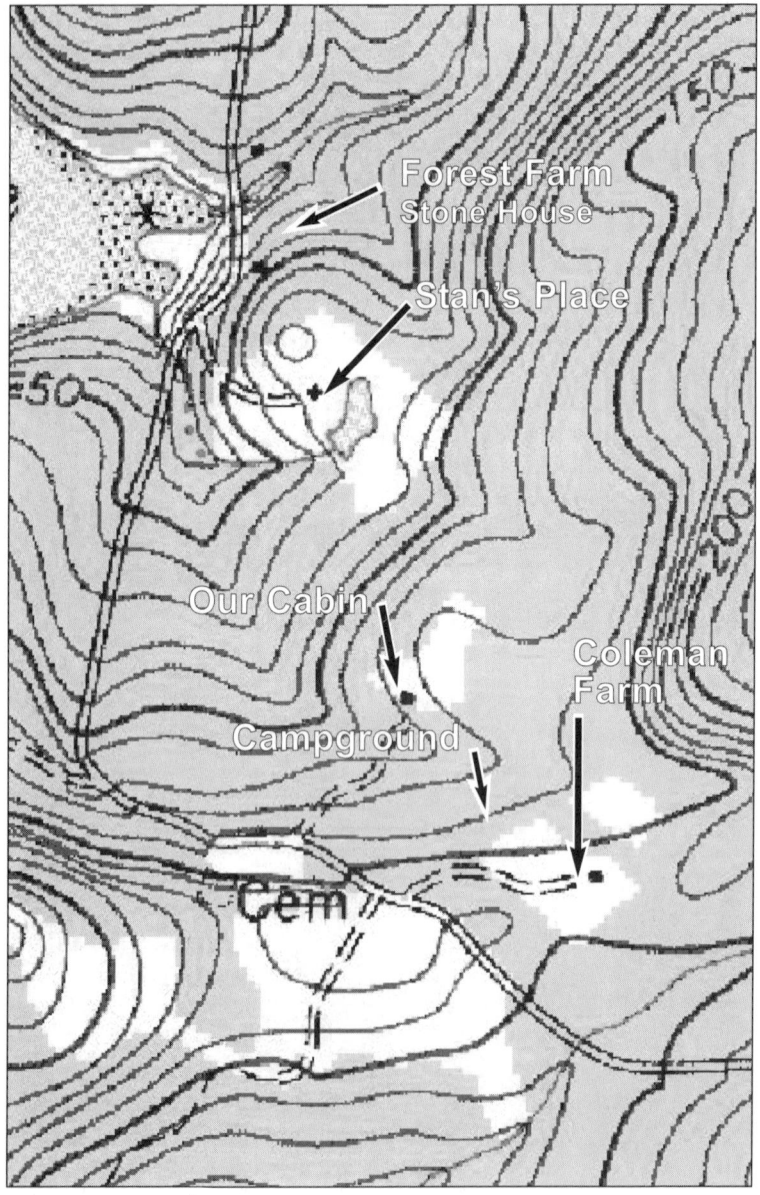

A portion of the topographical map of the Cape Rosier ME area
source: U.S. Geological Survey
July, 1985

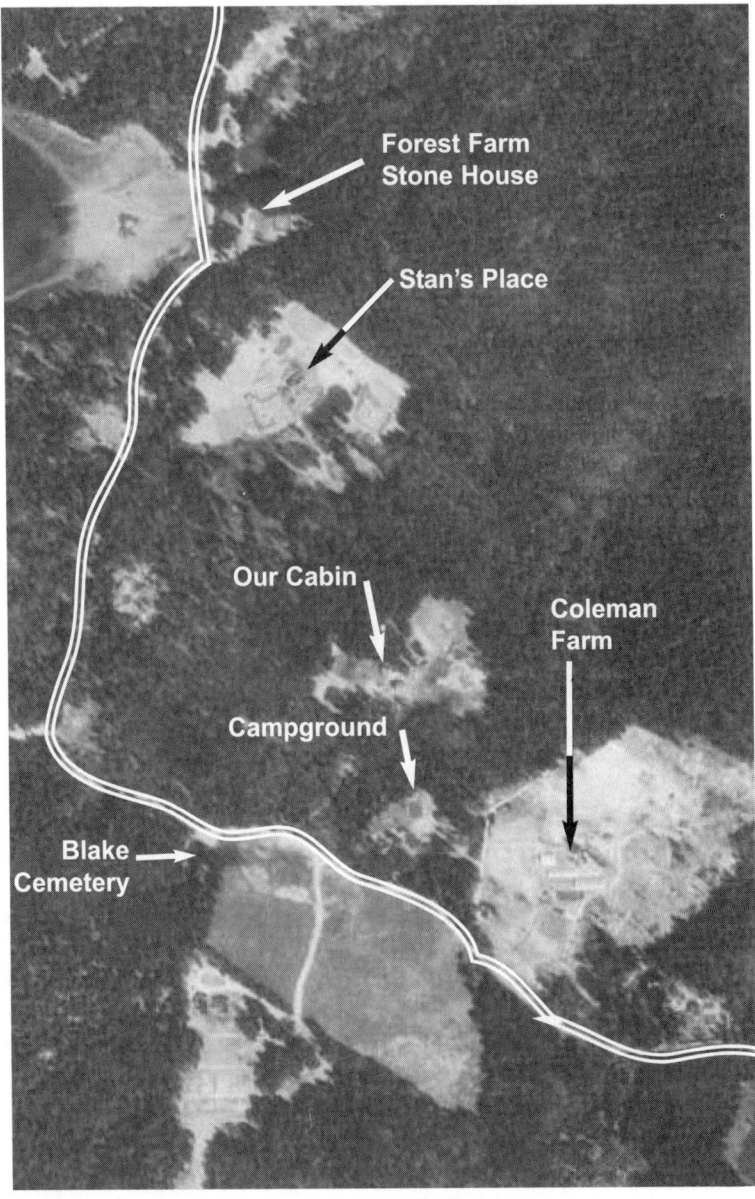

A portion of the aerial photograph of the Cape Rosier ME area
source: U.S. Geological Survey
May 1996

Chapter 1
Stan

I drove to the Cape like a horse to the barn. It had become so automatic over the past two decades. Despite the roads in town that circled around and came back on themselves, overlapping each other like Venn diagrams, I did not have to stop and think about what shortcut to take, or which unmarked side road, suddenly appearing to the right or left on a curve, would get us to our destination.

As I turned the car onto Cape Rosier, that peninsula sticking out into Penobscot Bay about half-way up the Maine coast, I nodded to the familiar rugged, gnarled, unhappy-looking fir trees that clung to the rocks and to the acidic, thin soil. They always looked so sad to me, poverty-stricken in their home environment, with not a thing they could do about it.

And then, as always happened shortly after turning onto the Cape Rosier road, I was struck once again by the palpable change in energy. It was a strange sensation, one I can't explain other than by saying it feels like entering a different force field. It was always there, even when I wasn't looking for it. I could be chattering away, engaged in conversation, or daydreaming off in a world of my own, but when I drove onto the Cape, I could feel it. I would take a deep breath, centering myself, and then I could continue on my journey.

The energy change was so noticeable that I never doubted the story that Helen's amulet had picked it up, telling her and Scott where to move next. I could just never figure out how that energy was transferred to the map over which the amulet had been passed, like a dowsing rod, in their time of decision.

I could see a few changes, but only a few, from when I had first driven down this road nearly a quarter-century before. A few new houses had popped up, some old ones had seen some sprucing. Most remarkable was the new vista at the first cove in Harborside — acres of woods turned, with the help of heavy equipment, into scenic pasture. And then there was that last stretch of tarred and/or dirt town road, which in my day had been always rough and reluctantly tended. It was now freshly paved, neat, and square-edged.

As we passed the first cove, the road rose steeply and we entered the dark stretch of forest between the two coves. Halfway up the hill, I glanced back and could still see the healed scar on the uphill side of the fir tree. The gash in its side had been made long ago, by our serendipital Renault after it had slid off the icy, unsanded hill with Keith and daughter Becca, then a toddler, inside. I had been in town when the road iced over and the accident happened. Coming home, I stopped in a panic at the crumpled car — only to find a note on the window that they were both fine and at home waiting for me.

The road leveled out, the tree branches making a dark canopy over the narrow pathway. Up ahead, at the second sharp curve in the road, another tree bore a similar scar, this one made by Eliot Coleman in his Jeep, doing the same slow-motion, sideways, icy dance during a different winter. He too was unhurt in his crash, but the tree would bear witness to the event for years to come.

Just two little memories, among hundreds, thousands, that this part of the world held for me.

And then we were suddenly out of the woods, with the car pointed straight at the middle of the second cove, where a huge, beautiful boulder eternally jutted. Just before the precipitous cliff, the road turned sharply to the left down into the gully, then just as steeply up the other side, then continued past the driveway entrance that was our destination.

I squeezed my car into an empty space in the line of vehicles parked along the side of the narrow town road. For a moment I stood in the middle of that road, gazing solemnly at that second cove, Orr Cove on the map, what Helen and Scott called Spirit Cove. I took yet another look at the scrubby firs that lined the edges of the cliff above the cove. Taking a deep breath, I turned and grabbed David's hand, and we walked up the long curving dirt driveway leading to the farm.

As we approached the clearing half-way up the driveway, the first thing to come into view was the high stone wall, painstakingly built by hand to keep the critters out of the quarter-acre garden. Then there was the one-car garage, and next to it, the old two-story wood-framed farmhouse.

Behind the garage and house we could see Stan's sod-roofed sauna. It stood on a tiny island in the middle of a shallow pond. The pond had been hand-dug, one wheelbarrow at a time, during the prior owner's tenure.

Stan built the sauna shortly after he bought the property, and it soon became nothing short of legendary. Stan invited everyone in the world to use it frequently.

Even though I liked a good sauna, I never partook at Stan's, primarily because of his tendency to cajole people into posing for group photographs in the steamy buff, pictures which he would gleefully drag out at the next event.

On the farm's hill to the left as we rounded the curve was the May pole, with last year's colorful but faded bunting still wrapped around it. A large American flag was flying at half-staff on the pole. It flapped in the breeze coming off the water, billowing toward the crowd milling around the tables of food set up just outside the stone-walled garden.

Talk about a punch in the gut. I expected to see the people, but I wasn't prepared for the May pole.

It was a few minutes after 10 a.m., May 3, 1995, and the memorial service for Stanley Stern Joseph of Harborside, Maine, was about to begin.

I had heard about Stan's death the way real news reaches people in small communities these days — by phone. Within hours of Stan's death, I got a call from Susan, who had heard it from Jane, who heard it from Nancy, who had gotten a call from Helen, who had learned of it from Ana, who had been living with Stan, Helen's next-door neighbor.

Stan had died on April 28, 1995. His obituary had appeared in the ***Bangor Daily News***, the only daily paper in these parts, the day after May Day, the day after the day that had become Stan's day.

For the first few years Stan actually invited people to his May Day party. But then somehow it became clear to everyone that you were just supposed to show up at Stan's on May 1st. A party would be in progress.

But not this year. My stomach knotted as I tried not to look at the pole.

As we walked through the crowd gathering on the hillside, I introduced David, the new man in my life, to dozens of my old friends and neighbors, some of whom I had talked with the past week, others whom I hadn't seen in years. To David, each face familiar to me was a new face for him to try to fit into the mosaic of my life. To me, each familiar face brought back a flood of memories, connections, personal stories, ironies and tragedies going back twenty or more years. I was soon on overload.

Stan was known for his music, particularly done on percussion instruments. In one of my earliest memories of him, he set up what looked like an eight-foot-long wooden xylophone in his living room, and insisted that everyone give it a go. It was impossible, even for us musical deadbeats, not to make beautiful sounds on that thing.

One of the ironies was that Stan's mother had grown deaf as his music had grown more important to him. Out of respect for that infirmity, it was announced that the eulogies were being tape recorded, and a transcript would be made for Stan's mother.

"So speak into the mike."

A baker from a town in New York, speaking into that microphone, remembered how Stan had called him up one fall and asked if he could come down for the winter and learn how to bake bread.

"Since he usually spent the winter in Bali or Greece," the baker said, "I felt quite honored."

A young woman whom Stan had hired to help with his firewood remembered the rhythm of the work: "Split wood, play badminton, split wood, go for a swim, split wood."

Stan was also known for his hats, which hung all about his house. Neighbor Barbara Damrosch (Eliot Coleman's third wife) said she relished showing off a new hat to Stan, because of his sincere and unabashed enjoyment of that particular type of apparel. Barbara and Stan were neighbors in more ways than one — her highly-popular book *Garden Primer* shared the same shelf space at the local library with *Maine Farm: A Year of Country Life*, the book written by Stan and his then-wife Lynn Karlin.

The eulogies were many, delivered by men in long ponytails and women in polyester suits with black nylons. Tom Hoey, the proprietor of Sow's Ear Winery, a funky down home sort of place at the other end of town, was almost unrecognizable in a tie and three-piece suit. A man in a beard showed up in a loose-fitting mumu and sandals. People wore their best, and their irreverent worst, all in memory of the Stan they knew.

They remembered Stan's gnarled hands, his dancing eyes.

Stan the clown, a failure at cross-dressing.

Stan, who freely admitted that his worse feature was his pair of big ugly feet. The same Stan who had once told a young woman — who had bothered to ask the question — that his best feature was his soul.

Stan, the man who had organized an adult Friday night softball team, and arranged for having the team name silk-screened onto long-sleeved T-shirts (Maine's vicious black flies, you know). The logo consisted of the word "Holy" and the image of what any fisherman in these parts would recognize as a mackerel.

"I would wear the shirt running," one woman said, "and sometimes people would yell out 'Holy Fish?' Every now and then someone would get it, and say, 'Oh yeah, Holy Mackerel!'"

That was Stan, I thought. He always seemed to be saying to the world:

It is what it is.
Read it any way you want.
Some of you might even get it.
Meanwhile, I'm off and running on something else.

As the eulogies continued to pour forth, I turned and focused on the dirt driveway David and I had walked up a few minutes before. I forced myself to remember the very first time I had been there, a much happier time, a time more than 23 years before, when this old farmhouse was owned by Helen and Scott Nearing....

The old Nearing homestead as it appeared in the early 1950s.

Chapter 2
The First Time

It was the week between Christmas and New Year's of 1971. I was on a week's vacation from my Girl Friday job at the **Providence Journal** newspaper in Rhode Island, and Keith and I were hunting for land. We had just snow-shoed over a 100-acre woodlot in the small town of Stetson, west of Bangor. Fronting on a paved state road, the parcel sported some nice-sized evergreen trees which appeared ripe for turning into a post-and-beam owner-built house. The land looked promising.

Cost: $7,000, the entire amount we had in savings.

We were heady with the real possibility of becoming landowners, but were not quite prepared to sign on the dotted line until we had looked at a few more pieces. But our week was almost up. Keith said he wanted to top off our trip north with a motivating experience.

"Let's stop in and see the Nearings," he said. "I think they live around here somewhere."

Some four decades earlier, Helen and Scott Nearing had gone on a similar quest for land in Vermont, and ended up near Stratton Mountain. They said in a book they wrote about that experience that they decided it was better to be poor in the country than poor in the city. They explained their move to Vermont not only as a means of simple survival, but also as a way of keeping their radical philosophies intact in a hostile world. It was a matter of setting your own rules. If the universities fired you for your outspokenness, teach outside the universities. Grow your own food so they can't starve you into compliance. Cut expenses to the bone. Provide for your own needs as directly as possible. Have one cash crop that will take care of the things that only money can buy. Above all, PAY AS YOU GO.

So, at ages 30 and 50, they moved to the country and bought a run-down farm for $300 cash and assumed an $800 mortgage. They cut their own firewood, bought clothing at second-hand stores, made maple syrup as a cash crop, and set aside as much time as possible for writing, lecturing, and general proselytizing.

Twenty years later, tired of the local hostility toward their odd ideas, the Nearings packed up their Puritan work ethic and set out for Maine to start the process all over again. But they took the time to write the book that would change my life.

The Nearings first published *Living the Good Life* in 1954. But it

Chapter 2 — The First Time

wasn't until Schocken Books republished it in 1970 that its popularity took off. The book has been in print continuously since then, and at last count had sold more than 250,000 copies.

"We can't do that!" I protested Keith's suggestion. "It's not polite, dropping in on someone unannounced."

"Well, we know they don't have a phone," Keith said, "so we can't call to ask if it's okay. Besides, they're probably not home this time of year anyway. I just want to see their place, even if they aren't there."

"But they're famous people," I said. "I'm sure they don't want people just dropping in on them all the time."

"Sure they do," Keith countered. "They as much as say so in the back of their book."

He pulled our well-worn copy of *Living the Good Life* out from under the Strout Realty catalog, and opened to the afterword at the end of the 1970 hard-cover (second printing) Schocken edition.

> Nineteen years of experimental homesteading in Vermont provided the material that went into the writing of **Living the Good Life**.
>
> Eighteen years of homesteading in Maine have rounded out our Vermont experience, matured it, and assured us that the life possibilities which we had explored in the Green Mountains of Vermont were equally available on the coast of another New England state.
>
> Flocks of young people have visited our Vermont and Maine homesteads. Many of them have been impressed by our way of life and have decided to try out homesteading for themselves.
>
> In the 1930's homesteading in the United States attracted a trickle of interest. Today the trickle has become a steady stream.
>
> We welcome the trend and assure our fellow homesteaders that audacity, courage, persistence, careful planning and plenty of good, hard work will bring abundant and satisfying rewards in this field as they have in so many other aspects of human experiment and experience.
>
> Helen and Scott Nearing
>
> Harborside, Maine
> April 1970

He was right. It certainly sounded like an open invitation. And it also sounded like we would be just a drop or two in the flow of people through their lives — particularly if we tried to be as unobtrusive as possible.

As we checked the map and headed our Volkswagen van toward Cape Rosier on Penobscot Bay, I realized I was pleased with this change of plans. In our relationship, I was the dependable, reliable, figure-it-out-ahead-of-time one. Raised in an immaculate house, I grew up as my mother's image of a nice girl, getting good grades, wearing the clothes my mother picked out for me, and not doing anything the neighbors could talk about. I was the middle kid (one older sister, one younger brother) of an intact working-class family. My dad was a foreman in one of the steel mills in Youngstown, Ohio; my mother worked off-and-on in a nearby factory sewing cloth toys (and as weigher and crane operator at U.S. Steel for 18 months during World War TWO, but that was before my time). I never had a hand raised to me.

Keith was the adventurer, the one willing to take chances, to act on any new idea unless he could be talked out of it first. We complemented each other well.

*　　　　　*　　　　　*　　　　　*　　　　　*

I met Keith in high school biology class, when I was a mere freshman and he was a mature sophomore. He was tall and handsome, a football player, albeit second string. I did not rebel at the assigned seating which put me next to what I considered this marvelous hunk of male humanity.

To my amazement, Keith paid attention to me, something new in my bookish, introverted existence.

Over that year, I learned that Keith was the oldest of his father's nine children by two wives. His life, which fluctuated between his father's and mother's homes, was complicated and difficult, but certainly more interesting than my own predictable, stable, loving — but boring — existence. I listened to his tales of woe, happy that I could be supportive, and enchanted at a view of life so different from my own.

We were a couple all through high school.

Graduating in 1964, Keith tried college, but dropped out after one semester, and got a job at a gas station. When I got my diploma the following year, money was tight, but I had it all figured out. If I got a daytime office job in downtown Youngstown, I could take a full load of classes at night at Youngstown University (now YSU).

A job in the order department at the Youngstown Public Library System, which paid $200.35 per month after taxes, did the trick. It was enough money to pay for college tuition, books and other fees, but not enough to also buy a car to get me the 12 miles between home and work/campus. My folks didn't have a car they could spare, and public transportation didn't stretch that far into the suburbs. But a room at the YWCA was very cheap, and, located as it was on the edge of campus and a block from the library, convenient to both work and class.

So that's what I did.

Chapter 2 — The First Time

Meanwhile, the Vietnam War was heating up. Keith was able-bodied and, no longer in college, was fodder for the draft. He pulled a relatively low number. It was clear his time would soon come.

We got engaged and started making wedding plans. My folks offered to pay for my college education if we would put off the wedding until after I graduated. I declined. I was 18, gainfully employed, and capable of making my own decisions.

Apparently Keith felt the same way. Without consulting me or anyone else, he went into the Navy recruiting office and enlisted as a Seabee, for a four-year hitch. Although surprised at this development, (how could he possibly figure that four years in the Navy was better than two years in the Army as a draftee?) I knew I would just have to deal with it. After all, men made decisions like that all the time, and I was in love with this one. And besides, the move would get us both out of Ohio. If Keith didn't get killed in the process, we might even have a good time.

We were married on April 16, 1966, and spent our brief honeymoon in Paris — Paris, Tennessee, where Keith's paternal grandparents had a cabin on a lake.

I would give the honeymoon mixed reviews.

Mammoth Caves, the underground caverns full of stalagmites and stalactites, were marvelous. Such wonder and beauty, hidden beneath what looked like ordinary rolling fields — sort of how I felt about Keith at the time.

It was spawning season on the lake to which Keith's grandparents had retired. Five-pound carp were everywhere in the shallows. Keith declared aboriginal urges and said we were going spear fishing. Borrowing deep boots, we waded in. He took a long sharpened stick and speared several. That done, I was ready to go back to the cabin. After all, how many carp could one eat?

"Well, probably none," he said. "Carp is too full of tiny bones to eat."
Then why kill them? I asked.

"Because they are here," he said. "It's fun. And look, there are so many, we couldn't make a dent" in their numbers.

He seemed more primed for military duty than I was comfortable with.

Later, while Keith was off with his grandfather, I had a cup of tea at the Formica-topped kitchen table with Keith's grandmother, a frail, smiling woman not five feet tall. I thanked her for their hospitality and the use of their A-frame visitor's cabin behind their lakefront home. I asked her how she liked retirement living in western Tennessee.

She liked the area fine, she said, but the area didn't like her and her husband.

I didn't understand. Was it allergies? Or the weather, which had to be hotter and stickier in the summer than the Ohio they had left? Didn't they have air conditioning?

"Oh, no dear, that's not it at all," she said. "It's because we're Catholic."

"Catholic. So what if you're Catholic? Why would that be anybody's business but yours?"

"Well, they don't trust Catholics in these parts. It makes it hard."

"What do you mean?" I asked. "What do they think Catholics do that they don't do? Weird rituals or something?"

"Oh, no, dear," said this wisp of a woman with a meek voice to match, "they think we're conspiring to take over the world."

That June, Keith started boot camp. After a short training period at Port Hueneme, California, he was transferred to Gulfport, Mississippi, to prepare to ship out to Vietnam. We rented out the back half of a drafty, rickety old wooden duplex propped up on cement blocks, with dozens of fire ant towers in the backyard and two-inch-long cockroaches always finding their way into the trash.

That duplex, a few miles up the coastal highway from the spot where actress Jayne Mansfield had met her death in a 1966 Buick Electra that had been driven forcefully under a tractor-trailer rig, was actually our second apartment in Gulfport. We had to leave the first — half of a partially-furnished run-down house with curling linoleum and a big four-poster bed dominating the living room — after we humiliated our sweet little old landlady by not only inviting one of Keith's black Navy buddies over for a pre-deployment dinner, but then actually sitting out on her front porch with him afterwards, where everyone could see.

She had thought we were such nice young people.

Keith was soon deployed to Southeast Asia, and I became part of the cadre of young wives in the community waiting for our men to come back home. The young women who spent those long months on the fringes of the military bases weren't into the patriotism, the flag-waving and the brass. But we also weren't into the protest marches, because that would be construed as lack of support for the men, OUR men, who, by whatever means of coercion, intimidation or patriotism got them there, were putting their lives on the line at that very moment.

We young wives, in our late teens or early twenties, were just passing the time until our loves came back to us, hopefully breathing and intact, and we could get on with living happily ever after. Vietnam was something our government was inflicting on its young men. It was something to endure, but not to think too deeply about. It was not safe to think too much.

Chapter 2 — The First Time

I got a job in the admissions office at the local hospital. It was just three tumultuous years after the 1964 Civil Rights Act had been passed. One of my responsibilities in my new job was to actively integrate sick people — black, white and brown — even those who didn't want to be integrated. For some reason I had no sympathy for the whining of the whites, but I could not ignore the terror in the eyes of a few elderly blacks who refused to be assigned to double rooms with whites.

"I won't sleep a wink," one sick old black man told me, hacking away. I could see he meant it. And, despite my lack of medical training, I knew that wouldn't help his condition one bit.

"Ah know ma place," I can still hear that frail elderly woman say as she held her ground, sitting in her wheelchair in my office. Her eyes were open wide in fear at the prospect of having to negotiate the hidden land mines in the unfamiliar territory of being a legal equal in the same room with a white woman.

I probably broke the law, but I found other rooms to put them in.

Half-way through one of Keith's two tours of duty, I met him in Hawaii on R&R. The whole week was nothing short of bizarre. There we were, two lonely people, one coming from a state of worried boredom, the other fresh off the front lines of a war zone, both grasping at the memories of a relationship that neither of us would ever have again.

In that tropical Hawaiian paradise, I was looking for comfort and connection in the arms of the man I loved; he was jumping at every noise, his eyes darting into the dark corners of every room, acting for all the world like a hunted animal.

Between the pineapple fields and entertainer Don Ho, I sought the emotional connection that was impossible to maintain through letters; he talked about Vietnam, and the tank he had come upon moments after it had hit an anti-tank mine that had torn it — and its crew — apart.

I wanted reassurance that everything would be all right; he explained how, as a telephone and electric lineman stringing and repairing wires, he was a prime target for any sniper in the area, a sitting duck all the time he was up on those poles.

At that time, two tours in Vietnam in a row was the limit for servicemen in Keith's outfit. A few days after he was back from his second tour, I woke up and felt comforted by his warm, firm, intact body in the bed next to me. He was safe, he was home, we could return to what passed for normal, at least until we learned where he would be assigned next. We would leave the horrors of the war behind us. The headlines would belong to others.

I slipped out of bed, headed to the kitchen to make some coffee. My ankle caught on something in my path. I stumbled. Suddenly pots and pans were clattering down around me, and Keith was sitting up in bed, laughing.

"What?" I asked in confusion, on my knees by the side of the bed.

"A trip wire," he said, grinning strangely. "Like the ones we had to look out for in 'Nam. Don't worry, no explosives. Just a lot of noise. I wouldn't do anything to hurt you, you know that, hon."

To my puzzled look, he smiled, "I just wanted you to understand what it was like over there, having to watch every step. I rigged them before I came to bed last night."

"Them?" I asked, incredulously. "Are there any more?"

"Not telling," he said.

He was transferred to Davisville, Rhode Island, and shortly thereafter an early-out program was announced. He was honorably discharged, and the Vietnam War was behind us, or so I thought.

Keith had come home in one piece, at least physically. But he had changed. He was moody, unfocused, mad at the world.

Keith started back to college at the University of Rhode Island, while I went to work for the ***Providence Journal*** in its South County bureau, as an administrative assistant. That meant I combed the town offices all over the county, ferreting out real estate transfers, building permits, births, marriage intentions and returns, writing them up for publication. In the process, I discovered I had a nose for news. I tipped reporters about projects that hadn't hit anyone's radar screen, gave them bits of information from official sources that pointed to a good story.

I also liked to write memorable obituaries, a concept new to the local funeral directors. Once they got over the shock of me asking so many questions, they rose to the challenge, pumping family members for more details to spice up the pieces. Conspiratorially, we tried to capture the essence of the person, no matter how humble, to make friends and relatives smile in remembrance. We had the freedom to do this (within reason) because the ***Providence Journal*** treated obituaries as news items, printing them free of charge.

After I got my feet under me, I started freelancing feature stories as time would allow. Among the pieces I wrote (for extra pay) were a cover piece for the paper's Sunday ***Rhode Islander*** on the restoration of several historic houses in the area, and a color piece on Keith's fix-up project involving an old boat in the entire length of our small living room.

That living room was in the tiny two-bedroom house we had rented in a hillside subdivision in Narragansett. With the landlord's permission, we turned the backyard into an incredibly productive organic garden. To add variety to our home-grown diet, and with "Stalking the Wild Asparagus" at ready reference, Keith scavenged the countryside for all kinds of exotic food. He dove for fat oysters in the brackish (and no doubt polluted) river that ran past our housing subdivision at the bottom of the hill. He found, analyzed, and we ate dozens of different kinds of mushrooms. He went hunting, fishing, and clamming, bringing back ducks, squirrels, and the biggest quahogs I have ever seen. Above all else, we ate well.

But he came down with a case of tularemia, probably caught from one of the squirrels. He was weak, bedridden, groggy and demoralized for six months. Getting to, or getting anything out of, college classes became an impossibility.

About then Keith started talking about how he had been born in the wrong century, that he didn't fit into today's society, that he would have really liked to have been a pioneer, opening up the west, using his hunting and fishing skills to provide for his family. The refrain intensified as the months passed, even as his illness receded.

After his recovery, he signed on as a crew member to a fishing boat out of Point Judith. I thought it was perfect for him — the thrill of the hunt, the rhythm of a steady job, as well as a welcome addition to the family budget. But he came home off the boat at all hours of the day and night, with wildly fluctuating sums in his paycheck. He had tales of rough weather out at sea, and poor, unpredictable catches. He slept fitfully. I worried about his health.

Just at that point in this strange string of events that has been my life, I read about Helen and Scott Nearing in **Parade** magazine. Here were two people who had not fit in with normal society, who had gone into the woods and back to the land, and had written a book about it. It sounded like the perfect solution to Keith's personal predicament. And I have to admit I was intrigued by the whole idea.

We were then members of the very middle-class Book of the Month Club. I ordered **Living the Good Life: How to Live Sanely and Simply in a Troubled World.** It was not on their alternate book list, but they eventually found a copy. It was the last book we ever bought from them.

Living the Good Life seemed to have been written just for us. Getting away from the crowds, living in the woods, figuring it all out and pulling it all together, sounded like an exciting challenge. If we decided to follow suit, we would be 20th century pioneers, in the true wild west sense of the word — pack everything we owned into the Volkswagen van and head north into the wilderness.

Keith's ready enthusiasm for the idea was a welcome change from his bouts of depression and restlessness.

And the whole idea was something I could sink my teeth into. It wasn't that monumental a step, I convinced myself. I lived mostly in my head. I didn't care about clothes or furnishings. I didn't need fancy appliances or status cars. I could do with a lot less than we had, and we didn't have much.

I saw homesteading as a way of getting down to basics, back to nature, finding out the essence of what life was all about. Forever curious, I really wanted to learn how people had functioned before electricity and all the gadgets had been invented. What was it like to plan your diet a year in advance and then proceed to grow it all? How much land does it take for a year's worth of potatoes? How do you make butter? Cook and heat with wood?

Just how self-sufficient could a couple of strong, young people really be in this day and age? Just how lightly could we tread on this earth? And was it actually possible to do all this, tend to all our own needs, in only four hours a day, as the Nearings said they did? Was the concept of a 40-hour workweek really a corporate plot, as some had claimed?

And could we really bring with us only the good parts of what passed for civilization?

I was more than ready to give it a try. Besides, I always carried the glimmer in the back of my brain that if it didn't all work out, we could just re-emerge from the treeline and pick up where we had left off.

So, in the fall of 1971, we started hunting for a chunk of land.

The climate in Rhode Island was wonderful, but the state was and is thickly packed with people. Keith said he felt suffocated. Massachusetts, sitting atop Rhode Island, was just as bad. Besides, in both states land was incredibly expensive. Buying a big enough chunk to give us the elbow room Keith needed was out of the question on our budget.

So we kept heading north, up I-95 past the 16 miles of built-up coast in New Hampshire, and on into Maine. We knew that north of Portland we would find cheap land prices and access to what we thought was a non-industrial saltwater coast. That access was very important to us landlubbers from Ohio who had recently discovered seafood.

*　　　*　　　*　　　*　　　*　　　*

From Stetson, it was more than an hour's drive to Cape Rosier. By the time we had made our decision to visit the Nearings and had gotten to within a dozen miles of Forest Farm, darkness had fallen. It does that about 4 o'clock in the afternoon that time of year in that part of Maine.

Chapter 2 — The First Time

We pulled off the road and spent the incredibly cold night bundled up in our VW camper. The next morning we had to scrape a thick layer of frost off the INSIDE of the van's windows before we could start out. After deciphering the winding roads of Brooksville, which all seemed to turn back on themselves, we found the only road leading to Cape Rosier. Four miles later we faced a towering Rosier Grange hall guarding a fork in the road.

Looking left and right, we decided to take the road most traveled. Two miles later it stopped at a "T" intersection. Someone had scratched "RACY" next to the symbol on the highway sign warning of the "T" intersection. Facing that "T" intersection was the Howard homestead, where we found octogenarian Tracy Howard in residence.

"First drive on the left after the second cove," came back his obviously well-practiced line when we asked for directions. He looked us up and down, glanced at the VW van, smiled, and went back into his house.

Over the years I have often wondered what young vandal had taken the time to deface that road sign in Tracy Howard's honor. Somehow I doubted he had done it himself.

The narrow town road shortly turned to a mixture of gravel and broken-up old asphalt paving. About two miles, and exactly two coves, later, we found the drive. A small hand-painted sign tacked onto a tree declared it to be "Forest Farm." We had found what we were looking for, and after all that driving around with the van's heater going full blast, I was finally warmed up from our bitter-cold night. It was by then late morning.

The landscape was covered with old snow, yet only a few tire tracks were in evidence in the furrow lines that marked the long curving dirt driveway. We drove up it and saw that the drive ended at a small garage. The Nearings' quarter-acre, stone-walled garden was to the right of the garage. To the left and a few feet away from the garage was an old wooden two-story clapboard house.

Scott Nearing was up on the small rise between the house and the cove. Long, straight, sapling-sized poles, vertically stacked in a number of teepee-shaped piles, cut the sky behind him. He was busy with his small hand saw, one by one turning those long, thin sticks of drying timber into stove-length firewood.

"Hello, Mr. Nearing!" Keith's booming voice called out as he pulled his 6'4" frame out of our respectable two-tone green and tan Volkswagen van (we had traded in our hand-painted zebra-striped one a few years before).

Scott, who was then 88 and had a face with at least that many well-earned wrinkles, waved at the intruding vehicle, but did not stop his work.

"Just ask him if we can look around," I whispered loudly to Keith from the front seat.

Keith went up to Scott, spoke briefly with him, then came back to the van and started digging around for the axe, one of the pieces of equipment we felt we would need for our trip into what we suburbanites considered the uncharted wilderness that was Maine.

"Come on and meet him," Keith said, axe in hand. "I'm going to split a little wood."

Nothing cools down faster than a Volkswagen with its engine off — or me in cold weather when I'm not moving. And, sitting there in the van, I was not moving. I gladly accepted his invitation, and followed Keith up the small hill, rubbing my gloved hands together as I went.

After preliminary introductions, Keith and Scott set about their muscle-warming tasks. I looked the situation over and did not see where I could do anything useful. The set-up was a one-person operation already stretched to two. I repeatedly tromped the ground, pounding non-sticking snow off my boots and gave myself a good hug.

Scott finally tuned into my predicament and suggested that I go down to the house and introduce myself to Helen. Aromatic smoke from burning wood was billowing from one of the house's two chimneys. I readily complied.

"Hello, hello, hello! Come in, come in, come in," Helen greeted me at the back door in what I would learn was her trademark triple cadence.

How odd, I thought. I haven't even introduced myself, she has no idea who I am or why I'm here, yet she is inviting me into her home. I know I probably look harmless, but still — this wasn't the way we did it in Ohio.

The back door led into an unheated room that spanned the distance between the brimming, neatly stacked woodshed and the heated main part of the house. An old refrigerator, like the one my folks put in their basement when they got a new one, was unobtrusive behind a stack of boxes.

The house itself was simple and spare, with a kitchen and living room of about equal size downstairs and, I would learn later, two bedrooms upstairs. A full bath with a toilet and an old-fashioned claw foot tub was tucked into a corner of the first floor just off the central stairway. Each downstairs room had large non-thermal windows on three sides — a plus for light and view, but a killer for heating, I immediately thought.

But heat was not a problem that day. The squarish wood-burning cookstove (black top, enameled white sides), was keeping the place quite cozy. A large, worn, stainless steel teapot sat simmering in one back corner. The heavy lid of a black cast-iron pot occasionally rattled off a little vegetable-smelling steam. Bunches of dried herbs and dried corn still on the cobs hung from the exposed wooden beams. The kitchen counter sported a stainless steel sink. A long, heavy, obviously hand-made, simple trestle table dominated the other side of the room. An electric lamp stood near the table by what had to be the master chair. Another handmade chair and crude milk stools made up the other seating around the table. The floor was of wide dark wooden boards, worn uneven by decades of foot traffic.

The kitchen had a simplicity usually associated with the Shakers — except, that is, for the east wall.

The wooden kitchen cabinets on the east wall were colorful and perky, with Dutch boys and girls in full regalia painted in bright primary colors. Since the usual kitchen billboard (the refrigerator) was parked out of the way in the cold room, recent newspaper clippings were instead taped to some of the cabinet doors and nearby walls. Most of the black and white headlines and photos screamed the latest horrors of the Vietnam War — children being napalmed, civilians being murdered by soldiers — a sharp contrast to the whimsical ornamentation they were covering.

I turned away from the headlines — after all, Keith and I had left that war behind — and thanked my host for her warm hospitality, with emphasis on the WARM.

"It's a real pleasure to meet you, Mrs. Nearing," I said. "We've read your book, and we're really excited about doing something like that ourselves."

"Please, call me Helen. And you can call Scott Scott."

Conundrum number one. I was raised to respect my elders, and one of the ways to do that was to refer to those elders as Mr. or Mrs. But another rule about elders had to do with respecting their preferences.

So I started calling her "Helen," as everyone did. And a strange thing happened. Despite nearly a half-century difference in our ages (Helen was then 69, I was 24), the years melted away and I was suddenly her peer. And despite their world prominence and prestige (in some quarters), with that one simple request, the prophets turned into human beings.

The stove's warmth and the hot herbal tea Helen served me felt wonderful, but I knew I was intruding. I tried to be as pleasant and invisible as possible. I had already figured out that this elderly pair, in this drafty century-old house with electric lights and a full bathroom, were no longer living the self-sufficient lifestyle they had described in their book. Except for the wood heat, and the stone wall around their home vegetable garden, their trappings looked very similar to those of other retired people I knew. That was fine, considering the book in question had been written some 17 years before about a place two states away. And they were certainly allowed some slack because of their ages.

But having rendered that judgment, and, since I had read their book and therefore knew all there was to possibly know about them, I decided that Keith and I should take our leave as soon as it was gracefully possible. With lunchtime fast approaching, I took a mental inventory of what was left of our food supply in the van.

Helen, however, had other plans. I pulled out of my private thoughts to find her in the midst of a strange dialog that I would only realize much later was a prospecting interview.

As Keith and Scott continued to labor on the hill outside the window, Helen first explained how lucky we were to have found them home, that they usually left for the winter on speaking and writing tours in warmer climates. She said visitors were scarce that time of the year, but that during the summer it was not uncommon to have two or three dozen folks come through in a day. She had long ago stopped taking down their names, she said, but she still tried to keep a head count. She showed me her record book. Forty people came one day, 24 the next, then maybe 11, then back up to 36. They came each day, every day, most of them unannounced, expecting personal attention and inspiration.

The total that year then stood at 1,371. She dutifully added our head count to her book.

Then she started to quiz me down. She wanted to know all about us — how long we had been married, what we thought of the war, where we were looking for land, if we planned to have any kids. I was really vague on that last one, primarily because I didn't see that it was any of her business.

*   *   *   *   *

At that point we had been married more than five years. Except for the months Keith was in Vietnam, I had been on the birth-control pill. (Historical note: It was only in 1965, the year before Keith and I were married, that the U.S. Supreme Court in Griswold v. Connecticut struck down state laws prohibiting the dispensing of contraceptives of any sort, or even information about contraceptives, to married people. As I was talking to Helen in her kitchen in December 1971, the Supreme Court's landmark abortion ruling in Roe v. Wade was still some 13 months away.)

Keith and I had decided against bringing babies into the messed-up world we lived in. But I had learned not to be up-front about that. My mother, anticipating grandchildren, didn't want to hear our rationalizations. But she was not the only one. I had once mentioned our decision while chitchatting with a friendly clerk in one of the town offices on my rounds picking up public records for the *Providence Journal*.

"That's selfish," said the clerk, a Mrs. Pease, whose lawn at home sported a "Pease in a Pod" sign. From her perspective, not having children when you were physically able was selfish, because then you could do anything you wanted with your money and didn't have to learn to put anyone else's wants and needs first.

I on the other hand, defended myself by opining that people who had kids were selfish because the only reason to have kids these days was because you wanted them, which was certainly putting your desires before those of a world that clearly didn't need any more of us.

*   *   *   *   *

"With Keith in the service and gone so much," I said to Helen, "we really didn't think it was the right time. I suppose once we got settled down on our own place we might think about it again."

That's when Helen told me about Eliot and Sue Coleman, a young couple a few years older than us who lived just up the road with their small daughter, Melissa.

"Too bad you can't meet them," she said. "They're away visiting relatives for the holidays."

It turned out the Nearings had sold the Colemans 60 acres of land a few years before, in 1968. The Colemans had plunged right in, built a small cabin, and had begun to raise their own food. They had grown and sold $1,200-worth of extra produce, enough to pay all their bills and to buy the few food items they couldn't grow themselves. They were doing well, Helen said, but were hoping that some people with kids would move into the neighborhood soon so Melissa wouldn't be so lonely.

Her remark surprised me. I had just assumed that any available homesteading land within spitting distance of the Nearings would have been snapped up already.

"Is there land for sale around here?" I asked.

"None that we know of," Helen said obliquely. "We get that question a lot."

It almost felt like I had been manipulated into asking the question. Even so, in my innocence, I took her answer at face value.

About then Keith and Scott came stomping in, and it was clear that Keith was on first-name basis with Scott. I then learned that Helen had been planning all along on feeding us lunch.

We were instructed to pick out a wooden bowl and spoon from the rack by the door. These we used for the entire meal of vegetable soup, baked squash, apples, apple sauce, supplemented by jars of blueberry jam, peanut butter and carrot marmalade to spread on anything able to take it, like apple slices. Tomato juice was served in glasses.

The vegetarian fare was delicious and surprisingly filling to us omnivores.

We were also introduced to the "carrot croaker," a strange cookie Helen insisted on concocting from the pulp she had left over after juicing carrots. She would add molasses, some flour, raisins, and anything else handy, shape the mix into small bars, bake them in the always-hot oven until hard and inedible, and serve them in a bowl to all comers. I think it was her way of testing people's dental health.

Wooden bowls on a rack in the kitchen of Forest Farm.

Chapter 2 — The First Time

After lunch, we were directed to the kitchen sink and told to simply rinse out our bowls and spoons under warm water and set them in the sink to drain. I had been a biology major in college, and was thus a firm believer in the germ theory of disease. I marveled at what I saw as this lack of sanitation. Here were two elderly people exposing themselves to any number of strange germs that happened to walk up their drive. But Helen and Scott were proud of not having seen a doctor in years.

Maybe they kept their own bowls separate, exposing only their guests to unfriendly communal infections. Whatever the case, it was too late for us to worry about it. And I was not about to challenge their kitchen procedures.

As I was busy considering how to gracefully bid our hosts adieu, Helen asked if we wanted to see the Coleman place. Even though Eliot and Sue were gone, she assured us they wouldn't mind.

While Scott went off to take a nap, Helen led us up the path behind the house, about half a mile through a stretch of woods, and out into a large clearing with a neat, square, owner-built cabin plunked down in the middle of it. We could see likewise neat and square patterns of garden sections under the covering of light snow around the cabin. The cabin's single-pitch shed roof, lower in the back, higher in the front, angled to meet the low sun in the northern Maine sky. It is an architectural style which I personally find unappealing, since it always reminds me of my grandmother's chicken coop.

Helen showed us into the unlocked house ("You're sure it's okay?") which was neat, spare and immaculate — and surprisingly warm for having been unheated for several days. To the immediate left of the door was the wood-burning cookstove, flued to the east wall and handy to the outside for hauling wood. The L-shaped kitchen counter ran along half the south wall, turning into the room to divide the kitchen area from the eating area. The other half of the south wall, facing the sun, was made of heat-capturing glass. A picnic table sat beneath that bank of windows. What passed for chairs was simplicity itself — 18-inch sections of round tree trunks, debarked and set upright. A wall of bookshelves dominated the west wall, with built-in benches underneath and on half of the back (north) wall. The sleeping area to the right of the door was a bed built in at shoulder height, with storage area underneath. The root cellar was under the house, entered through a trap door in the floor.

From inside the Coleman cabin, the ceiling soared to meet the sun. And I suddenly realized that in one respect shed-roof buildings are a lot like house trailers — they look worse from the outside than they do from the inside. I couldn't help but feel my spirit lift along with the ceiling.

Standing at the home-made wooden table, soaking up the rays coming through the window, a sense of peace and well-being came over me. Keith and I looked at each other. Here was the actualization of the Nearing theory. Helen and Scott had electricity, for which they often apologized. (Helen said electricity was already in their Maine house when they bought it. And they didn't use much, only for lighting, refrigeration — and their electric popcorn popper.)

But Eliot and Sue's home was self-contained and non-electric. And their homestead still seemed warm (important in December) and hospitable. It was really possible to do this, after all. One could be civilized while cutting the umbilical cords of civilization.

I think we floated all the way home to Rhode Island, with visions of gardens and bees and orchards and cozy little cabins in the woods dancing in our heads. Keith said he didn't think he could be a vegetarian, but we could raise rabbits and chickens. Plans for a house, one that could be built in sections and expanded as our needs and finances dictated, started forming in our minds.

All we needed now was a place to park our dreams.

A couple of weeks later, we wrote the Nearings a letter, thanking them again for their hospitality. We would be taking another look at that piece of land in Stetson the following week, this time with a realtor. Could we stop in and see them on our way back?

I swear, not three days later we got a postcard from Helen proclaiming, "Yes! Come ahead! But don't sign anything until you come see us!"

"What do you think she means by that?"

"They probably just want to warn us about buying land when the ground is frozen," Keith said. "Bogs can be awfully firm in the wintertime, you know."

"You think that's all it is?"

"What else could she mean?"

"You're right," I said.

Quietly, I admonished myself: You're just a couple of kids from Youngstown, Ohio. You're nothing special. Don't ever expect anything out of the ordinary to happen, and you won't be disappointed.

At the end of a pleasant second visit, during which Helen quaintly read both of our palms, the Nearings offered us a piece of their farm. They had mapped out a 30-acre piece, more or less (it turned out to be less) situated between their house and the Colemans. Sale price — $2,000. The parcel was smaller, rougher and rockier than the land in Stetson. It would be harder to homestead. But the price per acre was the same (about $70), we were within spitting distance of salt water, and we would have incredible neighbors — all the advice we would ever need right next door in either direction. And, with the $5,000 we had left from our savings, we could afford to build our house right away, instead of spending years saving up more money from my job in Rhode Island.

Before the full impact of their offer could sink in, they took us to meet Eliot and Sue Coleman and their small daughter Melissa. Eliot was short and wiry, like Scott. And outgoing. Like Scott, he could talk up a storm.

Susan was pleasant but detached, smiling but not about to be distracted from her work. She was busy hauling water from a well about 200 feet from their cabin. I thought it odd that Eliot, who was giving us a tour of his frozen gardens, did not offer to carry one or both of the heavy five-gallon water buckets, weighing about 40 pounds each, back to their cabin. I looked at Keith, knowing he would normally have stepped in to help. He shrugged his shoulders and kept quiet.

Inside the cabin, as Melissa played quietly in the corner or hugged her mother shyly, Eliot commented on how nice it would be if his daughter had other children to play with. I noted his comment.

As we walked back through the woods to our van parked at the Nearings, once again Keith and I had that sense of rightness descend upon us. This was definitely do-able. This was it. This was what we had been looking for.

Still thinking I would wake up from a dream, we accepted the Nearings' offer.

In all, the Nearings sold pieces of what they had thought was a 140-acre farm (but which also turned out to be smaller) to only a handful of people. Over the decades some other chunks were sectioned off by those new owners to a few of their friends, resulting in about a dozen houses, cabins and homesteads being built along the mile of road frontage of what had been the Nearings' original farm.

Years later, after both the good and the bad and I was no longer living out there, I asked Helen on one of my visits if she could tell me why she and Scott had picked Keith and me, out of the thousands who had come through their lives in those times, to share their land. She said she couldn't explain it to me, it was just something she and Scott had seen in us.

For many years I figured their decision had a lot to do with Keith's demonstrated skill with an axe — and with his military haircut and shaved face. Only recently did I begin to wonder if my job at the ***Providence Journal***, with its commensurate typing and filing skills, had anything to do with it.

Chapter 3
Getting Ready

We plunged right into our preparations. We raided all the junk shops we could find, in both Maine and Rhode Island. Our timing was good, because most of the places we patronized would soon disappear to make way for shopping malls or would metamorphosize into pricey antique shops.

First off, I scooped up cast iron skillets and Dutch ovens for use on/in a wood-burning cookstove.

I then discovered a set of clothes irons, used for ironing clothes. I thought they were so cute. They looked like little, squat, electric irons, but they were really heavy. They came in a set of two, so one could be heating on the wood-burning stove while the other was in use at the ironing board. The handle was detachable. When the one you were using cooled off, you parked it on the hot stove, detached the handle, and picked up the other one which was ready to go.

"You intend to iron clothes, living in the woods?" my mother asked.

"Maybe not, but if we need a pressed shirt for a special occasion, like if somebody dies, I'll be ready. Just in case," I said.

What I didn't tell her was that the irons were something I had to have, just to have. After all, they were historical items, and unlike Doritos, they were not making any more of them.

We stocked up on some of the many do-it-yourself books that were then coming out — *Organic Gardening*; cooperative extension service information on the family cow and chicken flock; *All Creatures Great and Small*; a pamphlet on how to butcher a pig; *Five Acres and Independence*; *How to Have a Green Thumb Without an Aching Back;* *Let's Eat Right to Keep Fit*; *Diet for a Small Planet*; and on and on.

Keith's brother Darryl, who had just joined the Navy, gave us a copy of *The Last Whole Earth Catalog* for Christmas. Flipping through it made it clear we were not alone in our quest for rural simplicity.

Since the electric line stopped at the end of Nearings' driveway, the first things we ordered from that catalog were Aladdin kerosene lanterns. They were promised to give off just about as much light as an electric lamp. And they were portable. To go to another room, you just picked up the lamp and took it with you. You didn't have to unplug it or anything. We had heard that a lot of people used them in their Maine hunting camps — a fact that did not impress my mother.

"So they rough it for a week or two during hunting season," she said. "I can do just about anything for a week or two. You're talking about doing this all the time."

She had good reasons for her skepticism. Mom had grown up on a small farm during the Depression, a time when her father could not find paid work for a full decade. She mostly remembered the hard work needed to keep the family of six fed and warm. And the mean horse.

She was thus not too pleased with our plans.

I tried to get her to focus on her more pleasant memories. I was hoping to pick up ideas, clues, hints of what it was like to live like that. Our junk-shop finds often served as the catalyst for those discussions.

"We've been checking out all the barn sales," I rhapsodized, "and we've found all kinds of useful things — old hoes and shovels; a classic set of ice tongs…"

"You'll need ice tongs?"

"Sure. For lifting blocks of ice out of the pond. If you pack them in lots of sawdust, the blocks are supposed to last most of the summer. Didn't you have an icebox on the farm when you were a kid?"

"Our aunt did, but we didn't. We put stuff in the milkhouse. You remember, that little cement house covered with ivy?"

"I knew you called it a milkhouse, but there was never any milk in it.

That's me at 20 months of age, standing in front of my grandmother's vine-covered milkhouse. I'm blocking the view of my sister, Barbara.

I always thought it was a magic playhouse. But you're right, it was always cold in there. I never played in there long."

"The cow was gone long before you came along," she reminisced. "But we still used the milkhouse after that, instead of an icebox. The cement walls and floor kept out any animals, mice and the like, and kept things cool, but mostly the cold came from the water. You remember that big hand pump outside Grandma's back door, don't you?"

"Yeah, I remember it being about as tall as I was."

"The water from that hand pump was pretty cold, even in summer. We pumped water for the house into a bucket that we hung from the spout. We didn't get an electric pump installed until I was much older.

"I remember them digging the well deeper by hand one year when it dried up," she continued. "I get the shivers thinking about your Grandpa in that hole 30 feet down with a shovel, with us hauling up dirt in buckets attached to a rope. I don't know what we would have done if the sides had caved in on him before he got them all rocked up. Or if someone lost his grip and dropped a loaded bucket of dirt back down on him.

"Anyway, when they got done digging the well and put the hand pump in, Uncle Teddy [her older brother] rigged it so the drain right under the spout didn't drain the water right back into the ground. It ran into a catch basin, and then into a pipe that went into the trough in the milkhouse. Your Grandma would pump the hand pump until the trough was full of water, then take the milk pail straight from the cow, strain the milk through cheesecloth to get out any pieces of hay, and then set the pail into the trough to cool."

"So that's what that two-foot-high wall was at one end!"

"Yes, and remember the lily pond?"

"Oh sure. It was right next to the milkhouse, on the side of Grandma's house toward the pasture. I loved the lilies. It probably wasn't as big as I remember it being."

"No, it was maybe 10 feet across, and about three feet deep."

"Three feet? I remember that you said it was so deep that it didn't have a bottom, and that if we ever fell in we would drown. I was afraid to go near it."

"Good. We didn't want you to go near it. A few years before you were born, the grandson of Grandma's next-door neighbor did almost drown in it."

"I didn't know that!"

"Yeah, he was probably three years old. His mother was visiting her mother, and they didn't even notice he was gone. He had wandered over and fell in and couldn't get out. Grandma just happened to be coming out of the house, and she heard him sputtering. Their house was right next door, on the other side of the driveway, so he didn't go far, but you never know with little kids, they just take off."

She gave me a knowing sideways glance, then continued.

"Grandma pulled him out, got him to stop gagging, and took him back next door. They were shocked. It was just coincidence that Grandma came out of the house just then. I hate to think what would have happened if she hadn't."

"Wow, you never told me that! So Grandma was a hero!"

"Yeah, I guess. But that's why we warned you kids away from the lily pond under threat of death. After all, you weren't more than three feet tall when you were that age. We didn't think any more of it, but that family sure didn't forget about it. When that kid grew up and got married, at the wedding reception they reminded us, and announced to everyone that Grandma had saved his life when he was little."

She smiled at the memory.

"Anyway, the reason I brought it up is that Teddy designed it so the overflow water from the trough in the milkhouse drained out into the lily pond. Grandma liked the lilies, so that hand pump got a work-out pretty regularly, to keep the pond full, even after Grandpa installed an electric pump to put water into the house."

"That's very clever. I hope we think up creative things like that in Maine."

Mom sighed and shook her head.

"I was just a kid during the Depression. Since we had a farm, we never went hungry. But it was a hard life. I don't like the idea of you going back in time."

Rather than get into an argument about what constitutes progress, and whether it made sense to spend a lifetime working, as my dad did, in a noisy steel mill which wrecked his hearing and his health, I diverted her attention to a 1909 Singer treadle sewing machine on a cast-iron base that Keith had found for $5. The old 1909 sewing machine that came with it functioned more or less, but it didn't have zig-zag, and that was the feature I used the most, primarily for patching rips in jeans. But then we discovered that the mounting screws on my portable electric Singer zigzag sewing machine precisely matched the screw holes in the treadle base. We switched machines, added a new leather belt to connect the foot treadle to the external pulley on the new sewing machine, and we were in business.

I excitedly told Mom about the great deal Keith got on ten used beehives. The supers had to be cleaned up and painted, but they were in pretty good shape, and the price was right.

Then Mom learned that the nearest private phone was even farther away than the nearest electric line.

"You won't have a phone? Oh my God. I'll never hear from you again."

"Maybe not, but if you can still read, I understand the U. S. Postal Service penetrates the wilderness, even in Maine. Although, not quite all the way. They tell us we'll have to pick up our mail at the post office in Harborside. Something about us being too rural for Rural Free Delivery..."

....."Remember that big grindstone that Grandpa had for sharpening knives and things, where you would sit on that hard metal seat like a bicycle seat, and pedal and have water drip from a can onto the wheel as it went around?" I asked my mother.

"Yes, he kept it out by the chicken coop."

"I remember that. Well, we found one like that, I think it measures 22 inches across, for $20. So we'll be able to sharpen all those axes and hatchets we've been collecting.

"And in one amazing junk shop piled high with all kinds of things, we came across this beautiful, but all beat-up, black cast-iron wood-burning cookstove. It was completely encrusted with rust and caked grease. Did you have a cookstove like that when you were a kid?"

"Yes, but we burned coal in it, not wood. Remember that filthy coal bin in the basement?"

"Vaguely. I remember you didn't let us go down there very often. Anyway, Keith took that cookstove all apart, and, one piece at a time, took off all the crud down to the bare metal. He used a wire brush attachment on his power drill, out in the back yard. We bolted it back together and stove-blacked it up proper. It looks beautiful! I'm so excited about taking it to Maine and using it."

Another great junk shop find of mine was the perfect chamber pot. Only 50 cents. It had a nice, graceful curve to it, white enamel over metal, with an intact wire-and-wood-handled bail, and a nice tight-fitting lid. It was a good foot tall, had a comfortable wide, flat lip, and only one small chip in the enamel, near the top. I would say it held about two gallons.

I think my oohing and aahhing over the fact that it had a matching lid clued the junk shop owner in to the fact that I wasn't going to use it as a flower pot. When he took my money, he made a point of saying, "You know, that's not for cooking."

I said, "I know." But apparently he was still worried. As I was walking away, he said really loudly, "That's not a stew pot there."

I said "I know" again.

"He couldn't quite bring himself to tell me what it WAS used for," I laughed as I told my mother the story. "I think he was afraid he would have lost the sale if he had."

For the uninitiated, a chamber pot is an in-house outhouse, sort of a portable potty-chair for grown-ups. It could be used at night or in the cold of winter, and then taken outside and emptied into the outhouse whenever it was convenient.

As it turned out, I was the only one who took advantage of that not-so-modern convenience. Keith was too macho to let a little sleet, snow, cold or dark of night keep him from the simple slit-trench that passed for our outhouse our first few years in Maine.

When I went to empty the chamber pot, I would take a boiling teakettle along with me in the other hand. I would dump the load, then use the hot water first as a rinse-and-flush, and then a second time to sterilize the container. The process worked fine, and was no more unpleasant than changing a diaper.

While we're on the topic, I confess there was a limit to the back-to-nature bit, even for me. I wasn't ready to use freshly-gathered sphagnum moss to replace toilet paper, as the Colemans were doing.

And then it was May and time to turn our focus and energies to Maine.

The Nearings by then had had the eclectic, multi-angled property lines to our pending parcel staked out and surveyed. With the deed description in hand, Keith and I walked the property, making plans. We pinpointed rock outcroppings and wet areas, some huge pine trees, a few medium-sized but tap-able maple trees, and the most beautiful yellow birch grove we had seen anywhere. We found some magical places with mossy rocks and overhanging branches. We picked out a house site — almost a natural clearing with a lot of small trees, situated about in the middle of the property, just south of a protective knoll, and next to the beautiful running brook. We decided on a general direction for the driveway out.

This was really going to work.

Helen insisted on a 10-year right of first refusal — if we decided to sell within 10 years, she could buy back our property "for the same price and on the same terms" as we were willing to accept "from any person." That was just fine with us. We were in this for the long haul.

On May 23, 1972, Helen, as the owner of record, signed the deed and Scott signed off his interest as her husband. And we became land-owners for the first time in our young lives.

I had scheduled a two-week vacation to start then, and Keith and I, along with our mixed-breed-but-mostly-beagle dog Brandy, immediately moved onto the land and set up camp. We had the bulk of our treasures already scavenged and $5,000 still in the bank. We were ready to roll.

The plan was to start right away clearing a house site. Then we would cut a path through the woods for a driveway, coming out on the town road about midway between the Nearing and Coleman drives. Our driveway would of course curve around enough to hide our little nirvana from public view and the casually curious. No hint of suburbia for us.

After we did that, we would hand-dig a root cellar, and then a trench in which to pour the cement for the house footings. After the cement work for the footings and root cellar was done, we would start felling trees for our 25-foot-square, post-and-beam, gambrel-roofed cabin.

At the end of those first two weeks, I would go back to Rhode Island and keep working at the paper until November to keep the money coming in. I would come up every weekend (a six hour drive each way) to help out, while Keith stayed on-site to keep the project moving forward.

In keeping with our new and pure philosophy, we of course would use only hand-tools — no smelly, polluting, fossil-fuel-burning chainsaws for us. We would mix the cement by hand, as the Nearings had done. To further preclude any temptation to use the VW van or to hire heavy equipment to move big trees or rocks, we would clear the land from the inside out.

Really, that was the plan.

Our critter-proof VW van worked reasonably well for short-term food storage, with enough room left in the back for an actual mattress for sleeping. But in inclement weather, when campfires and dry clothes were out of the question, we waited out the storm in John's cabin up the road.

John Tani was one of the earliest Nearing settlers. I didn't know much about him other than that he had built a cabin on the farthest piece of the Nearing farm, beyond the Coleman cabin, on what was by then part of the Coleman 60 acres. John owned the cabin, the Colemans owned the land. Curiously, no deed changed hands.

It was obvious even to a casual observer that John had done a lot of work. He had cleared a crude road as far as he could to his house site. Then, hauling in lumber and materials on his back the rest of the way, he built the cabin half-way up a steep hill. He then cleared and planted a garden in a small but very rocky area below the cabin. And then, his first Spring, with the seedlings just popping through the ground, he disappeared into the sunset, off to build boats.

The cabin was spare and crude, but it had a decent wood-burning cookstove, thin mattresses on the bunk beds, a home-made table with stools — and no lock on the door. The neighborhood used it as the overflow guest quarters. Just add food and firewood, and it was quite cozy.

The unwritten rule was that John's place was to be left as clean as it was found, or better. Over time an odd assortment of plates, utensils and cooking pots had built up. A few books were left on the shelf. Hooks were rigged to hang the lanterns for better light.

Everyone seemed to agree that, as the new permanent residents in the area, we had dibs on the place if we needed it, second in line only to John, should he ever return.

With both of us going at it with hand saws, the house site started to open up. The small trees and wild shrubs we cut down were stacked into several large brush piles, to be burned in the dead of winter when snow was on the ground.

As soon as we had cleared enough ground, we marked and staked out the corners of the future cabin. From then on we surveyed our domain through imaginary windows, ate meals in our imaginary dining room, finalized the rest of the homestead's layout in our heads.

That area down there would be the first garden, the flat area behind the house would come later. Fruit trees would go here, and there. The beehives would be protected from the winter winds if we put them over here. The driveway would come into the clearing from over there.

But things were not going as quickly as we had hoped. When I left two weeks later to go back to my day job, only the clearing for the house-site and first garden area could be crossed off our long list.

It would be the first of many work/time miscalculations.

But Keith was gearing up to lay out the road. I hoped to find a cleared swath to walk down when I got back the next weekend.

Instead, a week later I was met with a tale of frustration over the lack of progress.

"The path looks okay for a ways in on either end," he said of the driveway plan. "Where it comes off the town road is fine, and where it comes into the clearing here. But when I started to flag it on the ground — well, we've got huge logistics problems in the middle. For starters, the land in that direction is a whole series of ridges and ravines. I counted 22 places that will need culverts. A couple of the ravines are deep enough that they will need actual bridges. And we've got some huge trees and big boulders that I can't figure out how we can avoid. We're talking either heavy equipment or a whole lot of heavy back labor. If we don't go with heavy equipment, and assuming I can figure out how to do all this, it'll take so long we'll never get our house built by winter."

I pondered the situation. Philosophically we had been hoping to avoid hiring bulldozers or backhoes, and besides, it wasn't in our budget. But time was also a critical factor. What to do when neither of Keith's alternatives was acceptable?

"OK, we need to find another way out," I finally concluded.

Keith was skeptical. I perused the edges of the clearing.

"How about right up here?" I pointed to a gradual incline on the other side of the flowing creek.

We headed in that direction, and walked a gently curving path up a slight rise through the woods. About 600 feet later, we came out on the town road and found ourselves about a hundred feet from our property line marker. The entrance to the Colemans' long gravel driveway was a few dozen feet beyond that marker.

The path we had just walked was about half the length of our original route. It had only a few big trees. No need for culverts or a bulldozer, just a few loads of trucked-in fill. The house clearing would still not be visible from the road. And the larger trees that were in the way were mostly straight and tall and could be used in constructing the house. We would still need to build a bridge to cross the creek at the edge of the house clearing, but since the creek cut right through the middle of the property, we would need to do that no matter which way we came in.

"Too much like suburbia," Keith started to say, voicing disdain for side-by-side driveways. In about a minute and a half, however, as the possibilities sunk in, that contempt bit the dust of reality, and Keith became visibly relieved.

Then, gently patting one of the large spruce trees that stood in the middle of our proposed driveway, he asked, "Do you know how long it takes to cut down a full-grown tree with a cross-cut saw?"

Shortly thereafter, he bought his first chainsaw.

Chapter 4
Trees, Transients and Transplants

Sometimes, no matter how many books or pamphlets you read, the only way to understand how to do something is to just do it.

For me, trees were like that.

I have to admit that up to that point in my life, I looked at trees like any suburban nature lover, admiring their majestic beauty and drinking in their changing ornamentation in spring, summer and fall. I mourned the ones that I could see from the roadside when they were felled by wind, lightning, or new construction, or disfigured by electric line crews. But, despite spontaneously hugging one here and there, and helping to rake up the fall's accumulation of leaves in the back yard, I didn't have a personal relationship with any of them.

That changed the first time I helped cut one down. And we had to cut them down. Some were growing in the path of our driveway. Others would be used to build our home, to heat that home, to cook our food. Those beautiful trees were the essential raw material from which useful beams, boards, furniture stock and firewood were wrought.

At a gut level I came to appreciate that, in their death, trees were in fact the starting point for much of what we know as civilization.

Our first task was to learn how to fell trees without killing ourselves. And the first thing to learn in that regard was just how heavy trees are.

They are very, very heavy.

The force of a full-grown, standing tree as it falls to the ground still strikes awe and fear in me. Those huge wooden sticks weigh tons. Literally. And they are not always predictable in the path they take to the ground. That's certainly the case with trees cut down in the open, but is even more true when trying to cull out one tree in a close-standing clump.

Through trial and several errors, Keith and I learned to size up a tree's symmetry, and to figure out the placement and angle of a cut at its base that would get the tree to fall where we wanted. We learned that a slight miscalculation on the angle of the cut, or a gust of wind at the wrong time, would send the tree falling against another tree. Or twist it around in another direction. Or kick the butt up into the face of the logger.

I became a tree-cutting chicken. I knew the trees needed to be cut, and I knew only Keith and I would be doing it. But I decided I didn't need to tempt fate. After all, I had no manhood to prove here.

As we calculated our cutting maneuvers on a given tree, I would in addition gauge the height of the tree in question, and would plan the path through the woods that would get me at least that length away from its base in the opposite direction. In the last moments of a tree-felling, with only a final push of the saw or whacks with an axe to go (or when the tree got ahead of us and shifted with a groan on its almost-severed base), I unabashedly ran for cover. Peaking out from behind another substantial, protective, sylvan specimen, I would witness wide-eyed the powerful death throes of that grand wooden plant hitting the ground with a thundering crunch.

And I would check to make sure Keith was all right. He always was.

Once the trees were down and the trunks cut to length, they needed to be hauled out and turned into posts and beams for the house. Posts could be round, and needed only to be debarked. Beams that would have boards nailed to them had to be flattened on the appropriate sides.

I got pretty adept at turning a round log into a square timberframe, using a broad hatchet, a good eye and a piece of string for guidance. Normal axes are beveled on both sides, which is fine for splitting wood. A broad axe, or hewing axe, and its smaller cousin, the broad hatchet, are flat on one side, and so cut a flat edge.

That's me squaring a log with a hewing axe

Those tool-makers were so clever.

There is a way of squaring up a log using a chainsaw and a flat board, but the beams would be showing in our home, and we didn't want to have to stare up at the marks of mechanical civilization as we lay exhausted in our bed at night.

Such principles.

Meanwhile, people were coming to Cape Rosier in droves, as Keith and I had the previous winter, to check out the Nearings.

When we first crossed their path, Helen and Scott Nearing had been living by their wits in rural America, working hard, physically and mentally, getting a lot done, for more than 40 years. Wherever they had lived and lectured, they had been sought out by small clusters of people who shared their strong and acerbic philosophy and politics.

In 1970, the type and tenor of those people changed. After ***Living the Good Life*** was re-issued, the Nearings suddenly became cult figures. Spontaneously and mysteriously, the Nearing homestead in Harborside become part of The Tour, one stop on a national, and sometimes international, pilgrimage to find one's soul. The waves of people — unrelated and unorganized — came from someplace else, washed over Cape Rosier, and then rolled onto the next political or spiritual beachhead. Singly or in a group, the would-be disciples came with nothing but a wistful sense of wonderment in their hearts (and usually Dad's credit card in their back pockets). The people, mostly but not all young, arrived by thumb or Volkswagen van, to touch the hems of the Nearing robes, to pick up on their magic.

The Nearings had difficulty adjusting to both the adoration and the superficiality of many of their visitors. Once, a few years into the new phenomenon, Scott was asked what he thought of the adoring masses.

"I wish they were out doing something useful, like hoeing potatoes," he spit out.

After living for nearly three years on the outskirts of military bases, I could recognize a uniform when I saw one. And these new visitors had them — long hair, braids, ponytails, untrimmed beards, long flowing skirts or ragged shorts, sandals or Birkenstocks, tie-dyed T-shirts, wild scarves. Since I grew up in Ohio, where long hair is still an issue today, I was not accustomed to the hirsuteness. But I liked the colors, and admired the ease with which these friendly people wore those outrageous outfits.

I dressed in more practical sweatshirts and blue jeans, which did not rip as easily and could get dirty without looking inappropriate.

When they had a project going, the Nearings would accept offers of help from the passers-through. In fact they were masters at harnessing the free energy. Of course, not all of the workers were up to snuff, but some of them were trainable. One of the few who passed the Nearing test of industriousness was a woman named Susie Hall. Then 21, and from Maryland, the Nearings described her as the best worker, male or female, they had ever had visit them.

Eliot Coleman took his cue from the Nearings in the free-labor department. At first he simply pointed equipped travelers into the woods to pound some tent stakes and then invited them to come and learn a little gardening at his place.

One such couple who brought their own tent were Robin and Tony. I don't know whatever happened to Tony, but Robin went on shortly thereafter to work for newspaper publisher Nat Barrows in the fishing village of Stonington, Maine, on the next peninsula over. A few years later she and Nat founded the highly-acclaimed ***Commercial Fisheries News***, and 20 years after that, Robin Alden became Maine's first female Commissioner of Marine Resources.

As the crowds grew, it became obvious that more in the way of local accommodations were needed. Eliot talked the Nearings into financing construction of a campground area with a small A-frame cabin and all the amenities (its own outhouse, barbecue grill, and an outdoor shower complete with a solar-heated five-gallon bucket of water and a sprinkler nozzle). The only problem was, the place he wanted to put it was partially on our property. So he also talked the Nearings into convincing us to give up five oddly-shaped, long and narrow acres between our two driveways, cutting down our original land base from 30 to 25 acres.

We were more than a little reluctant at first, because it would put the noisy campground just a few hundred feet from our front door. And I wasn't convinced that Eliot couldn't find some suitable spot on his 60 acres for what amounted to a camp for his agricultural workers.

But our abutting neighbors on both sides were insistent. To help alleviate our concerns, they suggested we put into the deed a perpetual right of first refusal, and a restriction that the land would "not be divided for purposes of occupation or lease and no part of the said lot less than the whole shall be leased except for agricultural purposes." We acquiesced to keep the neighborhood peace.

The area was cleared, the campground built. As sometimes happened out there on the Cape, construction preceded legalities by a few years. It was 1975 before we finally signed the deed, casting the new property lines in stone. No money changed hands. Odder still, it took Eliot nine years to record that five-acre land transfer in the Hancock County Registry of Deeds.

Chapter 4 — Trees, Transients and Transplants

Most of the campground residents spent their time at the two big draws, the Nearings and Colemans. Those transient workers who were most interested in construction, or who had overstayed their welcome at the Colemans, were sent in our direction.

And so it came to pass, that very first summer, our budding homestead became part of The Tour.

Some of the folks who showed up on our yet-to-be-built doorstep pitched right in, asking questions as they went along.

Others were looking for inspiration and just wanted to talk, or to watch. Most of the time that was OK, as long as they didn't slow us down.

Some of the visitors became long-time friends. Most we never saw again.

A couple of them left lasting impressions.

*   *   *   *   *

It was late summer, and Keith and I were waist-high in the narrow trench that was to become the cabin's foundation. The subsoil was gravel, and condensed into a compact layer known as hardpan. We were deepening the trench inch by inch with heavy pick-axes, swinging mattocks rhythmically at the rocky ground to loosen it to the point where a shovel would be effective. It was a tight fit, trying to work in that narrow space, especially down more than a foot or so from the top.

"Hi there."

We looked up to see a tall and strapping fellow in dark hair and black beard, just crossing the bridge at the creek. Judging from the size of his pack, he was prepared to set up camp anywhere in the world.

"They said up the road that you could use some help."

"Help would be nice," Keith said.

"Well, here I am, in all my glory. Name's George. What can I help you with?"

"Do you see what I'm doing?" Keith asked.

George nodded solemnly.

"This trench is for the house foundation. It has to be four feet deep to get below the frost line, so the foundation won't shift when the ground thaws in the spring. We're going to fill the trench with cement, so it has to be straight-sided and as smooth as possible. We don't want the dirt to fall from the sides into the wet cement when we pour it. I use the mattock to break up the sod and dirt, then the shovel to get it out of the trench. Got it?"

"Sure, sure," George grinned.

"There's another mattock. You can start over there, where I've taken off the sod. Just hack away, around the corner there, where you won't hit either of us on the back-swing. Just follow the outline."

George swung off his huge backpack and enthusiastically grabbed the designated tool. We went back to our labors at two other places along the trench.

George jumped into the shallow part of the trench, took careful aim, and swung. Thunk. So far, so good. Another swing, another thunk.

George paused, put the mattock head-down in the trench, and leaned on the top of the handle, not saying a word for a full minute or so. We watched him obliquely as we picked away — swing, thunk, swing, thunk — at our respective tasks.

Finally George nodded his head firmly.

"Well, I'm going to California," he announced matter-of-factly.

"That so?" Keith said, keeping up his steady rhythm — swing, thunk, swing, thunk. "I've been there." Swing, thunk. "Nice place." Swing, thunk, swing, thunk. "When you leaving?" Swing, thunk, swing, thunk.

George contemplated the question for a few seconds.

"Why, I do believe this is as good a time as any!" he said.

In one graceful motion, George dropped the mattock he had been leaning on, grabbed his backpack, and slipped it onto his back. "See you later," he called, and went whistling up the driveway.

That was a stopper for us. We leaned on our mattock handles, George-fashion, and watched him go. We shook our heads to clear George away, and went back to work.

Swing, thunk, swing, thunk.

Tuck was the other case. He came trundling down the drive about a year later as I was feeding a bonfire, burning up the brush from the garden clearing. Keith was off on an errand.

"Hello," he said cheerily, as he scoped out the clearing. "My name is Tuck."

He was a short man, in his early forties, with a weathered look about him. Hobbit-like. I looked at his feet. He wore sneakers. I decided the name fit.

"Hello," I replied. "What can I do for you?"

"Well, I was hoping to meet the Nearings, but they weren't home."

"Yes, they left this morning," I said. "They'll be gone for few days. Too bad you missed them."

He again perused the clearing, apparently not finding anything of interest. "I wanted to talk to them about my plan."

Feeding a brush fire doesn't take a lot of concentration. I bit.

"OK," I said. "What's your plan."
"I'm going to sail around the world on a sailboat I'm building myself," he said.
Nice idea, I thought. Leisurely cruising the corals, dipping the fishing line in at appropriate spots...
"...and I'm going to live entirely on wheat grass and alfalfa sprouts." The coral reef disappeared.
"Wheat grass and alfalfa sprouts," I repeated flatly.
"Yes, that's right," he said, beaming.
"Ummm...Why would you want to do that?"
Tuck looked crushed.
"Why, to prove that it can be done," he said, obviously amazed at my stupidity.
"To prove WHAT can be done?"
"That a human being can be healthy while living for long periods of time on nothing but wheat grass and alfalfa sprouts. And some water, of course."
I threw a branch on the fire.
"Don't you see, if I can prove that, it'll revolutionize the world." Tuck insisted. "Just think, all these people in the starving countries of the world won't need to starve anymore."
"Uh, that's nice." More brush on the burning pile. Tuck made no move to help. He also made no move to leave.
"How long do you think it would take you?" was the only thing I could think to finally ask.
"I figure about nine months at least," he said, his excitement rising. "I've got this boat in the works already." He described the vessel in great detail to the landlubber before him.
"Of course, I would have to have publicity and documentation on every stop I made. To make sure I wasn't stashing any other food away, you know."
"Why go on a boat?" I asked. "Why not just do the same thing anywhere, in a laboratory or a locked house or something?"
"Because a boat is foolproof. If I leave on a boat, with only water, and alfalfa seed and wheat berries, and I'm gone for several months, people are more apt to believe that that was all I lived on, than if I said I did it at home."
I resurrected the thought I had had a few minutes before, of a fishing line dropped over the side of the boat, sinking into a fin-filled coral reef.
"Um, have you ever done this diet for any length of time?"
"Oh, yes! Lots of times!"
I looked at the man. He was not thin.

"No problems?"

"No problems"

Neither of us spoke for awhile. I focused on my task, wondering where people like this came from.

"I would think that diet would get awfully boring after awhile," I finally said.

"Well, you're right there. After awhile I do get these incredible cravings. After I've been on that diet for a month or so. And I always crave the same thing."

I contemplated what I would crave most after a month of eating baby grass and tickly sprouts. Fried chicken? Avocados? A fresh-baked muffin covered with...

"You're going to find this hard to believe, but every time I came off the diet because I just had to have a hot fudge sundae. With nuts and whipped cream and a maraschino cherry. Washed down with lots of hot coffee."

He wiped some saliva from the corner of his mouth.

"Wouldn't sleep for days because of the coffee. The caffeine, you know. After that I'd be all right and I could stick to it for a long time again."

I smiled weakly at him, speechless. Hot fudge sundaes were a particular weakness of mine, but a maraschino cherry? Didn't sound organic to me. I kept stoking the fire.

"Well, I can see you're busy."

Finally.

He reached into his pocket, pulled out a handful of mismatched business cards, and shuffled through them for a few seconds.

"Here, give my card to the Nearings, would you? And tell them what I said? I'm really sorry I missed them. I guess I'll be heading out now. It's almost lunchtime anyhow."

I deliberately did not ask him what he planned to eat for lunch.

As he pranced up the drive to his car, I looked at what he had handed me. It was a dog-eared business card for a master plumber in Canfield, Ohio. The name "Tuck" was nowhere to be found.

I threw the card onto the fire.

A few weeks later Helen reported that Tuck had come around again and caught them at home. He was looking for money, financial support for his project, she said with a frown. He didn't get any from them.

*   *   *   *   *

But back to that first summer.

It passed quickly with me driving up every Friday night or early

Chapter 4 — Trees, Transients and Transplants 41

Saturday, both of us working full-bore on Saturday and Sunday, and me returning to Rhode Island late Sunday night. I was usually exhausted at work all day Monday, recuperated by Tuesday, did the laundry, shopping and garden tending after work on Wednesday and Thursday, and got refreshed and raring to go by the time Friday night rolled around.

In those weeks we cleared the road, built a log bridge over the narrow creek, and had started to hand-dig the root cellar and, of course, the foundation trenches.

Digging the root cellar was one example of a project that is best not done alone. The first few feet went fine. But then the hole became too deep for Keith to simply pitch out the shovels full of dirt. The only thing he could do when I wasn't there was set up a pulley on a tripod over the hole, with a rope and a hook strong enough to handle a five-gallon bucket full of dirt. He would climb into the hole, fill several buckets with dirt, climb out of the hole, haul up the buckets one at a time, dump them, put the buckets back into the hole, crawl back down, and fill them up again.

Slow going. I couldn't help but think of my grandfather hand-digging that well deeper.

Despite all that, Keith had gotten a pretty good-sized cellar hole dug — when a storm passed through and it filled up with water. And it stayed filled up with water. The water was seeping in from the nearby hill, but it wasn't seeping out again.

Keith did the math on this real-life math story problem — if it was so far to a point on the creek low enough to drain the bottom of the as-yet-to-be-dug 10-foot-deep root cellar, and he could hand-dig just so many square feet of dirt in a day, how many days would it take to hand-dig a drain for the root cellar?

At that point yet another philosophical resolve bit the dust. Keith hired a local fellow with a backhoe.

No cement trucks for us, however. Forget the fact that not even an empty cement truck could have made it down our crude road, or could have crossed the narrow log bridge over the creek without collapsing it. The four-foot-deep trench foundation, along with the walls for the 10-foot by 12-foot root cellar, were to be built by the Nearing method (actually the Flagg method) — a composite of sand, local rocks and hand-mixed cement, one wheelbarrow at a time.

On a Saturday in September, I was headed for a week's "vacation" in Maine. We were going to get a whole lot done. I was tooling along on I-95, and had gotten as far as New Hampshire, when the old VW bug blew a piston rod just as I was approaching a toll booth. I managed to limp to a VW garage the toll-taker pointed me toward, about three miles away, where the mechanic said he could fix the car for between $300 and $375, or he could buy it off me for parts for $50.

There I was, 140 miles from one home in Rhode Island, and 230 from Keith and the other home in Maine. In this time before cell phones, I considered my options.

I could probably leave the car in New Hampshire to be fixed, and get back to Rhode Island by bus. But that would leave me stranded in Rhode Island at a time when I was badly needed in Maine. Even if I could find a bus going north, I was sure I couldn't get public transportation to take me further than Bangor, which was 50 or more miles from Harborside. And what would I do then? Keith was at least two miles from the nearest telephone. How could I get a message to him?

Names. I tried to think of names of people in Maine who had phones. Helen and Scott didn't have one. Neither did the Colemans. Directory Assistance had no phone listing for the Harborside post office. Tracy Howard was not only hard of hearing and feeble, but, in

The wooden bridge over our creek. Photo was taken from the cabin-side of the creek, looking toward the town road.

his 80s, I didn't think he drove anymore.

I racked my brain and finally remembered the name of a local woman, a subsistence farmer people kept telling us we had to meet someday.

Dottie Gray not only took the collect call, dear heart, but she said she knew where Keith was working in the woods, and would go out and get him and have him call me back at the VW garage.

This may not seem all that unusual for a friendly neighbor to do until you realize that, from her farm to our budding homestead, we're talking a distance of about six miles. It was my first taste of the realities of small town living, my first hint that, far from us packing civilization into the wilderness, civilization was already there — and knew every move we were making.

Keith called me back, and came down to get me with a 1966 Jeep Wagoneer that he'd bought that week for a few hundred dollars. We rented a tow bar from U-Haul for $11 and hauled the little German beetle up to Maine.

Turns out the clutch and transmission on the VW bus had been going for some time, which had prompted the purchase of the Jeep when the opportunity presented itself. But the engine of the bus worked just fine. And the engine in the bug obviously didn't.

So, Keith and an itinerant helper whose name I don't remember proceeded to do an engine transplant in less than sterile conditions in the middle of a clearing in the Maine woods.

The two of them took the engine out of the bus and put it into the bug. Then they threw in the better starter, the bus radio (the bug didn't have one), and swapped two almost-new tires from the bus. The only expense was $6 for a special tool to change the fly wheel on the clutch, or something. The 1964 beetle not only sprang to life, it started getting 30 miles to the gallon, better than either VW got before the transplant.

But it was already September, and the mechanical surgery had cost us four valuable days, half of my week's vacation. Fall was fast approaching, and the foundation of the house had yet to be poured. Time was at a premium. The push was on.

At the end of September, we stopped long enough to reassess our situation. The cellar hole and all the foundation trenches were finally all dug and ready for cement, the cellar drain had been laid and mostly covered back up, and we had hauled in sand and rocks in preparation for the first cement pour. But the flow of visitors had slowed to a trickle, and with it any chance for free labor.

Clearly, Keith needed me on-site if we were going to make it before winter set in.

That Monday, six weeks before my boss had expected it, I gave my two-week notice. After a flurry of garden-canning and house-packing, we moved all our belongings to Maine, storing our non-essentials in an unlocked bay of Tracy Howard's rickety garage/barn, in one of six horse stalls he rented out for $5 a month.

Carefully stacked in that stall was more than 700 square feet of window-glass — all that we would need for the house and maybe a small greenhouse. Keith had gotten the glass, including four huge ¼-inch-thick storefront windows, for $54 from the demolition contractor who was in charge of a new federally-funded urban renewal project just starting in Narragansett, RI. It was tricky getting the storefront windows to Maine intact, but three of those large panes ended up as sun-absorbing picture windows in the southwest corner of our new home.

Also among the mix was the set of Noritake china, still in its packing boxes, that Keith had bought for me on a military special during one of his Vietnam tours.

Keith had been in Maine full-time since May. On October 13, 1972, I officially became a "from away" Maine transplant.

I'm on the left, giving Scott and a friend a tour of our construction site.
Helen is bending over, checking out our cement form work.

Chapter 5
The CIA and a Real Jewish Princess

Right about the time I became a full-time resident, Helen announced that she and Scott would be leaving the first part of November for New York to do research for their next book, and would be away all winter. They needed someone to stay in their house, feed their beloved Puss-O (yes, despite their condemnation of animal slavery, Helen had a cat), keep the home fires burning so the water pipes wouldn't freeze, and, oh yes, deal with their mail and fill any orders for their books.

Didn't I once work for a newspaper? Was I willing to do that kind of paperwork? They would even pay me $100 a month for my part-time services.

The offer was unexpected — and welcome, especially at a time when the frame of our hand-hewn post-and-beam house was still masquerading as a bunch of standing trees.

We had been planning on camping out on-site as long as the weather allowed, and then moving to John Tani's cabin (hauling in firewood as we went) once the weather got more severe. Having a warm, comfortable base camp within a short walk to our work-site would be very helpful. And, since I had quit my job earlier than we had planned, the money offered for work done after-hours by electric light wouldn't hurt either.

"Let's go through today's mail," Helen said a week or so before they left. We were sitting at that huge table in her kitchen. "I'll explain what to do with each piece."

She first sorted out the magazines, newsletters and newspapers, most of which I had never seen before.

"Put all of these in this box," she said. "We'll go through them when we get back. Here's the stack of mail. And here's the list of books and what they cost."

Living the Good Life and **The Maple Sugar Book** were prominent on that list. But many of the orders I was to fill were for Scott's twenty-some other books and pamphlets, which they had self-published and sold under the non-profit foundation name of Social Science Institute.

"Put the bank statements here. You don't have to deal with them. This basket is for personal mail that doesn't have to be answered right away — I'll take care of that when we get back. If they need to hear from us right away, write them a note telling them where we are. Here, let me show you what I do..."

Helen grabbed a hand-addressed envelope off the top of the pile. Letter-opener in hand, she hesitated, fingered the envelope, and smiled.

Turning the envelope over, she pointed with the letter-opener to a tear in the envelope that had been obviously patched with several pieces of cellophane.

"See this tape?" she asked.

"Yes," I said, quizzically.

"The CIA is checking our mail," she said. "But don't worry about it. Just ignore it."

"The CIA?"

"Or the FBI, one of them. Maybe both." She casually slit open the envelope.

"Good, it's a book order." She reached for one of the order forms.

"You're not upset?"

"About the book order?"

"No, about the CIA."

"Not any more. They've been checking our mail for decades. You'd think they'd be pretty bored by now."

This information about the mail tampering was not conveyed with any sense of outrage or injustice. It was just a simple fact. Normal for the Nearings. Mild compared to other violations they had been forced to tolerate over the years. These were people the government was nervous enough about to keep an eye on. Not to worry.

"But how, why?" I was taken aback. My government? Spying on these sweet, old, proudly wrinkled retired gardeners?

Being a *Readers' Digest* fan, (I couldn't understand why my high school guidance counselor advised against listing that magazine on college applications that asked for recent reading material), I was wide-eyed at her attitude. I hadn't had the time yet to read Scott's latest book, **The Making of a Radical**, which had just been published, to find out why the government felt so nervous:

Fired in 1917 from the University of Toledo as a traitor for his pacifist speeches against going to war (this was after his 1915 dismissal from the Wharton School of Economics at the University of Pennsylvania for coming out against child labor), Scott had been indicted under the Espionage Act by a federal grand jury on charges of insubordination, disloyalty, mutiny, and encouraging resistance to the World War I draft.

In February 1919, a few months after he lost a Congressional race to incumbent Fiorello LaGuardia (yes, the same guy they named the New York City airport after), Scott found himself defending his First Amendment right to free speech in the publication of his 44-page pamphlet *The Great Madness*. After an eloquent personal appeal to the jury, he was acquitted of all charges. But the Rand School, which had printed the pamphlet, was convicted of publishing what Scott had written, and was fined $3,000. Go figure.

As a point of reference — in early 1919, when he was on trial, our neighbor Scott Nearing was 35 years old.

Our government apparently had a long memory.

The Harborside postmaster, Dorothy Crockett, the widow of a military veteran and a veteran herself, had not worked for the post office before she was named Harborside Postmaster in 1968. Back then, such duties were awarded by picking from among those who were willing to accept the responsibility, which usually involved sectioning off a portion of one's home for exclusive postal business.

When Harborside Postmaster Jessie Howard retired, Dottie got the commission, and made the necessary modifications to the Harborside home she and her husband had bought in 1947.

Although everyone recognized the legitimacy of the appointment, and her need for the income, community spirit was not helped in any way by the abrupt and caustic nature of the newly appointed public servant.

Boldly patriotic and suspicious of the most casual remark, the new postmaster (who got incensed if she was referred to as a postmistress) was in the perfect position to check out the kind of information the Nearings were getting and dishing out. Helen said she could only assume the woman was a government plant, named specifically to keep an eye on her and Scott.

I had to admit it was possible.

What Helen thought was so strange about the situation was the lack of finesse.

"It's just so obvious that they've opened them and sealed them up again," she said.

"Couldn't the senders have done it? I mean, I know sometimes I'll think of something I forgot to say, and open up a letter before it goes out. If I already have a stamp on it, I just tape it shut again."

"Yes, well, we checked that out a couple of times," Helen said. "We asked some of our friends if they had done just what you said. They hadn't. The letters were opened after they mailed them. Now, here's what you do when you get a book order..."

Meanwhile, next door, our cabin foundation was progressing nicely, thanks to a volunteer named Gary who showed up Oct. 25, ready to work. Gary had stopped in for a day or two in mid-summer, and said he would be back in the fall, when he had a couple of weeks clear, to help us out on any construction project we still had going. We said that would be great. But, having had other promises of free labor that never materialized, we knew better than to count on his help until we heard his boots on the bridge.

But return he did, and he and Keith were working well together on all sorts of two-man jobs. Like pouring the foundation. Like felling trees and laying the sills.

Normally foundation trenches are dug wide enough to accommodate large removable cement forms. We had dug ours narrowly and with great difficulty specifically so we could fill the whole trench to ground level with cement and carefully-placed stones without using forms. The two-foot-high movable forms like ones the Nearings described in *Living the Good Life* were used above-ground, and for the interior walls of the root cellar. The idea of sticking local rocks into the cement was not just because it made for an interesting surface to look at, or because rocks are inherently strong, but also because they took up space, so less cement was necessary. That last point was an important consideration, since Keith and Gary were mixing the cement by hand in a wheelbarrow.

I once tried the mixing shovel, but didn't get past the first wheelbar-

A close-up of the movable forms used to build the concrete walls.
Notice the size of the rocks we used.

row. So I took over lighter physical tasks — hauling water, strategically placing rocks, tamping wet cement to work out air pockets, stuff like that.

Unfortunately, the physical stress of hand-mixing that heavy, wet cement resulted in a painful swelling of the nerves in Keith's wrists, called carpal tunnel syndrome. But he kept going, invincible as he was in his mid-twenties. An emergency cortisone shot in one wrist also helped.

So it was early November before Keith, Gary, and I finally finished the house foundation, a fact which, looking back, I find astonishing. Of course, we hadn't yet lived through a Maine winter, and didn't understand what a time crunch we were then in. But I do know we were all very relieved when that part of the project was done.

November 3, 1972 letter to Mom
... Had my first yoga lesson yesterday from Gary. Wasn't too impressed, but maybe I just didn't get into it enough....

Only then did we start to seriously fell the rest of the trees for the house. But considering everything, that part went rather quickly. Within a week we had hewed and squared up the beams for the sill, the set of logs that sits on the foundation. While Gary and Keith worked with the adz and hewing axe, I smoothed out the final surface with the smaller hewing hatchet.

We squared those sill beams on three sides. It made sense to only flatten the sides that needed flat surfaces. A sill beam needed to be flat on the bottom, to meet the top of the foundation. It needed a flat outside surface to nail boarding boards to. And it needed a flat top, to make for a level floor. But we did not need to flatten the fourth side, which would be hidden inside the foundation perimeter and under the floor.

I also started working on the ends of the beams, making tricky mortises and tenons that actually fit together.

Along about then we realized we only had enough time to cut and trim the trees we would need to frame the skeleton of the house. We did not have enough time before winter set in to fell more trees and get them sawn into boards for the floors, roof and walls. We ordered a truckload of rough-sawn lumber from R. Leon Williams Lumber Company in Orrington, about 40 miles away. The driver who delivered it unceremoniously dumped the whole load in the driveway, splitting and crushing many of the boards.

The sills are on, and the wooden ceiling in the root cellar is in place.

I also busied myself stuffing and organizing our new root cellar (which by then had a thick wooden cover to compensate for not having a house over it). It was a sight to behold — that tiny room packed full of food from its gravel floor to its insulated ceiling.

At the bottom of the homemade ladder, the light from a kerosene lamp bouncing off the glass canning jars provided a startling burst of color in the otherwise dark pit. The bright red of the canned tomatoes jumped out first. Then the warm yellow color of the peaches drew the eye. The sparkling jars of tomato sauce and pickles and jam from our Rhode Island garden were neatly arranged on shelves made of thick, un-planed wood.

There on the floor was the pale green of the cabbages all in a neat row, still with their roots on. (Eliot had offered us 52 heads free for the coming and getting. We went and got.)

Tucked under the shelves, the orange shoulders of the carrots from our Rhode Island garden, plus those from the Coleman and Nearing gardens, could be seen in the shallow wooden boxes I had built. The carrots were topless but sticking upright just like they grew in the garden, packed in with damp, sifted sand from the old hillside gravel pit across the town road opposite our driveway entrance. (If the sand is kept damp and cool, carrots will keep for months that way.)

Bountiful was the only word to describe my emotions as I looked at our hoard of food. I felt positively wealthy.

Those days it was Christmas every afternoon when I took stock of what we had accomplished that day — the trees the guys had felled, the logs that were piling up in the clearing, the timbers that were being cut and squared to fit the giant tinker-toy house we had designed.

Exciting and fulfilling as all this work was, more rewarding to me was the realization that the dynamic between Keith and me was working again. Gone was the post-Vietnam broodiness. Gone was his frustration of not fitting back into civilization. He had found his niche. He was happy. We were doing it. Together.

I felt I had my man back again.

As I went down to the house a few days later to see the Nearings off on their journey, I discovered my job description had changed slightly. There would still be mail and paperwork to contend with, but, Helen explained, I wouldn't have to worry about tending the fire in the middle of the day for the first couple of weeks because a young woman, whom I will call Idora, would also be staying at the house with us.

A dark-haired woman about my age, Idora wore brightly-colored loose-fitting clothing that I knew would snag on just about every low branch or bush in a simple walk through the woods.

I assumed that their friendship was well established. That concept was quickly dispelled as we waved goodbye to the famous couple.

"Aren't they something?" Idora commented to me. "They don't know me from Adam. Or Eve, as the case may be. Oh well, I could stand a hot bath. A whole two weeks! Heaven."

Idora, I would later learn, was into meditation, Yoga, and other forms of physical and mental enrichment. She would show me funny charts with strange images on them, and even try to explain some of them to me. She taught me about auras. She explained the importance of colors on the psyche, justifying the bright scarves she always wore.

But that would all come later. At that point, with the Nearings fresh out of sight, Idora proceeded to the bathroom and started to run the tub full of hot water. I focused on the pile of mail on the table.

But my concentration was soon broken by gagging noises emanating from the bathroom. Or were they vomiting noises?

I pounded on the bathroom door.

"You all right in there?" It sounded like she was coughing up her lungs, like the tuberculosis patients I heard in the hospital in Gulfport, Mississippi.

"Yes, hon, I'm fine. (gag, snort) I'm just washing out my nose. (sniff, hard blow) It's been too long, and it's all full of gunk. (gag, hack) Don't mind me. (spit) I'll be done in a minute. (cough, choke)."

I turned away and swallowed hard. The gagging and hacking noises reverberated throughout the house. I decided it was a good time to help Keith up at our house site.

The next morning, as Keith and Gary were off cutting more trees, I started the process of moving our everyday belongings from our campsite to the Nearings' house next door, albeit a half-mile down the road. After I had unpacked the first load, I again began to tackle the stack of mail I had deserted the previous day, settling down in Helen's kitchen just in time to be greeted with more gagging resonance from the bathroom.

"Do you know how awful that sounds?" I asked her when she had finished her toilette.

"Do you realize how much awful stuff people accumulate in the back of their noses every day?" Idora shot back. "The nose filters out all this icky stuff from the air all day, all the pollution, and it builds up and builds up and when it builds up to the point that the nose can't hold any more, it spills over the back and into your throat and people swallow that stuff. Now, THAT'S awful."

I couldn't help myself. Even as I gagged at her words, I had to know more.

"So what exactly do you do in there? How does one go about washing out one's nose?"

"Well, I start by pouring some water up my nose, and then just blowing it back into the sink. Then I do it again, and see if I can go deeper, and catch the flush water as it goes over that lip at the back of your nose, you know, and into your throat. I spit that stuff out. It tastes terrible, I'll tell you. I don't like that part. But it makes me more determined not to swallow that stuff."

I found myself swallowing hard.

"And then if I REALLY feel stopped up, like there's a big hunk of gunk back there, I use dental floss."

"Come again?"

"Yeah, I floss my sinuses. I feed a piece of dental floss — it's waxed with natural beeswax, you know, to make it stiff — anyway, I feed it up my nose and over that back lip and down into the throat. Sometimes that tickles. And then I reach in my mouth with my first finger, like this, and catch the end of the dental floss. And then I do like you do with your teeth, I tug on both ends of the dental floss until I dislodge whatever is in there, in the back of my nose. And then I flush that out."

First one nostril, then the other. Every morning. A simple Yoga technique, she explained nonchalantly.

I was still swallowing hard, now contemplating all the crud that my automatic reflex was sending into my undeserving stomach. I couldn't help it.

"Aren't you afraid of drowning? I mean, I hear that can happen in as little as two tablespoons of water."

"Nah, I'm careful," she said. She put another piece of wood into the kitchen cookstove.

(Years later a new friend explained that the ritual often went further. She had been taught to swallow a long strip of cheesecloth, gagging all the way, until enough reached the stomach. It was supposed to act like a bottle brush. A few swishes, and the cheesecloth was pulled up, bringing the contents of the stomach up with it. If Idora had explained that procedure to me, I must have repressed it. The brain protects us by only allowing in information we can deal with.)

"Well, I'm going to do my yoga now," she said. "I'll be in the other room, so I won't bother you."

"Before you go, could you look at this letter? I can't make out the handwriting on this part."

"Sorry," she said, "but I'm not wearing my glasses."

"Did you leave them in the bathroom?"

"No. I know where they are," she said impatiently. "I'm just not wearing them. I'm trying to make my eyes stronger."

"And not wearing your glasses will do that?"

"Oh sure. Glasses make your eyes lazy. With the glasses doing all the work, the eyes don't have to use their own muscles. So they atrophy, you know, and get weaker. And the weaker they get the more you need stronger glasses. So I'm not wearing my glasses. The idea is to get my eye muscles built up. And then I won't have to ever wear glasses ever again."

"Is it working?"

"Well, not so far."

But her eyes were pretty bad and she couldn't really see what she was doing unless she used her glasses, which she found very frustrating because it proved she wasn't doing it right, but she couldn't figure out what she was doing wrong, you know? But she knew it was something she could control if only she could work out what the problem was.

"But then I haven't been doing it very long, just a couple of weeks."

I began to feel that I was being caught in a current and I didn't know how to swim.

"I always thought people wore glasses because their eyes were shaped the wrong way," I offered, "which means their eye muscles can't stretch far enough to get things in focus."

"Well, that too," she said. "That's why I do eye exercises. Like this."

And she demonstrated the contortions she put her eyes through, hard right, hard left, up so high into the eye socket as to lose the iris. Then she jammed her fists into her eyes, pushing them back into her head, holding that pose for several long seconds. When she let go and looked up, her head shook reflexively, as her eyes tried desperately to focus.

"Trouble is, I haven't been able to keep it up. Every now and then, I dunno, I just can't help myself, I REALLY need to read something or see something and I put my glasses back on, just for a few minutes, and it wrecks all that training, and I have to start all over again."

She shrugged.

"Oh well, until it works, I'll just have to get used to not seeing things clearly. Off to my yoga."

Yoga. Gary had tried to teach me a little of that, without success. I wondered what he would think of Idora. The two had not yet met. My match-making tendencies leapt to the fore.

"Um, Idora," I said. "One more question."

"Shoot."

"I don't know anything about you. For instance, where you're from, how old you are, your nationality, your religion.... are you single, married....seeing someone? Sorry, guess that's more than one question."

She looked at me a bit pensively, but, not surprisingly, her eyes didn't quite focus on me. It was a few seconds before she responded.

"I'm 24, I grew up in Chicago, and my family is Jewish."

Twenty-four I had already figured. Chicago I could find on a map. As for Jewish....

*   *   *   *   *

Although the institution and I had long since parted company, I had been raised a Catholic. Until I was 10, I was under the impression that all religions were Christian — either Catholic or Protestant. Then, we moved across town and I started sixth grade at a new school.

Imagine my shock when some of my classmates told me they were Jewish. Jewish? How could they be? I was very confused. Hadn't I been taught that Jesus on the Cross turned all the Jews into Christians? What do you mean, you don't believe that story? It's not a story, it's a fact. Isn't it?

And then, to compound my problem, my new teacher turned out to be not only Jewish, but would soon be married in a TEMPLE. Thanks to bad Saturday movies, my only concept of a temple was something explorers discovered in the jungles, covered with vines and monkeys.

But my greatest shock was yet to come.

Three years later, when I was in junior high, I remember getting into a serious discussion of some sort on the school bus home. A Jewish friend who got off three stops before me made a pointed reference to the Holocaust. She was absolutely aghast to learn that I didn't have a clue what she was talking about. Luckily, we reached her house before I was completely humiliated.

When I asked at home and found out what she was talking about, I was very angry. How could I have gotten to the ripe old age of 14 without anyone having told me about the deliberate extermination — in gas chambers and crematoriums, yet — of six million people, Jews or otherwise? Wasn't that a crucial piece of history? As far as the Catholic nuns had taught me in Sunday Catechism, the grisly fate of Jesus, along with the Christians the Romans had tossed to the lions, were the totality of religious persecution in recorded history. Why was the Holocaust such an integral part of Jewish education, and so totally lacking in Catholic teachings?

But, more importantly, why was the Holocaust not a part of my normal, public education? What was going on here? What else was I deliberately not being told?

My outrage over institutional secrecy was born in that brief school bus conversation. For which I am forever grateful.

*   *   *   *   *

Idora turned to leave. And I hadn't found out the last critical piece of information that I needed if I was to be matchmaker between her and Gary.

"Um, so, how about the last part?"

"The last part?" she said dreamily.

"Yes. Are you married or single?"

"Well," she said in a strange voice, "I don't exactly know."

"You don't know if you're married or single?" I mustered all my polite forces, but I couldn't hide my incredulity. "What do you mean you don't know?"

She looked at me with an impatient smile.

"Well, since you are so insistent, I'll tell you. But you must promise not to ever tell my folks, because they don't know yet and if they did they would just die, and I don't know if I'll ever have the courage to tell them."

Nodding in stunned agreement, I said, "So you're married."

"I didn't say that, now did I?" she chided me. She sat down in Helen's chair and got comfortable before continuing. Then it all came out in a gush.

"Well, it's like this, see. I was on an Indian philosophy schtick and all that, you know, and joined this ashram and all that, and I had this guru that I really dug. Know what I mean?"

I nodded even though I didn't.

"Anyway, this guru, who is really a great guy, told us all these wonderful things and got us to commune with our inner spirits and stuff. I was really into it. I was with this group of women, a whole big bunch of us, and this guru [I'm sure she gave me a name, but I wasn't in a state of mind to remember], we'd been studying meditation and stuff with him, see. Anyway, so after a few months, he gets this great idea of us actually going over to India on this holy pilgrimage, to fly over to this ashram, see? Dig it. So we all went over there, all together, just like he said. And when we got there, there were all these Indian princes over there waiting for us, see. Then our guru said, to make it even more spiritual, and save our eternal souls, we should marry these holy Indian princes."

India, guru, ashram. Toto, I'm SURE we're not in Ohio anymore.

"Anyway, after a few days over there we finally got to meet the guys, the Indian princes, the ones our great guru had picked out for us, and that was cool too. The guy he picked out for me seemed OK, at least at first. Even kind of cute. We were there for about a month, communing with each other, no sex or even touching, you know, that was part of the deal. Just communing with each other, mind and spirit connections, that kind of stuff.

"And after about a month, the great guru said it was time for the weddings. And most of us said fine, cool. A few chickened out at that point and went home. But I didn't. I should have."

She paused, and seemed to drift away in thought.

"So it was all right with you?" I asked, as calmly as I could. My eyes must have been as wide as saucers.

"Well, sure," she bounced out of her trance. "I mean, he was our spiritual leader and all, and we trusted him, with our very lives and all, and he said it was a great idea. And we did these negotiations and all. We were going to get married, but not touch each other for 30 days after the wedding. We all agreed that we would have this group ceremony, and then each couple would spend a month in isolation. Just the two of us, still not touching, no sex, just getting our spirits lined up one-on-one. For a whole month. Only after all that, would we be ready to discuss if we wanted the physical part of the relationship. We would spend 30 days praying and meditating together, you know. Sort of a spiritual bonding first, and so we could really get to know each other. It would only be a spiritual marriage, unless we agreed to go to the physical level, you understand, that's what he told us. A consummation of the minds and the souls. And they were holy men, and the guru was a holy man, and everything was going to be so spiritual, you know? Sounded great to us. Well, to most of us. That's when some of the women ducked out."

"How many of you stayed?"

"Oh, about 30. And it was really great. I mean, we were really getting it together. I was so happy, I was going to surprise my folks. I mean, they knew I was in India, but after some of the guys I brought home, I figured they would be delighted with an Indian prince. I think they would have accepted anyone I brought home except a black guy. Not that they're prejudiced or anything. I was going with a black guy once, but I didn't tell them."

She trailed off in thought.

"Then what happened?" I whispered, my eyes bugging out of my head.

She startled back into the present, growled, tossed her eyes to the ceiling, and started to pace the room.

"Well, he did it. Our guru married all of us, in one big beautiful ceremony. It was great, really beautiful. And then we each went off with our husbands to this beautiful apartment where we were supposed to be so spiritual and all, to start this 30 days of spirituality. And as soon as the door closed behind us — Oh, god, it was awful" She paced.

"What!"

"He was a slimeball. He started grabbing at me. Just grabbing at me! He wouldn't stop. Grab, grab, grab, grab. I really freaked.

She paced some more around the Nearings' big kitchen, flailing her arms.

"From the minute we were alone together, it was touchy, feely, touchy feely. He wouldn't take his hands off me. I couldn't to get him to stop. I kept pushing his hands off me, but he wouldn't stop. Grab, grab, grab, grab. It was awful.

"What did you do!?"

"I said 'You can't do this.' And he said, 'You're my wife.'

"Then I said, 'But you promised!' And he said, 'All you American women want is sex, sex, sex. Just admit it.'

"I said, 'I'll leave! I'll fly home.' He said, 'I won't let you. I am your husband now.'

"I said, 'I'll get an annulment. We haven't consummated anything.' He said, 'I'll fight it. It'll cost you big bucks.' That's what he said. 'Big bucks.'

"I said, 'I don't have any money.' He said, 'You're lying. All Americans are rich.' He was getting all this stuff from the American movies, see. He had seen all these American movies, and figured all American women were loaded with money. Rich, rich, rich. Plus, I don't have any idea what the guru had told him about us.

"That's when I ran out of the room. I went straight to my guru, and told him what had happened and demanded that he make my prince behave."

"What did he do?"

"Nothing, the prick. He just raised his hands, like there was nothing he could do, you know? I told him to send me back to the States. He didn't want to, said I should stick it out. It was awful. He said I hadn't given it a chance, that I had made an eternal commitment in a solemn, sacred ceremony, and that I should go back to the apartment."

"Did you?"

"Hell no. I beat it out of the country, as soon as I could get a ticket."

"Then what?"

"Then I looked up a lawyer friend of mine, a guy I went to school with. He said he would try to get a divorce or an annulment, but that it was tricky because it was international, and he's a prince, and if he didn't want a divorce he could make all kinds of trouble, and all that kind of thing. He tells me it's real complicated. He's doing what he can, but it's taking more time than he figured."

"What about your folks?"

"My folks! God, they don't know anything about this. They would die. I don't want them to ever know I got married. It would kill them. And besides, I think my prince is probably after their money, so they have to stay out of this totally. The good part is, as far as I can tell, he doesn't know who they are. Which is how it has to stay until this whole thing is over with."

She took a deep breath and looked as straight at me as her eyes would allow.

"Anyway, I got so upset by the whole thing that I hit the road, and just left my lawyer friend to take care of it. I haven't talked to him in a month or so — I probably should call him — but I don't know if he's done yet, if he got the divorce finalized or annulled or whatever. So, in answer to your question, I don't know if I'm married or single."

"Oh," was about all I could muster.

I wrestled with it a little. But finally I decided that a divorce or annulment in the works and a husband in another country was close enough to being single. I told Gary that he might want to meet Idora. I said they had yoga in common.

Huge mistake.

Not that they didn't hit it off. They did. Big time.

But it turned out that Gary was the moonstruck type. We would be working on shaping the house beams, and suddenly Gary's hammer and chisel would stop. Keith and I would look up and there Gary would be, gazing into the sunset. Or the sunrise. It didn't seem to matter what time of day it was. Gary would go down to the Nearings for lunch and come back three hours later, straddle a log and start skinning it with a draw knife, only to stop, moon away some more, idle tool in hand.

He moved into the Nearings' house with us and Idora, and would show up at our clearing later and later every morning. And even when he managed to drag his leaden feet up the hill to our house site, his enthusiasm for house-building faded long before the early November sun washed out in mid-afternoon. It was simply amazing to watch. Like the Cheshire cat, the only thing left of him that we could see was the grin.

Gary couldn't get Idora out of his mind, and while she was there, nothing else could get in. I started to count the days until her scheduled departure.

But, of course, I should have figured it out — Idora's disappearance did not mean we would get our willing worker back. Gary would be leaving with her. They had decided to head out to California in Gary's van. They would stop in Chicago, so Gary could meet Idora's folks.

By that time I had determined that the nearest public phone was at Leach's country store, about a half-mile from the grange hall. I say it was a public phone because it wasn't a pay phone. It was a regular phone that could be used by the neighbors to make local calls. Long-distance calls required reversal of charges. And it was all very clear to everyone which of the two one was doing, because the phone was located in the small public area between the belled door and the tiny checkout counter, on the wall opposite the painted wooden table perpetually staffed by the town's retired male gossips perpetually drinking lukewarm coffee. Everyone inside the walls of the small store could hear every word that was said.

So it came to pass that, about a week later, Idora announced that she needed to call her folks to tell them she and Gary were coming. I eagerly offered to drive her to Leach's. I was curious how Idora's parents would take Gary, with his shaggy beard and long reddish-brown ponytail. Judging by her description of them, they seemed pretty uptight, straitlaced (read: Midwestern) people. I was getting more used to the sight of men in long hair, but I knew my mother in Ohio frowned on it. In fact, she still does.

I wasn't about to miss that conversation on a bet.

"Hi, Mom. Yes, it's me. I won't be long. I just wanted to let you know that I'll be coming by next week. Yes. And I'll be with a friend. We'll be in his van.

"Of course I'll tell you about him. His name is Gary, I met him here in Maine. He's really nice, Mom. You'll like him. How tall? Oh, about 5'10' I would say. He's skinny, lots of muscles, and he's a hard worker. He's got long brown hair. I said, his hair is long. Yes, he wears it in a ponytail. And he's got a beard.

"Now Mom, I have to tell you something else about Gary, but you have to be sitting down. Are you sitting down? Are you? Good."

"Mom, he's Jewish!"

There was a 10 second pause in her soliloquy. Then:

"What do you mean, am I sure?"

Weeks later the mail brought word that the pair and the van made it successfully to Chicago, where apparently Gary passed the parental muster. But they never quite made it to California, at least as a team — car and other troubles got in the way. Months later word filtered back that Idora did end up on the West Coast, where she found work as a masseuse to make some money, then went back to school in a heavy-duty field. Last I heard, which was years and years ago, she had gone into something like psychotherapy. As a profession.

Gary and his grin disappeared into the sunset.

Since I saw nothing scandalous in the Nearings' mail during my stint as secretary, I thought the job of watchdog must be awfully boring. I think Helen thought so too.

Over the years, Helen became renown for her garden sweet peas. When they were in bloom, they were everywhere. She did not hoard them. After she had filled all the vases in the house, she would make up bunches and distribute them around the village, to Deaf Alice and old Tracy Howard and anyone else she thought would enjoy them.

Helen made sure the Harborside postmaster got a bouquet. Every time.

I've wondered if those bouquets were an innocent attempt by Helen to soften her up. More likely, I think, Helen's gestures were in the spirit of those flower children of that era who put the stems of daisies down the barrels of guns held by soldiers lined up at attention at protest marches, prepared to protect the world from their pacifism.

If it was Helen's attempt to weaken her resolve, it didn't work. Years later, when a Japanese guest of Helen's was visiting, he took pictures of everything in sight (now there's a stereotype for you). But, Helen said, he made the mistake of snapping a picture of the Harborside Post Office.

The postmaster stormed out of her office, marched across the small parking lot, screamed at the visitor, who was standing in the middle of the public road, and demanded that he give her his film. Not knowing what federal law he had inadvertently broken (none whatsoever), he handed her his camera. She opened it and exposed all the film, handed the empty camera back to him, and stormed back into her house.

This behavior was rationalized in the community because they knew the postmaster and her husband had been stationed in Pearl Harbor in 1941, and had lived through the Japanese attack there.

Helen didn't seem to mind the purported CIA/FBI connection, especially if it meant that Harborside had its own post office. The other post office on Cape Rosier had been closed down in the late 1960s due to lack of business, and the next post office was off the Cape in South Brooksville, eight miles away. That would have been quite a daily trek.

Not wanting Post Office Central to overrule the CIA and/or FBI and close the tiny outpost for a similar lack of business, Helen kept the postmaster as busy as she could by sending lots of letters and shipping out lots of books. Social Science Institute, the front organization for the Nearings' self-published works, was the Harborside post office's biggest customer. Helen also made a point of keeping up her subscriptions to left-wing publications, some of them from overseas.

I also felt that there was a sense of pride involved. It was a matter of their reputation. If the Nearings were still being watched, they were still doing their job.

I had already made several visits to the tiny post office, located in a small ell on the side of an old, yellow, Cape Cod-style house in the middle of the tiny village of Harborside. And I couldn't find anything to refute Helen's contention. The postmaster wore a perpetual scowl and left the clear impression that you were bothering her, even if you just wanted to buy a stamp. She was efficient and went strictly by the book, but would not bend one iota beyond that. A smile was not part of her job description.

The mystique around the postmaster only increased when, a year or so after we arrived, word got around that she was fully certified in a second career — as a mortician. We joked behind her back that she must be expecting a transfer to the dead letter office. And we wondered, uneasily, what REAL use she would make of those unusual skills.

This time, my curiosity would not contain itself. I did get up enough courage, once, in the post office, to ask her if the mortician story was true. She said yes, smiled strangely and turned away.

And then, on June 11, 1975, not quite three years after that letter-opening conversation with Helen, the ***Bangor Daily News*** front page headline screamed:

Report hits illegal CIA acts.

The Rockefeller Commission report charged the CIA with engaging in "plainly unlawful and improper" domestic activities. The United Press International news account stated:

> For the first time, the report officially confirmed reports — and with

details — that the CIA opened mail, tapped phones and kept names of tens of thousands of Americans on file during the angry days of antiwar and other protest movements, demonstrations and riots."

A sidebar Associated Press story in the same paper read in total:

> For nearly 20 years, Central Intelligence Agency officials hid from postal authorities the fact they were opening thousands of letters sent to or mailed by American citizens, the Rockefeller Commission report disclosed Tuesday.
>
> The commission concluded the mail-opening programs of the CIA were illegal and also violated individual rights guaranteed by the First and Fourth Amendments to the Constitution. The program ended in 1973.
>
> In 1952, the CIA, with the cooperation of postal officials, began examining mail flowing through the New York post office to and from the Soviet Union, the commission reported.

In early October of 1975, the FBI too admitted to examining "large volumes" of letters from the outside between 1959 and 1966, looking for unspecified "indicators." At least a thousand of those letters were reportedly then opened by the FBI. The FBI also admitted receiving information from letters that had been opened by the CIA as part of its own mail surveillance program, according to an AP account.

By October 22, 1975, the CIA's admitted mail-tampering numbers were calculated in the millions. According to a UPI account:

> The envelopes of 2,705,726 letters were photographed and 215,820 were opened. Of the opened letters, copies of 67,846 items were turned over to the FBI and the remainder to the CIA Soviet section and other agency departments.

And then there's this:

To tie up some loose ends for this book, I stopped in to see Phil Farr, Brooksville's longtime fire chief and superintendent of Holbrook Island Sanctuary on Cape Rosier. Phil is the son of Lura Farr, who was the last postmaster at the long-closed Cape Rosier Post Office. Since his mother had already passed away, I asked Phil if she had ever mentioned anything about the FBI watching the Nearings' mail.

"Oh yes," he immediately replied.

Once or twice a year, every year, he said, an FBI agent would show up and ask his mother if she had anything to report about the Nearings. Since her post office did not handle the Nearing mail, her response was always the same: nothing to report. She would then send him on his way down the road to the Harborside Post Office, where the Nearing mail was processed.

"If she had had anything to report, would she have?" I asked.

"It was the FBI," he said. "What do you think?"

From there I went to pay a visit to Dottie Crockett at the Harborside Post Office. It was more than a quarter-century since my first conversation with Helen about postal surveillance, Dottie was well past normal retirement age, but she was still on the job. I asked her if she knew whether Helen's suspicions were true.

"No," she said tersely, "and I wouldn't tell you if I did."

I relayed to her what Phil Farr had told me about FBI agents. What did she know about that?

"I don't discuss post office business with anyone," she replied, refusing to confirm or deny any such visits. "You're not going to get a thing out of me, Jean."

She would not even tell me when she had become Harborside Postmaster, even after I pointed out, and she agreed, that the date was public information.

When I got home, I called post office officials and asked them for that starting date. I was told that some time ago Dottie had put a hold on her file, and that no information could be given out. I pushed the issue. Finally, after I had been shuffled around to four different people over five days, someone made the determination that the information I wanted was indeed a public record, and could not be withheld despite the Harborside Postmaster's request.

She started that job on June 28, 1968.

Meanwhile, I filed a Freedom of Information Act request with the FBI in 1997, to get their side of the Nearing story. I asked for their entire FBI file on Scott Nearing, but also asked specifically about the Post Office connection. Over the years I have repeatedly checked with the FBI, where my request has survived an administrative appeal, an address change (they sent a notice to my old address, and closed the file when I didn't immediately respond), several successive levels of bureaucracy and different contact agents. The latest hold-up, I learned, was because, after several months of searching, they could not find "Section 1" of their Code 61 (Treason) file on Scott. The most recent agent I talked with, in August of 2003, could not determine how long "Section 1" had been missing.

Despite that gap, she said, her office had decided to forward what they had to the Disclosure Unit for final review. The Disclosure Unit, she explained, had the job of determining how much information they could reveal, under national security guidelines, about this man who had died 20 years before at the age of 100.

Chapter 6
Feet First

Life in the Nearing woods was certainly turning out to be interesting. It was in some respects like an exploding star — my universe was expanding rapidly in all directions. The resulting shifts in perspective were astonishing. History, politics, culture, normalcy itself, were suddenly being redefined before my eyes.

I soon learned that the best way to approach each new experience was with caution, but an open mind.

One day someone said it was time for a foot massage, and we were to all gather at John's cabin down the road that afternoon.

I had never had a massage. I hadn't thought about it much, but I knew massage and sex were somehow linked, and it wasn't good.

In high school, the message from both the church and home was that a young girl's body was her own worst enemy. Nasty males, young or old, were lying in wait to inflict pain, suffering, or pregnancy on lithe spirits. Tomboys were asking for it. So were cheerleaders. And remember, girls who wanted to take woodworking shop or auto mechanics were really just boy-crazy tramps, and were of course barred from the courses for their own protection.

The rule was: No public display of affection. If you would do that in public (hold hands, for instance), what would the neighbors think you were doing in private?

Since we were at best on nodding acquaintance with these amorphous neighbors who held such power over my behavior, I always thought that logic was a bit screwy. But nevertheless, the assumed opinions of the unspecified neighbors were the ultimate criterion.

Under such tutelage, shoulders become hunched. To pull one's shoulders back, to stick out those breasts for the guys to ogle, was to ask for it. After all, back then that was still a viable defense in rape cases — dressing like that, walking like that, she was asking for it, what did she expect?

As a result, a rift developed between my mind and body. Reality was the stuff going on in my head. My body became simply the vehicle for carrying around my thoughts. There was the thinnest of threads connecting the image I saw in the mirror with the person I perceived myself to be.

So it came as a shock to me month after month in my new home in

Maine to see so many people parading through our backyard who were so blatantly PHYSICAL. Shoulders back, wearing flowing colorful clothes, dangling jewelry, hanging all over each other. And, even worse, they clearly ENJOYED it, and didn't seem to care a rip what I, or anyone else, thought about it.

Not care what the neighbors think? Can they do that?

I loved it, but it was like loving a parade. It didn't mean I had to be part of it, or that it had anything to do with me. It was just fun to watch.

(I came up the back path from the Nearings one day and saw three people standing in our back field waving in slow motion to me. I waved back. All three turned 90 degrees in unison, raised one knee slowly, and did some other arm motions, also slowly and also in unison. It was my introduction to Tai Chi Chuan, an Oriental meditation-exercise program. I felt kind of stupid standing there with my salutatious arm hanging in the air.)

So, what should I do with this foot massage business?

Well, I guess that would be OK. It wasn't really a REAL massage (as in massage parlors...you know). There would be lots of people there, and my feet were far enough from the rest of my body to make it safe.

Most of my memories of that afternoon are hazy, like a brushed photograph. I recall about a dozen people, Keith and me, maybe the Colemans, and several people from Eliot's burgeoning campground-for-itinerant-volunteers.

We assembled at dusk. The fire in the wood cookstove was going. We had been advised to wear comfortable, loose-fitting clothing. We laid face-up on a variety of mats, rugs and tables, got covered with blankets, and got our feet naked. The Aladdin kerosene lamps gave the place a soft glow. I think there was even some incense burning. (Red flag! Red flag!)

Several people were doing the massaging, one per person. The woman working on me first washed my feet. Warm water, soft towels, gentle caresses. I was beginning to think I would like this. She let me sniff the hand lotion, to make sure I approved of the gentle scent. Then she applied some to her hands and to my feet. Next she held up her hands like a magician does to show she was hiding nothing, and quietly pointed to her short evenly-cut nails. I nodded. And she then went to work.

From that point on, I mostly remember the pain.

Slowly, one toe was pinched, pulled and then pushed. Then the next toe, pinch, pull, push, to the very extremes of where those poor little protuberances could stretch. Then, methodically, ever so slowly, one small section at a time, the whole foot was probed for any little crevice between the muscles, the bones and the tendons which would cause pain.

First the pad under the toes, then along the edge, then in the arch, under the heel, by the Achilles tendon. An excruciatingly tiny section at a time.

It felt like her fingernails were an inch long and made of elephant tusk, and were pushing their way like dull knives into the spaces between all those tiny bones.

"That hurt? Oh, that just means we need to work on it a little more. I'll work it out. That hurt? You must have a cold. That means your sinuses are stuffed up."

How's that again?

"Have you ever heard of acupuncture?"

Vaguely. Wasn't that one of those quack-o hocus-pocus mind tricks the Chinese pulled on each other with needles?

"The Chinese believe we each have lines of energy connecting different parts of the body," she was saying. "When those energy lines get stopped up, you get sick. In acupuncture, they stick little needles in you to try to unplug the energy lines."

"Sort of like a Roto-Rooter?"

"Something like that. Anyway. These energy lines all end in the feet. In foot reflexology, we don't use needles, but we think along the same lines. We believe that the feet are where a lot of these energy lines get plugged up. When the lines get sluggish, little granular crystals collect in your feet. When I give a massage, I can feel where the crystals have built up and are stopping the energy flow."

Crystals. In my feet.

"And that's where it's the touchiest. Where the crystals are. It's the sharp edges of the crystals that are causing the pain. Not my fingernails. See, I don't have any nails. But if I massage those crystals, they break up, sort of dissolve into small enough pieces and get back into circulation."

I tried to picture it, without much success.

"This part of your foot corresponds with your sinus cavities. If it's sensitive, it's because your sinuses need cleaned out. This..."

Oh! Ah! Let go of my foot!

"...will loosen some of that up....That's touchy too? Gee, do you have menstrual problems? Or maybe you're just sexually uptight."

I don't think I like this. Massages were supposed to feel good. This is crazy. Get the hell out of my subconscious.

"Well, I get cramps..." I mumbled. She moved her steel fingernails to another spot.

"Go barefoot as much as you can. Outside. The uneven ground pushes on these crystals and gets them moving when you aren't even looking."

Right. In Maine. In the stubby woods full of sticks, rocks and

Chapter 6 — Feet First

brambles. Fat chance. I gritted my teeth and hung on, trying to look as casual as I could.

When it was over, a half-hour or more later, I was surprised to realize that it really did feel great. And it wasn't just the great that comes when you stop beating your head against the wall. Things felt looser, my feet, and my insides too. More relaxed. And there was a definite spring to my step.

Hey, I might be willing to do that again — someday.

One foot-reflexology session under my belt, and I was psychologically prepared for my next lesson in the body politic. How great a leap could it be from getting a foot massage with the neighbors to taking a sauna with the neighbors? Stark naked?

Dick Chase and his wife Mary, who was Swedish, had a sauna and bathhouse on the shore of their saltwater farm just off the Cape, and the sociability to invite a bunch of us back-to-the-landers without inside plumbing over to use their facilities a couple of times a month. I'm sure their sensitivities were both social and olfactory. (To my knowledge, the Nearings never attended these sessions.)

The events included a pot-luck supper, with use of the sauna optional. I refused to go the first few times, but finally agreed to at least be part of the pot-luck supper.

It was a little disconcerting to be munching on a carrot at the buffet table in the bathhouse main room, and have a naked neighbor bop out of the sauna, pink and steaming in the cool room, grab a carrot stick from the platter, remark about how great the sauna felt, and then turn and jump into the deep pool of cold water just outside the sauna door. Especially when the neighbor was male and I was a married lady and not supposed to see such things. But I was supposed to act as if it was the most natural thing in the world to do. And, God forbid I should be so gauche as to LOOK.

In my casualness I swallowed my carrot stick whole.

OK, I said to myself. Self, you are being a prude. These are nice people. You know every one of them. Not a pervert in the crowd. Think this through rationally. If God had wanted us to be naked, we would have been born that way.

In Sweden, I reminded myself, saunas are just a part of life. The Indians have their sweat lodges. And skinny-dipping is an all-American term. There is a precedence and history to all this.

By this time a half-dozen people, male and female, young and old, had come through and grabbed a taste of something off the platter. For some, one round of hot sauna and cold water was enough. They showered in lukewarm water, and were getting dressed. Others, Keith among them, thought three times through was about right, and disappeared behind the heavily insulated wooden door for another go at the heat. The really adventurous ones took a quick hike down a short path and actually jumped into the secluded salt-water cove. Their shrieks could be heard clearly through the trees.

They all told me that I was really missing something wonderful.

So, next time around, I said I would give it a go.

The dressing room next to the sauna had clothes hooks and benches. The room was full when I entered, and people were busy stripping off bluejeans, sweatshirts, T-shirts, work boots. Some even had underwear to remove.

A fire was already burning in the small woodstove inside the sauna. Dick had started the fire about an hour before, to get the room and the rocks in the metal basket next to the stove nice and hot. The room was not considered worth bothering with until the temperature got to at least 150 degrees.

I seemed to have a lot of trouble unlacing my boots, so I was the last one left in the dressing room. I stripped down, wrapped my towel around me, and headed for the sauna door. One of the first-rounders was just coming out, and was making the split-second decision of whether to jump in the deep tank of frigid water just outside the sauna, or to go jump in the cove. He looked at my towel and said simply, "You won't need that in there."

Define need, I thought to myself, still clutching the towel.

But he was ignoring me. He jumped into the deep tub, letting out a loud, spontaneous WHOA-WHA!! when he hit the cold water.

Show-off, I thought. I would never shriek like that.

A naked woman came out of the sauna and headed for the cove.

You are a real prude, aren't you?, I said to myself. What the hell, Jean, just do it.

I flung the towel someplace, and quickly opened the door. I would have shut my eyes, but I needed to see where I was going.

A chorus of "Close the door!" greeted me. Rule number one — be quick and don't let the heat out.

I was struck by a wall of heat, closely confined. I of course was familiar with the heat from a wood stove, or a closed car sitting out in the hot sun for hours, but had never been surrounded by it in the buff. It was tingling, hot but pleasant. The dressing room had been quite cool.

The sauna room measured maybe eight feet square, with the hot stove opposite the door and three tiers of slatted wooden benches running the length of the room to the right. A small window and a thermometer were on the wall opposite the door.

I hesitated with the closed door at my back. Now what? Someone told me to pick a spot, that the hottest places were closest to the stove and on the third tier up. The thermometer was then about 180 degrees. I reminded myself that 212 degrees was the boiling point of water.

I chose a spot down low, near the door, gripped the edge of the bench, and closed my eyes. The room was strangely quiet. I peeked to see if I was missing something.

The other occupants were busy being self-absorbed, deciding their comfort level, occasionally shifting to a better location or position. Eliot started espousing some new way to grow something in the garden. I tried to be nonchalant as I looked over the crowd. Not a bathing beauty among us, although Keith looked pretty good. But then I was prejudiced.

So this is who these people really are. No façades here, no societal barriers of clothing or jewelry.

(Rule number two — no jewelry. Metal absorbs heat and could get hot enough to burn skin.)

My nose was beginning to tingle and burn.

"Anyone want some steam?" someone asked. A few people nodded. A dipper of water was scooped from a bucket and dribbled on the hot rocks next to the stove. The sudden humidity made the room instantly feel 20 degrees hotter. The tip of my nose was feeling singed, and my nostrils were protesting the inhalation of that steam. I also realized I was feeling lightheaded.

About then someone said, "First time in you have to go easy. Just a couple of minutes. When you get lightheaded, it's time to get out."

I got out. Closed the door quickly behind me. Then decided that the four-foot-deep tub of water was the safest, if I passed out and needed to be rescued. I held the end of my burning nose and jumped in feet first.

"WHOA-WAA!" I shrieked. Turns out that's an involuntary pronouncement.

And then I realized I felt great, as I bobbed up and down in the tub.

"Don't stay in the tub too long, you'll get chilled," I was advised. "Thirty seconds seems to be about right. Depends on how it feels."

Wow! I suddenly felt perky, vibrant, wide awake, ALIVE! Great! Wonderful!

I climbed out of the tub and stood on the slatted floor, watching the cold water turn to steamy vapor on my red skin.

"I'm going to do that again," I said, grinning. I darted for the sauna door.

My mother was not very understanding.

"Not my Jeanie!!!!!!!!!!!!!!!" her letter screamed.

I tried to tell her it wasn't like that at all, but how graphic can you be with your mother? If the guys were thinking sex in there, they managed to keep it under control. I mean, it would have been OBVIOUS. I suspect the intense heat, not to mention the frigid cold water, helped considerably.

Not only that, but she was talking sex and I wasn't. It just simply was not a sexual experience. And in a way it was reassuring to me to see other people's bodies. When the only exposure someone has to nakedness is in art or **Playboy** magazine, that someone can get a very distorted picture of what is normal — and how one measures up. These people considered themselves normal, and they came in all kinds of shapes. So did I. What a relief!

But my mother was not alone in her feelings about group and/or public nudity.

A few years later, Eliot's crowd of farm volunteers included several who were vying for the best overall tan. It was in a grocery store 20 miles away in Blue Hill that I first heard about the female crew riding topless through town high up on the loaded hay wagon being hauled to Eliot's. The only thing I could imagine was a back full of prickles from the sticky, scratchy pieces of hay. Yuck. But the storytellers were obviously impressed — by what they saw, or by the very idea of doing it, I wasn't sure.

And it didn't help the heart palpitations of several little old ladies who had gone out of their way to visit Eliot's remote farm to buy some of his excellent produce — only to see a batch of co-ed naked pea-pickers in the back field. After the haying incident, Eliot had tried to establish the rule to cover up for company, but the pickers hadn't heard the light tread from the delicate feet and canes of the elderly women as they approached the stand. Besides, they were early. The stand hadn't opened yet for the day. It wasn't their fault.

As far as I know, no award was given for the best overall tan, but the contenders were talked about in town for years afterward.

And Eliot lost some good customers.

Chapter 7
Building a Life

Living on the head of the Cape gave me a whole new perspective on raising children. I was fascinated by the interaction between Eliot and Sue Coleman and their daughter Melissa.

With them, it wasn't a matter of doing what all the books said and passing some sort of test. It wasn't a case of making sure they had every toy and every flash card the kid next door had. It wasn't about cartoons and commercials, cute clothes and a fully-decorated room of one's own.

It was more a matter of sharing a life.

Melissa was a bright, although lonely, little girl. Homemade toys and a lively imagination got her through the day. Even at five, she was a help in the kitchen and garden. She did real work that had real consequences. Her family ate the carrot she had planted two months before, or the salad greens she had picked and washed for dinner. She helped her mother milk the goats, and understood where cheese and yogurt came from. Her efforts were appreciated and nurtured. She was part of the system.

She was taught whatever she wanted to learn and could absorb. Library books abounded. So did loving patience. Household stuff like pots and pans became temporary toys that made heavy demands on the imagination.

Melissa was encouraged to explore her world and be independent. When she wanted to go barefoot into the new snow, she was told it was not a good idea, but was not forbidden to do it. When her feet got cold after about two minutes, she was back inside, getting warm socks and boots on. She was not scolded for disobeying her parents. It was a lesson in cause and effect. Decision and consequences.

That first fall, when we were busy building our new home, Melissa was looking forward to being a little less lonely in hers, because her mother was pregnant.

Susan carried her pregnancy with rugged grace. She was obviously happy about the prospect of another new life, but she did not see any reason to slow down. Being pregnant was a part of living. Natural. Healthy. To be taken in stride. Nothing to fuss about. No reason to give her any special attention.

Since she had gone down this road before, she knew what she needed. About five dozen cloth diapers. A few baby smocks. A snugly cloth baby carrier that would hold an infant close to the chest, leaving the hands free.

And that was it. No bottles. She would be breast-feeding. No bassinet. A wooden box with some bedding would do just fine until the baby graduated to the homemade bunk bed Eliot would build. No jump-chairs or high chairs. No competition to get into the most prestigious day-care.

Maybe an extra length on the clothesline. Eventually another rope swing on the big hovering tree next to the house.

It all seemed so simple — and so foreign to my suburban culture. I was suddenly aware how senseless all that garish clutter had seemed to me, and why I had never been able to garner any enthusiasm for parenthood.

I found myself getting comfortable with another of my assumptions turned on its ear.

From a letter sent to Mom:

October 26, 1972

...I thought I mentioned to you about Sue Coleman's new baby. She intends to have it in the cabin, like she had Melissa. They have a woman doctor who will do the delivering — I guess they'll call her from the nearest phone to come down here. Eliot says with Melissa, Sue's mother paid for two months of Pampers, and then Susie did all the diapers by hand, but he doesn't think she'll be fooling with the Pampers this time. Sue is a really remarkable woman.

Shortly after I mailed that letter, Eliot came down and told us Susie would be having her baby in the hospital after all. The doctor who had delivered Melissa suddenly decided she was tired of doing home deliveries. Eliot said he briefly considered delivering the baby himself, but decided against it. However, he had gotten the local hospital to agree to allow natural delivery, with Eliot in the delivery room. This was a relatively new phenomenon in hospital births, so we were impressed. But he couldn't get them to agree to allow Melissa in on the experience.

Sue's mother of course was delighted that a hospital was in the picture. But Susie was not pleased at her mother's delight. She really didn't want to go to the hospital for the birth, and was firm in her conviction that she would stay there a mere 12 hours, and only because the doctor insisted on that.

Then Eliot told us about the placenta. It seems that right after Melissa was born, Susie followed the example of many animals and ate bits of the baby's placenta, or afterbirth. He said they had heard about the idea before the birth, and Susie had been willing to consider it when the time came. And when the time came, Eliot said, Susie said she really felt a craving for it. He sliced off some tiny pieces and sautéed them lightly

(Eliot said it looked a lot like fried liver), and vegetarian Susie wolfed them down. The rest of the placenta was ceremoniously buried. Supposedly the placenta has a hormone in it that helps the uterus contract to normal size. Eliot said the doctor was amazed to see that it actually worked.

In hospital births, new mothers usually receive an injection of that hormone to help the process along. Eliot said that, despite their success in clearing other hospital hurdles, they hadn't yet had the nerve to bring up the possibility of direct placental ingestion.

"I'm really coming up against some strange ideas here," I wrote my mom.

The Colemans did not have medical insurance. Neither did we. My mother didn't like that idea one bit. About then, Blue Cross sent me a notice that if I wanted to continue the coverage I had with the **Providence Journal**, the premium was $166.20 a quarter, or more than $600 a year. We decided to take our chances.

October 26, 1972
...You asked about hospitalization. I had it at the Journal and we only used it once. We figure that if we just keep an emergency fund and be careful, we should be able to handle any doctor bills that come along. Health insurance is just so expensive for the little that past experience has shown that we'll need it. If we sock away the amount we would put towards premiums, we would soon have a healthy sum at our disposal, which it wouldn't be with an insurance plan. Once an insurance premium is paid and you aren't hospitalized for that period, the money is gone. It's like a perpetual hospital bill. The Journal paid for all the company's coverage, it didn't come out of my pay.

Keith's problem with his wrist cleared right up with that cortisone shot. I think that maybe one of the reasons he was losing weight was from lack of sleep. We're getting a good solid 10 hours every night now, from about 8 p.m. to 6 a.m.

...Got to go now. And stop worrying. We'll be fine.

By the second week in December, Keith and I had the first story of our house all framed up, ready for the outside boards. The main beams for the second floor were in place, and we were starting to put up the rafters. The roof would not be far behind.

It was not bad working in the cold if I kept moving, and we had plenty of things to do to keep me moving. As the frame went up, the house looked a lot bigger than I thought it would. We would have lots of room.

The post and bean frame of our cabin was coming together nicely.

December 9, 1972
... I'm confined to the house today with a cold I picked up from Eliot and Melissa Coleman. So far Susan hasn't gotten it.

Meanwhile, we had established a comfortable base camp in the Nearings' house.

Right away we joined a milk cooperative to get raw milk from local farmer Dick Chase, (the sauna owner). The milk was unpasteurized and unhomogenized. But the cows were tested because Dick also sold to a regular creamery, so we figured it was safe. And it sure was good, tastier than any I had ever had from the store. We started off with only a gallon a week. I experimented, and managed to make butter, whipped cream and cheese from the stuff.

I started to bake all our bread too, because we just didn't have the time to go running to the distant store every few days or every week. Using a sourdough starter, I would make up the loaves in the morning, and leave them to rise while we were at the housesite working. They rose pretty slowly, not only because it was sourdough, but also because once Idora left, the Nearings' house cooled off with no one to stoke the fire all day. But that worked fine, because the loaves would be perfect, ready to go into the oven at night when we got back.

I discovered that cooking on Helen's wood-burning cookstove was a real delight. That is, once you get past the necessity of establishing a firewood pile, building a fire, waiting for the contraption to heat up (about 15 minutes from a cold start), and dealing with the ashes.

Ben Franklin invented the metal stove as a way of keeping the open hearth's smoke from seeping into the room, as well as to capture more of the heat that was going up the big drafty chimney. It was an invention that forever changed the course of home cooking.

In most woodburning cookstoves, the fire is built inside a firebox on the left-hand side. The fire heats the flat top of the stove from left to right, hot to simmer. The broad expanse of the hot stove top is a real luxury. You could put on five or six pots all at once if you wanted. Eggs frying too quickly? Move the frying pan a foot to the right. Simmer that chicken stock for soup? About in the middle. Reheat that cup of tea? Sure, set the cup right there on the far end — unless of course it's a plastic cup, in which case it will melt.

Not only does the fire give the cook an infinite selection of heats, but it also circulates the heat around the oven, which means that when a cookstove is going, the oven is on. Having a hot oven available at every meal is highly inspirational, and explained all those pies and biscuits in all those pioneer books I read as a kid. It was a very different mindset from worrying about a hike in the gas or electric bill every time I made a pie.

But the heat that heats the oven also heats the outside of the cookstove, meaning that ornate cast iron is a cozy place to lean up against in January, but makes for a sweaty kitchen crew in the summer. Hence the old tradition of a "summer kitchen," with the cookstove moved to the porch or even into a separate airy building.

December 17, 1972

...We've been busy confined to the house. Helen sent me orders for 131 books to fill. It sure does make a pile of books! The money is nice in this job, and it sure is great to have a warm roof over our heads right now, but I think that as soon as we can swing it financially, I'll back out of it. I don't like being so personally involved in someone else's lives, and that's what it amounts to, being responsible for all the mail, most of it gushingly adoring.

...My cold is gone, so don't even worry about that. Keith is fine, except that his right wrist is bothering him now. He got that cortisone shot in his left wrist, and that seems to be all right. He's thinking about going to the

doctor about it, but it isn't slowing him down any. The weather at the moment is slowing us down though.

By that point we had boarded over the better part of the nice big gambrel roof frame. The plan was to put all our sawmill lumber under the roof to keep it dry and snow-free. The roof overhang would also protect us from any rain or snow as we went about boarding up the sides. We had bought cedar shingles to put on the roof, but we figured we didn't have the time to nail them on one at a time and still get the rest of the house closed in before bad weather. So we decided to put tarpaper on over the roof's boarding boards, holding the felt strips down with narrow battens. We could do the roof up properly with shingles in early spring when the weather warmed up.

The third week of December, we had just finished getting the roof boarded over, and had started to put on the tarpaper. The job was going quickly, but we had only secured three strips before the snow hit. It was a real sudden blizzard, with the wind blowing up a fury. Within minutes, the roof got too slippery and we had to come down. If it had held off for only an hour more we would have been all set. Worried by the storm's sudden appearance and intensity, we wondered how long our project would be delayed.

Luckily, the snow was just like powder. The wind died down the next day, and we were back up there, sweeping off the snow, and finishing our task. By Christmas, we had half the building closed in.

About 5 p.m. New Year's Eve, Eliot and Sue dropped Melissa off at our encampment at the Nearings. Susie was in labor, and we would be taking care of Melissa for the duration.

Susan had a New Year's baby, a girl, born at 1:45 a.m., January 1, 1973. When Eliot picked up Melissa later that New Year's morning, he said that if they ever had another baby, they'd have it at home whether they could get a doctor out to the house or not. He said the doctor was busy putting on his gloves when the baby was born.

Then he and Melissa went home to do the milking.

Susan and the baby came home that afternoon, as she had planned, about 12 hours after the delivery. She was radiant. The tiny baby was all wrinkled and beautiful. Everyone was healthy. Everything was normal, to be taken in stride. Don't make a fuss.

They were so sure it was going to be a boy that it took them three days to decide on a name — Heidi. Susan was proud of the fact that she had only missed one milking.

About then, Keith's brother Darryl showed up for a two-week stay. By the time we put him on the bus the second week in January and sent him back to the Navy, the four outside walls had been boarded up, and the windows, including the big storefront ones that we had gotten from the urban renewal project in Rhode Island, were neatly in place.

January 13, 1973

...By the way, I'm off the pill. We didn't like the idea of trying to eat good unpolluted foods and then my turning around and taking artificial hormones every day. And more and more stuff seems to be coming out in the paper about possible long term effects. And (you'd better sit down) we're talking about having kids in a couple of years. We both seem to have mellowed quite a bit since we've been up here, and it just doesn't seem like such a bad idea any more.

It was then time to work on the floors. The main beams were in place — those went in with the rest of the skeleton, before the roof went on. But the smaller floor joists for both floors had to be fitted and placed. And then the sub-flooring could go down.

We had the logs all cut and carried down to the site, so the week after Darryl left, Keith and I hewed and skinned and cut mortise and tenon joints and set the joists in place. We put flooring on the second story first. The idea was to close off the upstairs so we could put heat downstairs.

In two weeks time, we almost had the floors done, when the Nearings returned to Harborside from New York, via Albania. It was the first week in February.

They both looked nice and healthy, but had different reactions to coming home after their long winter trip away. Scott was mild-mannered for a change, almost jolly, while Helen seemed especially grating and pushy.

It was a wonderful feeling, moving out of their house and into our own. It felt like we were finally coming home, even though the bottom floor wasn't quite done when we first moved in. The house had sawdust and chips all over the place, but otherwise it was livable and comfortable, if still a bit primitive.

Although we were grateful for the housing, it was really a relief not to have to take care of Nearings' place anymore. It had taken more time out of our days than we had realized, and when they got back, it seemed to both of us that a lot of pressure had been removed.

Once we were in our own home, we knew it would be just a matter of making it comfortable, with walls and shelving and cabinets and the like. We still had most of our stuff in the garage in the village because we still had the finish flooring, insulation and inside walls to do.

In many respects our first days in our new home amounted to fairly glorified camping, only with a regular bed and stove.

We hooked up the cookstove that we had found in that old junk shop in Rhode Island, the one that Keith had taken completely apart and had cleaned, scraped and ground spotless down to bare metal, one piece at a time. It worked really great, a lot better than Helen's and I liked hers while I was using it.

But a strange thing happened the first time we lit a fire in it. The fire drew well on the metal stovepipe chimney, a good start. Then I set a pot of water on to heat, and we went about our work. But suddenly we both sniffed and looked at each other.

"Do you smell ham?"

"No, more like roast beef."

I went over and checked the pot. There was still just water in it.

Despite Keith's more than thorough cleaning, we were catching ghosts of meals cooked long ago. It was a little unsettling. But then I decided it was nice to have a stove with its own history and character.

Our new cookstove did triple duty. It heated our house, cooked our food and humidified our dry winter air whenever we set a pan of water on it. I learned to listen for that certain pitch to the water as it heated to evaporation, just shy of boiling. It lets off sort of a sub-primal high-pitched scream as it passes from liquid to vapor.

I also got so I could tell when the fire needed to be replenished, not so much by feeling the heat coming off it, as by listening to the sound of the stove. There is a certain series of clicking or pinging sounds associated with that much cast iron, bolted together, as it heats and cools in response to the fire in its belly. Accelerating clicks means the fire has caught on well. Too many clicks too fast means you'd better turn the damper down or you'll have a chimney fire on your hands. Decelerating clicks, down to a few per minute, and it is time to add more wood. If you can't hear the stove at all, you've let the fire go out and you've made unnecessary work for yourself, having to get it started all over again.

There is a certain basic connectedness with wood heat. Not only your comfort, but possibly your very survival, depends on your constant awareness, at some level, of what is happening inside that ornate and funny looking cast iron contraption over against the wall.

All this becomes almost subconscious as you live with a wood stove as your sole source of heat during a winter in Maine. It is a part of your reality, like knowing when there is someone else in the house, even if she is not making any noise.

Chapter 7 — Building a Life 79

Our experienced Glenwood cook stove.

Every day we worked hard and every day we could see our progress. We flopped exhausted into bed every night. Until we had put up the insulation, we slept huddled under layers of comforters and down sleeping bags, nearly fully clothed, with wool hats on.

> "Ma in her kerchief and I in my cap,
> Had just settled down for a long winter's nap..."

February 8, 1973
...The weather has been kind to us here this winter. We had two cold snaps with the temperature below zero for a few days, but mostly it's been balmy, in the 20's, 30's and 40's. They're calling it the long hot winter. We did go skating yesterday on Nearings' pond and had a lot of fun....

Chapter 8
Setting Up

With the Nearings back home, and our new house insulated and officially occupied, we took a vacation back out into the real world. We visited relatives in Ohio who had been collecting odd canning jars and more non-electric gadgets for us. On the way back we stopped in Rhode Island to pick up our first livestock, a strange mixture of young hens and a pair of mis-matched roosters, from a poultry connoisseur we had gotten to know when we lived there.

We were straight out of the Beverly Hillbillies as we tooled along Interstate 95, with our station wagon and trailer piled high with all that useful junk. The spectacle was complete with our oddly colored chickens peering out the back window from their wire cages, gawking back at the finger-pointing kids who passed us giggling and screeching in the left lane.

We got back fine, despite the fact that one tire on the overloaded trailer went flat on us — twice.

We put the chickens temporarily in our dead Volkswagen van, sectioning off the back from the front seat with chicken wiring, in an attempt to confine the mess to the working end of the bus. We threw in some straw, and constructed some roosts and nests toward the back.

Immediately, we found that two roosters were a bit of a problem. As soon as they found themselves in the same space, the big black and white one (Keith said it was a Wyandotte) started picking on the little, colorful Bantam that we got because he was free and pretty (he had a white feather in his tail). We had to rescue the poor little thing.

Keith said we could keep him in the house until we figured out what to do. He checked the bird over closely and said it didn't have any bugs. Since it was his idea, he got to clean up after the bird. The chicken turned out to not be nearly as messy or smelly as I expected, and he became quite a pet. Keith tried teaching him tricks, and the chicken even managed to tolerate dog Brandy's curious advances. Intrusive sniffs from a big furry critter were much preferable to certain torture back in the van. We named him Ferguson.

March 3, 1973
...The big rooster crows long and loud, starting at 5:15 a.m. Ferguson doesn't start to sound off until well after 7, and then almost quietly.
...Helen Nearing is an accomplished violinist, and she found out I played

in school. So she's talking about giving me lessons. It might be nice, but I doubt that I'd have the time for awhile. And Keith is terrified at the thought of me practicing.

...Tried out my skis the other day, going up to Colemans. Fumbled around for awhile and really didn't do too well. Colemans said they'll show us how sometime (Eliot was a ski instructor part-time in college), but now with the snow melting, we'll probably have to wait till next year....

Keith finally decided to partition the bus, and to put Ferguson back in, with three hens in his section to keep him company. Ferguson was happy with the arrangement, but the other rooster tried his darndest to get at him from the other side of the chicken wire. In psychology there is a term, first observed in chickens, called the "pecking order." I wasn't aware that it could get to be so vicious. But I guess that's what cockfights are all about.

Two weeks later, we started getting eggs. Finding the first one was really a thrill. And I discovered the hens certainly do let it be known when they were laying — lots of cackling.

Sometime about then, a young couple visited us with their three-year-old, Amy. It was a sobering visit. The Nearings had sent them up to us, so they could see homesteading in the flesh. They were headed for Minnesota to look for cheap land.

After they were gone, Keith and I both remarked that it was a shame they didn't like their little girl. She was getting slapped constantly, not brutally, but abruptly. It was, "Amy, don't do that." "Be quiet Amy, we're talking." (She was singing to herself) "Amy, stop that."

All I could see was that she was such a nice little kid. She took a tissue to blow her nose, then politely asked where our wastebasket was. When I told her we didn't have one, and showed her how we burned all our paper in the stove, she was fascinated.

We invited them to dinner. I set about making a pie, and asked her mother to peel the apples. I ground the flour in our hand grinder mounted on the countertop, and then asked Amy if she would sift it for me, to get out the coarser pieces that would make the pie crust crumble when it was rolled out.

Her mother seemed irritated by my suggestion, and "helped" Amy a lot. Poor kid, she had never seen a pie made before, and obviously wasn't allowed to do anything for herself.

It was one of those times when we could have said, "you can leave her here if you want," and really meant it. Oh well.

Chapter 8 — Setting Up

March 15, 1973

...I'm re-typing one of Scott's manuscripts for submission to a publisher. It's **Man's Search For the Good Life**. It's supposed to be a companion book to **Living the Good Life**, but it is so pitifully dull, boring, and poorly written. I will be surprised if it is accepted for publication, but maybe it will be, on his reputation alone. It's an overly-long, drawn-out essay on why Scott Nearing thinks people look for the good life, and how they do or can't do it. Very wordy and says little. I was frankly surprised. I thought he was a good writer.

...I've got to get to bed. It's raining, and sounds so nice on the roof.

P.S. Have you heard the one about a truck driver driving through a big city? Every three blocks he would stop his truck, run around the back of it with a big stick, beat the back of the truck, run to the cab, jump in, drive three blocks, and repeat it again.

A cop was following him and curiosity got the better of him. He pulled the truck over and said, "You're not doing anything wrong, but can you tell me why you beat on your truck so often?"

The driver replied, "Well, you see officer, this is a two-ton truck and I've got four tons of canaries in the back here. So I've got to keep half of them flying all the time."

We started nailing up the wooden boards that would serve as paneling on the inside of the house. As we finished the kitchen and dining area, built a dandy woodbox and headed for the living room area, I thrilled at not reading "Fiberglas" everywhere we looked. Next would come the temporary kitchen counter and cabinets.

It was perfect maple sugaring weather — warm during the day, below freezing at night — and I had wanted to get at our five small stands of maple trees. But we had just too many projects burning to divert our energies just to satisfy a sweet tooth for a luxury item. As we learned in the Nearings' **Maple Sugar Book**, it takes 40 gallons of sap to make one gallon of syrup. It would be free for the taking if we could get to it and boil it down on our cookstove, so we were determined to try it — sometime.

In early April we moved the chickens out of the damp VW van and into a chicken coop that Keith built. It really looked nice, roomy, up on the hill where they would get lots of sun — and where, incidentally, they were almost out of earshot. We called it the Harborside Hilton.

The hens seemed to love it. We started getting six or seven eggs a day, and once we got eight, out of nine hens. The two white hens laid large or extra-large eggs, while the eggs from the black hens were small. But it was more than we needed, so we started a system with the Colemans, swapping eggs for goat's milk.

The roosters, however, had a different reaction to being moved to their new quarters. We had the Bantam in a separate section in the bus, but we decided not to fuss with that again. So we put the two roosters in the coop together. It took the big one about 90 seconds to start attacking the Bantam. Really picked on him awful.

So we ate the little guy.

The first Harborside Hilton.

I was expecting all kinds of bad feelings about killing it, especially since we live between two vegetarian families. But I was frankly surprised to find that it had bothered me more when Keith sawed down a magnificent tree to build the house than it did when we killed and cleaned that chicken.

I thought a lot about it, and the more I did, the more I was unable to understand the difference, morally, between cutting off the head of a chicken or a cabbage. Why is one form of life so much more precious than another, as vegetarians claim?

We hadn't gotten very deeply into the philosophy behind vegetarianism with our neighbors yet, but I decided I would — some day.

One day we tried letting the hens and the one remaining rooster out of the coop. The idea was to give them free range, fresh air and exercise. I had always heard that one of the functions of a rooster was to protect and keep his ladies in line, but they roamed all over the place. One tried to nest in the woods. We decided not to do that again. Keith made plans to fence in an area for them, maybe one that was portable so he could move it around, to give them new ground to scratch on every now and then. Until then, they would stay in the coop.

Then one of the black Bantam hens turned broody, refusing to get off her eggs. We had planned on ordering 50 chicks from Sears soon, but we thought we'd seize the opportunity, and try setting a few of the big eggs from the white hens under the broody hen and see if they would hatch.

According to Eliot and Scott, the weather that April was roughly two or three weeks ahead of a normal season. We had beautifully sunny, warm spring days for a few weeks. The snow disappeared, and we started to clear for the garden. By Ohio standards, it seemed late to be just starting garden work, but we learned that local gardens weren't usually planted until mid-May, or even Memorial Day weekend.

But then the season righted itself and we got the normal chilly weather, freezing rain and cold wind. We were all feeling pretty soggy. Tending our seedlings on a shelf under the big storefront windows in the corner of our cabin helped my mood.

April 8, 1973

…I'm getting a little tired of doing Helen Nearing's busy work, even if it is only for three mornings a week. I'm starting to feel the urge to write for publication again.

…Scott, and maybe Helen, are going to China next month with a group of mostly Canadians. They've gotten clearance from the Chinese, one of the first groups in recent years to do that. I think the Nearings were there in the '50s, so it will be interesting to hear his comments and comparisons.

…You and I must have the same sense of humor. I thought it was funny, but Keith reacted to the truck-full-of-canaries joke like [brother] Joey and Daddy did.

By mid-April we had made good progress on clearing enough land for a garden. Forget about planting anything, we were still felling trees and removing brush. And despite the weather being back to warm and sunny, the ground was still frozen two inches down under the trees we were felling. We couldn't get a shovel into it. We figured it would take at least a week of good weather and sunshine for it to thaw, and by then Darryl would arrive for another two-week stay.

One of those branches we were clearing out brushed against Keith's eye, scratching it. It was a painful, irritating, albeit minor injury, but it was enough to prompt another exchange about hospitalization with my mother.

I tried to explain to her that I worried just as much about Keith getting hurt when we had insurance as when we didn't. It wasn't the bills that concerned me. It was the strange accidents that we didn't see coming, the ones that could change our lives forever. I reminded her that the best insurance policy in the world hadn't saved Ray, an old family friend, from falling off a high ladder while volunteering at a church in Ohio, badly crushing many bones and putting him in pain for the rest of his life.

April 17, 1973
...We treated ourselves to a pork dinner for our anniversary. And I must say that this stove cooks a mean pork roast! Crisp on the outside, and oh so juicy on the inside. I think, personally, that the stove has had a lot more experience at this type of thing than I have, and knows just what to do.
...Sure, our cousins are welcome here. We have a nice parking lot on our drive where they can park their trailer. The spot is just out of sight of the house. But I think you'd better warn them about the crowd that the Nearings draw. Long-hair, hippie types, mostly vegetarians, some into yoga, weird clothes. Some very straight kids in military haircuts and tailored clothes do show up, but not often. Mostly a great bunch of people if their appearance doesn't turn you off. (Helen admits an irrational dislike for long hair — ponytail length — on guys.) Anyway, our drive passes within a few hundred feet of where some of these people will be camping out. No incidents, but we expect some noise on occasion.

The first week of May we opened our two active beehives and inspected the swarms Keith had captured the summer before. One hive was very strong, but the other looked like it hadn't made it through the winter very well.

By then we had three broody hens setting on two eggs each that would start hatching that weekend. With those three no longer laying, we only had six hens producing — barely enough to keep us in eggs. The 50 chicks we had ordered from Sears, both for laying and eating, were due to arrive on June 19. The chicks cost 28 cents each. Chicken scratch and laying mash cost about $7 per 100 lb. bag, with one bag of each lasting more than two months for so few birds. Not too bad. And we figured the cost would go down in the summer when we fed them scrap greens from the garden..

We had covered over the new small chicken yard with chicken wire, a precaution we were glad we had taken when a huge bald eagle flew low over the coop. The chickens were terrified. We also had seen evidence of fox and raccoons and we made sure to lock our flock up well at night.

About then the Colemans' goats started to kid. The deal was that if they had more than three females, we would get one. They did, and we did. She was cute as a button. We named her Muffin. The first few days it was a struggle to get her used to the bottle, but then she became a guzzler and I had to limit her rations.

Feeding baby Muffin.

On rainy days Keith began putting in a steep stairway to the root cellar. That made it so much easier than crawling down that small hole in the floor while grabbing onto the rungs of a ladder for balance.

May 9, 1973

Happy Mother's Day!

...Keith's wrists have begun to bother him again, so we tried heavy doses of vitamins C & D, plus calcium, and he is sleeping better at night. He used to wake up every hour or so in pain. Hopefully the condition will gradually improve, so he won't need an operation to correct it, as one doctor recommended...

By the first week in June, we started to feel we were on top of the garden work. By that I mean we had planted more seeds than we had left to plant, in the two 20 x 40 ft. garden patches we had managed to eke out. (That was the size of the garden plots Eliot used.) We had corn, peas, tomatoes, onions, lettuce, beans, beets, parsnips, cabbage, cauliflower, spinach, broccoli, Swiss chard, and some herbs already in the ground. Also, we borrowed a 20x40 plot at John's up the road by his vacant cabin, and planted it all to potatoes. And the seedlings in the flats were looking good.

Of course, our meager patches couldn't compare with what was happening at the Colemans, where they were almost ready to open their farmstand for the season. But at least we didn't feel depressed anymore when we went up there for a visit. We still had hopes of getting three more 20 x 40 ft. patches worked up that year, one for vine crops like squash, cucumbers and pumpkins, and the others for all kinds of things, like our winter cabbage, and more corn and lettuce.

The broody hens hatched five new chicks out of those six eggs we had put under them. But as they pranced around with their mini-broods, two more hens went broody. We were down to 3-5 eggs a day, enough for our hearty appetites if we scrimped. Since Sears had moved back our delivery date for chicks, Keith put 15 eggs under each of the new broody hens. He said we might as well make good use of the birds if we were going to lose them as layers anyhow.

June 5, 1973

...You will like Muffin. She's a real charmer. We used to let her out of her pen when we were working in the yard, but we don't have the garden fenced in yet, so she stays confined now, away from the nice green peas and tomatoes and cabbage. She gets weaned in about two weeks.

...I'm looking forward to your visit.

We got our 51 Rhode Island Red chicks from Sears in the mail on June 21, the same day our three broody hens hatched 15 chicks out of the 30 eggs we had set under them. We decided to put all the chicks together under the new mother hens, and see how they did. It worked slick. The hens took good care of their huge flocks, and looked rather proud of themselves, if not a little surprised, for having done such a good job of hatching 66 chicks from 30 eggs. From our perspective, it sure was simpler than worrying about a kerosene brooder keeping the chicks warm until they were old enough to fend for themselves.

Building a new chicken coop was suddenly high on our priority list.

June 30, 1973

It certainly was nice to see all of you, but I sure wished you could have stayed longer...

That [news] story about the Colemans was interesting. Thanks for sending it. It caused some commotion around here. The story, short that it was, was all wrong. Eliot was never a stockbroker, although he had worked for a year on Wall Street, much as I worked for the **Providence Journal**. And he was quoted as saying things he never said...

At the end of June, the Colemans' third goat had triplets, two nannies and a billy. We prepared for our second goat, either one of the new kids or Muffin's sister, whichever Eliot and Sue didn't want to keep. They liked the coloring on one of the newest kids. I was all for getting Muffin's sister, even though they called her Turnip, mostly because she was at the weaning stage. If we got one of the newborn kids we would have had another two months of bottle-feeding to look forward to. Muffin had just been weaned, and it sure was nice not having to face heating a bottle the first thing in the morning, as well as a couple more times during the day.

Word was getting around that we kept bees. That week a fellow about two miles down the road, someone we had never met, came and got us to go to capture a swarm in his front yard. It was huge. Keith suited up and got it with no trouble, and the bees seemed to settle into their new hive quite nicely.

So we then had four beehives. Two had wintered over successfully, but one of those had gotten so strong and crowded that it was getting ready to swarm. We ordered a new queen bee from a place in Georgia, and split the hive in two.

The garden started to flood on the last day of a rainy week. Keith did some emergency ditching and trenching, and saved the garden. But when sandy soil is soggy, you can tell it's been raining for awhile.

It stopped raining for a few days, but didn't clear up. We hadn't seen the sun in weeks and rain was again in the forecast. All the wet weather was giving Eliot fits. The tips of his pea vines were rotting off, and some pea pods were developing spots. He was really cursing the weather. I was glad that year that we weren't depending on a crop for income. Our plants were growing slowly, but they were all right. We were eating lettuce, mustard greens, radishes, and a few strawberries out of the garden.

Wednesday, July 4, 1973

We'll be getting Muffin's sister tomorrow, Colemans have decided. I'll still have to bottle feed her for a week or so until she learns to eat grain. (She's still nursing her mother.) But that's not bad. Remember that inn in the village that you asked me about when you were here?...

The inn in Harborside Village at one point was a commercial operation, but was now jointly owned by a large well-to-do family who kept it to house all of them during their yearly reunions. But it was getting old, and was not in the best of condition. In fact, that year half of it had shifted on its foundation, making it more than a little unstable. The family checked around for someone to tear that unstable half down, keeping the good half intact. Eliot suggested it to Keith, who said he would do it if Eliot helped.

The pay wasn't great, just a few hundred dollars, but Keith and Eliot would have salvage rights on all the lumber, beams, wire, and plumbing fixtures including five old claw-foot bathtubs. With the price of lumber skyrocketing, and us needing a woodshed and Colemans needing a barn, the idea was appealing. In addition, there was a 1,000-gallon water tank in the attic that we had our eyes on.

Keith calculated that the job would take about a month to do, and if they did it right, there wouldn't be much scrap.

July 14, 1973

...We did get Muffin's sister for our second goat, and we renamed her Sasha. (Sasha Goat!) They've really taken to each other, although Sasha is still nervous around people. But Muffin isn't lonely and she doesn't cry now every time we leave her. That certainly was a pleasant change. Sasha was weaned pretty easily too, so no more bottle feedings. Hurrah!

By mid-July, Keith's sister Cassie had arrived for the summer, and our garden was finally in for the year, with the winter cabbage seedlings the last thing to go into the ground. Everything but the spinach looked great.

We were counting our blessings because we hadn't had any bunny trouble — unlike Eliot, who had been plagued with them in his unfenced patches. We gave our dog Brandy credit for our success. He had already caught two rabbits that we knew about. Unfortunately, he wasn't discerning in what he went after. One night he ran into a skunk, and probably saved our chickens, but he smelled up the whole place. He got a royal bath for his efforts.

Despite the garden setbacks that year, by mid-July Colemans' garden was again beautiful. At Nearings' suggestion Eliot set up Thursday evening as an informal class on gardening. It was sort of a counter-point to the Nearings' Monday Night Meetings, which usually dealt with social or political issues. Eliot's sessions were really informative for us novices, and we took a lot of notes.

Meanwhile, we built a new, bigger chicken yard, 40 feet square, out back near the bees. And Keith was quite a bit along in the building of a combination chicken coop/winter goat barn.

That's when another technological advance entered our lives.

...We've decided to get a roto-tiller, a Troy-Bilt. It's expensive and noisy, but it sure would save a lot of time, which on occasion would really help out. We know we can do it by hand, because we are doing it. But we're going to give it a try. Eliot says he couldn't garden on the scale he does without one. It doesn't break sod too well, but for turning under manure, autumn leaves, or green cover crops, he says you can't beat it. We'll let you know what we think of it.

The Troy-Bilt roto-tiller was of course bright red. We called it Keith's toy. It certainly worked beautifully. In 15 minutes and with no effort it turned under a whole patch of freshly manured garden, something that took us a whole afternoon to do before. And it was surprisingly quiet in operation. Eliot's was so loud we could hear it at our house, but I could barely hear ours when I was up feeding the goats.

It was August before we got around to nailing those cedar shingles onto the roof, over the tarpaper that had gotten us through the winter. The shingles made the place look classy. By then the outside boards on the walls had shrunk as much as they were going to, by an inch in some places, and were ready for battens to be nailed over the cracks.

That same month we discovered that the whole back hill, behind the house where we had planned to put the orchard, was one huge raspberry patch. And across the road, behind the commercial blueberry field, was an even bigger wild plot. It was time to start canning.

Raspberry picking sure did bring back memories of Grandma's farm and her raspberry patch at the edge of the pasture. That was where I learned that I could stoop low and look up under the leaves to see a whole lot more berries than I could see standing up. I was pleased to see that the trick still worked.

First I put up 62 jars of raspberry and blueberry juice. To do that I put a cup and a half of berries and a tablespoon of honey in a quart jar, then filled it to the top with boiling water and screwed down the rubber-ringed canning lid. This was the Coleman technique, and when we had some of theirs the previous winter, it really perked us up.

Then I started making jam, but didn't get very far because by then the season was almost over, and it was hard to take time away from everything else that needed to be done to go berry picking.

We had started picking our first peas the last week in July, about a month after Colemans. They tasted so good and sweet we ate them all raw. First servings of the string beans and summer squash were a week away. By August, the tomato vines finally had green tomatoes on them.

Meanwhile, our bees had been going nuts. After Keith captured a swarm at a neighbor's down the road, two of our own hives swarmed. One settled about 15 feet up in one tree, and the other swarm landed 25 feet up in another tree. Keith was able to cut off the tree limb with the lower swarm, and get it into an empty hive body.

The swarm higher up was a real challenge. Bees swarm in a clump like a big raindrop, and are about as delicate as one. A bump could send the whole thing dropping to the ground. Keith didn't think he could get the swarm down from that height without dropping it. So, while it was still daylight, he built a platform in the tree underneath the swarm, put an empty hive body on it, and then carefully moved the swarm down the short distance to the empty hive. He went back after dark when all the bees had moved into their pre-fab housing and had settled down for the night. He stopped up the entrance, and moved the wooden hive body to where we wanted it. Slick.

That meant we had six hives, but we knew the last two would probably not make it through the winter because they didn't have enough time to make enough honey to get them through.

While we left it to the bees to provide their own winter fodder, we bought 54 bales of hay, a whole winter's worth of food for the goats, at 45 cents a bale. We put the bales in the dry upstairs of the house, next to our Rhode Island treasures that we had finally cleaned out of Tracy Howard's garage, and beside the leftover lumber that was racked and drying. The house smelled wonderfully of fresh hay and raw wood.

Speaking of hay, in exchange for help cutting and raking it up, we got half the loose hay from a field just off the Cape. Many fields in the area were cut once in mid-summer just to keep the brush from growing back. Most of those fields were so depleted that the hay would not have had much nutritional value even if it had been cut in its prime, before the seed-heads developed. The hay in this field was cut so old that it wasn't good for feed, but it would be great for mulching in the garden, putting in the compost piles, and bedding down the goats.

But this hay was loose, not baled. So we decided to build a haystack. That turned into a more complicated undertaking than I had imagined. The hay in a proper haystack should be stacked just so, one layered forkful at a time, and then combed with a pitchfork to direct the rainwater down and away. If water soaked into the stack, it would rot the whole thing.

It was miserable working in all that dust and pollen as we moved the hay off the trailer and onto the haystack. After we were done, we had a pile about 10 feet high and 12 feet in diameter. We put a tarp over the very top. The pile settled a couple of feet overnight.

August 1, 1973

...Muffin and Sasha are getting so big. Sasha has calmed right down. Now she'll let you brush her, although she isn't as lovey as Muffin, who will crawl in your lap if you'll let her. At about 50 or 60 pounds, that's no small feat anymore.

We're going to breed one of them in February at about 10 months of age, and the other one in September next year so we'll get milk year round. It takes them five months to kid, so with luck we'll get milk next July. There seems to be a demand around here for dairy goats, so we shouldn't have any trouble getting rid of the nanny kids. But we haven't decided what to do with the billies. Colemans drown theirs at birth. We've thought of raising one for a month for meat, but they look so cute at that stage that we don't think we could eat it.

...Cassandra will be leaving for home a week from Thursday, and then will come back for a week or so with Keith's mom in September before college starts. She sure has been nice to have around. She works like a horse. We tell her she's here for a vacation, but she certainly pulls her share around here, weeding, shingling, hauling manure and the like. Her spaghetti sauce is out of this world! We'll hate to see her go.

...Lots more to write, but I've got to get this in the mail, so I'll skip to the important news -

I'm Pregnant!

We just found out last Thursday when I went to the hospital for a test. I haven't seen a doctor yet (Aug. 20) but by my calculations it will be the first week in March. ...I feel great, with only a twinge of nausea every now and then, but I'm still eating like a horse. Lots of fruit and fresh raw vegetables. And we're catching mackerel for fish and another chicken will hit the table this week. I'm really surprised I don't feel sick or anything. In fact, other than missing my periods, I feel normal, so I had to have a test to find out.

Keith is so happy (I am too!) that when he heard he climbed up on the roof and crowed like a rooster. That night the Colemans mentioned they heard our rooster and he sounded a little sick.

Susan has loaned me all her pregnancy books and I'll have the same doctor she did, Dr. Brownlow. His fee is $210 for the whole pregnancy through the six-week checkup, and we figure about $100 for a one-day hospital stay. Not bad. I'm only a little worried about telling Keith's mom. She's already a compulsive knitter. I'm afraid we'll be deluged with baby sweaters.

It'll be quite a change for us. I'm just starting to get used to the idea. ...I've never felt healthier in my life.

I hope you're as happy as we are about it. Quite a change from a few short years ago when we were never going to have kids, isn't it? We weren't *ready for them then, and having them then would have been a disaster. But we're ready now, older and more down to earth. It makes all the difference in the world.*

I love you all.

Meanwhile, the harvest continued. I ended up with 10 jelly jars (half-pints) of raspberry jam, 29 of blueberry, and 25 of peach. The blueberries were mostly from Nearings' highbush patch. They had a pick-your-own deal that appealed to us — pick four quarts, keep one free-of-charge and give the Nearings the other three to sell. They were so much bigger and easier to pick than the wild ones that we went that route. A quart of Nearings' blueberries made two jelly jars of jam.

We bought the peaches at Payne Gardens, a fruit and vegetable stand near Bangor, $5.95 for a bushel basket. We got five baskets, ate a lot fresh, made jam, skinned and halved the rest and put up 52 pints and 25 quart jars.

The few that were left we dried on a screen over the stove.

By the end of August I had also canned 58 pints of snap beans, and was glad to see them dying down in the garden. I also made 9 pints of sweet pickles, but the cucumber patch was getting too much shade and wasn't doing as well as I'd hoped.

August 25, 1973

...The winter squash and pumpkins look great, and we'll be eating our first corn this week. We've been eating our own chicken and it sure is tasty. We can't afford to buy any. Last time I looked roasters were 97 cents a pound....

...Yes I have a sink. It's in a box upstairs.

The tool and wood shed construction was penciled in for September. The water system was scheduled for October — 300 feet of ditch to bring water from the source of the brook to the cabin kitchen.

At that point we were hauling water from a free-flowing tap we had set up at the edge of the creek near the house, just above the bridge. We had sunk a bottomless, wooden springbox into the ground at the beginning of the creek in the woods above the house, just at the point where the natural spring broke through to the surface.

Then, we ran a 300-foot roll of one-inch plastic pipe from that box down the creek toward the house, securing the lower end to a waist-high stanchion. After we got the siphon going, gravity pulled the water down the pipe, where at first it just spilled out continuously onto a wooden platform. Any time we needed water, it was a simple matter of taking an empty bucket out to the pipe, waiting for it to fill, and then walking it back the 100 or so feet to the cabin.

After awhile, and in the tradition of my grandmother's milk house, Keith built a long narrow box with a hinged top. We diverted some of the cold piped water into one end of the box, where it would swirl around and cool down any container — like a glass gallon jar of milk — that didn't mind sitting in water. The constantly-running water would then flow out though a hole at the other end, falling back into the creek from whence it had come.

This, of course, only worked when the weather was above freezing. So getting that pipe sunk into the ground below the frost line and having it flow year-round with the turn of a kitchen faucet was the long-term goal.

August 25, 1973 (cont'd)

I went to the doctor last week, and he put a tentative date down of Feb. 27 for delivery. I frankly don't think I'm that far along, so I've been saying the first part of March.

The hospital is small, seems to be a nice place, and their attitude about delivery frankly surprised me. They even have a course for natural childbirth and seem to assume that the father will be in the delivery room. I was expecting all kinds of resistance but found the road well-paved.

In case you haven't guessed, I do plan to breastfeed. It just seems so much simpler than heating a bottle on a woodstove in the middle of the night, just to mention a for-instance. Less expensive, too, not having to buy bottles or formula. It's supposed to be better for the baby too. It's nice having Susan Coleman so close for advice in case I run into troubles. She's so down to earth about raising kids, a lot like you are.

Around Labor Day, our goat herd suddenly doubled. One of Eliot's customers needed wintertime housing for her Nubian milking does and kids (Nubian goats are the ones with floppy ears), and she was looking for a permanent home for her two milking Alpine does. Eliot, being one to never miss an opportunity, offered her his pasture and ours, no charge, if she would buy the winter feed. Colemans would take the Nubians, and we would keep the Alpines.

But housing the herd proved to be no simple task.

We picked out a quarter-acre sloping spot north of the cabin, and proceeded to clear the perimeter for a battery-powered electric fence. Then we had to deal with the ancient and rotting piles of dry slash left by loggers, which were full of protruding sharp sticks that would rip open udders when (not if) the goats climbed on them. Since the nearby forest was too dry that time of year to get a brush-burning permit from the fire department, we had to get the slash out of there, pile it up somewhere, and burn it in the winter when snow was on the ground.

That project turned out to be a full week's work. But once the area was clear, the electric fence went up fast, in a couple of hours. We moved the goats' little A-frame shed to the new pasture, put the old, smaller chicken coop out there too, and added a milking shed to the coop to make everyone nice and comfy. We threw in our two goat kids, and waited expectantly.

Our new herd showed up on Labor Day, six of them all piled into a Volkswagen van. The four Nubians went to our waiting neighbors, and we welcomed our two beautiful Alpine milkers. Juno was 5 years old, and her daughter Nicky was 3. Nicky had kidded that past spring, but Juno was 18 months into her lactation cycle, long by any standard. They were each giving about half a gallon of milk a day.

Susie had to teach me how to milk. Unlike cows, whose udders have four teats, goats have only two. I learned that, also unlike cows, when you milk goats, you don't pull down on the teats, you push up. Eliot's customer explained that she milked both teats at once, instead of alternating one after the other as Susie had been doing. Susie had never seen that, so she tried it, and said it worked so much easier. So I learned that way. It really was easy to pick up, after a day or two.

Susie told me that when she first learned to milk, her hands were sore for about a month until her muscles got built up. My hands were only sore for the first day, which made me wonder if I was doing it right.

The goats had a stand that they jumped up on to be fed and milked. Ours was about chair seat height, Colemans' was a little lower. I would sit on the edge of the platform with my left shoulder nudged into the left side of the goat, to let her know what I was doing, and milk from there. Grown goats, even our Alpines, which are bigger than other breeds, just aren't very big. Ours weighed about 145-150 lbs., and Muffin and Sasha wouldn't get bigger than 110 lbs. That size is more manageable than a cow, and for the volume of milk they give, goats eat less.

The new goats and our two kids got used to each other pretty quickly. And we were suddenly getting a gallon of milk a day and loving it.

We bred Juno, the older goat, that September, figuring she would kid in mid-February. Our plan was to keep the milk flowing year-round, which could be a little tricky, since goats are like deer, and only breed in the fall and winter, from about September to February. Cows can be bred year-round.

I told Keith he'd have both Juno and me to worry about at the same time.

Once the pasture-building and goat-getting business died down, we realized we were three weeks behind in our fall plans for a woodshed and the water system. But then it was the wild creatures' turn to demolish our schedule — among other things.

September 15-18, 1973
...Please excuse all the typing errors. I'm doing this in the dark, and can't see a thing. Keith is out in the garden waiting for the raccoons to hit the corn patch — they got about a quarter to a third of our crop so far — and apparently Keith can hear them but they won't go into the open if there's a light in the house. Our lamps won't hold enough kerosene to stay lit all night, so we're trying to catch the coons themselves.

They've really wrecked havoc with Helen's blueberries, tearing off choice branches and doing a lot of permanent damage, and they're decimating Colemans' cornfield too. Traps don't seem to work, so we're going to try the .22 for a few nights.

This was about the time Keith became a hired gun for the Nearings. Up to that point, Scott would only call upon Keith to shoot and kill the occasional skunk that had been caught in the steel-jaw leghold traps Scott set to catch varmints, because he didn't want to have to deal with the smell. Scott would take care of the rest of the offending critters himself, mostly porcupines and an occasional woodchuck — by beating them over the head with a club until dead. We thought claw traps and lethal blunt force were interesting techniques for a nature-loving pacifist to use on the wild creatures he professed to cherish and admire.

But the damage being done that year in the blueberry patch far outweighed anything they had seen before. The fellow who usually coon hunted on the Cape every year with his dogs had been sick that year, and the raccoons were running rampant.

Scott convinced Keith to stake out their highbush blueberry patch. One night, after several sleep-losing but uneventful stints, Keith said sometime after midnight he heard this incredible noise, banshee-like screeching, right in the blueberry patch. It made his hair stand on end, it was so awful — and so near. He turned on his powerful flashlight and saw a whole bunch of raccoons, who proceeded to scatter in the wire-fenced, quarter-acre patch.

Keith said he got off a couple of good shots. He hit one raccoon square, it dropped like a rock in the row between the bushes, onto the packed sawdust walkway. Keith said he stepped over that carcass and shot at another animal farther down the row. It yelled, so he thought he hit it too. But when he went down to check it out, he couldn't find the second animal. And when he walked back up the row, the carcass he had stepped over was gone. In fact, not a trace of a raccoon could be found anywhere. The whole scene freaked him out so badly he never did a stakeout for them again.

Back in our patch, Keith got two porcupines that Sunday night, and he said he could hear the raccoons but they didn't show up. We went to bed — and heard them about three in the morning. We considered putting Brandy in the corn patch. But if we didn't tie him there he would run off. And if we tied him up and he got in a fight with a raccoon, he would be at a disadvantage.

Then we heard some people down the road had shot a few coons, and Nearings caught a couple in their traps in the blueberry patch. So we figured the excitement was about over. But by then there wasn't much corn left for them to get anyhow. We had managed to salvage two meals. We decided that the next year we'd have an electric fence around the corn patch. We heard that kept them out.

September 18, 1973 (cont'd)

We've canned 18 quarts and 20 pints of pears, and 19 pints and 7 quarts of dill pickles, and I'm starting in on the tomatoes. I got some pickings from Colemans, enough to make 30 quarts. And ours are just now starting to come in — not nearly as many as I would have liked. I was hoping for 100 quarts since we used up the 70 quarts I canned last year in no time.

Colemans had let us pick from two rows of their cherry tomatoes. Processing those were a lot more work because all those little tomatoes were a devil to scald and skin. Susie didn't skin hers, but I found several spoiled ones that looked fine until I took the skins off, so I didn't take the chance.

By the time I was done, I had 88 quarts put up, with all but 10 coming from their garden.

By early October we'd had four frosts. The first one came on Sept. 21, the first day of fall, and it was a lulu, got down to 25 degrees. But we had everything covered with spare bedspreads and blankets and came through fine.

As for the rest of the garden report, the lima beans didn't do a thing, but the dry beans were okay. The carrots were wonderful, plentiful and sweet. We harvested enough squash and pumpkins to get us through the winter. We dug up about 325 pounds of decent potatoes from John's garden, but another 75 pounds were ruined by something that looked like the potato froze, only it was brown, not black, and even hit potatoes buried deep. We figured it was some kind of disease. Eliot had never seen anything like it.

Our root cellar was really getting full, with jars and produce. It sure was a nice feeling having a whole year's supply of food put away.

October 3, 1973
...Yes, I have been up to my neck in canning, and believe it or not, it looks like we'll come close to using up all those canning jars, several hundred of them.

We bought 150 pounds of big beautiful onions at the local wholesale food outlet in Bangor, at $4.50 for 50 pounds, or about 9 cents a pound. Then we got all our grains delivered from Boston — 150 lbs. of wheat, 50 lbs. of rolled oats, 50 lbs. of sunflower seeds, 25 lbs. of brown rice, among other things. We were prepared to hibernate for the winter if we had to. We were really enjoying the fall season, quite a contrast from the year before when we were worrying about having a roof over our heads.

Keith was well along on building the woodshed, his wrist problem a thing of the past. Just as author Adele Davis (***Let's Eat Right to Keep Fit***) had predicted, it took four months for the heavy-dose vitamin therapy I put him on to work. We were more than a little relieved, since the alternative was a debilitating operation that would put him out of commission for two months and might not even work.

October 5, 1973 (same letter)
A few weeks ago we had a couple people visiting Nearings who stayed in the campground. They both pulled out fiddles and started playing jigs. After dinner the whole neighborhood just kind of congregated for an impromptu concert. Lots of fun. Since then I've dug out my fiddle, and Keith has offered all the encouragement I need to keep practicing it. I picked up a book of Irish music...

It seems that we're going to be interviewed by the **New York Times** in a few weeks, for an article they want on young people homesteading. The reporter wrote Helen a letter asking her to suggest candidates, and she mentioned us, after checking with us first. Probably won't amount to too much, but then Colemans got an invitation to appear on Dick Cavette when they were first written up in the Wall Street Journal. It'll be interesting. She (the reporter) is supposed to be here on Oct. 22.

As the cold weather of October settled in, the goats started giving less milk. We were down to three quarts a day, enough for the two of us unless we got a lot of company. Whenever I could get enough together, I would make cottage cheese or cream cheese, which could be made in small batches.

I was finding that goat's milk handled a lot differently than the cow's milk we had been buying from Dick Chase. Although it's higher in butterfat than most cow's milk, it's also naturally homogenized, so the cream doesn't rise to the top. We started looking around for a cream separator, but new ones cost $130, and I was told they had so many parts they were a pain to clean.

Sue Coleman had four goats milking, which gave her enough to make a batch of cheddar. Two gallons is a minimum for cheddar, since it has to age, and then the protective hard rind comes off. If the wheel is too small, there isn't enough edible cheese left to bother with after the rind is cut away.

Susie brought our chickens the whey, the liquid that separates from the curds (remember Little Miss Muffitt?), which is loaded with calcium and vitamins.

Our chickens were growing well, but the young hens hadn't started laying yet, and our egg count on the older birds was down to a couple a day, due to the cold weather and the diminishing light. Once they are old enough, hens need lots of light to lay eggs. Most commercial egg farms in the north light up their coops.

The roosters were just starting to weigh in at 3 pounds dressed, perfect roasting size.

October 28, 1973

...So with the goats, the roosters and the garden, we're eating pretty well down on the farm. It's a good feeling having your food supply for the winter all stashed away and accounted for. With the price of food up here, we couldn't afford to eat as well any other way.

We got 55 to 60 pounds of honey out of our hives that fall, about a 5-gallon bucket full. Our honey extractor worked beautifully. With a special "capping" knife that we heated on the stove, we cut off the very tops the honeycomb, on both sides of the frame, and then put two frames full of honey in the barrel-sized extractor.

Cranking the handle sent the frames spinning, centrifugal force splattering the honey against the insides of the barrel. It dripped down to the bottom and came out a spigot in the bottom right into the jar. The extractor did such a good job, the frames of empty honeycomb were almost dry when we were done.

Afterward the empty frames went back to the bees in the hives for them to clean up the little honey that still stuck to the comb, and to start filling them up again. We left the bees about 70-100 lbs. of honey in each hive, for them to eat during the winter. We figured our three strong hives would make it through the winter fine.

We used about 150 lbs. of honey a year, so we were far from being honey self-sufficient. We used it unpasteurized, unstrained, and unheated. Raw honey is better because it has vitamins and enzymes in it that help digest it. Heating honey also makes it lose some of its "body," flavor or what-have-you. Ours was a little strong, but I liked it that way.

October 28, 1973 (cont'd)
...About four people the past few weeks have thought Keith and I are newlyweds. We really get a kick out of that. A fellow we met briefly, when he saw Keith again later, said, "Give my regards to your bride." We've started a Lamaze natural childbirth course at the hospital, and the teacher made some comment about Keith's attentiveness changing in a few years. We all laughed when we found out we had been married longer than anyone there, including the teacher. It's really kind of flattering that people think that. I hope it stays that way.

The last couple of weeks I have really started to show. I've gained about 13 pounds, and have finally decided that I'm not passing enough gas to account for all those gurgles in my abdomen.

Nobody had told me that's what a baby's first kicking felt like.

October 28, 1973 (cont'd)
Keith was listening for a heartbeat last night and got kicked in the ear. He was so thrilled! I told him he won't be so thrilled when he got pushed out of bed that way in a few months. He's just so sweet and understanding, especially when I get tired and lie down in the middle of the day. I feel guilty and he tells me not to — and means it.

Keith's brother Darryl popped in on us in October, dragging along an old Navy buddy. So naturally Keith put them both to work. We finally insulated the downstairs ceiling/upstairs floor. The previous winter when we put in the floor between the two stories, we just cut and laid down two layers of boards, not nailing them because green lumber shrinks so much. That week we took up the boards, fit them tight against each other, nailed down the first layer, put 2x4's between the first and second layers, put Fiberglas insulation between the horizontal studs, then nailed down the second layer.

All this entailed shifting an awful lot of hay, boxes, and drying, stacked lumber around up there to get at the floor. But it was noticeably warmer immediately thereafter, for a given amount of fire in the wood stove.

October 28, 1973 (cont'd)

Just got a note in the mail. The **New York Times** is putting the story off till spring. We'll probably never see a reporter. Guess I'll just have to write it myself.

Chapter 9

The Invasion of People Who Take Aim

In our first few years on Cape Rosier, we found ourselves hard up against a local culture whose concept of their God-given property rights was far different from ours.

I'm talking about hunters.

In Maine, November is hunting season. More specifically, it means deer hunting season, with guns. Bow-and-arrow hunting season stretches a few weeks before, moose hunting is in early fall and other animals get their weeks in the sights at other times. But for most people on Cape Rosier, hunting season meant deer and guns and the month of November.

It is a month for people to change their behaviors, whether they are hunters or not. For many new residents, it meant violating all the personal habits they had developed to merge with the back-to-nature forces they had come into the wilderness to find.

In November in Maine in the woods you wear bright blaze orange, talk loudly, turn up your portable radio if you have one, sing or whistle if you don't, and forgo any attempts to commune with nature. Don't wear white mittens or hats because a hunter might mistake them for the back-side of a white-tailed deer, and you might end up dead. (This actually occurred in Maine in the 1980s. The hunter was acquitted of manslaughter by a local jury, which understood how such a tragic accident could happen to anyone.)

The law says a hunter can only hunt from sun-up to sun-down, but every hunter knows that the best time to get a deer is in the dimness just before dawn and at dusk — when neither the deer nor the hunters can see very well.

We learned that neither deer nor hunters recognized land ownership, even in the daylight. Property lines were simply irrelevant. And the hunters (if not the deer) were backed up by the law. The law in Maine in the 1970s said that a hunter could hunt on anyone's property, unless that property was specifically posted with clear signs every 50 feet along the entire boundary.

If those cardboard signs blew off in a storm, or mysteriously disappeared, the hunter could successfully plead ignorance. That is, he could plead ignorance if you, without a gun, caught him, the guy with a gun, on your property, and managed to hold him there while you called for a game warden and the game warden got there. Which might take hours, since you lived so far out in the boonies and the warden covered such a wide area.

(If you attempted to hold the trespassing hunter there by pointing a rifle at him, you would be charged with criminal threatening with a firearm.)

And when (if) the game warden got there, he would warn the hunter that he could be charged with a hefty $25 or $50 fine for trespassing if he didn't apologize to the landowner. But the warden didn't want to really write up a ticket because, hey, there was no harm done, he was just walking on your property shooting at something he is allowed under state law to shoot at. It is your responsibility as a landowner to stay out of his way. And, besides, do you want this sharpshooter mad at you?

(Unspoken, of course, was the fact that a good part of the warden's salary was being paid by hunting-license fees. It would be counter-productive to make hunters pay attention to the law that appeased only the non-hunters. Might discourage the hunters from buying a license the next year.)

This was all mind-boggling to me, coming from a part of the world that valued grass over children, where people hollered at kids who retrieved balls on their lawn, or paperboys who cut a path from door to door instead of walking down one drive and up the next. Staying within the lines was one of those things that predated kindergarten and was imprinted in my brain — until we moved to Maine.

So, OK, we were new kids on the block (minus the block, which implies sidewalks — or at least paved roads). And our isolated property was a favorite hunting spot, not only for the natives, but for folks who came from hundreds of miles away to practice their sport.

How were we to gracefully fit into the community, which viewed the Nearing enclave with suspicion anyway, while protecting our very life and limb, not to mention our deer-colored goats which were not within sight of the house in the back pasture?

We were told that if we simply posted our property, we would be resented as unfriendly newcomers who unreasonably cut off the winter meat supply for needy natives. And we would be adding to the perception that all these people "from away" say they like it in Maine, but then try to impose their odd ways of thinking on Mainers and change Maine into what the newcomers had left behind.

It would be considered a personal affront. Everyone had always hunted in our neck of the woods, and therefore that was the way it should always be. We were advised not to make trouble for ourselves.

But if we didn't post our property, we would be ducking bullets from hunters who didn't come out our way more than once a year, and who had no idea our new home was on the other side of all those trees and bushes.

We decided that the hoopla was exaggerated, that hunters were basically responsible, and that we could (ha, ha) duck the bullets. We managed to hold this view until the day we saw a set of trucks with Massachusetts plates parked at the edge of our road, and a bullet hit the tree above Keith's head as he was crouched at the slit trench at the edge of our clearing, about 150 feet from our house. The bullet's impact greatly facilitated the process in which Keith was already engaged.

So we decided to post.

We came up with what we hoped would be a middle ground. We took some old cardboard boxes and made crude signs with felt-tipped pens, and posted the signs along the road to let the hunters know we were down there, in the woods, off the road. The signs read:

Caution — Inhabited Land, Farm Animals
Caution — Men Working in Woods
Caution — Milk Goats In Pasture

We didn't have enough for every 50 feet, but we posted them along the road as evenly as we could.

Some people thought they were stupid. Others recognized that the signs did not forbid entry (which would get the hackles up on any true-blooded American hunter), but simply asked for caution (appealing to their native intelligence and innate desire to avoid a personal injury lawsuit).

The next time I stopped for gas at Horseshoe Market, the lone pumping station on the Cape, proprietor Perry Smith asked where our house was on the property. And I knew we were in. Here was a hunter's question from a man who did not have the time or the inclination to hunt. In small towns, such proprietors substitute for the local newspaper. My guess is that someone asked him about the signs, and he said he would find out the next time we came by. It's an information dissemination process that works very well.

I told the grocer we would give any potential hunter a tour of our property. We did, once or twice, made some friends, and never had a problem again. And I was no longer afraid to visit our outdoor facilities.

Several years later the Blue Hill Farm Inn had a sign hanging in its kitchen which I would have liked to have used. The owners said they had found it in a flea market. It read:

NO HUNTING
Due To The New Folks
Being a Bit
Queer In Their Ways

Chapter 10
Energy Highs and Lows

We had a nice Thanksgiving dinner — our own chicken, stuffed and roasted; potatoes, corn, cranberry sauce, candied carrots, gravy, and a pumpkin and an apple pie. And except for the corn and apples, it was all home grown.

Thanksgiving that year coincided with the 10th anniversary of the assassination of John F. Kennedy. Since Kennedy was from Massachusetts, the Boston radio station we listened to had a day-long special. (Our battery-powered radio picked up the station clearly from 250 miles away over the unimpeded watery expanse of the Gulf of Maine.) That program sure did bring back memories. They tried to avoid reference to it, but I couldn't help comparing the feeling of optimism when Kennedy was president with the disaster that passed for a presidency in 1973. JFK wasn't perfect, but he seemed to bring out the best in people, while Nixon seemed to bring out the worst.

When Keith started taking down half of the Lodge in the village, he spotted a beat-up rocking chair in one of the spare rooms and asked the owner about it. The seat was bad on it, so she just gave it to us. Keith rewove the seat, using some rope he had lying around upstairs. It was really comfortable, with arms and a high back for resting the head. By then it was the only chair I could sit in comfortably.

Thanksgiving Day, November 22, 1973
…I'm getting awfully big of late. At least I feel awfully big, even though I don't show as much as anyone else in our class. The teacher is pregnant, due on Jan. 10 (I'm due Feb. 27), and I've gained 16 lbs. to her 15, but she sticks out awfully far. Keith says she walks to accentuate it, but I think it might be related to firmness. I'm surprised at how hard and solid my belly is. I guess I expected to get like a beer belly, soft and floppy.

I've been feeling pretty good, but I'm definitely slowing down. I'll have to start making some new clothes. The jeans don't fit, but a pair of slacks you gave me do, so thanks. Susie Coleman has already given me some used baby clothes and some slacks.

The baby is really kicking like crazy already. That's a strange feeling. I think we're finally getting used to the idea that we're actually going to have a baby.

Three more days of hunting season left….

Keith is getting all the garden work in he can. Next spring it'll be pretty hec-

tic around here with a new baby. He's started in on the chicken yard, pulling stumps and turning the ground. We'll move the chicken yard next spring and plant in the old one that they've been fertilizing all summer and fall.

Darryl and Cassie will be coming up in a few weeks for Christmas over the college semester break ... By the way, all we're planning on giving this year for Christmas (all we can afford) is some of our preserves, like blueberry jam you wouldn't believe. We'll be sending them back with Cass and Darryl, so you'll get them a little late. To send them by mail would cost more than they're worth....

Susan Hall has left for the winter, to try it out with a boyfriend in a commune in Vermont. She may be back here next spring, working with Colemans. We had a going-away party for her last week...

I'm resting in the rocking chair from the Lodge. Note the bags of animal feed stacked to the ceiling, and the pumpkins under the bed.

By then the nation's energy crisis was in full swing. OPEC, the Organization of Petroleum Exporting Countries, had finally organized its members, getting them to cut back on production to send prices for any kind of petroleum products sky-high. Not only was gasoline and home heating oil affected, but so were power companies, who needed industrial-grade oil to run their electric generators. Outdoor Christmas lights were at first discouraged, and then banned outright. Homeowners were asked to lower their thermostats, and businesses were ordered to do so. Long lines formed for the little gasoline that was available, at any price. For the first time, the nation as a whole realized just how vulnerable and energy-dependent we were. Before long, appliance manufacturers were required to post the energy-efficiency of their products. New car engines had new minimum mileage standards to meet. Scientists developed a sudden interest in solar power.

Meanwhile, we were warm and cozy in our little house in the woods.

November 30, 1973

...I'll bet your street looks awfully dim this Christmas. Had you already put up the lights outside? Have you lowered your thermostat? We really seem kind of detached from the whole energy crisis back here in the back woods — all except for gasoline. Last time we needed gas, we had to go all the way to Blue Hill (22 miles) because everyone was out. We're keeping some extra on hand now. We've heard of old World War TWO taxis in France, steam cars, powered by wood. If things get much worse, Keith is talking seriously about looking into that, maybe converting the VW. I'm all for that, if we can do it. Might save us a lot of money.

December 18, 1973 (same letter)

...The roosters are weighing between 4 and 6 lbs. dressed, and are really delicious. We're thinking of trying to can a few in a few weeks to cut down somewhat on our feed bill. Until we start getting enough eggs to sell, the feed bills are hurting us.

Keith is getting a funny look (kind of misty) in his eyes now every time he feels the baby kick. He's going to make a great papa...

I'm working for the Nearings, but very part-time. They've given me an expense account and I'm responsible for their ad campaign. I put small ads in papers and magazines. Only takes a few hours a week at the typewriter, and I don't have to go down there except for consultation. But even at that I'm having trouble finding time when my head is clear enough to do a decent job of it. But they seem happy about the response they're getting from the ads, so I guess I'll keep it up for awhile. They're not traveling at all this winter. They are planning to write another book though, on their 20 years in Maine — a sequel to their book about Vermont.

Eliot got his picture on the current issue of Organic Gardening. I haven't seen the article yet, but Susie says it's a lot like the one in the Observer — not very good in other words. But after the cover of Organic Gardening, what's left?

Have a nice holiday (or two). We'll be cutting our own tree in a day or two, and stringing popcorn and cranberries and such to decorate it.

December 26, 1973
Thanks for the Christmas money. We'll probably end up putting it toward the baby's doctor bill. That fund is coming along nicely. The whole thing should cost us about $500. That's still cheaper than it would cost us if we had insurance, because when I was working in the hospital, all but the most expensive plans only allowed $150 total for maternity stay. A year's premiums would cost more than that.

Helen sent up some books, on house building and a cookbook for me. The books don't look new, but it was still nice of her, since they don't celebrate Christmas. We gave them some kiffles and kolachi.

Colemans are visiting relatives and I'm milking four of their goats. We're getting about a gallon a day, and with four of us, we're using it all up. Colemans have 11 goats up there. The milking isn't so bad, but all the pushing and shoving and making sure everyone gets fed her grain ration can get confusing. I think we'll try to stick to about six goats maximum. Colemans should be back Saturday night.

Chapter 11
We're NBC News, and We're Here to Make You Famous

December 26, 1973 (cont'd)

Have you seen our blurb yet on TV? I wore one of your outfits. When we came back from town, when I called you, they were waiting for us. Seems the other two families they wanted to interview weren't home, so we were it, and they wanted more footage. The guy said it might be a week or two before it's shown. The producer may decide that the blurb on the Nearings, and one on windmills here in Maine, might be too similar. They might want to space them out a little. Oh well, we learned a lot about TV news. I can't help but expect the whole thing to be a fiasco.

Turns out hunters were not the only creatures we had to deal with who took aim. Potentially less lethal, but unfortunately not confined to any season, were the camera-wielding reporters.

The Nearings were masters at getting publicity. They had been doing it, and doing things which attracted it, for more than 40 years — Scott for more than 60.

For them it was a useful medium. They were able to get their unconventional views out, and the exposure usually prompted a spate of book sales, which helped on the income side of the ledger.

Sometimes we or the Colemans would be back-up stories, ways for media organizations to get two bangs for their hefty transportation bucks to our outrageously isolated location.

("Eight miles from the nearest stop sign! Can you imagine?" "What do you mean, there's no place to eat for 20 miles? I only want a burger.")

Eliot, a natural ham with a couple of unwritten books in the back of his brain, looked forward to the exposure.

We, on the other hand, tolerated it. Or cringed. I had already figured out from seeing what happened to the Nearings and the Colemans that fame was not all it was cracked up to be. I was torn between hiding in the woods, and letting people know that ordinary folks really could do what we were doing.

(If a philosopher lives in the woods, and nobody is around to notice, how can he have an impact?)

But hiding in the woods in Harborside, Maine in the early 1970s was not an option for us.

The media circus finally hit our household in December 1973 when an NBC film crew came knocking.

NBC National News was doing an interview with Helen and Scott. When the reporter had asked Helen for suggestions of homesteaders to interview before they left Maine, she told us she sent them to us rather than to Colemans because Eliot had been getting too much attention of late.

This crew actually showed up, although they probably wished they hadn't.

A news reporter named Norm was accompanied by a camerawoman and one other man dragging some lights. This being 1973, I was pleasantly surprised to see the young woman hefting that camera around on her shoulder. I also smiled when I saw the guy carrying the lights.

The first order of business was of course to interview us.

"Okay, you can sit there," Norm said pointing to a spot in our living room. "And I'll interview you from here."

Keith and I were amenable.

"Uh, where do I plug in the lights?" the young man asked.

"You don't," I said, grinning. "No electricity."

Panic set in. It was now mid-afternoon, and in Maine in December, that meant dark was fast approaching.

Batteries for film cameras in those days were heavy, big and didn't carry much charge. And the charge on theirs was low.

"Well, we'll have to shoot first and ask our questions later," Norm said.

So that was what that saying meant.

They rushed outside, pointed the camera at the house, panned on us standing in front of it. They zoomed in on Norm, microphone in hand. Norm asked us some non sequitur questions which I'm sure he figured on patching into the tape, but which were a bit difficult to answer.

He wanted one-word answers to questions like "Why are you here?"

I have trouble being eloquent even when I am not being rushed. I was feeling manipulated, and I was sure that Keith and I looked ridiculous.

Anything else visual? And be quick about it.

Well, it was about time to milk the goats.

Yes, Yes!!

I looked at the camerawoman's low pumps, and thought of the very "visual" but aggressively friendly goats.

But, oh, isn't your rough pasture and slapped-together milking shed quaint! That's a great milk pail you've got, terrific, get a shot of that. Oh, look, that goat wants to get into the milk shed so bad she's trying to knock down the door, that's the funniest thing I've ever seen in my life!

Chapter 11 — We're NBC News, and We're Here to Make You Famous

Back in the house, by the light of the kerosene lamps, the cameras were packed away.

"Now we can talk for a few minutes. What did you say you names were?"

Norm interviewed us — Jack Webb style, notebook in hand, "Just the facts ma'am" — for a total of about five minutes. It was not exactly a philosophical meeting of the minds. And then...

> What fate!
> We're late,
> for our next appointment, date,
> no time to find out how or why,
> we're late,
> can't wait,
> 'sbeen great.

And they were gone, off to interview two other homesteaders the next day, along with a few Maine people tilting with windmills as the energy crisis advanced. Or so they said.

I sighed deeply, and whispered a silent prayer for the other homesteading couples.

The next day while I was at the grocery store in Blue Hill, I called Mom to tell her about the whole farce, particularly the ringmaster's orchestration of our command performance. Mom said she would get her tape recorder ready (the VCR had been invented, but was not yet epidemic and my folks didn't have one), and would watch faithfully. It wouldn't be on for more than a minute or two, I told her, so you'll have to look quick.

I said I couldn't imagine what the piece would end up looking like, with that skimpy, truncated interview. So that's how a national TV reporter does his job. I heard they get paid big bucks. I could have done the job a lot better. But whatever he got out of the experience, it would be on national television. I hoped it wouldn't be like Eliot and those interviews with him that were published full of errors.

When I got back from calling Mom, the NBC crew was waiting for us — in daylight, with charged batteries and proper boots. Their connections with other homesteaders had fallen through, so we were to carry the standard for the whole movement.

No pressure there.

Yes, the root cellar is great, looks colorful. Can you get that camera down there OK? What else would be a good shot? What do you do that's different here in the house, something — grind your own grain? Yeah, that would be great, can you crank that thing for a minute or two? Perfect. What else? Maybe we can get you to light one of your kerosene lamps? We can do this.

So now, Norm finally wanted to know, and this time at a leisurely pace, what's this homesteading schtick all about?

The two-minute piece showed up on the Today show on Christmas morning, December 25, 1973, and again at noon on NBC news affiliates. Mom caught most of it on the tape recorder. It had to be the strangest Christmas present she ever got.

Having neither a television nor a phone at that point, I of course didn't know the segment had already aired when I wrote her a letter the next day.

When she played it for us later, the piece sounded OK, better than I had expected. We didn't embarrass ourselves, Mom said it looked fine, she got to see the house and goats, Keith and I looked nice and healthy. She was quite pleased. I think my aunt also saw it, and maybe a few other relatives.

But coming as it did at a time when most people were totally immersed in the grand finale of the buying spree that accounts for 40 percent of all U.S. retail sales, the audience was small, to say the least. We got two letters from people who wanted to know more about homesteading.

The hand-cranked grain mill (as seen on TV)

A third letter was from Rhode Island.

It seems that the TV was on in the background that Christmas morning as presents were being opened in the household with the "Pease in a Pod" sign on the lawn. Mrs. Pease, my multiply-unselfish clerk friend, saw me out of the corner of her eye. She bolted to attention.

Her first reaction was: "I know her! I know her!"

"And then they showed you cranking that whatever on the counter, and I said to my husband — SHE'S PREGNANT!!"

Chapter 12
The Calm Before

January 15, 1974
...A farmer near here, Dottie Gray, came and got Keith today to help slaughter her sheep. He expressed an interest in the skins. Apparently they just threw them away. We hope to be able to make a sheepskin coat or two from them, but have to find out just how to process them first. They did ten sheep in about four hours, and he came back with all the hides plus a small lamb carcass — 20 pounds worth. Not bad for half a day's work. It'll be a nice change from chicken, that's for sure. It's now hanging in our root cellar, aging for a bit.

Keith said he's never done sheep before, yet when he went there he seemed to know just what to do. And he did it better (neater) and quicker than the fellow who was supposed to know what he was doing. I think Keith is just a born farmer. An animal farmer more than a plant farmer like Colemans. A farm just doesn't seem to me to be a farm without animals....

By mid-January, the new woodshed had been roofed over. Our firewood would stay dry. As soon as Keith got enough good boards out of the Lodge he was still in the process of tearing down, he planned to close off half the woodshed for a workshop. I was looking forward to getting his tools out of the house, where they were spread all over.

The Ashley heater was up and running, and with the place fully insulated, it worked just dandy. We put one or two large logs in it at night, and despite below-zero weather, the coldest we found ourselves in the morning was about 52 degrees. More normally it was between 60 and 65 degrees when we woke up, and rose to about 70 during the day with the cookstove going.

By the heat of the fire, we ordered our year's supply of seeds. The bill came to $50.

January 15, 1974 (Cont'd)
We had liver from that lamb today and it was absolutely delicious, the best I have ever tasted. Keith said it was just because it was so fresh. I sure do talk a lot about food, don't I? Sure is grand to eat so high on a pauper's budget.

Speaking of pauper's budget, we broke the barrier last year. Counting everything, we earned $2,700 last year, so we don't have to file an income tax return. We spent more than that, because we used some of our savings as we'd planned, for some big items, like the tiller. This year, since we'll be three, we can earn something like $3,500 tax free. We can live pretty high on that, now that most of our capital investments are out of the way — and now that the farm is starting to pay its way.

Mom, I'm really so happy. Everything looks like it is all falling into place and is going to work out fine.

It's quite a high to see your dreams materialize...

Ashley stove

Chapter 13
Having Your Baby

Just when I started to put on a little weight with the baby, and the maternal instinct started kicking in, politics entered the picture.

A pregnant woman is a magnet which draws other women to tell their stories. They came from all directions, and from all generations. To a woman, they had wonderful moments in their pregnancies, incredible experiences in labor — and awful tales about the dumb tradition-bound doctors.

I had paid only slight attention to the issues around Susan's pregnancy — midwife versus hospital, nature's way versus governmental regulation. After all, it didn't concern me.

But then suddenly, it did.

Today rooming-in is fairly standard, and some hospitals have birthing rooms (as opposed to delivery rooms) where the baby is welcomed in the presence of family, video cameras and colorful wallpaper. The internet was added just recently.

Believe me, ladies, it wasn't always so.

Back in 1973, doctors and hospitals were just beginning to grapple with the women's movement. The attitude was still pervasive that it was doctors, not women, who delivered babies. The almost-exclusively-male medical profession back then viewed women as the truckers who brought the babies to the hospital so the doctors could do what they were destined, by God and the AMA, to do — bring the babies into the world. Where they brought a baby into the world FROM was irrelevant. Or, if not irrelevant, then weak and whining and complaining all the time.

Under this scenario, babies were the products of well-trained doctors, and came into being in environments which were sterile, except for the truckers. After delivery, and while the doctors were still in charge, babies had to be protected from the germ-laden vehicles which got them there. Keep them in the sterile nursery. OK, let the mother feed it, if she insists. Breast-feeding? Gross. Animalistic. Unscientific. That's not what breasts are for. Besides, breast-feeding will make her tits sag. Tell her that and watch her change her mind.

Cow's milk is fine. Allergies? Well, we have this wonderful new laboratory-produced formula which is particularly designed for good health and nutrition.

She still insists on breast-feeding? Tell her I need to know if the kid is eating well. I've got it, tell her to weigh the baby before and after it nurses, and mark it down for me to see. I need hard data to know if the kid is doing OK. Not just her animal instincts. Raw data.

These women are so ignorant. They haven't had a decade of medical school. What do they know about being pregnant and having kids? They had better do as I say.

But there was a new and growing ripple in my generation, which said we weren't going to take it any more. Tiny Blue Hill Memorial Hospital had started to respond to that voice.

In the early 1970s, as a first step, BHMH sponsored natural childbirth classes. They covered more than training in Lamaze. We had doctors and nurses talk to us, we toured the delivery room and nursery, and reviewed various hospital policies. We learned the hospital didn't have a separate labor room. Mothers went through labor in their hospital rooms, went to the delivery room from there, and then back to their rooms after delivery. The hospital was small, only 25 beds. (The one I had worked for in Mississippi had 200 beds.)

Some of the nurses were Lamaze alumni, so they knew what to tell us. They explained, for instance, that right after delivery, we could expect to get awfully cold. We were advised to pack wool socks. They were trying to get the hospital to provide heated blankets.

We were told to anticipate the sensation, more than half-way through labor, of "wanting out of here," of trying to get away from it all, of having had enough. Some women want to jump out of bed and pack a suitcase at that point, even if they are already in the hospital.

Most of the course dealt with Lamaze, a French form of natural childbirth which requires the woman to concentrate, to focus on her body, and to regulate her breathing in ways which help her ride out the overwhelming contractions bringing her child through the birth canal. In Lamaze, the mother, not the doctor, is the star.

Central to Lamaze training is learning how and when to breathe. Deep breaths are appropriate during some stages, shallow rapid panting is invaluable in "riding the crest" of a contraction. (Lamaze avoids using the term "labor pains.")

The advantage of all this training is that a woman knows what to expect, she is aware of the total experience, and neither she nor the baby is drugged. Giving birth can then be viewed as an incredible opportunity for a unique, mystical experience, a physically taxing but liberating event which unites the family of women in sisterhood — rather than as an unpleasant ordeal for which one is best anesthetized out of consciousness.

We knew the whole world was not following the beat of our different drumming when word reached our class in Blue Hill that a doctor in Ellsworth, at the next hospital down the coast, had threatened a Lamaze alumnus that he would walk out of her delivery if he caught her panting.

Another component of Lamaze is the involvement of the father — if he is willing. In the classes he learns all about the process he set in motion so many months before, and in the delivery room he acts as his partner's "coach."

Keith loved the whole idea of impending fatherhood. He was attentive in ways I hadn't seen in years. He took pictures of my burgeoning belly. He stared at me wistfully. But Keith didn't like some of the women in the class (there were about six of us) because they were such strong feminists. I found them all interesting, and looked forward to those eight Fridays in October and November. I was the least pregnant, so to speak, but there was not another class scheduled before I delivered.

Otherwise, I busied myself by collecting five dozen cloth diapers and a few cotton smocks, and telling my mother she ought to be glad we weren't going to have a home birth. (Picture it, Mom — in the woods, with a midwife, no phone and no running water. Don't you feel better already?)

Anticipating a late February, or early March birth, Dr. Brownlow and I discussed my view on pain killers, vitamin K shots, rooming-in, breast-feeding. Everything was all set and understood.

January 15, 1974 (Cont'd)

One of the girls in our childbirth classes had her baby last month, just over 5 lbs. We went to see them and she kept saying: "It works! It really works!"

She was in labor 12 hours and had the whole thing naturally. Her husband sat there and grinned the whole time we were there -- a proud papa to the core. I guess after 12 hours they were both pretty exhausted, but said it's the only way to go. I was really encouraged to hear all about it.

...They raised two pigs last year. We're getting pointers from them for this spring, and they've invited us over for pork dinner next week. We're kind of isolated here between two vegetarian families when it comes to animal husbandry. Sure is nice to find some kindred spirits....

That pork dinner turned out to be crucial. As they passed around the baked beans that went so well with the home-grown pork, Judy and Jeremy Stewart laughed at how the last time they had been served beans was at another friend's home, the day before Ian was born, ha, ha, three and a half weeks early. And gee, there you are, pregnant and all, and we're feeding you beans, ha ha.

It was delicious. I ate like a horse. I could do that because it seemed that I had more room in my stomach at mealtimes the past few days, despite my weight gain of 21 pounds. The baby had definitely shifted, but the doctor insisted the baby hadn't dropped. It was too early. Besides, we hadn't decided yet on a name. I was looking at girls names for "her," while Keith was mulling over what to call "him."

I woke up at 2:25 a.m. the next morning, discharging a little bit of water, maybe a quarter-cup, and a few small blood clots. About 10 minutes later I started getting some mild contractions, every six to 10 minutes. I really expected them to stop, since it was a full five weeks from my due date.

About a quarter to four, the contractions were still coming, although not any harder, but I thought I'd better wake up Keith. He said he never woke up quicker in his life. But we both still thought it was a false alarm, and didn't want to go all the way into the hospital and not have anything happen.

By now the contractions were about five minutes apart, with some good hard ones. But others were so mild I wasn't sure if I should even count them.

At about 6:30, on Adele Davis' advice (***Let's Eat Right to Keep Fit***), I had a big glass of milk and some vitamin C, E, and calcium tablets. The vitamin E was for the baby — supposedly it reduces the cells' need for oxygen, helping the baby if the labor were long and she somehow couldn't get the usual supply, like if the placenta were to detach a little early, or if she didn't breath right away. The vitamin C helps the circulation and helps the small blood vessels stay elastic so they won't rupture so easily. The calcium tablets were for pain. And the milk was because the women I talked to who had already delivered all said that they were starved during labor or right after delivery and the hospital wouldn't even give them water until it was all over.

Around 7 the contractions stopped for 15 to 20 minutes. Keith went up and fed the animals (the goats were all dry by then and didn't need milking). He popped over to Colemans and asked them to feed the animals in the evening if we weren't home.

The contractions picked up a bit harder, but were very sporadic, anywhere from 3 to 15 minutes apart. Keith packed my hospital bag.

At 9:30, Keith went into the village to call the hospital.

After he left to make the call, I started having some really strong contractions. I decided it was definitely time to leave.

No Keith.

I got dressed for the trip. My water broke, soaking my fancy maternity bell-bottomed pants. It took two towels to clean up the mess.

No Keith.

I changed my slacks, tucked a towel into the crotch of my dry slacks, and paced the room.

No Keith.

I started searching for a suitcase to pack, even though mine was by the door. I wanted out of there, to leave. I had had enough. But Keith had our only working vehicle. I was in a panic, by myself in the house with no phone, and no car.

About an hour later, Keith finally returned.

I screamed at him.

"I couldn't just make a phone call and turn around and leave," he said. "It wouldn't have been polite."

He said they told him Dr. Brownlow was out of town for two days, and that Dr. Murray, who was covering for him, was in the operating room until 11.

By that point I was beyond sitting up in the car. I stretched out in the back seat of our Jeep Wagoneer, and hung on for dear life, as Keith floored it. We hadn't even reached the grange hall at the fork in the road when I got my first strong urge to bear down. Twenty miles of frozen, twisted, snow-covered backwoods Maine roads were between me and that hospital.

"I have to push!" I yelled.

"Don't push, don't push! Pant! Pant! For God's sake I'm driving as fast as I can!"

Keith stopped at Dottie Gray's farmhouse long enough to ask her to call the hospital, which I didn't understand because that's what I thought he had been doing for that long hour earlier in the morning.

From then on Keith drove as fast as he could. The roads not being the best or the straightest around there, I remember concentrating on staying in place in the back seat more than on the contractions. The intense fear of being in a car accident as the result of being driven what felt like 70 miles per hour on slippery, winding roads designed for 35 slowed my other processes down a bit. I only had the urge to push (a sensation different from a contraction) three times during the half-hour trip. The contractions, however, were getting hard to ignore. They were good ones, and they were 2 to 3 minutes apart.

Breathing and panting like they taught us in Lamaze classes was probably the only thing that kept the baby from being born in the car.

We walked from the car to the hospital, Keith carrying the suitcase and most of me. I almost made it in without a contraction but had to stop for one at the nurses' station. Dottie said later that she got through to the hospital, but when we got there, they clearly didn't know we were coming.

Despite that, they reacted pretty well.

I was whisked into a wheelchair, and they guided me to the nearest semi-private room, where I saw one of the women from my Lamaze class. I smiled at her, and managed to say, "We wanted rooming-in. Doesn't that mean a private room?" or something like that.

So we all turned around, me waddling with a towel in my pants, and went down the hall to an empty private room. Three of them stripped off my clothes, duly noting the soaked towel, and got a hospital gown on me as I collapsed in bed with another contraction.

They dragged Dr. Murray in from the hall, where apparently he was just coming out of surgery. He was a rather staid, proper gentleman-type, and asked me in his stiff British-sounding accent to tell him when I had my next contraction. I said, "Now," he stuck a gloved finger up my rectum to examine me, looked at Keith, then at the nurses, and said, "If we hurry, we might make it."

As he walked quickly to the door, I yelled out, "Might make what?"

He turned and said with a straight face, "To the delivery room." And he left.

Keith left too, to go with him to put on a gown for the delivery room.

I wiggled from the bed, which I hadn't even had time to wrinkle, and onto the gurney, down the hall to the delivery room and onto the table. It was now about 11:30 a.m. I was still panting and blowing to keep from bearing down.

Considering the circumstances — no charts, no history, no preferences, a doctor who had never seen me before — the crew did a remarkable job. They gently but urgently shouted questions at me, about allergies, whether I wanted a Vitamin K shot, other stuff that had been written down someplace during a quiet interview. They hurriedly explained simple routines, and gave me choices.

Lamaze was the magic word. They had their parts of this drama memorized, especially the nurses, and just because the star arrived midway into the performance, the final act was still going to come off as rehearsed.

As I got my legs in the stirrups and they tried to drape and prep me, I asked if I should bear down with the next one. The doctor said yes, and to let him know when it was coming.

He was still adjusting his equipment on the first one.

He said, "That was a good one."

Keith said, "I can see the top of his head. He's got dark hair."

I thought, "This isn't all happening. They're going to send me home and tell me to come back later."

On the delivery table the contractions changed. They went from waves of unpleasant, but not quite painful, cramps to simply an overwhelming urge to push down. No pain at all. I was surprised. I relaxed completely between contractions.

Keith was at my head, charged by the doctor with keeping my hands off his precious sterile drapes, which the doctor seemed to think were awfully important. I thought this was more than a little silly, considering the mass of germs in such close proximity to that part of my anatomy which was then the center of everyone's attention.

It was wonderful having Keith there. The experience wasn't like either of us had expected it would be. Mostly it went a whole lot quicker.

In the delivery room I had a backache for one contraction, and for another one I felt like I might throw up, but I didn't, and it was gone just that quickly. Anyway, I had 8 or 10 more strong contractions, during which Keith said the crown of the baby's head would bulge out, but not quite enough for the baby's whole head to come out. At that point the doctor gave me a very liberal episiotomy, which Keith said he didn't think was totally warranted. But what do you do in a situation like that?

On the next good push, Keith said I let out a grunt-groan-growl that he wouldn't have believed would have come out of little ole me, and the doctor said, "I've got its head, now I'm getting its left shoulder."

And she was out.

And up on my tummy, all dark purple, crying, and feeling so heavy on my stomach, and looking so big! She came out all in one contraction, which I didn't expect. Even though they had a mirror, I didn't see her come out, I was too busy bearing down. But I felt her, and Keith saw it all. The only real pain I had was then and it was like the pain from a cut just as she came out, but not where the doctor had cut me. And that was all.

We managed to ask the doctor a few things we had cleared with Dr. Brownlow, about having the baby room-in right away instead of after 12 hours in the nursery. He said fine.

And about nursing on the delivery table while he sewed up the episiotomy. (The doctor was willing, but the baby wasn't.)

And we remembered the Rh factor soon enough for him to get some blood for testing from the umbilical cord. (I didn't need to get a shot because she turned out to be Rh-Neg too.)

We started to mention the placenta, but decided to settle for a shot instead.

They got me on the gurney, bundled the baby and put her on it with me, and we went wheeling back to the room, where they cleaned and weighed her (5 lbs. 14 oz.), and I called my mom and told her that Rebecca Jean had been born at 12:25 p.m. It was Wednesday, Jan. 23, 1974.

About an hour later, I felt the need to go to the bathroom, stood up, and fainted for the first time in my life. Luckily Keith was right there to catch me. I felt a lot better after I got some hot soup down me. A nurse took my blood pressure, and it was fine. Fainting was the only bad part of the whole experience.

Dr. Brownlow apparently just missed the whole thing. He was supposed to be out of town, but decided against it because of bad weather at his destination. So he was home about noon Wednesday. I think he was disappointed — he liked delivering babies. He said next time (!) he would teach Keith how to examine me for dilation, and that I'd better get to the hospital as soon after the first contraction as possible.

We went home about 2 p.m. the next day, about 27 hours after I got there. I was 16 pounds lighter than when I went in (not counting Becca, of course). My tummy was almost gone, but it was soft and mushy. I understand we were the talk of the hospital for a day or two. The hospital bill was about $175, about half the normal bill for half the normal stay. The doctor charged $210.

Helen and Scott came to the cabin to see the baby, one of the very few times I can remember them coming to visit. Helen read Becca's palms. I didn't know you could do that with newborn babies. When she asked if she could, I suddenly remembered that Helen had read both Keith and my palms before they had offered to sell us some property. I remembered her saying that Keith had the deepest heart (love) line she had ever seen, straight and true. My life line was short when we first got to Maine, telling her I wouldn't live long, but it had gotten longer by the time Becca arrived. I didn't know palm lines changed.

Helen said Becca's palm lines showed she would be very even-tempered, not emotional, and that she has a great head line, which meant a thinker and probably a career.

Since Keith thought he still had plenty of time to make that cradle and hadn't gotten around to it, a neighbor, Carolyn Robinson, loaned us a cradle that looked old-fashioned. Her son had built it for his daughter Rebecca several years ago, but her granddaughter had long outgrown it, and it had been gathering dust in her attic.

(Carolyn lived at Undercliff, a waterfront portion of Cape Rosier around the corner from the grange hall. She had more than a little in common with Helen and Scott. In fact, the book she wrote with her then-husband Ed, ***The Have-More Plan: A Little Land - A Lot of Living***, published in 1945, predated the first edition of ***Living the Good Life*** by nearly a decade. Detailing how to live an independent lifestyle on a few acres, the book reportedly sold more than 700,000 copies over the course of 20 printings in those stability-seeking years after World War TWO. Helped by the book royalties, the Robinsons bought Undercliff Farm in 1949, while the Nearings were still in Vermont. When she and Ed divorced in 1958, Carolyn kept that property.)

We got a sample box of disposable diapers at the hospital, picked up five dozen at Grants, and got two dozen as a gift. They gave Becca a diaper rash. After a couple of weeks, I decided to use them only at night, when I would be more apt to stick her with a pin putting on a cloth diaper in the dark.

About five dozen cloth diapers lasted her until she was house-broken. And they were the easiest things to wash, even by hand using an old-fashioned hand-crank ringer. In the early 1970s, before disposable diapers completely took hold, you could buy things called diaper liners, which were soft but tough pieces of fabric much like paper towels. Anything solid in a diaper could be lifted right out in one lump and disposed of normally, leaving behind a smelly but not messy diaper. I suspect some of the tougher paper towels would work as well today.

Nowadays disposable diapers are considered the norm, with tons of human waste and strange chemical absorbers ending up in landfills and incinerators — not a healthy situation. And they cost so much! I saw one program recently that detailed the expenses of a young mother who was working full-time at a minimum-wage job. Out of her take-home pay of less than $200 a week, $40 went for disposable diapers for her two-year-old daughter.

I saw two things wrong with that scenario:

1. If two weeks worth of spending on disposable diapers ($80) were spent instead on cloth diapers, that mother would have only a slight increase in laundry bills, but an immediate 20 percent increase in her spendable cash. At that income level, more disposable income is much preferable to more disposable diapers.

2. What the heck is a two-year-old still doing in diapers?

But I digress.

Breast-feeding worked great. It was not only cheap and easy, particularly in the middle of the night, but it was also supposed to be a pretty effective means of birth control as long as the baby was nursing and not eating anything else. The hormones released by that activity, or whatever, are said to suppress periods. Susie Coleman said it worked for her for two years.

But I was not convinced, and had an IUD inserted at my six-week check-up.

Mother and daughter got along fine all winter and spring, both resorting to rejuvenating naps, followed by incredible bursts of activity.

The southwest corner of the cabin with its large sun-catching windows.

Chapter 14
Loaves and Fishes

February 20, 1974

Sure has been hectic around here lately. Scott has me typing another manuscript for him that a publisher wants to see next month, so I've been pushing at that every spare minute. I only get 50 cents a typed page, but it adds up. So with that, nursing Becca every 2 or 3 hours, and trying to keep the dishes done, I haven't been writing many letters...

The stitches have long since healed. They didn't have to be taken out, they dissolved in place, which is nice. I imagine they're made of something like those seed tapes. Still a little touchy there, but not bad. It could have been a lot worse.

I'm not surprised someone asked you if we were married. I think it's funny. "Living together" is common among people who decide to live like we do. Most of them are younger than us, though. I don't know of one couple who've succeeded at this who isn't married. I think you need stability out here, and getting married is a part of that — it's a commitment that a lot of young kids aren't ready for ...

...Becca is nursing now (again), so I have a few minutes while she finishes the left side. Can't write while she nurses the right side.

She's doing great. ... I got a copy of Dr. Spock's baby book, and stopped reading it half way through. I can understand why a lot of mothers are neurotic if they try to listen to him. He would have them running to their doctor for advice on everything from using a pacifier on down. Doesn't give the mother any credit for common sense. And a lot of stuff he would make me worry about if I didn't know better. I certainly wouldn't recommend him to anyone. If I believed everything he said about breast-feeding, I would have been afraid to even try it...

(*Author's Note: In 1975, Dr. Benjamin Spock, in announcing the third revision of his book, apologized for the sexist language and tone in prior editions, and promised the new edition would be less offensive to women. When he died in March 1998, he was praised for having told a generation of women to trust their own instincts.*)

The hens we had bought as chicks from Sears were in high gear. We got 17 dozen eggs that week in February, and all we didn't eat I sold for 85 cents a dozen. We just let the word out, and got a lot of takers — could have sold more if we had them. The eggs were usually between large and extra large, with an occasional jumbo and double-yolker. The orange yolks were a far cry from the pale yellow ones in the local grocery store, and people appreciated the freshness. I was pleased that the income would start paying the feed bill, with a little left over.

Exactly a month after Becca had been born, on Feb. 23, our Alpine goat Juno kidded, twice, at 10:30 and 11:30 p.m. She had a nanny and a billy, in that order. We named the nanny Windy and her brother just Billy because we had decided to eat him.

But then problems developed. By the next morning Juno hadn't expelled the second placenta and seemed to be getting weaker. We knew something was wrong, so we called a vet, which being Sunday meant the one across the Bay, 50 miles by road. Diagnosis — milk fever. More common in high production dairy lines like hers, it was quite often fatal if not caught in time. Juno's system had geared up so highly for milk production that it drained calcium from other parts of her body to put it into the milk. Since calcium is needed for muscle coordination, including that of the heart and lungs, she was in serious trouble.

But there was something he could do, the vet said, if we got her to him in time.

Keith and Eliot rushed Juno to the vet while I tried to feed her kids with a nipple, an eyedropper, and finally a pan, which worked. Meanwhile, across the bay, the vet gave Juno an intravenous shot of calcium gluconate. Keith said 15 minutes later she was out of her coma and on her feet — the system responds that quickly to calcium.

So they brought her back and we thought the excitement was over. But the next day she seemed to have a relapse. Being Monday, Keith got an IV solution of calcium gluconate from a closer vet and gave her enough for a cow. She responded, but not as quickly.

For days, she wouldn't eat. I tried to entice her with anything I could think of. She nibbled on seaweed and water, then cabbage, carrots, and apples, and finally, a little grain. For three weeks I hand-fed her, a tidbit at a time, three or four times a day. Colemans supplied us with milk from their own herd for the first two weeks to feed Juno's kids — they insisted on it because it's best for newborn kids. We were taking their whole supply, about half a gallon a day, for over a week with their blessing.

Since Juno was incapable of performing her motherly duties, we brought the goat kids into the house to keep them warm. Keith built a small pen in the corner to confine them, which didn't always work.

Juno finally got on her feet. As she got stronger I started milking her a little at a time. I was getting just barely enough to feed her kids. She looked so thin. We wondered if we would lose her, even then. Her daughter Nicky was due to kid the middle of April. We got a supply of IV solution, in case we needed it. And I watched their diet closer.

With dog Brandy standing guard, the baby goats use the couch to test their climbing skills. Month-old Becca is more interested in other things.

In mid-March we added two baby pigs to our farm inventory. They were seven weeks old, had just been weaned, and weighed about 20 pounds apiece. They cost $25 each. It was cold out when we got them so we thought we'd keep them in the house for a few days until the weather broke. With Juno reunited with her offspring in the goat pasture, we put the piglets in the pen the goat kids had just vacated.

I had heard that pigs are really clean animals. Well, they may be, but, unlike goats, their manure stinks to high heaven. They didn't stay in the house long. We put them in a sectioned-off part of the chicken coop, with access to a small penned area outside. They would be getting better quarters in a month or so when they outgrew that coop space.

They were cute, but I was counting my hams already. The English call pigs mortgage lifters. We debated whether to sell one in the fall to cover our costs — in effect to get one for free — but with our hearty appetites and the steady stream of visitors, we knew we might want to keep them both.

The little pigs got fed three times a day when I fed the goat kids. Windy and Billy never did learn to suckle Juno. It was something of a bother, heating up the pans of milk, but that way we were able to see how Juno was doing and make sure the kids were getting enough milk. Feeding all those new babies, human and otherwise, kept me hopping.

March 17, 1974
...Keith has three people lined up who want to pay him to roto-till their gardens for them. It would be nice to get some cash money back on our investment in that beast.

I think that book about our project here will be a long time coming, if ever. I can't even seem to find enough time to write my mother a letter. Can you imagine that?...

Within weeks the pigs had doubled in size. Keith built a nice pen for them out of cedar posts and spruce bars, about 2 or 2½ feet high, based on the principle that pigs can't jump.

Good theory, but one got so excited when I went to feed them one morning that she jumped up at the slop bucket, got more than half way over the top bar and fell out. No trouble getting her back in, where the food was, but Keith put up another tier of railing.

April 9, 1974
We're finally getting rural mail delivery, starting Saturday. They wouldn't approve an extension beyond Nearings' driveway because of the bad road, so we'll have to walk down there to pick it up. But that's still better than going all the way into town. It'll save a lot of gas.

The town is supposed to fix our section of the road this summer, so we'll try to get the route extended to our drive when they do. The road gets very rutty when it rains, or thaws, or both, which is where it is right now.

Gee, that's strange, but that's really the big event around here.

Saturday evening, April 13, right on schedule, it looked like Nicky's birthing was imminent. She was breathing heavy and straining occasionally. We stayed up till midnight, checking her every hour or so, finally went to bed. Keith got up at 3 a.m. to check her, and I went up at 6. No change. Her vulva area got really soft and mushy, then started to get firm again.

We mentioned that to Eliot, who went home to check his goat book. He came back telling us we had trouble, that when that happens it usually means a Cesarean section will be needed.

Chapter 14 — Loaves and Fishes

Nicky by then had gone weak-kneed, stiff-legged and looked like she was going into shock. We resorted to drastic measures. I went up her birth canal with a surgical glove and some Vaseline, and found the cervix only big enough to get four fingertips into it. Nicky by now was flat out on the ground, and offered no resistance, but groaned when I tried to stretch her cervix.

Keith went down to the house to get some surgical equipment his mother had given us (scalpel, etc.) and his gun in case he needed it. Meanwhile, I was trying to stretch the cervix, and finally it started to loosen. I got my hand in, and the kid was right there, feet and head in the right position. By this time Keith had come back. The water sac broke, I grabbed the feet and pulled the first kid out. It was a little nanny. Nicky came right out of her slump and licked the kid off.

We decided to let her try to do it herself for the second one. We didn't want to interfere with nature any more than necessary. Maybe that was a mistake, but it was 9:30 p.m. when she kidded, we stayed with her until about midnight, and since she didn't seem to be in any distress, or even discomfort, we left her till morning.

By morning she seemed to be in labor, straining periodically, but no progress. Then she started to look like she was getting weak, so I went in again. I found the second kid, had some difficulty trying to decide if the feet were front or hind. It came out back legs first, not unusual for the second, but the water sac had already broken and he (a billy) was dead. In fact, it looked like he had already started to decompose. Since it takes more than a few hours for that to happen, he had probably been dead for a week or so. I went in again and found Number Three. He was in a cock-eyed angle with his head back and I couldn't turn it around to face forward. The head is supposed to come out between the legs, like taking a dive.

Well, Nicky looked like she couldn't take much more, so Keith took over, despite his big hands. He got in with difficulty, turned the kid around and pulled it out. It was another billy, also dead, but not decomposed. Keith went in again to check for another one, but that was it. We flushed her out with a mild vinegar douche. In town that day, Eliot picked up a pill for us to put inside her womb to combat infection.

The next day Nicky was up and around, looking very bruised from behind, but otherwise apparently okay. So far so good. The little nanny, however, was awfully weak. She still had trouble standing, which usually happens just a few minutes after birth. After licking her off at birth, Nicky had just ignored her. Since we only wanted strong goats in our herd, we decided to sell the baby. Until we found a buyer, we put her in that pen in the house to keep an eye on her, feeding her Nicky's colostrum out of a pan.

By then Keith had about enough of goats, said if we had to go through all this trauma every time a goat kidded, the milk wasn't worth the trouble. Maybe purebred Alpines weren't such a good deal after all.

But then again, Nicky did have an awful lot of milk in her udder.

April 16, 1974
...It just dawned on us a little while ago that our savings account is earning 5 percent interest while inflation is 8-12 percent a year. In other words, the value of our money in the bank is going down instead of up.

So we decided to take some of that money and buy things now that we had planned to budget for later — like a better chain saw and another wheelbarrow, and a whole lot of tools.

I think I mentioned John Tani to you, the fellow who built the cabin down the road on the other side of Colemans', then just left it. He came back last fall, and turned out to be a nice enough fellow. Did a lot of clearing, hauled manure and made compost.

But there's something about Spring that he apparently can't take, and he's off again wanting to build another boat. (That's where he went last time.) But I guess this time he's gone for good. He wants the money back that he put in the place, and I guess Helen Nearing is willing to buy it [the cabin] from him.

So now Colemans are all excited again about maybe finding another couple, hopefully with kids, to homestead here. Apparently Helen already has a prospect in mind...

Spring is here again, with its mud. Becca is sleeping for six hours or so at night now, so I get my sleep and don't usually have to nap during the day anymore. I sure do get a lot more done now. The house looks half-way decent more than half the time. That's progress!

For my first Mother's Day that May, Keith installed my sink. On the side where my temporary counter had been was now a beautiful birds-eye maple countertop with a stainless steel double sink, four drawers, and a shelf, with a storage area under the sink. It looked absolutely stunning.

Two other countertops, along the other two walls in the kitchen, were in the plans, when Keith found the time. He had managed to figure out that the spring at the source of our brook was high enough to bring water right to the sink by gravity feed, without the need for a pump. In fact we had about a foot in height to spare. I was really looking forward to that.

May 8, 1974

...Becca is growing like a weed! I took her for her first shots on April 24, and she weighed 10 lbs. 12 oz. And was 23 inches long....Sometimes I can't help but wonder what the future holds for her, and for me and her. I want to teach her so much...

Nicky the goat was doing well, giving about five quarts of milk a day, to Juno's two to three. So we were getting just under two gallons a day. We managed to drink most of it, although I set aside enough to make three small wheels of cheddar and two batches of cottage cheese.

Carolyn Robinson, the same neighbor who loaned us the cradle, dug through her attic and came up with a cream separator she used when they had goats. The screw adjustment was stuck on heavy cream. We would get about a cup of cream from a gallon of milk, and it was so thick that it set up stiff when it cooled down, almost to the consistency of soft butter or cream cheese. We used it like butter as it was, without churning it. It was also great on baked potatoes, in tomato soup, and in an omelet. Delicious. I made cheese with the skim milk, and the whey went to the pigs. Great eating, and nothing was wasted.

May 8, 1974 (cont'd)

I hereby interrupt this letter to add my wind to the trumpet. Happy anniversary and happy Mother's Day as well! I sure am glad you were a mother cause I got Jean out of the deal. I also think you're great other than that. At one time I was pretty leery though I think you'll recall you had me pretty skittish way back when! Now I'm convinced I've got a gem of a mother-in-law. Keith

How about that!?

...We've managed to snag one of the helpers that came to see Nearings and Colemans. Keith says he's a good worker, unusual in that bunch, and he doesn't talk all the time while he's working, another unusual trait. Name is Greg Summers. Nice guy. Hope he stays around awhile.

We're busy planting and transplanting. The weather for the most part has been rainy, drizzly and cool, unseasonably so...

By the end of May we had both running water and a drywell for the graywater. The backhoe we hired worked awfully fast. What we thought would take three days took only 11½ hours. That was a nice surprise since he charged $12 an hour.

The first day, he took out an awful lot of stumps that would have taken Keith several months to do by hand. The newly-stumpless field looked almost rock-free — probably the best place for a garden on the whole place. Then he used the loader on the front to grade our road up the hill behind the house to the goat pasture, digging some fruit tree holes on the way. Next he graded some piles of clay around the house left over from the foundation dig and the cellar drainage line. It really neatened up the yard.

The second day he spent two hours digging a 4-foot-deep trench from the woods to the corner of the house for the water line, and a big hole near the house for the drywell. He was a real artist, it was a pleasure to watch him work. Unfortunately, he couldn't get the backhoe into the woods to dig the trench all the way to the spring, so Keith resigned himself to digging that portion by hand.

While the backhoe was up at Colemans pulling stumps, Keith and Greg laid the water pipe and filled the drywell for the drain with rocks and stones. The third day the guy came back after finishing up at Colemans and spent an hour filling in the trenches. The part of the pipe from the edge of the field to the spring was laid on top of the ground through the woods.

The guys got the siphon going in the pipe, and we were in business. The flow wasn't very fast, but it was plenty for what we used. And what a joy it was not to have to haul water either in or out! I reveled in washing diapers that day, with my hand-crank wringer screwed down to the partition between the double sink. I got to rinse them really well, for a change. We still had to heat water on the stove until Keith got the parts and the time to hook up the hot water tank to the wood stove. But what luxury!

The goats had settled down, and we were still getting just over seven quarts of milk a day. Eggs were 69 cents a dozen in the stores, 49 cents with a coupon. But the feed prices were the same. On top of that the hens were molting so we only had seven dozen extra eggs a week to sell. But we still managed to break even.

By the end of May, our first garden area below the house was almost planted for the season except for the potatoes. After a rabbit got three of our small cabbage plants, we fenced in the garden with chicken wire on post frames, following Eliot's example.

We planted 89 tomato plants, nine 20-foot rows of onions, four of garlic, two of lettuce, about five of cabbage and cauliflower, and the rest in beets, radishes, leeks, chives, parsnips, carrots, spinach, chard, Fava beans, and I forget what else. The peas planted in the upper garden, behind the house, were up and doing well. Our strawberry bed had some flowers, and 75 asparagus roots had just arrived, along with 15 fruit and nut trees — apple, peach, plum, cherry (sweet and sour), Chinese chestnuts, and filberts. Only one beehive survived the winter, but it seemed to be doing well.

When they weren't working on the homestead, the guys were in the village, where the lodge was coming down nicely. Greg and Keith had gotten an awful lot of work done in the three weeks since he turned up. We found out that he bought some land near Bangor during the winter that had turned into a swamp when spring came. He was trying to get his money back from the seller, and in the meantime he was helping us.

Greg came packing a big pile of canvas, sewed into a teepee shape. He and Keith cut and skinned 20 long, thin poles, and set up his teepee on the hill near the goat pasture. It was just beautiful — and functional. A fire in the middle of it heated the space so well, yet all the smoke went out the top. It was the nicest campfire I ever sat around.

Greg was 24, from Michigan, and was a commercial artist by training. He seemed very level-headed, and was a good worker. We appreciated his help.

By the end of June, I was baking bread to sell at Eliot's farmstand. I had gotten quite a reputation for my loaves and other baked goodies, and Eliot said it would be a nice addition to what he had to offer. I figured if I was going to be more or less confined to the house anyhow, I might as well do something that would bring in some money.

It helped immeasurably that Keith's sister Cassie was back for the summer and was a willing co-conspirator. She made the cinnamon rolls, which were outstanding and an instant success.

Keith made me a very nice display case, a wooden box with a hinged, glass top. It sat on the counter at the stand, where people could help themselves. I had a separate change jar, so Colemans didn't have to worry about keeping track of the money.

We started out with three loaves and a dozen cinnamon rolls a day, increasing our inventory as the traffic at the stand increased. Over the summer we added French bread, pumpernickel, and my mother's specialty, braided Ukrainian Easter bread.

We experimented and discovered that we could start the yeast dough the night before, right before bed, and put it downstairs in the cool root cellar to rise overnight. The one-rising varieties, the French bread and the pumpernickel loaves, we shaped into loaves before tucking them in for the night. The next morning those were ready to pop into the oven as soon as it was hot enough. Meanwhile, we punched down the other bread dough, shaped the loaves and rolls, let them rise at their leisure while we ate breakfast, and had everything baked and on the stand by the time it opened at 10 a.m.

It was quite a sight, Becca in a carrier on my back, me hefting baskets of hot bread covered with bright towels, traipsing through the woods to Eliot's stand.

By the end of July we were selling six whole wheat bread loaves, four sourdough French long loaves, four pumpernickel round loaves, and about 24 cinnamon rolls (or what was known in this part of the world as "sticky buns") every day. All baked on a wood-burning stove. The sticky buns were loaded with raisins and walnuts and just smelled irresistible. We sold them for 15 cents each. The whole wheat bread (1½ pounds) we priced at 95 cents, the pumpernickel was 80 cents and the French 70 cents. Cass made the Easter bread, and it usually sold, at $1.75 a loaf, before it had a chance to cool down.

The prices were high by Ohio standards, but comparable to local home-baked goods.

The goat's milk and hen's eggs that we didn't use ourselves all went into the bread. On top of that we got to eat all the loaves that were a little too brown on top or the few during the week that didn't sell.

June 29, 1974 Friday

... I wouldn't want to do this year-round, but when you can see the end of it, it's really lots of fun. I enjoy baking, much more than I do cooking, for some reason. This will go on till about Labor Day, maybe a few days after that, when all the summer people go back to work in the big cities. So for about two months this summer we'll be working our tails off.

...The strawberries are just starting to bear. The season is so late here. But the rest of the garden is looking really super, all green and leafy. The pigs are getting big too. In fact, everything is looking fine this year. A lot less hectic than last year.

That lodge Keith is taking down seems to be taking forever, but we can see the end of it now. All that's left is to take apart the bottom floor, burn all the rotten wood, and have people cart off the lumber at 10 cents a board foot.....

Greg Summers, the guy who was helping Keith and who built the teepee, has bought John Tani's place, the cabin and land on the other side of Colemans. He bought [the cabin] from Nearings and is now helping them for pay to pay for it. So he's not here anymore.

July 21, 1974 Sunday

...The garden is beautiful, and it'll be in its prime when you get here. We're eating well out of it. The peas are out of this world. Canning season has arrived. We got two boxes of peaches from a nearby wholesale farm-

stand and put up 39 pints of those, and ate all the rest. We're going to go back for more...

Keith got a whole load of fresh mackerel from a fisherman just down the road who couldn't get rid of them, so we've canned 60 pints of them in the pressure canner. It looks like we'll be having fish at least once a week all year. That will be nice. Mackerel is great in a casserole, a lot like tuna fish.

The pigs are fine, big and solid. We think we're going to breed one of them this fall, and sell all but two of the litter hopefully next January before we butcher the mother. We already have people who say they'll buy from us if we do that. That would make the whole thing a paying proposition.

Keith finished tearing down the lodge about two weeks ago. That was really a load off his back. Now he's selling the lumber like mad, not really great stuff, but people are paying 10 cents a board foot for it, boarding boards and 2x4s and such. It's nice to be putting money into the bank.

Now Keith has a job for a few weeks working for the contractor who is building Helen Nearing's new house. He doesn't get along with Helen too well anymore, but he's not working for her but for her contractor, Fred Dyer. He's the fellow we sold a goat to last April, so we're good friends with them.

Chapter 15

We Have Seen the Enemy And They Are Part of Us

I was raised on the germ theory of disease. My mother believed in them, and fought them continuously with liberal doses of soap and water. Our house was nothing if not clean.

In grade school I learned that ever since the invention of the microscope, germs had been seen, identified, classified, linked to specific diseases. The germ for tuberculosis was different from the germ that caused yellow fever or malaria. You wouldn't catch measles from a germ that caused mumps.

When I was a kid, vaccinations for diphtheria, tetanus, and pertussis (whooping cough) were standard, and came bundled all together in the DPT shots even then routinely given to infants, including me. Everyone I knew had a round dotted smallpox vaccination mark somewhere on their body.

In the mid-1950s, not one but two vaccines were developed for polio, that devastating neurological infection which had been running rampant among the population — all the way to the White House and Franklin Delano Roosevelt. I got both the Salk dead vaccine by injection in a doctor's office, and the Sabin live vaccine on a sugar cube administered en masse after school (with parental permission) a few years later. In all the controversy over which was most effective, my mother, who believed that scientists were smart and wise and that science would protect us from all evils, figured that twice was better than none at all.

The measles vaccine would come along in the mid-1960s, after I already had natural immunity. Ditto for mumps.

In high school and college biology classes I learned that vaccines try to trigger natural immunity without actually causing the disease. In that way they are different from antibiotics, which are designed to kill all but the strongest germs already at work — thereby inadvertently creating a master race of a deadly disease organism when the few tough surviving germs proceed to go forth and multiply. The theoretical vaccination scenario was this: If just one generation of germs for a given disease could be prevented from reproducing all at the same time all over the world, the disease would disappear.

So when it came time to vaccinate my first child, I thought the situation was a closed topic. After all, what was there to discuss?

That's when I learned that the Colemans didn't exactly believe in the germ theory of disease. Health, they said, was not the absence of disease, but a state of being that warded off affronts to its integrity. The ideal way to prevent disease was to stay healthy. The various germs identified in scientific literature were just tiny opportunists, taking advantage of a weakened physical condition.

Eliot said it made no sense to work so hard to change one's lifestyle so profoundly, to live a healthy, rural, vegetarian lifestyle, eating only organically-raised food, breathing clean country air (we did not know then that the prevailing winds made Maine the exhaust pipe for our entire industrialized nation), and then turn around and inject germ samples directly into the bloodstreams of our innocent children, supposedly to protect them from diseases which have been practically eliminated from the face of the earth.

I listened to this argument with interest. I knew the Nearings agreed with that concept. After all, in *Living the Good Life* they had quoted two authors who raised that very point.

In their chapter on Eating for Health, they say:

> Instead of spending his time on the subject of sickness, Dr. [G. T.] Wrench [in The Wheel of Health, London: C.W. Daniel 1938] asked, "What is health? Why are people well? Where can I find the healthiest people to study?" After much inquiry and research, Wrench concluded that the Hunzas, a tribe occupying a small valley in the border area between India and Tibet are the world's healthiest. Much of his book is devoted to an examination of the reasons for their state of well-being. He concluded that "Diseases only attack those whose outer circumstances, particularly food, are faulty...The prevention and banishment of disease are primarily matters of food; secondarily, of suitable conditions of environment. Antiseptics, medicaments, inoculations, and extirpating operations evade the real problem. Disease is the censor pointing out the humans, animals and plants who are imperfectly nourished."

Two dozen pages later, they quote Dr. D. T. Quigley, who in *The National Malnutrition* (1948), wrote:

> The Indians in the back country who did not have access to the white man's food kept their good health; had no tuberculosis or any of the other diseases mentioned.

I thought of those rinsed-but-not-washed wooden bowls down at the Nearings, and wondered.

Other parents in our larger community, who professed a belief in the germ theory of disease, nevertheless said they did not want their children vaccinated because of the statistically small, but still very real, possibility that the vaccines, particularly the live ones, could trigger either the disease itself or an unacceptable adverse reaction. Besides, there was some talk of possible long-term effects, of other diseases triggered later in life from resident virus particles. Those parents did not want to bear the responsibility, however small, of possibly harming their children in their well-intentioned attempts to safeguard them.

Susan contended that the chances of her children having an adverse reaction to the shots was greater than their chances of catching the diseases in the wild. Statistically, she was right, since most children in the United States in 1974 were routinely immunized. I appreciated that fear. But I also couldn't help see the larger picture.

First of all, I agree that healthy bodies have stronger immune systems, which are better able to fight off invasions of unacceptable organisms. And I believe that eating healthy food is important in maintaining a healthy body.

The devil, however, is in the details. Food grown on a mish-mash of decaying organic matter and various minerals (i.e. compost), water and sunshine get varying degrees of the nutrients they need to grow and therefore have themselves varying degrees of health. Did they get enough boron, calcium, water, phosphorus? If not, how do we know? Some foods like acid soils, some like alkaline. When we grow both kinds of food in our home garden, are some or all of them lacking in what they need? Is there such a thing as a perfect food or a perfect diet?

Many times it's just that we don't know enough about what we're doing, and how it may be affecting our own health. The Romans built their clever water systems with lead pipes, and caused their own downfall with mass lead poisoning. The Nearings mentioned that they long ago stopped using aluminum cooking pots because it "probably acts as a slow poison in the human system." They were right — some studies have suggested aluminum, even that found in popular deodorants, may be a factor in Alzheimer's disease. Questions have been raised about contaminants in mercury-based dental fillings — or the amalgam alternatives — as well as in drinking water from now-popular plastic water pipes.

Eliot claimed that eating healthy foods would keep a body healthy. He grew and ate healthy foods. Yet he occasionally got sick, caught colds, and was known to pass them on to the neighbors. If he stood by his theory, then he was obviously doing something wrong. If he couldn't get it right, who could?

As for Wrench and Quigley, what they either did not know, or refused to consider, was that those isolated pockets of healthy native populations they found were not saved from disease by the absence of white man's food, but by the absence of white man's germs. OF COURSE, back woods Indians without access to tuberculosis germs would not come down with tuberculosis. How could they?

The healthy American Indians proved that point quite well, when Europeans arrived and smallpox immediately decimated our nation's native population. All those Indians didn't have time to get unhealthy by eating white man's food or drinking white man's whiskey. If you will remember your lessons about Thanksgiving, the earliest settlers didn't have any food when they got here, and relied on the American Indians to teach them how to grow native species. And those deeply religious early settlers didn't have any whiskey or hard liquor to lead the natives astray because their religion forbade it.

I have also wondered, although I have never seen the question raised, if any of the many deaths the earliest colonists suffered the first year or two on these shores might have been caused by their exposure to germs of unknown and unnamed diseases innocently passed to them by immune American Indians.

For that matter, did anyone go back to those isolated tribes studied by Wrench and Quigley to see if they had been affected by the germs the white researchers had inadvertently passed around?

It has been assumed by many that most of the smallpox epidemic among our native population was due to natural infection, the result of strange germs thrust upon unprepared immune systems. But some letters penned by Lord Jeffrey Amherst, after whom the town and college in Massachusetts are named, suggest that Lord Amherst recognized their vulnerability and used smallpox-infected blankets as germ warfare against American Indians in 1763, at the close of the French and Indian War.

The bottom line I came to is this: the decision to keep children vaccine-free can only work for a small number of isolated children in a world otherwise full of vaccinated or naturally immune people.

Ironically, those cautious parents are the ones who provide the world with the weak links, the only living hosts in which the deadly germs can hope to survive. It is un-immune and unvaccinated populations that make not only epidemics, but germ warfare, possible.

I took Becca to the free clinic for her shots, held my breath each time and prayed she would have no reactions. She was fine. Still is, as far as I can tell, nearly three decades later.

However, back there in the mid-1970s, I got real, solid reinforcement for my decision to vaccinate my daughter not long after she had gotten her shots.

The message was clear. The unlikely messenger was a backhoe's claw.

The backhoe operator was working in the gravel pit directly across the town road opposite our driveway. Workers were expanding the pit, making a flat area level with the gravel town road by digging vertically into a 20-foot-high hill. The backhoe was working about 100 feet in from the road, using its bucket claw to eat away at the sheer back wall of the sand and gravel hillside. The claw was feeding the face of the cliff into the backs of huge dump trucks, to be hauled away and transformed into driveways and drainage fields.

On that eventful day, the backhoe operator aimed high and took yet another bite out of the back wall of the pit. Only this time, about six feet below the crest of the hill, the claw hit something other than sand or gravel. It was wooden. A box. No, not a box — a casket.

What the hey?
Oh my God! Fellas! Geez! How did that get there! Call someone, quick!
Look! There's a whole cemetery up here! In the woods! Did anyone know about this?
Well, I'll be. Look at all those old gravestones, in amongst all those full-grown spruce trees. What do you make a that?
Creepy.

Town officials were mortified. How could they have lost track of a whole cemetery? And not a small one at that. Well, it wasn't more than a quarter-acre in size, maybe 100 by 100 feet. But it was a whole lot bigger than some of the town's old family farm plots that everybody knew about. There were at least a few dozen stones in there. Old ones, going back a hundred years or more. How could this have happened?

The gravel pit was immediately and officially closed. And the town fathers, who took their town history and responsibilities very seriously, organized a work party for the next weekend to fell the 10-inch-wide trees that had grown up among the headstones, and to reset the fallen and broken markers.

Not long after they had removed all the debris and cleaned up the site, I went over to check it out. It was pretty impressive — worn, hundred-year-old marble and granite headstones, for people who had died old and for youngsters cut down in their prime. Some had just names and dates, others were remembered with whole poems beautifully carved in stone.

I worked my way to the back of the plot, reading the memorials as I went. Farthest away from the road, I looked up to see a small four-sided

Chapter 15 — We Have Seen the Enemy And They Are Part of Us 143

granite obelisk. About six feet high, it was surrounded by a shaky wrought-iron fence. The stately spire seemed to draw me to it.

The Blake family grave marker.

I read the first side, which had two names:

Daniel Blake
Born Feb. 7, 1812
Died Jan. 28, 1894

Christina F. His Wife
Born Jan. 7, 1817
Died Jan. 28, 1894

That's curious, I thought. They both died on the same day. I did the math. She was 77 and he was 82. They were old.

I wondered if they had died tragically, maybe in a fire. Maybe they had frozen to death that cold January, only to be found days later. Maybe, after they were discovered, people only surmised that they had died the same day.

On another face of the obelisk was a list of four names — Sons of Daniel and Christina Blake. A third face held four more names — Daughters of Daniel and Christina Blake.

Sons of Daniel & Christina F. Blake
Hiram	Died Dec. 1, 1863	AE 11 yrs. 7 mos & 7 days
Albion	Died Dec. 7, 1863	AE 9 yrs 9 mos & 7 days
Andrew J.	Died Dec. 14, 1863	AE 1 yr. 3 mos. & 20 days
George L.		Lost at Sea

Daughters of Daniel & Christina F. Blake
Joanna	Died Nov. 23, 1863	AE 15 yrs. 25 ds.
Margaret	Died Nov. 29, 1863	AE 14 yrs. 5 mos.
Abbie M.	Died Nov. 30, 1863	AE 4 yrs. 9 mos.
Eliza AE		1 yr. 3 mo.

All had died decades before their parents.

Still so new a mother, I wondered how it must have felt to have lost eight children to death in that last century, in...when? This one says 1863. That was during the Civil War. Were any of them in that war? Did they die because of it? Let's see, son George was lost at sea...

As I started to compare the dates, the horror of it sunk in.

Six of the eight children listed on the stone monument had died in 1863. In fact, they had died within three weeks of each other, from November 23 to December 14, all in 1863.

Joanna was dead at 15, Margaret at 14. Hiram was only 11½, Albion nearly 10. Abbie was not quite 5, Andrew was just a baby at 15 months. No date of death was listed for baby Eliza, who had also lived only 15 months. Was she Andrew's twin?

The next time I had reason to go off the Cape, I sought out Louise Grindle, who had been Brooksville's town clerk since dirt. Never married, Louise Grindle would serve the town as treasurer and/or town clerk for 49 years, only relinquishing the reins in 1995 after the town built a new municipal office building several miles from her home. A town correspondent for the ***Bangor Daily News***, the ***Island Ad-Vantages*** and the ***Ellsworth American***, she regularly sent in tidbits on what was happening around town — who was visiting whom from out of state, reports of

Chapter 15 — We Have Seen the Enemy And They Are Part of Us

some residents' exotic vacations, who enlisted, who got engaged. Curiously, Louise served as host to many beloved cats, at the same time she owned 19 rocking chairs, which were scattered around her neat white clapboard home within sight of Walker's Pond, a huge fresh-water lake that drained into the Bagaduce River.

(It appeared that the bodies of water in Brooksville were named under the same standard by which the 40-room waterfront homes of the wealthy summer residents of nearby Bar Harbor were referred to as "cottages."

Walker's Pond was probably a mile long, and half a mile wide.

Richard's Lake, however, was about 15 feet across. Named for Richard Condon, Richard's Lake had been dug out beside Condon's Garage in South Brooksville — the same Condon's Garage memorialized in Robert McCloskey's children's book, **Blueberries for Sal** — and was used by the local fire department as an emergency water source for its tankers.)

Besides all those rocking chairs, Town Clerk Louise Grindle was also the proud possessor of the town's oldest known pickle, a condiment which would be featured in the town's 1982 annual report.

The cucumber that was the basis of the historical pickle had been coaxed into a narrow-mouthed glass bottle when Louise was just a girl and the cucumber was just a gherkin.

The cucumber grew to full size inside that bottle, only to have its fate sealed at the end of that summer with salted vinegar and a stopper. The picture of the pickle in the Town Report looked a bit fuzzy. But it was not a photographic fluke. After several decades in brine, the pickle itself was a bit fuzzy.

As town clerk, Louise of course was responsible for all the important historical records — births, deaths, marriages, real estate transfers — going back to the town's founding some two centuries before. She kept the huge bound volumes, with beautifully handwritten entries, in a pantry off her kitchen.

I had copied down the information on the obelisk. I showed it to her. What could she tell me about the Blake family?

Louise was a friendly sort and pulled out one of the oldest of the town's record books.

On page 160 of a huge, leather-bound volume, in fading brown ink, the children of Daniel and Christina Colson Blake were listed. A few notations appeared to have been added sometime later.

Brooksville Town Records

Daniel Blake and wife Christina Colson

Cordelia	April 25, 1836
Susan	January 7, 1839
Lorenzo B.	March 25, 1840
Lucy	June 7, 1842 (may be Jan. 7)
Daniel	November 13, 1843
George L. B.	February 2, 1845
Charlotte T.	April 12, 1846
Ivan	January 12, 1847 (died an infant)
Margaret	February 12, 1848
Eliza	March 12, 1854 (died an infant)
Hiram	May 8, 1853
Albion	January 4, 1855
Mary G.	April 1, 1856
James Buchanan	May, 1857
Abbie M.	February, 1859
Andrew Jackson	July, 1862
Eliza	July, 1862 (twin, renamed for sister)

So. The Blakes did not have just eight children, they had 17 — and possibly 18.

Looking a bit closer at the list of names, we noticed that Joanna, who was listed on the tombstone as having died first in the epidemic, did not appear on the birth records. Applying a little biology to the chronology of birth dates, Louise conjectured that Joanna was probably born around 1850, and was 13, not 15, when she died.

According to the marriage records, Daniel and Christina were married when Susan was seven months old. Louise speculated that Daniel had a first wife, whose name was not recorded, and who probably died giving birth to Susan in 1839, when daughter Cordelia was three years old.

It looked like Christina then proceeded to have 15 children, starting promptly with Lorenzo eight months after the wedding.

Baby Eliza was indeed Andrew's twin. She had been named for her sister who also had died as an infant, probably six years before she was born. Christina Blake was 45 when she had the twins.

I scanned down the list. Christina had 16 children in a span of 22 years, with only one set of twins. So much for breast-feeding being a natural and effective form of birth control.

"That's amazing," I said to Louise, in awe at the history jumping out

Chapter 15 — We Have Seen the Enemy And They Are Part of Us

at me from the page. "Do you have any records that could tell me what all the kids died from?"

"Why, diphtheria, dear," she said simply, abruptly, and matter-of-factly, in a manner that told me that, if I had not been "from away," surely I would have known. "There was a lot of that in town that year. It mostly affected the children."

In fact it appeared that only children under 16 were listed on the obelisk. We postulated that all of the older children had already gone off on their own. Of the younger children, only little Mary and James (who might also have been called John) seemed to have survived the epidemic.

While all this was fascinating from an historical and intellectual perspective, at another level the information was hitting me right between the eyes. Diphtheria — the "D" in the childhood DPT shots.

I thought of the pre-industrial clean air and water, and the most-likely organic food that these children had grown up eating, in those days before pesticides. Yet their healthy bodies had been unable to resist those deadly germs.

Picturing a ruptured casket hanging out of the cliff at the top of my driveway, I couldn't help but wonder how long diphtheria germs stayed viable. Could they last 100 years? Had the backhoe punctured a time bomb while mining for good road gravel?

I consoled myself with the thought that Becca, Keith and I would be safe — we had all had our shots.

We were on a roll. I pushed the envelope. Did the town clerk know how the parents came to die on the same day, some 30 years later?

Louise Grindle paused, racking her brain. She said she didn't believe they died in either of my scenarios, fire or ice. But the Blake family was still around. I should go talk to them. They would know. She gave me some names.

I filed all that information away, not having the time then to pursue it any further. But the story nagged at me. It was unfinished business.

Then, in late 1976, Frances Clark of Brewer donated her great-great-grandmother's diary to the Brooksville Historical Society. Written by Margaret Lord Varnum (Mrs. David Varnum Jr.) between Dec. 31, 1852 and Nov. 20, 1884, it contained this entry:

December 1863:
Diphtheria. Sickness and death is making awful ravages in our town. Mrs. Blake has lost six children to that awful disease diphtheria, and has two more sick. Three more children have died on the

Cape. Death, it respects neither age or sex.

Finally, in 1981, I decided to do something about that unfinished business.

First of all, I asked a friend who was then a physicians' assistant in Bucksport to tell me all he knew about diphtheria, particularly anything about how it was treated long ago. He dug out an old reference book, published in 1867, only a few years after the Blake deaths. The book vividly describes various attempts — from hot pepper tea to wood ash poultices and gargling with castile soap — used in the 1860s to break through the thick membrane that develops in the throats of diphtheria patients, gagging and suffocating them.

Dr. Chase's Recipes or Information for Every Body

Diphtheria — "I have had the treatment of several cases, and have uniformly been successful; the remedy is very simple. It is the external application of water to the throat, at degrees of temperature alternating from the highest that the human skin will bear, taken to almost zero. I am prepared to verify that by proof."

A. Henderson, MRCS England 13
Upper Seymour St., Portman Sq. London 1858

M. Roche mentions in L'Union Medicale that he had saved six patients in six cases of diphtheria by the following mode of treatment. The false membranes were first freely cauterized with lunar caustic and injections then made every hour against the fauces with a solution of common salt, the strength of the solution being such as not to create nausea. Chlorate of potash was also given internally; and tincture of iodine as a topical application was used in half of the cases; but M. Roche considers that the irrigations with the solution of common salt were the chief agents in the case.

Diphtheria — remedy for — Make two small bags to reach from ear to ear, and fill them with wood ashes and salt; dip them in hot water and wring them out so that they are not dripping and apply them to the throat; cover up the whole with a flannel cloth and change them as often as they become cool, until the throat becomes irritated, near blistering. For children it is necessary to put flannel cloths between the ashes and the throat to prevent blistering. When the ashes have been on a sufficient time take a wet flannel cloth and rub it with castile soap until it is covered with a thick lather; dip it in hot water and apply it to the throat and change as they cool, at the same time use a gargle made of one teaspoon of cayenne pepper, one of salt, one of molasses, in a tea-cup of hot water, and when cool, add one-quarter as much cider vinegar and gargle every 15 minutes until the patient requires sleep. A gargle made of castile soap is good to be used part of the time.

A correspondent in Maine, in sending the above remedy, says there had been a number of deaths from diphtheria until this remedy was used, since then all have recovered.

Diphtheria — A gentleman who has administered the following remedy for diphtheria says that is has always proved effectual. Take a tobacco pipe, place a live coal in the bowl, drop a little tar upon the coal, and let the patient draw smoke into the mouth and discharge it through the nostrils. Safe and simple.

Diphtheria — specific for — The Italian journals publish a letter from Dr. Giovanni Calligara, describing the remarkable success which has attended his treatment of diphtheria with phenic acid. He relates the losses he formerly experienced among his patients when treating them with emollients, solvents and cauterization with hydrochloric acid, and observed that this cauterization can no more eradicate the morbid principle than tearing the leaves off a plant will destroy the root. He now simply uses a gargle of phenic acid and distilled water, with external applications of new flannel with food and drink to be taken cold. After adoption of this treatment, Dr. Calligra lost but one patient out of 58. He requested the Italian journals to publish this discovery. Phenic acid is the agent which is now being used in this country as a remedy for cancer, and seems likely to affect an immense saving of lives formerly hopelessly sacrificed to that disease.

Armed with that information, I then pulled out the names of the people Louise Grindle had suggested years before, and managed to track down three of them.

Lorenzo's granddaughter, Doris Blake Johnson, was in her 80s and living in the Bucksport-Orland area.

After talking to me, she sent me to little Mary's daughter, Catherine Libby, who was then in her late 80s and living in an apartment building in Rockland, Maine.

I also talked to Lucy Venno in Brooksville, one of the town's noted historians.

Here are their remarkable stories:

Doris Blake Johnson
Interview, April 1981, Orland, Maine

Editor's Note: While Mrs. Johnson referred to her relatives as Uncle Dan, Uncle Hiram, Grandfather and Grandmother, it was clear each was her great-uncle, great-grandfather and great-grandmother. The exception was Lorenzo, whom she referred to either as "my grandfather" or by his first name.

I'll be 84 on May 1. My great-grandmother was Christina Blake. She and Daniel had 16 children. Nine died [in the fall of 1863]. Two names are missing from that stone.

I love dolls. One year they gave me two dolls and I wondered what to name them. I was an only child. My grandfather, Lorenzo Blake, said, "Why don't you call her Joanna? I had a little sister one time with that name and she died."

My grandfather was a tall man, not a fat one, but a big man. He wore a goatee beard; it was white. He had bright blue eyes, black-haired, with huge hands. He weighed 235 pounds. The Colsons were Irish. So were the Blakes, originally. My grandfather said it was spelled "Blaik" in Ireland, some people will say that means "by the lake." I understand my grandfather got his size from the Colsons.

He and Uncle Dan and their father, they all went to sea. They were Grand Banker fishermen, gone for weeks on end, on old sailing ships. They would drop anchor, the fishermen would go off in dories, team up, drag the nets. When a dory was loaded with fish, they would unload it into the hold. The crew on board would fix them, salt them down. Sometime they would get lost in the fog and never be found again. Uncle George was lost at sea.

Anyway, the story was, my grandfather [Lorenzo] came home from sea and found his mother with a house full of sick children. He said he hadn't talked to his mother five minutes when he knew it was diphtheria. None had died at that point. They promptly got a doctor and found out it was diphtheria.

A few days later Uncle Dan and his father came home from sea. They wouldn't let them in to see them. It was roped off, quarantined. Back then they would drive stakes all the way around the house and string a rope. They hung a red cloth off it, that meant quarantine. Neighbors cooked food and pushed it under the rope.

His mother was getting pretty worn out with the care of the children. Uncle Dan and Uncle Hiram, they would make the caskets in the barn across the road, put them under the ropes. He [Lorenzo] and his mother would get them ready. They would put the bodies in the caskets, seal them, push them under the ropes. And they would take them and bury them. Then they would have a mass funeral.

Strange to say, my grandfather didn't contract diphtheria. Some of the children died in his arms. It must have been a terrible, terrible two weeks. I can imagine. Whenever he would tell about it, the tears would come.

Lorenzo — One time he was shipwrecked, he lashed himself to the mast, they found him in Nova Scotia encased in ice. A year later he finally got in [back home]. He had shipped out down south before he had a chance to make it back to Bucksport.

My grandmother thought he was gone [dead]. She was working out in the garden in the spring when he came back. There was an awful racket, people blowing horns and ringing bells, they was bringing him in on their shoulders.

It took a long time for ships to come and go in those days. They lived a very precarious life, those old-time sailors. He got measles at sea, was taken to a woman in Newfoundland. After he had the measles, he lost much of his hair except for a line.

Daniel and Christina died the same day. Grandfather had had a shock [stroke], he had been in a wheelchair four years or so. The last of it had been quite a care for Grandmother. Grandfather was in bed, Grandmother was so tired they persuaded her to go lay down in the other room.

All at once she sat up.

"Daniel! Daniel! Something's wrong with Daniel! He's gone!"

And she dropped back down dead too.

Lorenzo and Mary Elizabeth Dunham were there with them. I don't know what very last thing happened to them. They died within minutes of each other. In those days they didn't call it the flu, they called it the grippe.

Lorenzo told me that when he was a little boy his mother taught him to read from the Bible, taught him his letters on a slate. My grandfather read the Bible through every winter. The Blake Bible was printed in 1828. In those days about the only books they had was the Bible and the almanac. Grandfather used to mention reading, so I presume they had other books.

My grandfather was a veteran. He was called Captain, but I don't know if he ever captained a boat. I was born in East Orland. Lorenzo went to sea from the time he was a boy at 14. Most people by the time they was 12 or 14 went as cabin boys and kept going on.

Catherine Libby
Interview, May 1981, Rockland, Maine

I was born in 1898, on August 26. My mother [Mary] was seven years old when half of the family died. My Uncle George Blake came home from sea and they think he brought the germ with him.

My mother said that he said, "When I come back, I'll bring you a new pair of shoes."

Then he went away, he went back to sea, and never came back. This was 1863, during the Civil War. Uncle George was a mate on a square rigger, a clipper ship. He was just a seaman I suppose. They said he was lost at sea, but they thought the cannibals got them because the ship was wrecked on the island where cannibals were. He was left on a piece of wreckage and the cannibals picked him up. Someone notified a family from Bath that he saw George on a piece of wreckage. This man was saved and he said he would try to tell what he knew. Uncle George wasn't married.

She [her mother, Mary] said the reason she always felt she didn't get the black diphtheria is because they gave her so much red pepper tea. Her stomach would burn from taking it. They gave her so much she thought she'd die, and she never liked anything like that afterward. She had it but didn't die, and Uncle John didn't die. He was probably three or four years old. Mother said she and Uncle John were saved. She said she had it lightly. Most of them filled right up.

The children would die one after the other. They couldn't get help very much. They had to go to Castine for a doctor. She said that Grandmother was all upset, they kept dying off. The houses weren't heated, they did the best they could to keep warm and comfortable.

Grandfather was a farmer, I believe, owned a lot of sheep, had a flock on Spectacle Island. There was an old apple tree in back of the old house. A barn was across the road on the side of the hill from where the house was. It don't look a bit like it did.

Grandmother and Grandfather sold a big chunk of land to a syndicate in New York that planned to develop that property because it had been the steamboat wharf. There are cottages down there now. That's an awful God-forsaken country down there, Cape Rosier. It wasn't populated in those days, no way to get out. My father had to walk from Brooksville to Bangor to board a ship, unless someone with a wagon would give him a ride. Grandfather went to sea between farming and what have you.

Grandfather had a shock in the barn, lived five years in a wheelchair. Their children would come home to help them when they could. They died within a few minutes of each other....My grandfather and grandmother died within an hour of each other. My mother said, that winter she was in the process of having one of her children, so she couldn't go to the funeral.

They said about the time Grandmother and Grandfather died that they [the 1863 caskets] were moved to a regular cemetery. They decided it would be best to move them. They were reburied from the family burial plot. There's a book in the library, ***On the Shores of the Penobscot***, that told about that cemetery on Cape Rosier being haunted. The leaves in the cemetery were always in motion. They said that the cattle used to go down around there and feed around the cemetery. They said the cemetery was haunted. I don't think Doris [Blake Johnson] knew about that.

They said the house was haunted, because of these children all dying, you know. My sister said she was scared to death. In those days they believed in spirits, a lot of them were superstitious. One day she [Mary, her mother] was alone in the house, after she was married, and she went down the cellar to get some potatoes. When she went down she heard footsteps in the kitchen, heavy boots and moving chairs. When she came back up, four men were sitting around the kitchen table, they just faded away. My father said it was just her imagination. A few nights after that she said they went somewhere, to Grange or whatever, and when they came back in sight of the house, every room was lighted up. They had kerosene lamps in those days. When they got home, everything was serene, quiet, not a soul around. She said, "We moved out the next day. We didn't stay there any longer." Coming from them, I know they must have seen something.

The house had a granite rock foundation. It was a Cape with a high knee wall and two chimneys. It was brick down in the cellar part. I kept a brick for a doorstop. It had been in a chimney.

My father went to sea, stopped when they started a family. He was a captain on one of the vessels that would go to the West Indies. It carried lumber from Bangor, came back with molasses. He signed off the ship about 1890, and he said he thought he wouldn't go to sea again. He took his luggage, and as he was getting off, a black shadow went over the ship. The ship went out with a load of lumber and was never seen again. He always said he felt that black shadow that came between him and the ship was an omen of something to come.

Mother was 17 when she married Captain Charles Chester, who was 19, from Chester, Pa. I'm the youngest one in the family. One died at 91 and my sister was 94 when she died last year. If they were alive they could tell you things, the history of the Blake family. My son majored in history. He's often told me I should write a book.

Lucy Venno
Interview, Summer 1981 Brooksville

My great-grandmother Eliza Colson, sister to Christina, married Henry Blake. Diphtheria was rampant around for a long time. My husband had diphtheria in Stockton Springs when he was about five. Some of it was brought home by the people who went to sea. They played with the other children. No one knew. I don't know if people tried to keep people separate, if they knew much about contagion.

People got diphtheria in the summer like they got polio. Quite a few died at one time. November and December was late for diphtheria. My grandfather helped out and got it, when the children were sick at the house. He craved red pepper, it evidently kept his throat clear so he wouldn't choke. That's what happens, you know.

Two children were buried down in the field by the Nickersons. No, no stones. They were not moved. I don't know what their names were. I don't think they died with diphtheria.

The parents lived where Dot Nickerson's house is now. It was an old Cape Cod-style house. Quite a bit of the farm was across the road. The barn was across the road. It was quite cleared, there was a field, they must have had cattle too. Much later on, the steamboat wharf was down there, in 1910. A storm took it away. In 1915, gone.

The roads were just so you could get a horse and buggy through, and that was all. There wasn't a decent road anywhere. When the automobile came, they had to do something about roads. The first autos were high up and could go over humps in the middle, where the grass grew, without hitting.

Their grandson, Charles, and Henrietta Blake were with them when Daniel and Christina died. They had been called to go down. The children had all moved away. They were sent a message to come and help out. They died within a few minutes of each other, of flu or pneumonia.

Before 1906, people met in schoolhouses for church services. After 1906, two churches were built, a Methodist over in the Creek, and a Unitarian church at Undercliff.

Otis Gray was a Civil War veteran. He had a large family. Someone brought home TB to the family. Most of the children contracted it and died of it. The so-called board of health at the time decided the house was not fit to live in because of what they felt was contamination. So they burned it.

Then they moved the Dan Blake house to that site. It was moved near to the Methodist Church, the road in there. I remember going through that old house before they took it down. It had one chimney, with bedrooms upstairs. Mrs. Veague was caretaker in the winter. She really believed. I think she was a spiritualist. She believed that on a certain date, she would find something out of place, something thrown. I remember going through there with her and my hair standing on end.

Spiritualists and mediums were quite the thing at one time. Table rapping, things like that. My mother used to tell about it. Her grandmother, Betsy Bakeman, had a spiritualist at her funeral.

I saw the Blake house after it was moved. It stood there for a long time. They burned it down to make room for the Holbrook Island Sanctuary. It was a very small Cape Cod house. On the Cape, most of the homes were removed, taken to other places and put up again.

The Colsons had a large family, they probably all moved away. The Colson place was down in the field where the Colemans' place is. The little Coleman child is buried in the cemetery where the Colson's child is. Mother was indignant when people said they just buried that child in the woods.

At one time they lived on the Hoffman property [about a mile further down the same road], went to sea whenever possible, on Bay coasters, sailing vessels that carried freight. They went to sea when they could, fished, but fish was so cheap they couldn't get enough for it. They farmed enough to keep their families. My grandfather Charles didn't go to sea. Salmon was very plentiful and cheap. It was subsistence living for the families. Perhaps each family had its own little patch of blueberries. They could sell quite a few things in Castine. All the children picked berries in season. Someone would row them to Castine, they could always sell them, either door to door or to boarding houses. They went by boat everywhere they went. Some people used to make butter and take it over there to sell it.

John, Daniel and Christina's son, got Spectacle Island from his father and mother, left it to two daughters, Christina Patten and Louise Blake Nichols. Cordelia moved to Bucksport and married someone named Sawyer. Lately I think the Pattens might still own their half, the other half was sold to a real estate person.

Around 1900 a company formed, the Boston Land Company. It bought a lot of those places with the idea of developing the Cape as a summer resort, sort of like Bar Harbor. A few people would not sell. Those who did moved away. It just petered out. George Ames, where the Nearings lived, was going to head it up. It just fell through, probably from lack of organization, the right people trying to promote it. All the cleared land grew up. Later it was bought by people who wanted to cut pulpwood.

Ferd Clifford said they were digging gravel when they hit the casket. It seems then the graves were cleaned up. Some headstones were taken a few years ago. A man, I think he's dead now, in South Brooksville, was carving in marble. He thought nobody cared and just took them.

Chapter 16
Canning Lids, the Achilles Heel

We thought we were being pretty independent, living out there in the woods and all, but the summer of 1974 showed us just how dependent we were on industry and infrastructure when simple canning lids — the flat lids with the rubber seal ring — suddenly were in short supply. Turns out that the energy crisis had scared a lot of people, who reverted to growing gardens and storing and hoarding food like never before. All the canning lid companies were caught by surprise by the intense demand all over the country, and belatedly put on extra shifts to fill orders — although there were some conspiracy theorists who figured it was just a plot to drive up the price.

The lids in question were designed only for a one-time use. They sometimes could be pressed into service a second time, but you couldn't count on the seal being good, and who wanted to risk botulism or spoiled food? All the canning jars I had were the type that took the flat lids with the screw-down rings. I did not have any glass-topped jars, which required only the rubber rings to seal. But it didn't matter, because even those rubber rings were becoming impossible to find.

August 6, 1974
Once again I only have a few minutes to write...

Sure has been hectic around here. The bread thing is doing quite well, starting to make a profit, but it sure does take a lot of time out of the summer, especially with canning season here in full force now. I've canned 51 pints and 24 quarts of peaches, about two dozen or better pints of peas, and the beans and summer squash are ready now. And I'm having the darndest time getting lids. Two places have my order for 60 dozen lids (60 boxes), and one of the places (Ball Corp.) has cashed my check already, so I'd better get the lids soon. I'm close to running out.

Muffin had a beautiful billy goat kid on Saturday, August 3, about 1 p.m. She did well, all by herself. As Colemans would say, those peasant goats don't have any trouble kidding, just the uppity purebreds. Muffin was only half purebred. Sue and I laughed and said that must be why we did so well birthing — peasant stock.

Keith slaughtered another pig for Dot Gray, and we got a quarter of the pig for payment. We cooked it all up and canned what we didn't eat right away. I used the pressure canner and got eight pints of darned good meat.

It was easier than I had expected. We dug into a couple of the jars almost immediately. Keith had been working a construction job for a few weeks and one day said he wanted some pork sandwiches for his lunch.

August 12, 1974

Can you see if you can find any canning lids for me out there? The situation is starting to get desperate around here. So many on order and no word yet, and things are ripening. We have about 3 dozen lids left from last year. I'm hoping the situation is just regional and that you can get them there. They just aren't to be had here for any price. Only thing available is jars with the lids, but no lids by themselves. Sure would appreciate it.

We closed down the bread business for the season Sept. 1, except for special orders. It sure was a relief to be done with the whole project. Cass and I cleared $400 almost to the penny, a nice sum, but not much for all the work two people put into it. But I learned an awful lot about making bread and about merchandising, so I rationalized that the education made up in part for the low profit.

Once that project was over and we didn't bake every day, I started getting all kinds of work done around the house.

Keith was also getting caught up on some projects. His boss didn't let his crew work in the rain, or on weekends or holidays. With a week of rainy weather, the VW was fixed and passed inspection. The electric fence got placed around the corn patch to ward off the coons. He and Darryl, up for the week, put a floor in the workshop part of the woodshed, framed the walls and windows. By not working for pay for a few days, Keith took pressure off himself rather than the other way around.

September 4, 1974

The tomatoes are starting to come in. I'm getting a good feeling about the harvest. We braided onions today, the ones that were cured, and got 11 nice long braids hanging by the ladder. And about the same amount yet to cure. That should be enough for us, and they look so nice hanging up…

The canning lids I ordered finally arrived….

October 6, 1974 Sunday

Canning season is just about over. I might get a few more quarts of tomatoes, but that's it. We didn't get as many tomatoes canned as I would have liked — 40 as opposed to 93 last year, but our fruit just wouldn't ripen. We have two or three bushels of green ones upstairs ripening, and some still coming in the garden, but not many. We've had a couple of good frosts, and most gardens around here are finished.

The root cellar is really filling up though. Except for tomatoes, I have loads more of everything canned — 20 pints of corn (none last year — coons got it all). We got loads of potatoes, about twice what we had last year, but slugs did a lot of damage — they were bad all over this year. All the bad and tiny potatoes will go to the pigs. We've been picking nice apples off trees that belong to summer people who are back in the city now. Some are misshapen and small, but those will go to the goats or pigs. We've got oodles of carrots, and the peppers, which aren't supposed to survive here at all, gave us a good yield. I canned some and we're drying the rest. Right now we're sitting on an awful lot of food. It's a good feeling.

The trees are vivid. Really beautiful New England weather, the kind I like best.

Yes, all the company is finally gone. It's good to be alone again, but things aren't getting done like they were with a few helpers. Darryl will be starting on a job down the [steel] mill this month to make some money to come up here and homestead. He's part-owner of that land his dad bought.

Keith quit working for Fred Dyer last week. He has a few jobs lined up to do yet (shingle a house, repair a roof, etc.), then he can start full-time on projects around here. We hope to get a finished floor down in here, his workshop done, kitchen cabinets, but I don't know if we'll be able to on top of all the regular farm work. We just had 7 dump-truck loads of manure delivered, five tons of lime and a ton of phosphate rock that has to be spread and tilled in, autumn leaves and seaweed to collect for the compost piles that have to be made, and so on. Lots to do. I hate to make lists, they're so depressing.

Fred Dyer told Keith he can come back anytime he wants and work for him again. So when we run out of money we do have a way of getting some more.

We just took one of our sows to be bred today. The other sow will be butchered, probably the end of next month. We're planning on smoking the pig. We'll probably can some of the meat too. That mackerel we did in July is delicious.

Rebecca is in to absolutely everything. She's making a half-way decent housekeeper out of me in spite of myself...

I'm making cheese again, doing a few little things differently, and it looks like it'll work out this time. My attempts last spring were all inedible. Now that the visitors are gone and we're not making bread, we've got extra milk again.

Keith just harvested honey again. We've got to extract it now, but it looks like maybe another 60 lbs. That will be 120 lbs. from one hive, more than we got from six last year. That hive is dynamite!

Finally got our logs cut up into lumber so Keith can finish his workshop. We've had the logs cut and sitting by the drive all summer, till the guy at the sawmill could find the time to cut them. Cost us 6¢ a board-foot.

November 3, 1974 Sunday
Sorry this letter is so late but it seems of late that everything takes so long to do. I don't know why, but even getting the dishes done is a big accomplishment anymore. Rebecca does take up a certain amount of time, I know, but she can't be the whole reason. I can't figure it out.

Rebecca has learned what hot is. She seemed to avoid the cookstove, but we just put the Ashley heater back in for the winter, and she was fascinated by it. We were careful with her and let her touch it just lightly once with her finger. So since she learned it's hot, she just ignores it. She's a pretty sharp kid.

Just finished all the fall housecleaning I'm going to do. The windows are washed, anyway. Sure does make a difference, to be able to see out. In a few weeks, after Keith gets the gardens ready for next spring, the next project on the list is another try at the water system [which had stopped flowing], and then putting down a real floor in here. That will be nice...

We had a nice Halloween, warm, and we got five trick-or-treaters. Colemans brought Melissa and Heidi down, and a family in the village brought their three girls over all decked out. We had some friends over for dinner too, so it was all very festive.

Butchered six hens last week because our eggs have really dropped off. Canned the meat and broth for soup. The hens didn't weigh very much for all they eat.

We just went out and bought six months supply of animal feed, 38 100-lb. bags. We figured prices would be lowest now right after harvest, and we won't be having any new money coming in for awhile, so it would be nice to have on hand. It's all upstairs, with our hay. Keith has reinforced the beams to hold the extra weight.

November 15, 1974 Friday
I've taken on a very part-time job for the holiday season — making wreaths. A local concern here supplies the wreath frame and the wire, and comes to pick up the wreaths. We supply the brush (lots of fir trees we want to get rid of) and put it all together. They pick them up in a huge stake truck, then they go to a big barn where cones and bows and stuff are added. Apparently it's a big cottage industry around here. We keep bumping into all kinds of people who are making them. If you're fast and can spend some time at it there's good money to be had. But I just can't seem to

get the hang of it. It takes Keith about 15 minutes to cut enough brush to keep me busy for 3 or 4 days. The guy who runs it sells them all over the country, to department stores and the like.

I am surprised your taxes are so low. Our whole place is assessed at $1,750, and our taxes this year were $75. That's over 4% of the valuation in taxes each year. I think that's quite high. So I don't think homesteading is quite the answer to your tax problem.

Keith is getting a reputation as a butcher. Last week he did five sheep, a pig and a goat for Dot Gray, and from that, two other people have asked him to do their pigs for pay. Keith says that kind of work doesn't bother him at all.

Speaking of which, he apparently had it out with Nearings a few days ago before they left for New York for the winter — told them just where we stand with them, in our meat-eating, and life-style and the like. Told them we can be friends, but can't be disciples of theirs since we disagree on so much. They didn't say much but I'm sure we'll hear about it sometime. I was surprised he was so frank and blunt with them, but I think it is the best way. There has been of late a strange feeling coming from them that we haven't been acting the way we should with them, so now it's all out in the open.

An Aladdin kerosene lamp illuminates the tools of a homesteading time/date management system.

Chapter 17
The Nukes and Me

Nineteen seventy-five and the two months leading up to it were all very strange.

The usual time warp we were living in then was odd enough. There we were, more than five years after our country had landed a man on the moon, and Keith and I were trying our darndest to master the technology of the mid-nineteenth century.

The oldest of our nearest neighbors had been born in the last century, and talked about important people he knew personally who had been dead long enough to have been in my high school history books.

(This really hit home a few years later when Scott turned up in a cameo appearance as a "witness" in "Reds," the controversial 1981 movie which Warren Beatty produced, directed, and starred in. The movie was about Scott's American friend John Reed and his involvement in the Russian Revolution of 1917. That revolution was three years before my father was born, but Scott Nearing was then in his mid-thirties.)

In that self-induced time warp, we back-to-the-landers spent a lot of time trying to reconcile the marvels of modern medicine with the grace and power of natural remedies. Raised on furnaces and central heating, we familiarized ourselves with the tricky workings of wood-burning stoves. In the process of hauling in seaweed and leaves to build up the garden, we found ancestral muscles unknown to supermarket shoppers. We were coming to recognize the high ecological value of horse manure, while driving vehicles that led to the widespread scarcity of that particular commodity.

And then, as 1974 ended and 1975 dawned, that ultimate irony.

Even though we were living in a place so remote the electric lines didn't penetrate, we found ourselves facing the prospects of a full-blown nuclear power plant, first on a nearby island, and then literally across the road from our few green, organic acres.

November 20, 1974
Central Maine Power Company is planning to build a nuclear power plant on an island six miles upwind from us. We're just starting to get involved in fighting it. Apparently they've found higher rates of birth defects and cancer downwind of other plants, and they're very dangerous to operate, with all that radioactivity, not only at the plant, but on the

highways as they ship it to and from. Sure they take precautions, but accidents do happen.

We went to a debate last night, and even the guy from the power company admits that the Atomic Energy Commission hasn't figured out a safe way to dispose of all the radioactive waste one of those things puts out. And apparently one of the wastes is radioactive plutonium, the most dangerous substance known to man. It doesn't occur in nature, only man makes it, and a speck the size of a pollen grain if inhaled will cause lung cancer. This plant is supposed to produce 400-600 _pounds_ of the stuff every year. Handling that much, you can't tell me they'll be able to account for every speck. They've just applied for a permit to build, so there's still a chance we can stop it.

It just sounds to me like an apartment dweller who decides to put a cow in the spare bedroom because he likes milk. He arranges to feed her, but hasn't figured out yet what to do with all that manure. But he gets the cow anyway, says he'll figure that out later. It just doesn't work that way.

It's a threat and it's scary. We came here to get away from that type of thing. I guess even if they did build it, it wouldn't be operational for 8 or 10 years. But if it does go into operation, we'll seriously consider selling and moving elsewhere, it worries us that much. But we're not alone in that, which means there is hope.

Friday AM. Found out last night that we're within the radius of that proposed atomic plant that they test the milk of dairy herds for radioactivity. If Strontium-90 gets out of the plant into the air, onto the pasture and into the milk, we drink the milk, and could get bone cancer. Nice. Guess we're on a list now because we have dairy goats to test. We're closer than I thought to that thing.

December 6, 1974 Friday

We got back from Barb's Tuesday night. We had a real nice time ... The car got good mileage the whole trip, between 30 and 35 miles to the gallon. So with the $20 you gave us and the $15 Barb gave us, we made out all right. An expense-paid vacation — what a Christmas present! Thanks so much.

The farm was fine when we got back. But we came home to the news that Central Maine Power Co. just bought an option to 412 acres of land across the road from us. No firm deal yet, and no plans, they say, but wow! How do you cope with something like that? This place is so lovely, and I can see it in 10 years absolutely ruined. I hope not, but I'm not counting on it. But where do we go from here? It can get depressing. But I guess the best thing to do is not to dwell on it and just sit tight and see what happens...

As was her way, Helen took the bull by the horns. She called up Central Maine Power Company headquarters, and politely asked if a spokesperson could possibly come out and make a presentation to the company's potentially new neighbors. About that option to buy, their plans and all. CMP said it would be happy to comply.

Piece of cake, I'm sure the poor man thought. He was nibbling at his carrot croaker and drinking his herbal tea as the neighborhood proceeded to congregate in Helen's kitchen.

As our numbers grew, we brought in more chairs and benches from other rooms, shuffling them into position to give him a proper audience. He finally stood, and leaned, almost sat, on that massive table in the kitchen, as we turned our eager faces up to his.

He said the option on those 412 acres, some of whose trees were visible through those kitchen windows, was a safeguard for the company, in case other locations they were pursuing for more power generation did not pan out. He said when the property came on the market, CMP felt compelled to seize the opportunity. It wasn't often that such a large waterfront parcel came up for sale, and the price was certainly right.

He said things were looking good for putting a nuclear power plant on Sears Island, part of the town of Searsport about six miles across the Bay, in which case the Cape Rosier property would get a lower priority, and might not be needed for many years to come. But they wanted to cover their bases. You understand.

Yes, indeed, they were looking at nuclear power, he said. Nuclear energy was an absolutely necessary ingredient to meet the growing needs of the population of Maine and New England.

"That's bullshit," someone finally interrupted him. "We don't want it and we don't need it."

Clearly the spokesman was confused. He had been expecting a warm reception, like the one he got from most homeowners in Wiscasset, further down the Maine coast, where the state's one and only nuclear power plant paid 90 percent of the town's property taxes. Or like the excitement he was then getting in Searsport, when he had presented the actual, laid-out, development plans for a nuclear power plant on Sears Island.

The spokesman shifted gears and tried to explain all the safety features built into the complicated designs for nuclear power plants, tried to educate this group of uninformed, superstitious, ignorant people. He promised construction jobs (all that he assumed we were capable of — highly-trained operators would of course have to be imported), along with better quality schools, and millions of dollars pumped into the local economy. If we didn't understand the complex science involved in nuclear energy, he figured, surely we would relate to self-serving economic issues.

We said we all had some college education, and apparently understood better than he did the risks involved in such an operation. A local fisherman (with a college degree) who lived on the other side of Cape Rosier said he had left the Wiscasset area to escape that nuclear power plant, and he didn't want to have to move again. Also, we said, the bulk of us were self-employed and didn't need jobs, the local schools were fine thank you, and we didn't want his company's dirty money.

"...There have to be trade-offs," the spokesman cajoled.

"Yeah, trade-offs. Your money for our health," came the spitted reply.

Finally he muttered the phrase that we had been waiting for him to say:

"...But you all use electricity..."

We looked at each other, looked at him, smiled up at the Big Central Maine Power Company Spokesman, and collectively shook our heads in the negative. After all, most of us lived beyond that last company pole down at the end of the Nearings' driveway.

The panic that came over the CMP rep's face at that point was for all the world that of an explorer who had stumbled across a flesh-eating cult — and who suddenly realized we were all between him and the door.

Not to worry. Except for Keith, the fisherman, and me, he was in a room full of vegetarians. But it was nice to see that healthy color in his office-whitened cheeks.

And then there was the time warp known as the Maine town meeting.

Instead of mayors or city councilors charged with coming up with a municipal budget under threat of voter rebellion in the next election, we had boards of selectmen who had to conform to the very specific spending instructions given them every year at the annual town meeting.

As old as the Republic itself, the Maine town meeting might be considered an anachronism if it weren't for the fact that it is one of the few remaining working examples of true democracy in the nation today. It is the chance for all registered voters in town to personally and collectively direct how much they are willing to pay in property taxes, and exactly where that money should go. Traditionally held on the first Monday in March, in the pre-crocus mud season, town meeting was also the perfect chance for neighbors who had been cooped up all winter to get together and catch up, in the guise of being good citizens.

And good citizenship was taken very seriously. The town report, printed in February and hand-delivered to every residence, was the operating document. The most closely perused section in that booklet was the listing of all delinquent taxpayers, those who hadn't paid their property taxes.

This simple fact of Maine life prompted at least one doctor a few towns away to pay his local property taxes in the same year he failed to pay his federal income taxes. He explained his reasoning — that he particularly wanted to avoid the embarrassment of getting his name listed in the town report — while on the witness stand during his federal trial for tax evasion. I know this because his remarks were printed in the local paper.

Also printed in the annual town report was a list of residents lost to death in the past year, documentation of the occasional pickle or other historical artifact, along with the town's annual budget and last year's expenditures. (For a few years, the list of expenditures included payments to Eliot Coleman for time spent as a road-crew worker, filling potholes and fixing roads. Not coincidentally, his annual wages for the days he worked came to just about what he paid in property taxes.)

The town report also listed the town business items of immediate concern, anywhere from a few dozen to a hundred "warrant articles" to be voted on by the attendees at the upcoming annual town meeting. Even though most of the budget items were predictable year to year (selectmen's salaries, pothole repair), that didn't mean the meetings were routine. The placement or removal of a single street light would often elicit more spirited discussion than the entire school budget.

Occasionally, something new would make an appearance. In 1975, CMP's option to land on Cape Rosier was the hot topic.

We were relieved when we first heard that someone outside the Nearing enclave had taken the initiative and had placed an article in the warrant to spot-zone the head of the Cape to forbid business or industrial activity. It made us feel that we were not alone in our opposition.

But when we got our town report, our joy turned to dismay. Instead of describing the forbidden zone in reference to the curving town road, whoever drafted the ordinance had drawn a straight line across the Cape from Orr Cove near Nearings' drive to Bakeman's Beach, what we called Hoffman's Beach, about two miles away. Yes, it included all 412 acres under CMP's option, but the resulting line also went straight through the middle of our property and through that portion of Colemans' land that included their farmstand.

Starting sometime after 7 p.m. (an annual imprecision which irritated Scott Nearing, who, looking at his pocket watch before one such town meeting, was overheard to loudly mutter, "The one good thing about the Nazis, they always started their meetings on time"), Brooksville's 1975 Town Meeting was a long, raucous meeting in the old wooden high school gymnasium converted for the occasion to town government's ground zero.

First we learned from the moderator, highly schooled in Roberts Rules of Order, that state election law prevented floor amendments or alterations to duly-posted town ordinances. It would be an up-or-down vote.

Since people in most Maine small towns thought they and their neighbors should be able to do as they pleased with their property, some were nervous about spot zoning, even if it meant keeping a giant monster at bay. The state-mandated subdivision regulations were irritating enough, but there wasn't a big call for subdivisions in Brooksville, so those rules didn't have a noticeable impact. This call for zoning, on the other hand, was locally-generated. That made it worse. The foot-in-the-door syndrome, you know. Before you can blink twice, the whole town would be zoned, and people wouldn't be able to move an outhouse without getting some bureaucrat's permission.

Someone else raised the issue of the legality of spot zoning, in a town which otherwise had none. Might cost the town some money if CMP decided to sue, and the town had to hire a lawyer.

Someone said they thought they had heard somewhere from somebody's cousin who used to work for the state that utilities were routinely exempt from local zoning ordinances, so even if we passed the ordinance, it wouldn't apply to the power company. Was all this an effort in futility?

The discussion was long, thoughtful, occasionally loud, and full of dissension.

We, of course, were torn between principle and the preservation of our ability to conduct some kind of business (bread-baking? furniture-making?) on our own property. Reluctantly, we decided that some other way would have to be found to stop CMP — maybe just another ordinance with a different map. We voted against the ordinance. So did a majority of the others at the packed town meeting.

I went out of my way the next several days to get a copy of the ***Bangor Daily News*** (no small feat out there in the boonies) to see how it reported on the story. I was hoping to see a story which not only captured the complexities of the conflict, but which would clear up some of the questions raised.

Papers for the next few days headlined the fact that Searsport voters had voted overwhelmingly — by nearly a 3-1 margin — to approve construction of a nuclear power plant on Sears Island. (Historical point of reference: This was just weeks before the front pages would announce the fall of Saigon and the end of the long Vietnam War.)

Finally, March 6, 1975, the Thursday after Brooksville's town meeting, these four paragraphs appeared in the Hancock County edition of the paper:

Brooksville votes fund of $192,079

BROOKSVILLE — A four and one-half hour annual town meeting here Monday saw voters tax themselves a total of $192,079 for the operation of schools and government services.

However, only $28,624 of that total tax burden will be needed for local government operation during the ensuing year.

Some 232 voters participated in the election and town meeting, which placed unopposed candidates in office and returned incumbents.

The only contest gave the victory to Victor Fowler as road commissioner.

I couldn't believe my eyes. My local daily paper had blown a terrific story.

I vowed that the next time I was in Ellsworth, the county seat some 35 miles distant from our humble abode, I would stop in at the Hancock County office of the ***Bangor Daily News*** and let them know what I thought of their incompetence. It wasn't worth the gas or the time to make a special trip.

My opportunity came up a week or so later, when I headed to Ellsworth to talk to the phone company. Money was by then getting tight. We needed $50 a week to live on. Keith said he could get more odd jobs if we had a phone so people could call him, but didn't think we could afford to have the phone company extend the line to our place. After all, the electric company wanted more than $5,000, involving a high monthly charge for five years, to extend their line up the road from the Nearings' driveway to our property.

Besides, Keith informed me, he liked living close to the edge. I should stop bugging him about money.

I said we were making assumptions, and we needed to know exactly what we were dealing with. I would try to pin down the phone company, to find out just how much it would cost us to get one installed.

Since it was on the way, I went first to the ***Bangor Daily News*** office, on the second floor above a hardware store, on the sunny side of Main Street, where I confronted Bureau Chief Maureen Williams.

"I used to work for the ***Providence Journal***," I said, introducing myself. "You missed a huge story in Brooksville." I gave her the details. "How could that possibly happen?"

"Well, for starters," Maureen said, "this whole bureau is me and one puncher," a fellow named Red who spent his time at the 60-words-per-minute teletype machine, transcribing press releases and Maureen's copy and sending it on to the main office in Bangor. "We cover about three dozen towns. Almost all of the town meetings are on the first Monday in March. I check the town reports ahead of time and try to spot what could be controversial. That's how I pick the town to cover in person. The next day I call the town clerks in the other towns to find out what happened. What they tell me is what gets in the paper."

Town Clerk. In Brooksville that meant Louise Grindle. This was beginning to make some sense.

"Now that you mention it, I don't think Louise sent me a town report this year," Maureen continued. "And she didn't tell me any of this when I called and talked to her."

Of course she wouldn't. Louise Grindle was under no obligation to embarrass the whole town by ratting to a reporter about how rowdy the crowd had been. Well, not exactly rowdy, but some voices had been raised. It would make her nice town look bad, or at least impolite. It was none of the paper's business. She had given out the important information, on the budget and the elections. That was all she could be expected to do. If the reporter didn't ask her why it took all those long hours and all those people to conduct so little business, well, that was not her problem. Besides, she wouldn't have told, even if the reporter had asked.

It was a perfect example of the problems with telephone journalism.

I was brought back from my mental reality check by Maureen's voice.

"The main office knows we're missing some important stuff. As a matter of fact, they've been talking about maybe hiring some part-time reporters. You said you had some newspaper experience? Would you be interested in a job?"

"Um, me? Part-time? Only in and around Brooksville?" I thought of our diminutive bank balance. "I'd have to talk to my husband. But I think I could do that. Sure."

"Good. When I get the details, I'll give you a call. What's your phone number."

"Well, as a matter of fact, I'm on my way to get one of those right now," I said.

As I closed the office door behind me, I had to stop and catch my breath. I had walked in with a complaint, and had walked out with a much-needed job that I hadn't even been looking for. It was just like the Nearings' offer of land — exciting, unanticipated, and inexplicable — a second astonishing turn of events.

I think I sensed, even then, that the conversation I had just had would forever change my life.

Chapter 18
On the Record

It was June before we got our phone. That was partially because the phone company had to remember how to plant phone poles. Their normal procedure, of course, was to piggy-back on the electric poles, but we didn't have any. Their regulations nevertheless said they had to run the first half-mile on a public road free of charge, and string the wire down two owner-installed poles on a private drive, likewise. Beyond those limits, it was $70 per pole, a one-time charge, on top of the usual $15 installation fee.

We were .65 miles from the last phone, which was in the neighbor's house on the other side of the Nearings, right at the sharp left turn and dip in the road at Orr Cove. The phone company charged us for one pole beyond their half-mile limit. One pole halfway down our driveway, fashioned from a tree Keith cut down, skinned, and set upright beside the drive, did the trick.

The entire installation cost $85.

I decided to test my journalistic wings by covering a meeting of the all-volunteer Brooksville Fire Department. Upon mounting the worn wooden steps to the second-floor conference room above the garage housing the town's two fire trucks, I was met with what would turn out to be a familiar refrain for the next year or two of my professional life.

"You're a what? For which paper? Gee, I dunno. Are we supposed to be doing something important here tonight? Is there something going on you fellas haven't told me?"

That first meeting was also memorable because of Herbie Hutchinson.

Herbie was a Mainer whose roots were so deep it was surprising he could move at all. In fact, he didn't move — he was living in the gray weathered house that had been in his family for generations. Herbie had a rugged, wrinkled, weather-beaten, ageless face and nearly toothless grin. I took him to be in his early forties, although he could have been 15 or 20 years on either side of that.

Herbie was very polite and friendly when I entered the room, moving over to the next folding chair, gesturing me to a convenient aisle seat. He was very solicitous, smiling, mouthing the usual amenities. He had a very thick Maine accent.

Unfortunately, it was so thick I couldn't understand a word he was saying.

I looked around desperately to see if someone would recognize my predicament and offer to translate. Nothing.

So I just nodded politely to Herbie and tried to focus on what Fire Chief Phil Farr, seated at the folding table facing the bank of 20 chairs, was saying. They were deciding which of two types of air tanks to buy with the $900 appropriated at the annual town meeting. I took my notes, left quickly, and went home to write up the story.

Shortly thereafter I got into my first journalistic controversy, when I quoted a new Methodist minister addressing a Brooksville parent-teacher meeting as saying, "Kids are walking down the corridors of Blue Hill Academy bombed out of their minds on marijuana." The minister said he was able to spot "a large concentration" of drug users on a recent visit to the high school, where most of Brooksville's secondary students attended classes.

This, of course, did not sit well with the local superintendent of schools, who accused the minister of doing "irreparable damage" to the community by making unsubstantiated charges.

The minister conceded he had not talked with school officials about his concerns, and was not privy to any confidential student records. After an initial protest to the ***Bangor Daily News*** editors, in which the minister charged he had been misquoted, he finally admitted he had made the statements I had attributed to him. He just didn't like the "tone" of the article.

He, like Louise Grindle, did not like the idea (which was apparently new to him) that what was said at a public meeting was on the record, and could well reappear in print, out there before God and everyone. You'd think a minister would know that.

It was about this point in time that Maureen called and told me they wanted to talk to me in Bangor. I remember going up there with Becca, some 50 miles north, and filling out some paperwork. But I also remember an intense discussion with Assistant Managing Editor Kent Ward, at his desk in the middle of a busy newsroom. A former Marine, Kent Ward was a consummate newsman, a Perry White equivalent except that Kent always sported a well-trimmed crewcut.

Becca, who was not yet 18 months old, was fussy after the hour-long drive into the big city. There were no kids around and nothing to play with in the newsroom. I wouldn't let her beyond arm's length as I tried to carry on an intelligent adult conversation with my new boss.

Totally bored and ready for a nap, Becca started making little grunting noises. Still talking, I instinctively lifted up the left corner of my shirt. Becca dove under and began to nurse.

I was in mid-sentence when I noticed the blank stare in Kent Ward's eyes. All conversation had ceased in the large newsroom. The face of the assistant managing editor, a lifelong bachelor, was turning beet red.

Oh yeah, I thought. I forgot. They don't do this in the real world. I've been living in the woods too long. I really do need a refresher course in civilized behavior.

Time warp.

I quickly interrupted Becca's snack, and excused us both. I said I would call when I got home.

Kent told me not to hurry.

I heard we were the topic of conversation for a few days in the Bangor newsroom.

Right from the start I enjoyed my part-time job. As a kid, I had never had enough of my questions answered. Here was a job where I was actually paid to ask the questions, interview interesting people, cover scandalous trials, report on nasty accidents.

And, much to my delight, all kinds of people felt compelled, even eager, to answer those questions — cops, fire chiefs, lawyers, superintendents, town managers.

It is also one of the most public jobs I can think of. Every single day, what you did the day before is out there for everyone to see and grade. Even politicians don't have that much exposure.

While school board meetings predominated in my reporting that first year, I also soon realized that the newspaper had given me incredible leeway to decide what was news. As a result, I was able to bring my homesteading world and local community into the mainstream media.

The newly-formed Blue Hill co-op got a nice feature story. I profiled five local craftspeople — a potter, a stained-glass maker, two furniture-makers, and a weaver — in a full-page spread, three photos and the headline:

Doing what you want... and making a living from it

I reported on the fundraising donkey-ball game, complete with donkeys, in which the winner of the women's half-time game of musical chairs was then, much to her surprise, proclaimed "Miss Jackass 1975." (That only works once.)

When a Hindi from India was visiting the Nearings under the sponsorship of the Social Science Institute, and gave a talk in his bare feet, long white shirt and skirt at Nearings' "Monday Night Meeting," I wrote up what he talked about.

When a dozen county extension agents converged on the Coleman farm as part of a course on organic farming sponsored by the Maine Organic Farmers and Gardeners Association (MOFGA) and the

Cooperative Extension Service, readers learned about that too.

In another case of time-warp syndrome, I seized the opportunity to document the ingenuity of Native Americans in the design of the teepee, which I had first discovered when Greg Summers parked his in our back yard. In an unusual convergence, that year several farm apprentices were using teepees as housing, some setting them up, with landowner's permission, in the village in open fields visible from the road.

It was very scenic, and far more startling than cows on the landscape. Not only that, in the evening when a fire was lit inside, the teepees would glow like huge Japanese lanterns.

The world needed to know more about these marvelous structures. I interviewed one worker and wrote this story:

Teepee provides cheap housing

HARBORSIDE (Aug. 22, 1975) — David Hudak of St. Albans, Vt., has been living here in a portable vacation home with a cathedral ceiling and a built-in fireplace. And the home costs only a few hundred dollars.

The home is a modern adaptation of the traditional Indian teepee. It is modern in that it is made of marine-treated canvas instead of animal hides. But all the other advantages, and there are many, have been retained.

Hudak, 27, has his home set up this summer on the farm of a friend while he studies at the Social Science Institute here.

He bought the canvas cover, liner and door frame for slightly more than $300 while he was a road construction worker in Flagstaff, Ariz. Doing road work, he needed a portable or mobile home. The traditional campers or homes on wheels did not appeal to him. He tried a tent for a while, he said, but found it much too crowded.

A teepee was an answer that he liked aesthetically and spatially.

The ceiling soars to 15 feet, giving a feeling of spaciousness in the structure that is 18 feet across at the base.

Although there are no windows, the canvas filters in enough light that the dwelling is illuminated better in the daytime than most houses. The low-slung door doubles as a window on good days, but can be closed when it storms.

It took Hudak and a friend about three hours to set up the teepee, including leveling the site, lifting the central tripod in place, arranging the 12 other 25-foot poles in the correct order around the tripod, stretching the canvas over the poles, tying it down, building a fireplace in the middle out of a few rocks and moving in.

The outside canvas cover does not quite touch the ground when it is stretched over the poles. A canvas liner about eight feet high is tied to the poles all around the inside. This does touch bottom inside the teepee. This creates a natural air draft coming from underneath the outside canvas, directed up behind the inside liner, and out the ventilation hole at the top. A fire in the middle of the structure burns warmly and well, but all the smoke goes out the top.

The doorway, and ventilation slot above it, traditionally faced east, because North American winds prevail from the west.

Hudak spent one winter in northern Arizona in the teepee, where the coldest temperature was five degrees. He said it was okay if the fire was going well and a good down sleeping bag was nice.

It's odd, says Hudak, that even with the door wide open at night he has no problem with mosquitoes. In fact, one night it was so beautiful, he said, he took his sleeping bag outdoors to sleep under the stars. But the bugs got so bad that about five minutes later he was back in his "home" just a few feet away, and they did not bother him at all, he said.

When it rains, he said, most of the water that hits the poles at the top of the teepee drips down special smoothed surfaces of the poles and right back outside at the bottom. A small amount drips in, but most of that falls into the fireplace pit and does no harm at all, he said.

A few months later I did a story on one of Colemans' farm apprentices who had been the U.S. national boomerang champion the year before. (Bet you didn't know we had one.) Under the instruction of Frank Schlosser of Emmaus, Pa., then 19, everyone in our Cape Rosier neighborhood was making and throwing boomerangs.

Swedish and early American cultures were the focus in a story I wrote about sauna owner Mary Chase who was trying to revive the art of growing and processing flax into beautiful linen fabric.

It was a homestead art — about the level of technology Keith and I were then aspiring to — which had faded out in the early 1800s when the industrial revolution and cheap cotton cloth came along. Mary had gone back to her ancestral Sweden for more than six months to learn the techniques, and had grown a quarter-acre of the tall crop on their waterfront farm. I sold a longer version of her how-to story to *Yankee Magazine*, which later put it in one of its Forgotten Arts books.

Of course I wasn't single-handedly bringing homesteading into public view. The numbers of young people flowing into Maine in those years were hard to ignore. Stories on our individual and collective efforts were showing up in just about every publication in the state.

It's just that, back there in the woods, I became keenly aware of the impact of my individual journalistic decisions on the flow of information to the outside world.

Meanwhile other historical events were taking place across Maine, including these two stories which ran on the front page of the July 20, 1975, *Bangor Daily News*.

Gals want to be smoke eaters

SKOWHEGAN — Chauvinist remarks aside, Susan Young and Leah Norton are determined to become Skowhegan's first female firefighters...

High court says woman may retain maiden name

PORTLAND, Maine (AP) — A Cumberland woman may change her married name to her maiden name, even though she remains married, the Maine Supreme Court ruled Friday.

In a 3-2 decision, the law court sustained the appeal of Susan E. Reben, whose petition to revert to her maiden name, Susan E. Hirsch, had been denied in Probate Court....

The decision noted that Mrs. Reben, in her appeal, was represented by her husband, which "clearly demonstrates his non-opposition."

The dissenting opinion, by Chief Justice Armand A. Dufresne Jr., cited common law doctrine calling for a common surname in marriage.

"Whether in this era of the women's rights movement it still makes sense to require that a woman upon marriage must assume her husband's surname ... is a matter more properly resting in legislative discretion," Dufresne wrote...

Not everyone agreed with my journalistic instincts over what constituted news. I hereby confess that I refused to take a picture of a carrot that Scott Nearing had found in his garden which had grown right through a discarded iron nut. The metal was girding the carrot around its middle. Scott was not pleased with my recalcitrance, and grew even more displeased when, a week later, the *Ellsworth American* ran a similar picture of a girded beet from someone else's garden.

And then in November 1975, I got to write this front page story:

N-Plant delay won't affect land option

CAPE ROSIER — Any plans that Central Maine Power Co. may have had for land on which it has an option here will apparently be unaffected by the company's postponement of construction of a nuclear power plant on Sears Island.

According to CMP spokesman Peter Thompson at Augusta Friday, the Sears Island plant is being postponed only until his company can get a definitive ruling on ambiguous wording of Nuclear Regulating Commission rules regarding building nuclear plants near geological faults.

CMP contends that the fault discovered on Sears Island is "glaciotectonic" or formed by shifting earth pressures caused as a major glacier retreated northward, and is not capable of current action.

But since the NRC regulations do not differentiate between different kinds of faults, CMP will be actively pursuing a clarification with the NRC before it proceeds any further with the Sears Island plant.

But even if the CMP appeal is ultimately disapproved by the NRC, the Cape Rosier site will not automatically be excluded, also. Nuclear regulations forbid the building of a plant within five miles of a capable fault, and Cape Rosier is about 7-3/4 miles by water from Sears Island. However, Thompson said he was not sure which direction the fault on Sears Island lays, or whether it comes closer to the Cape under water.

Thompson did say that the discovery of a fault on Sears Island may preclude a nuclear facility on Cape Rosier. At least CMP will be taking a much closer look at the site before deciding what to do with the land, assuming it purchases the 412 acres. The option CMP has on that land expires in May, 1976, and Thompson said the company would probably wait until close to that date to make a decision on buying the property, extending the option, or letting the option lapse.

He said the Cape Rosier property is only one of several pieces statewide on which CMP currently has options to buy. And the company is still hopeful for some progress on Sears Island and will not be making plans for any other power plant until the technical problem of the NRC regulations is resolved.

As things turned out, Cape Rosier's CMP story would end right where it began — in Helen Nearing's kitchen. Nearly two years after that contentious Brooksville town meeting about CMP, I wrote this story for the *Bangor Daily News* February 23, 1977, edition:

CMP to let option lapse on 412-acre Cape Rosier site

HARBORSIDE — Central Maine Power Co. does not plan "at this time to pick up the option again" which it holds on 412 acres on Cape Rosier in Brooksville, according to a company spokesman.

John H. Arnold, field coordinator at the CMP Sears Island Project Information Office, made his remark Monday at the home here of Helen and Scott Nearing to a small gathering of people, most of whom are landowners adjoining the optioned site.

CMP's option to the Cape Rosier land, originally obtained November 25, 1974, has been extended three times. The latest extension expires on March 25.

Arnold explained that any time such a large parcel of shorefront property with a deep water port becomes available, his company wants to take a look at it for possible use as a utility site. The option was repeatedly extended because the people who were in charge of "taking a look at it" were kept busy on the Sears Island project until recently. Reasons for the company's rejection of the Cape Rosier site centered mainly around its remoteness.

Even though only about seven miles of water separate Sears Island from Cape Rosier, their locations on opposite sides of Penobscot Bay make for worlds of difference.

"Cape Rosier is so doggone far from our electricity load centers," in Portland and Augusta, Arnold said. It has no established transportation facilities in the area, while a dock, a railroad and Route 1 are at the doorstep of Sears Island.

Sears Island is also about nine miles from a major north-south transportation line in the state. Power generated on Cape Rosier would have to be strung to Bucksport before it could tie in with that system, a procedure which would entail complicated and extensive right-of-way provisions.

Also, during the construction time of a power plant, either nuclear or coal, up to 1,650 people would be employed, but only for a short term of a few years. Sears Island, being near a major highway, and a more populated area, has a greater labor force on which to draw. Cape Rosier, a virtual dead-end, is in an area of low population density. The land under option borders on a dirt road. Arnold indicated that importing people to work on such a site for such a short period of time would wreak havoc with the local economy, both when it comes and when it leaves.

"Where do you put 1,650 people on Cape Rosier?" Arnold said.

Nuclear plants take about six years to build, with a peak in the labor force the last two or three years. Coal-fired electric generating plants take about five years to build, with a 1,150 labor force peak during about the last two years. Coal-fired plant construction does not require as many skilled people as nuclear plants, Arnold said.

Compared to the large construction force, the operating force of a nuclear plant like the one which had been planned for Sears Island is only about 110 people, a good percentage of them highly skilled, such as nuclear engineers. A coal-fired plant, such as the one now planned for Sears Island, can be operated by about 150 people, and not as many highly skilled.

And lastly, Cape Rosier is located in Bangor Hydro-Electric Company's service area.

Arnold said that Ernest and Helen Oliver of Camden, owner of the Cape Rosier site, have been informed of the company's plans to let the option lapse.

Chapter 18 — On the Record

At that meeting Arnold denied that local opposition, including threatened legal — or illegal — action if eminent domain was used to get power-line rights-of-way across old family homesteads, had anything to do with the company's decision.

Oh yes, one other remarkable thing happened in 1975. After dozens of meetings and interviews in Brooksville and a few surrounding towns, hours and hours in which I honed my listening skills while I struggled to remember some simple shorthand, I found myself sometime that fall, about six months after I started, once again ascending the stairs in the Brooksville Fire Department to report on another of their meetings.

Herbie Hutchinson was there again. He was as polite and friendly as ever. He had as thick a Maine accent as ever. He again moved over and offered me an aisle seat. He mouthed the usual amenities.

And once again I was speechless. But this time it was because I was in shock.

That's because I understood every word he said.

Chapter 19
Chicken Entrails
And Other Private Parts

The high priest in his white vestments solemnly cut open the dead chicken and inspected its entrails. He pointed to the tumorous growths on its kidneys, and to its shrunken testicles, and predicted a tumultuous year ahead.

Besides the many time warps in 1975, that particular year also had many layers. The last chapter dealt with the public parts of that year. This chapter tells you about that year's more private parts.

It was the first part of January 1975, and two of our chickens had dropped dead on us, a couple of weeks apart, for no apparent reason. We just found them stone cold in the chicken coop. I took the second one up to the University of Maine in Orono, north of Bangor, and the good doctor did an autopsy on it — then a free service.

"See these growths?" the white-coated University veterinarian asked. "We've seen three kinds of growths like that. They all cause the kidneys to eventually fail. We've determined that one kind is caused by a virus, but we don't yet know about the other two. We don't know how to prevent this stuff, or how to cure it. The birds just waste away. They're skinny, not meaty at all, and have poor comb development. This bird is how old? Six months? And weighs, let's see, only about two pounds. He should be three or four times that size by now. And look, here, these are his testicles. They're supposed to be about the size of an almond. Look, you can hardly make them out. He looks like a hen. Clearly he hasn't been pumping out the hormones."

When I got home, we checked the rest of the flock and found three more in puny condition. I home-autopsied one of them (shades of high school biology class) and found the same thing the doctor had. The chickens had been eating their share of the food, but for some reason they weren't able to convert the food into either eggs or meat for the soup pot.

Even though the doctor assured us the virus was probably not transmittable to humans, we decided not to eat the three skinny birds we had culled out. We threw their bodies into the compost heap. None of the other birds seemed to be affected.

Chapter 19 — Chicken Entrails and Other Private Parts

In an apparently unrelated event, but about the same time, Eliot Coleman came down with hyperthyroidism, an overactive thyroid. He started losing weight, and, since he was normally thin, he didn't have a lot extra to spare. His eyes looked all bugged-out. He said his heart would pound on occasion like he had been running in a race. His doctor told him that they couldn't control the condition with pills, that the only thing they could do for it would be to operate on his thyroid, and remove as much of that throat gland as necessary to get the excretion back to normal.

Defying doctors' advice, and not wanting to go under the knife, he decided to try beating it with vitamins and other nutritional measures, and right off the bat managed to put back three pounds. The doctors, of course, were amazed.

Since Eliot was concentrating on his health, and trying to get all the rest he could, he did not have the time or energy to plan, organize or supervise projects for Becky, his wintertime farm apprentice. So we inherited her.

Becky had come to Colemans in the fall, right after walking the whole Appalachian Trail from Georgia to Maine, a distance of some 2,150 miles. Unlike other transients, she did not disappear when the first snow fell. When the Colemans went off visiting relatives over the holidays, she had stayed in their cabin, hauling hay and cutting up apples for the goats. She did everything but the milking.

Becky was 25, a footloose college graduate, and hailed from Vermont. She recounted how she had recently hitchhiked across the country and back, just to do it.

She seemed to have an inordinate interest in bones and hides, as well as porcupine quills, which she collected at every opportunity. Road kill took on new meaning in her presence. She said she even tried to tan a skunk's hide once.

Among the things we later learned about Becky was that her mother had died in childbirth. It had been her mother's first pregnancy. Her father still lived in Vermont.

Becky started out her tenure with us by helping Keith build an addition onto the farrowing pen for the impending litter of piglets. They also slaughtered a steer and a sheep for two of our neighbors and then went to work on the shop.

Becky tended to be moody and was often cranky and irritable, traits that were usually innocuous in the isolation of the Maine woods.

But she occasionally helped me with the dishes, which I appreciated.

Our sow farrowed on Jan. 27, by the light of the full moon and in 15-degree weather. We managed to witness the birth of all but the first two of her ten babies (five of each sex). Number Two was the runt, with not much life to him at all. He just laid there, growing colder and colder. When even a hot water bottle didn't seem to do him any good, I resorted to stronger measures. I'd read somewhere that cows and goats lick their young to to stimulate them and get their circulations going. So I stuck the cute little piglet inside my coat and just started rubbing him as hard as I could all over, like you'd rub your hands together to get them warm. I did this, really roughing him up, for about 15 or 20 minutes straight. Keith thought I was nuts, then said I was being mean to a dying animal. I ignored him. The piglet was either going to die or live, but I wasn't going to sit by and do nothing.

It worked. He woke up. He perked up. When he finally started to protest his treatment, I put him back with his siblings, and he went right to nursing on his mama.

Apparently it was unusual in that part of the world for all the pigs in a litter to pull through. Keith said when people would ask, their first question was, "Has your pig popped her young-uns yet?" The second question was, "How many died?" None of ours died.

Keith castrated the males at four weeks, and we sold all but two of the piglets at eight weeks for $25 each.

In February we all had the flu for two weeks, Keith for three. Then, while Keith was working in a friend's shop making our kitchen cabinets, he had a run-in with a table saw. It took a good gouge out of the tip of his longest finger on his left hand. His old boss, Fred Dyer, a Pentacostal, came and prayed over the finger. Keith said he slept better that night. The wound never got infected, and healed to a small scar.

Keith came in the cabin all excited one day with the news that Becky had a $60,000 trust fund, proceeds from her mother's estate. It was the first time I had heard an actual figure for any trust fund that so many of the people passing through our backyard seemed to have. I was not impressed with the amount.

I said that's nice. That much money is small compensation for the loss of her mother, I said, but I guess it's better than nothing. I'm glad for her that she's got it, I said. Knowing that about her does make me feel better about not being able to pay her anything for the work she does around here.

Let's see, if the trust fund paid something like five percent a year, sounds like she's got about as much money coming in as we do, I said, only we have to work outside for ours.

If she's careful, I said, and I know she's careful — in fact she's more skin-flinty than anyone I've ever seen — she could live on the income from that kind of money indefinitely, I said. She has no housing costs, no car, and right now she's trading work for her room and board. Pretty good deal, I said.

If she lived like real people it would be gone in a couple of years, I said.

It sure explains how she can take off all over the country any time she wants, I said, hiking the Appalachian Trail or hitchhiking across the country and back like she did, I said.

That's okay. Life is like that, I said.

Sixty-thousand dollars, Keith said again.

After six weeks of heavy doses of all kinds of vitamins, it looked like Eliot had licked his hyperthyroidism. Not only did he gain back most of the weight he had lost, which the doctors said would be impossible, but he said his blood tests showed that he'd gotten so back to normal that he'd even started in the other direction. He said he still didn't feel quite right yet, and his hands still shook a little when he held them out, but he was over the hump. He told us his next task was to figure out which of the vitamins he could reduce or eliminate. He also said the doctors had just decided to leave him alone.

Then in April, Sue and Eliot had some words, and Susie took Heidi and went on an unplanned visit to her folks in Boston. Melissa stayed with her father. Eliot didn't say much about it, which was so unlike him we figured it must be serious.

Eliot was getting along fine without Susie, at least as far as the farm work was concerned, helped as he was by five or six unpaid workers, with five more expected for the summer. Becky worked at Colemans in the morning, and at our place in the afternoon, so we sort of knew what was going on.

But word had gotten around town about the split-up, and summer people arriving in late spring that year were whispering that, under the circumstances, they couldn't bring themselves to go to the farm when the stand opened in June.

We were concerned, since Eliot was viewed not only as a good organic gardener, but as a representative of the whole back-to-the-land movement. We knew that many people would take the long ride out to his remote farm not just to buy good vegetables, but to get a glimpse of the whole operation, and, by buying food there, become part of something grand.

Of course, some of them had already been turned off the previous summer, with the competition among the farm apprentices for the best overall tan.

Eliot was very cool toward us during Susie's absence. With other people he overreacted or acted strangely. Keith developed a case of isolationism, and cut another path through our woods so everybody from Eliot's campground wouldn't have to go right past our house and through our garden to get to Nearings. I looked around for another market for my bread, and tentatively found one at a farmstand about 12 miles away.

And then, in early June, Susie returned, in time for their ninth wedding anniversary. Turns out they were married the same year Keith and I had been.

June 6, 1975

...Enjoyed the article on the Nearings. Not as accurate as it could have been (such as Colemans being the next farm), but interesting. I about fell over when I read that Helen says they never needed any help. They couldn't survive very well without help, from what we can see. But they enjoy their little fantasies, and if they don't hurt anyone, I guess there's not too much harm in that. We probably weren't mentioned because we're not important enough. Eliot is nationally known too, like the Nearings. We're little nobodies here in the woods, and that's fine with us. And now that the community, such as it was, back here on the head of the Cape is breaking up, or seems to be lately, that's just as well.

I baked bread for both stands in June. When the pick-your-own strawberry season ended, demand for bread at the farther stand dropped abruptly, so I stopped baking for them. In mid-August I had trouble getting bulk flour from my supplier, so I closed down my bread operation at Eliot's too. I told Susie that when baking became a real drudge, it was time for a change, and that she should plan on finding someone else to bake bread the next summer. She didn't seem to understand.

Cass returned the end of July after summer school. The bees swarmed a few days later, and since my whole hand swelled up for three days the last time I got stung on the wrist, and since Keith wasn't home, Cass suited up and captured the ball. She also started doing the milking, since she hated feeding the chickens and pigs.

A friend of ours miscarried in mid-summer, three days after the town crew went past spraying 2,4-D to kill the weeds on the side of the road. She had been sitting on the stoop of her husband's woodworking shop, saw the crew spray the mist in her direction, smelled the sticky-sweet herbicide aroma. 2,4-D is one of the two herbicides in Agent Orange,

2,4,5-T being the other. That was the mixture which was sprayed so liberally over Vietnam, and which has been linked ever since to health problems in veterans and birth defects in their children and Vietnamese children. The doctor said the miscarriage was probably due to placenta previa, in which the placenta attaches too low in the uterus, and cuts off the blood supply as the fetus grows. Our friend was convinced it was the spray. She was three months along. It had been a planned pregnancy. They were very disappointed.

The backhoe was back in mid-August, doing preliminary work on our pond. We decided to block off the stream below the bridge, next to the lower garden, since the banks fell away quickly there and we could get a good depth fairly easily, without moving a whole lot of dirt. Our pond would be good size, maybe nine feet deep, and big enough for garden irrigation, swimming, maybe for stocking with fish, powering a water wheel, even fire-fighting, if our house ever needed a place for the Brooksville volunteer firefighters to drop the intake hose on their suction pump.

It would be far better than the Colemans' little irrigation pond next to their farmstand, which was handy since it was within a few steps of their thirsty, bucket-watered gardens, but which wasn't any bigger than my Grandma's old lily pond out by her milkhouse.

I weaned Rebecca at about 19 months, much to her displeasure.

As soon as town officials had learned that he could be reached by phone, Keith had been offered, and he accepted, an appointment as Clam Warden for the town, a paying position that required him to check the clam flats every now and then to make sure people had their permits and weren't digging beyond them. He had a patch for his sleeve and a badge and everything.

Digging with clam forks in the tidal muck for hidden shellfish is hard, backbreaking work. But for the industrious, it could be good money. And for some, it was the only way they knew how to make a living. Because of that, some flats farther south had been over-harvested, no longer yielding mollusks of marketable size. Other beaches had been closed due to raw sewage from summer homes or industrial pollution from chemical plants and paper mills.

Clam diggers from other towns had started to come into Brooksville, sometimes surreptitiously by boat, to work sections of the coast outside their permits. Everybody knew everybody else, and knew if diggers were not where they belonged. But they had to be caught in the act, since the twice-daily incoming tide always hid any evidence of trespass.

Normal tides in mid-coast Maine are about 11 feet, high to low, measured vertically. Depending on the grade in the clam flats, an 11-foot drop in the water level could expose from a dozen to several hundred feet of tidal ground. The Bay of Fundy between Nova Scotia and New Brunswick has seen twice-daily tides of 60 or more feet, prompting more than one study on the feasibility of harnessing that much waterpower for the generation of electricity.

To protect their mucky turfs, some clam diggers, both locals and those from down the coast, had resorted to carrying guns or clubs, and were known on occasion to use them. It was the closest thing Brooksville then had to the Crips and the Bloods. It was into this volatile situation that Keith could potentially walk, unarmed, any time he checked the flats in full Clam Warden uniform.

Then, just as he had predicted, word got around and the phone started ringing off the wall with people calling Keith to do odd jobs for them. Keith soon discovered he had less and less time to check the clam flats.

Our sow farrowed again in mid-summer, but had only four piglets. We couldn't figure out if she needed more Vitamin E, or if it was the boar. We decided to give her one more time before turning her into pork roast. As it turned out, we had trouble selling even those four. Nobody wanted to raise fall pigs. Seizing the opportunity, that fall we turned one of the piglets, then weighing about 60 pounds, into a dynamite outdoor pig barbecue, roasted on a spit over an open fire for eight hours. We invited all our carnivore friends.

On top of our unplanned pig herd, we were getting lots of pig parts from Keith's growing popularity as a pig slaughterer. Keith had done our pigs so well that our friends and neighbors, and then outright strangers, started calling to see if he would do theirs. We knew it was a hassle to cart pigs off to the slaughterhouse in Bangor. Not only that, but the commercial places in the area didn't exactly have a reputation for good record-keeping. One customer reportedly got back two left halves. The slaughterhouse, which has since closed, insisted that both halves belonged to that man's pig.

After a few stories like that, people stopped growing pigs. Why spend all that time and energy if you couldn't be sure you would get your own pig back?

When Keith decided to go into the business (he charged $30 per pig), those unused backyard pigpens suddenly filled up. In fact, after Keith got a client list going, people would call us in the spring, before they bought their backyard pig, to see if Keith was still in business, and to extract a

Chapter 19 — Chicken Entrails and Other Private Parts

promise that he would do their pig come fall. One year he did upwards of 60 pigs for people.

Infrastructure. It makes all the difference in the world.

To go to a pig-killing, Keith would tie his tripod and a big 55-gallon barrel down to whatever vehicle he was using and head for the pig, wherever the pig was on the face of the earth. It was a half-day process at best. He started by filling the barrel with at least 30 gallons of water, then building a fire under the barrel and heating the water to 155 degrees Fahrenheit — scalding temperature.

Other than tending the fire, this was chit-chat time. Keith got a lot of socializing done during these sessions.

When the water was hot, out came the rifle. The owner would slop the pig for its final meal. As the pig contentedly dove its head into the trough, Keith would lean over the pigpen fence and pop the pig right between the eyes. The pig would die happy.

Its brains scrambled, the pig would keel over and start kicking its death-throes. That was the time to jump into the pen and slit the animal's throat. With the heart still beating, the several pints of blood in the pig were soon pumped out through the wound in the neck. Only a few people tried to catch that precious liquid for blood pudding. (I tried making it once with blood from one of our pigs. I didn't like the gritty texture.)

Then Keith would haul the pig over to the scalding barrel, which by now had the tripod positioned over it. Keith would hook the carcass under the lower jaw, hoist it high with a rope and pulley, and dunk half of the pig into the scalding water, for anywhere from 1 to 3 minutes. The purpose of the hot water was to loosen the bristles on the pig's hide. The test was to tug on a tuft of bristles. As soon as the tuft could be pulled out by a slight tug, it was time to get the pig out of the water.

The carcass was hoisted out and then lowered onto a clean surface — such as a sheet of plywood or heavy marine canvas — where Keith would proceed to scrape the bristles off the hide with special bell-shaped scrapers. That done, it was time to hoist and dip the other half of the pig, this time with the hooks through the animal's back hocks.

Once the carcass was scraped clean, Keith would gut the animal, behead it, and then, using a meat saw, cut it in half down the length of the spine. And he was done. It was up to the pig's owner to dispose of the guts, and to see that the carcass halves were properly hung and cooled. In the late fall in Maine, the outdoor temperatures usually took care of the cooling. But it was wise to find a place where wild animals could not reach.

Cooling the carcass firmed up the meat. It is nearly impossible to cut up any hot, freshly killed animal, and pork is the slipperiest. But, unlike other meats, pork does not improve with aging. As soon as the carcass is cool and firm (overnight is good), it is time to cut it up.

Some pig owners butchered their own pigs. By that I mean they cut up the carcass halves into meal-size chunks. (Slaughtering and butchering are two separate functions.) Others took the halves to the local grocery store where it would be custom-butchered. Maine also had private smokehouses scattered across the landscape where hams and bacons could be custom-processed.

Before he packed up and left, Keith would ask the pig-owners if there were any parts of the animal, other than the intestines, that the owners did not want. He usually came away with the head, and sometimes the liver and heart. There's a goodly amount of meat on a pig's head, if you know where to look. And my mother taught me how to cook liver — quickly, in thin strips, with equal amounts of sauteed onions.

We ate well.

Despite our abundance of pork, that November Keith bagged a deer, a 10-point buck, the day before hunting season closed. He brought it down about a quarter of a mile from our house, across the road behind the blueberry field. It dressed out at about 165 pounds.

That was a lot of meat to deal with. A woodworker friend offered us floor space and an electric outlet in a room off his shop if we wanted to put in a freezer of our own. All we had to do was pay for the electricity. We jumped at the offer. The huge chest freezer we bought was soon filled.

That development greatly reduced our need for canning lids, along with eliminating the considerable hassle of canning meat in a pressure canner. But as a result we were once again relying upon a continual supply of electricity to the freezer to preserve a good part of our food supply.

That same November, when it came time to breed the sow again, we found out the boar we had used the previous spring had been turned into sausage. Then we heard about a pair of boars just off the Cape. The owner assured us his guys were the best in the business.

We told him our pig was big.

He said big was fine.

Keith built a sturdy pig crate to hold our 500-lb. darling for the trip over there in our trailer. It got interesting getting our sow into the crate, and then getting the crate into the trailer, but we did it.

When we got there, we found a massive mud hole and two little boars who were all excited at the prospects, but were not up to handling such a big mama.

Just couldn't reach.

In December, when the sow again came in heat, we took her to a place that had a sign up in the feed store. What a difference! The boar was as handsome as pigs get, and quite big enough to handle her. He had a record of fathering 12 or 13 pigs per litter. Theirs was a beautiful, if brief, relationship.

The part I liked was that there were four or five men there who just took the pig and her crate off our trailer, put her in the pen with the boar, put her back in the crate when the coupling was complete and put the crate back on the trailer for the ride home.

They complimented us on our sow's behavior. I complimented them on theirs.

We cut a small Christmas tree from the back of our property, and decorated it with strung popcorn, and with real candles for lights, which we didn't turn our backs on the whole time they were lit up. A candle-lit tree is a beautiful sight to behold.

In the exchange of down-home gifts, a friend gave us a couch pillow she had made with fabric she had hand-woven from wool yarn which had been hand-spun by another friend using a fleece from one of her own sheep.

It was that kind of place.

By the end of the year 1975, Susie and I, our friend who had miscarried — in fact just about every fertile woman we knew — were all pregnant.

Chapter 20
Cracks in the Façade

We learned many things from Helen and Scott. *Living the Good Life* was full of useful information, and had touched a deep cord with us. That was, after all, why we were homesteading in the woods of Maine.

But, after dealing with the Nearings on a regular basis for more than two years, one of the things we had come to learn was not to take everything they said or wrote at face value. By that time I knew I had been wrong that day when I first walked into Helen's kitchen — just because I had read their book, I didn't know everything about them. Not by a long shot.

Yes, there was no question they worked very hard, every day. Unquestionably they were robust, energetic, and deliberate, despite being well on in years. Undoubtedly they were principled human beings, and they wore their principles firmly and resolutely. And because of their organizational skills, they could get more free work out of a rag-tag bunch of inexperienced city gawkers than anyone would ever dream was possible.

That self-assuredness and confidence and worldliness and stubbornness that drew so many people in — they were, after all, living proof that it was possible to beat the system — made it all the harder to understand the inconsistencies that kept cropping up. So many times the Nearings drew a hard line in the sand that no one had drawn before, stepped over it, and then ignored or denied the mis-step, despite the footprints they had left behind. It then fell to the followers to decide whether the flaws, if noticed, were major or minor.

Some of the inconsistencies, even in their earlier writings, were obvious to many on the very first reading. The most frequently cited hypocrisy concerned their lambasting of "animal slavery" in all its forms — the owning of pets, as well as draft, dairy or meat animals. Yet in *Living the Good Life* the Nearings included a photo showing their garden being plowed by draft animals, while another photo showed Helen at the reins of a team of horses hauling maple sap through the snow. And they mention several times in *The Maple Sugar Book* that teams of horses and oxen were used in their sugar bush.

Did that mean their principles would fall to any expediency, or that they did not hold the principle as strongly as it sounded? Or was it something in between? If they did not actually own the animals in question, for instance, were they off the hook?

(I had a friend once who lived in the woods, far from any public transportation. He refused to own a car because the air pollution they created was wrecking the planet. Yet he hitch-hiked everywhere, and his wife, who had a full-time job, owned a car. Contrast that with a like-minded individual, someone who frequented organic farms as a willing worker in the 1980s. We called him "Walking John" because he refused on principle to ride in any petroleum-powered vehicle, regardless of who owned it. Under his rules, hitch-hiking was out of the question. Someone finally took pity on him and gave him a beat-up bicycle, which he put to good use.)

And then there was the issue of Puss-O, Helen's last cat.
In *Living the Good Life*, they (I suspect Scott) say:

> Cats and dogs live dependent subservient lives under the table tops of humans. Domestic pets kill and drive away wild creatures, whose independent, self-respecting lives seem far more admirable than those of docile, dish-fed retainers. We enjoy the wild creatures...

Scott disavowed ownership of Puss-O, thereby keeping his own record clean. I, being a cat person, understood Helen's affection for the animal. And I knew that, really, no one ever owns a cat. It is the cat who decides whether or not it will grace you with its presence.

Not only that, I knew that on any homestead with a garden, a root cellar and a pantry, a cat was really a necessity, the nicest insurance policy one could find to keep your stock of growing or stored food rodent-free. We always had a cat or two (or three or four) around.

The same thing could be said of dogs, in relation to larger garden invaders. Without a dog's protection, Eliot lost seedlings to rabbits, and we had our corn and the Nearings had their blueberries decimated by raccoons.

But rather than build a stone wall around his only cash crop, or at the very least install a cheap but effective battery-powered electric fence, Scott, that self-avowed non-violent pacifist, chose to use the cruelest form of entrapment — steel-jaw leghold-traps — to rid his income-producing quarter-acre blueberry patch of wild creatures who were only following their natural instincts.

We could only shake our heads in wonderment.

Some of the idiosyncrasies that I noticed in *Living the Good Life* were simply laughable. For instance, this is what Scott said about his own daily routine:

> Each day was divided into two main blocks of time — four morning hours and four afternoon hours. At breakfast time on week-days we first looked at the weather, then asked 'How shall we arrange the day?' Then by agreement we decided which of these blocks of time should be devoted to bread labor and which to personally determined activities. Of necessity the weather was the primary factor in making the decision.

Not three pages later, Scott soundly criticized his neighbors' work ethic, lambasting them for doing exactly what he himself was doing. He wrote:

> They were accustomed to a go-as-you-please existence....They got up and went to work, or did not go to work, as the result of accident or whim....When they did decide to work, they let inclination determine the object of their efforts.

Scott had "personally determined activities," while others "let inclination determine the object of their efforts." The only difference I can see is that Scott discussed his schedule ad-nauseum, and sometimes even put it in writing, while the natives held all their decision-making in their heads.

Scott was also highly critical of the local priorities:

> If someone came along and wanted to visit, they would turn from almost any job and chat, sometimes for hours.

To me, that meant the Vermont natives were more flexible, and recognized the value in being neighborly — visits from friends and neighbors took precedence over work which could most likely wait for another time.

Scott intellectualized about the importance of community, but he could not abide what he called "idle gossip," refusing to acknowledge that such information — about illness, couplings or uncouplings, accidents, births, deaths, job changes, who was in trouble and who needed help — is at the very foundation of any community activity.

Then there was the issue of diet.

The Nearings swore off alcoholic beverages. No problem there. Except that occasionally the cider they served had been around for awhile, and had a little fizz. Some of it actually had a good kick to it.

Helen made a point of saying that she never made bread, and seemed proud of that fact. As a bread-baker, I always thought that was a little sad. The rhythms, warmth, smells, and vibrancy of the bread-making process is just so wonderful, and I would have thought Helen would have found them appealing as well.

But from her often-repeated statement many assumed that Helen ate no bread. Not so. She bought some from me, more regularly from another woman in town, and lamented the softness of the store-bought varieties she sometimes resorted to.

The issue of leavened bread might be just a matter of personal preference, except for the fact that yeast is considered by many biologists to be on the animal side of the equation. After they have done their job of making bubbles, the yeast bodies growing in the bread dough are baked alive in a hot oven. (I once had this conversation with a bread customer of mine who had just informed me that he was a vegan. I thought we were having an interesting intellectual discussion, while he proceeded to have a philosophical melt-down before my eyes.)

Which leads us to the issue of vegetarianism, veganism and dairy products.

In *Living the Good Life*, they state:

> Long ago we decided to live in the vegetarian way, without killing or eating animals; and lately we have largely ceased to use dairy products and have allied ourselves with the vegans, who use and eat no animal products, butter, cheese, eggs or milk.

By "lately," I took it to mean the early 1950s, right before they wrote and self-published *Living the Good Life*. They certainly weren't vegans early in their Vermont sojourn:

> One of our first steps in Vermont was to ask the Lightfoots, who were our nearest neighbors and lived less than a quarter of a mile away, whether they would supply us with milk. They agreed, and one or another of the Lightfoot girls would come over each day and deliver it.

But after they cast in stone that vegan pronouncement in their book, how strongly did they hold to it?

In the 1970s dairy products regularly showed up in their private meals in the form of yogurt, cottage cheese, hard cheese, and especially ice cream, Helen's passion. A household tip in Helen's handwriting on how to keep cottage cheese (by storing it upside down in the refrigerator) was among the notes tucked away in her bookshelf. Several of Helen's recipes in her cookbook, *Simple Food for the Good Life*, published in 1980, call for dairy products. They were certainly not strangers to the stuff.

Keith and I had tried vegetarianism for a few months early-on, but we found we were not able to overcome a severe drop in energy levels despite what was supposed to be an adequate diet. We decided to take what for us was a more normal route — to have dairy animals, and to raise and kill our own meat, in the tradition of hundreds of years of family subsistence farming.

Our decision was a great disappointment to the Nearings. And they let us know it.

Their overt disapproval of our diet stuck in our craws, because we knew about the dairy products, especially ice cream, that they ate, and we knew that they were well aware of the link between dairy products and meat production.

For those who are not clear about that connection, here it is: Unlike hens, who can lay eggs without ever seeing a rooster, dairy animals only give milk after they get pregnant and give birth. Therefore, baby calves and goat kids are an essential part of the milk equation. And since about half those babies are male, and since only females can grow up to give more milk, the question arises as to what to do with the bull calves and billy goats and all those extra heifers (young female cows) and does (female goats) not needed for future milk production. The logical answer, in the world at large, is to turn them into meat.

Meat production, therefore, is a direct by-product of dairy production. One doesn't happen without the other.

At least Eliot was not two-faced about it. Vegetarians but not vegans, the Colemans had dairy goats, but Eliot drowned the male goats at birth, and buried the carcasses. That seemed like such a waste to me, but at least he took on the responsibility.

It was therefore interesting for me to read in ***Simple Food for the Good Life*** that the same disapproval they had heaped on us over our choice of food, they in turn had felt coming from others.

> We are looked down on with some scorn by purist friends for using any dairy products....If there is egg or milk in something while traveling, we'll eat it. If there's meat, we won't. Inconsistent? Certainly. Who isn't, about many things? Is there a thoroughly consistent person on earth?

(Before this part of the discussion, Helen in her cookbook stated bad biology and implied that if huge animals like elephants could live as vegetarians, then we should be able to also — completely ignoring the fact that elephants and other ruminants have multiple stomachs and other biological differences which allow them, and not us, to digest great masses of cellulose.)

Then, a page or two later, Helen gets to the heart of the matter, raising the issue that I had struggled with since we killed our first chicken:

I acknowledge that leaving off meat-eating means taking the lives of plants when we cut off their lives, swallow and digest them. And I apologize to the radish, the carrot, the head of lettuce, the apple, the orange, when eating them. Some day, I hope, we shall be able to live on sunlight absorbed through the skin and deep breaths of clean air — though that also is teeming with minuscule forms of life.

So far, eat we must, in order to survive. Therefore we should look to the less sentient forms of life for sustenance. Life is inherent in every food substance that we imbibe, and one has to kill to eat, whether it be an apple, a tomato, or a blade of grass. By what right do we consume these marvels of nature? Plants have an important place on earth. I salute the trees and apologize if I cut one down. I shrink from picking a daisy or a pansy, or biting into an apple or radish. Who am I to take their lives in their prime?

We should widen the range of human feeling until it encompasses all life on earth, doing the most good to the greatest number and the least harm to the least number. Standards and relative degrees of harm and harmlessness will vary with each one of us. Some will continue to eat fish and fowl while eschewing red meat; some will eat nothing that walks or wiggles — still eating dairy products; some will eat no products at all of the animal kingdom — no eggs, milk, cheese or honey. But we can all be constantly aware of the rights of others, be it baby lamb, bison, fly or cauliflower. We can modify our food habits so that we approach the ideal of living on fruits and nuts and seeds which have finished their life cycle and with which the tree or bush or plant is finished.

Unfortunately, the Nearings' contradictory pronouncements about their diet has had some unintended consequences in the scientific community. Take the issue of Vitamin B-12.

Not long ago, a friend of mine related how, in a college nutrition class she had taken at the University of Maine in the early 1990s, Scott Nearing's name had come up in a discussion about the body's long-term ability to conserve and preserve vitamin B-12, a nutrient essential to healthy human life and available only through animal sources. The reference was to tests done on Scott's vitamin B-12 levels in the last dozen years of his life. The clear assumption was that Scott had ingested no animal protein since his conversion to vegetarianism around the age of 50.

In my attempts to get more information about those tests, I ended up calling Dr. Roger Hurlburt, then in Stephens City, Virginia, who had been fresh out of college in the late 1960s and was running a research and development lab for the late Dr. Nelson Trowbridge.

Dr. Trowbridge, who then lived in Brewer, Maine, was an old friend of the Nearings, and when he asked to do some tests on them, they acquiesced.

Dredging up memories from 30 years before, Dr. Hurlburt said in that telephone interview that he didn't have any direct contact with Helen or Scott, but he remembered that Scott's blood test showed he had pernicious anemia, due to a vitamin B-12 deficiency. Dr. Trowbridge advised Scott to take monthly B-12 shots to get his levels up again. At the time, there were no B-12 dietary supplements or pills that would do the job.

"He said 'I don't think so,' that he would prefer to have his diet take care of it," Dr. Hurlburt said.

It was one of those lines in the sand. Helen included a letter from Scott to this doctor in her book, **Loving and Leaving the Good Life**, published in 1992.

> Thank you for your letter with concern on my health status. As I understand your proposal, you want me, each month, to furnish urine samples and have B-12 injections and other necessary medication and/or treatment.
>
> If I did this I would be trying to prolong my life under medical supervision for the rest of my life. Thank you, but I would rather die much earlier than follow such a course.
>
> My formula is to stay well and live as long as I can, in moderate health and vigor. If I cannot stay well by a normal diet and temperate living, the sooner I die, the better for me and the society of which I am a member.

So what happened?

"We monitored him, Dr. Trowbridge drew blood on an annual basis, and it actually corrected itself, although it [Scott's B-12 level] was getting low again toward the end of his life," Dr. Hurlburt said. "I think Dr. Trowbridge said he was eating seaweed or an extract of seaweed, something like that."

Dr. Richard A. Cook, Professor of Human Nutrition at the University of Maine in Orono, said seaweed itself does not contain B-12, but some of the plankton and other microorganisms that ride along on it do contain that essential vitamin.

But it wasn't seaweed that had done the trick, as Helen confessed in **Simple Food for the Good Life**:

Chapter 20 — Cracks in the Façade

Aware of the almost universal abuse of our animal brothers, Scott and I, as vegetarians, have lessened our dependence on animal products. We drink no milk, eat no eggs (except what may come in dishes served away from home), wear no animal skins or coats of leather, and try to get non-leather belts and shoes. We are not purists, nor entirely consistent in our avoidance of harm to animals. We both eat honey, stolen from the bees. Scott eats yogurt, although he is turning to tofu, a soybean product. Aware of the vegetarian's need for vitamin B-12, we both eat some cottage cheese. I have a predilection for Dutch cheeses, having lived long in Holland, and my mother being Dutch. I also have a well-known (to my friends) liking for ice cream: a remnant from my misguided youth. This addiction is indulged in occasionally, at birthdays and other celebrations, when I may fall from grace. I have used buttermilk in journey cakes, and cheese occasionally in a cooked vegetable dish.

Dr. Hurlburt said that cottage cheese and yogurt are both good sources of vitamin B-12, and was surprised to learn that the Nearings ate dairy products. He did not think Dr. Trowbridge had that understanding.

Dr. Cook, my friend's nutrition professor, also did not have that understanding. He was familiar with the tests done by Drs. Trowbridge and Hurlburt, of Scott's public pronouncements that he was a vegan, and his strong stance against B-12 shots as stated in that published letter.

As a result, for years Dr. Cook had been invoking Scott Nearing in his classes as an example of someone who could go a long period of time without ingesting any animal protein and still not end up with a deficiency. He concluded that it was possible for the body to conserve B-12 and recirculate it internally for years and years before using it all up.

He had made the mistake of taking Scott at his word.

But the Nearings did more than eat a little cottage cheese. Despite Scott's public and private disavowals of B-12 shots, both he and Helen were on the receiving end of those shots on a regular basis. Jeannie Gaudette, Nearing friend and neighbor of many years, commented at a Monday Night Meeting at the Nearing homestead in the summer of 2000 that a medical doctor friend of theirs who lived nearby came over every month for years to administer B-12 shots.

"She [the doctor] came over every full moon," Gaudette explained to the crowd. "Not that there was anything magical or mystical about the full moon. It was just a good way for her to remember that it was time to do it."

Dr. Mary Dietrich, the doctor in question, refused to comment on the issue, even though both Helen and Scott had died many years before our discussion. She was simply not interested in correcting a public misconception. I explained what was then being taught in nutrition classes at the University of Maine. She accused the professor of not having done his homework. When I pointed out that the professor was using Dr. Trowbridge's test results and Scott and Helen's own published words for his source material, this well-schooled medical doctor said she had no sympathy for people who believed everything they read in a book and then proceeded to run their lives by it.

In April 2002 at Forest Farm, while looking through "a bunch of index cards w/ quotes," Greg Joly came across a medical prescription form dated November 1984, written for Helen, then age 80, authorizing two 100 mcg Vitamin B-12 shots, to be administered Dec. 10, 1984 and Jan. 14, 1985. The prescription form was signed by M. M. Dietrich, MD.

Another issue of varying importance to different people was the Nearings' use of electricity. The Nearings talked eloquently about cutting the umbilical cords of society by going to live in the woods, and implied that they lived happily in Vermont without any electricity. Of course at the time they had no choice. Electric lines would not be extended to their corner of the world until more than a dozen years after their arrival.

In 1946, Helen and a lot of her neighbors signed utility right-of-way permits, and got power installed shortly after that. According to Darlene Palola, who now owns their stone house in Vermont, the Nearings were leading proponents of Vermont rural electrification.

But because an electric line dangling between a house and the road is the most visible umbilical cord of society, thousands of people naturally have been surprised to see that the Nearings had electricity in their home in Harborside. I too was surprised at first, but, I figured, in their old age they had earned a little convenience.

When asked, they dismissed their electric connection by saying it was there when they bought the place. But they never disconnected it either, and when they built their new stone house in Harborside, it was fully electrified.

They disavowed electric refrigeration in *Living the Good Life*, but the Nearings had a refrigerator when we first met them in Harborside. It was replaced shortly thereafter by a donated freezer, and was almost immediately filled with blueberries — and ice cream. This I certainly did not begrudge them. Refrigeration had turned out to be the trickiest part of non-electric food storage for us, particularly in the summer. So when that friend six miles away offered us floor space for our own freezer if we paid the electric bill, we jumped at the chance. It was so much easier to freeze meat than to pressure-can it. And we liked ice cream too.

Discussing the issue in *Our Home Made of Stone* (1983), Helen explained that it cost only $35 for the new house in Harborside to be hooked up to the line running along the road. She then quotes Frank Coffee in *The Self-Sufficient House* as saying:

> If an umbilical can be stretched to a power grid at reasonable cost, the convenience of a central system may be preferable to an alternative on-site system — even one that insulates you from an uncertain energy future.

This was despite having recently confronted the real possibility of a looming nuclear power plant across the road from her home, as well as the worldwide energy crisis that put traditional electricity production in jeopardy. And she did not mention at all, or apparently consider, solar power, that exciting renewable energy source then making headlines, even for such a simple thing as pre-heating water for their hot water tank.

All she would say was:

> A windmill would not have been as cheap for us. We succumbed to the lure of easy power.

Their new stone house in Harborside turned many of the Nearing's "Good Life" pronouncements on their heads. There in *Living the Good Life* was their disdain for architects and master craftsmen:

> If we are worth a snap of the fingers, we can build with lines as good or better than our great-grandfathers. If we cannot, we do not deserve to live in a well-designed house.

Even though Keith and I had designed and built our own home, and were very happy with the result, from the beginning I thought that statement doomed many otherwise nice people to living in badly-designed homes. Everybody had special talents. God forbid our lives should be confined to only those that we possess ourselves.

In *Our Home Made of Stone,* Helen insisted:

> We are not architects and never employed one.

It appears that "employed" is the operative word here, because later on in that same book, as well as in *Continuing the Good Life*, we have this statement:

A Dutch architect friend drew up the first plans from Helen's initial drawings. His name was E. M. Kraamer-Ferguson, and he worked at the Bureau of Interior Planning in Amsterdam, Holland. The only thing I can figure is that Mr. Kraamer-Ferguson must have donated his services, therefore he was not "employed." But why did the Nearings feel the need to play word games like that? And why did they then leave clues lying all around?

The four-year building project at the new house site began with construction of a stone outhouse, and then a garage/storage building. Keith did a lot of work on both buildings.

When it came to the house itself, it was bad enough that the Nearings shipped Douglas fir beams all the way from Oregon to the Pine Tree State of Maine, in direct contradiction to their insistence that homes be made of native and local material. But then they asked Keith to hand-hew half an inch off three sides of those huge machine-squared beams. Gritting his teeth, Keith began the job. But after awhile, he couldn't take the hypocrisy any more. It was one thing to use his talents to form square beams from round logs. That was useful work. It was quite another to cosmetically scarf up imported, machine-squared beams to make them appear to be what they were not.

The new stone house in Harborside is a beautiful and comfortable house, homey and cozy. And it had a lot of hands building it — master carpenter Brett Brubaker who did all the massive oak timber framing around the doors and windows using scavenged beams; Fred Dyer and his crew (including Keith) who drained the site, dug and poured the cellar with the help of a cement truck, and did all the carpentry that Brett didn't do; Forrest Tyson, a retired electrical engineer and professor of electronics who wired the house; an unnamed plumber who put in the piping and the Swedish Clivus Multrum earth-closet (composting toilet).

And then there were the dozens, hundreds of volunteers, free laborers who came for an hour or two or a summer or two, hauling rocks, hoisting wet cement to the top of the forms, shoveling gravel, getting very sweaty and very dirty in the process. The site often looked like a beehive of activity. Helen and Scott were indeed masters at organizing inexperienced but willing help.

In 1977, Bullfrog Films did a half-hour documentary on Helen and Scott, which was shown several times on Maine Public Television. In it, Helen says very clearly and deliberately that Scott mixed most of the cement for the new house himself in a wheelbarrow, and that she laid every stone. She then proclaims it to be a one-man, one-woman house. She doesn't mention Keith, or Brett, or Fred Dyer and his crew, or the cement truck, or Forrest Tyson, or the hundreds of unpaid volunteers. Someone watching the documentary could only be led to believe that Helen and Scott, she then in her 70s and he in his 90s, had built that huge stone house all by themselves.

It was pure myth, the concept of Super Couple, and Helen was unabashedly promoting it, at the expense of the real workers of the world.

The unanswered question is why?

Hundreds of people knew the truth, because they had been there. The Nearings certainly didn't need the myths to build their reputations. That was firmly documented in public sources. No question they did work hard on the house, harder than most people their ages would have or could have done. That couldn't be taken away from them. What they were doing, what they had already accomplished, the inspiration they were still providing people on a daily basis, was truly remarkable.

Why did they need to create a myth when reality would have done quite well?

Continuing the Good Life was published in 1979, two years after the Bullfrog Film, and ***Our Home Made of Stone***, a construction picture-book of the project, came out in 1983. Both told a very different story than Helen did in the film, finally giving credit to Keith, Brett, Fred Dyer, and all the others. Says ***Continuing the Good Life***:

> Our outhouse was designed and built with hand-hewn timbers, a metal roof and a heavy Dutch door. Keith, our near neighbor, and Scott did the foundation; Helen did all the stonework; Keith hewed the timbers and did the other necessary woodwork. It turned out to be a beautiful edifice and has been called "the prettiest outhouse in five counties."

As for the garage:

> Keith did the hand hewing of the timbers, the form work and general carpentry on this building. He stayed with us up to plate level. Then we had to put on the roof. Fred Dyer and his team did the job…

As for the house:

Our work team consisted of the two of us if no one else was around; many particularly enjoyable days we quietly worked away together, with no outside help. But we get endless visitors and they usually want to help with whatever we are doing. The majority of them, boys and girls, men and women, have had little or no experience with such work, but they learn the ropes fairly quickly and many times become useful members of a smoothly functioning team. Or else they remember some errand they had to do in town and leave suddenly.

When we found how many workers were available on any set day, we paired them off. A couple of people made the mixes in the wheelbarrows and wheeled them to the job. One or two people were needed to keep the master mason (Helen) supplied with stone, which she insisted on handling herself...

Brett was the genius of the place and did single-handedly all the woodwork that had to be done. We and various visitors did all the stonework; Brett took care of the setting up and building of the forms. He proved an indefatigable and meticulous worker, a perfectionist of the

The garage/workshop at the new Forest Farm, seen from the garden

Chapter 20 — Cracks in the Façade

first order. Perhaps we can best sum up this contribution by describing him as a one-man precision job, comprehensive and outstanding.

Two individuals really built the house. With Helen insisting on laying every stone, from outhouse through two large buildings to the high chimney, and with Brett tackling the careful carpentry and the cabinetwork alone, it might be termed a one-man, one-woman house...She handled every stone personally, choosing it, trying it out and putting it in its permanent place in the wall. Scott was allowed to mix the concrete in his favorite wheelbarrow, and dozens of unnamed helpers put in many days' work here and there on the house construction. But it was Helen's and Brett's house.

So now the one-man, one-woman house was Helen's and Brett's, not hers and Scott's. I consider those paragraphs to be a public apology for the mis-statements in the documentary, for Helen's neglecting to mention all the non-Nearing talent and muscle that built their wonderful house.

One other thing. The new Forest Farm in Harborside was not a cheap house to build. It cost many thousands of dollars, more than $80,000 for

The rear of the stone house. The greenhouse is on the right

the house itself, more than $100,000 for the entire complex including the garage, outhouse, walled garden and greenhouse.

It cost real money for the materials, the professionally poured concrete cellar foundation, the bagged cement used for the walls, the Douglas fir beams shipped cross-country, the Swedish Clivus Multrum composting toilet, the electrical wiring, the wood stoves, the slate flooring, the windows, and the many hours of paid labor by skilled craftsmen.

Where did that money come from? Certainly not from their quarter-acre of blueberries. How about their books?

We find the answer tucked in half a sentence in ***Our Home Made of Stone***, when Helen writes:

> I was the instigator, the planner, the chooser of the site, the designer, the interior decorator, and through a kind legacy from an old Los Angeles friend, the one who paid the bills.

What friend? She doesn't say. She only hints, drops a clue.

Only many years later would I learn that the California legacy that bought and paid for their new Harborside house was not the first substantial windfall to dramatically change Helen and Scott's life.

Chapter 21
More News and Letters

In January 1976, Keith finished installing our kitchen cabinets and the bathtub. At the same time. In the same place. The full-sized bathtub was under one length of the counter, with the countertop hinged for a lid. With the lid down, you'd never know there was a tub under there.

It was a real luxury to take a hot bath indoors. Not the best arrangement for company, we knew, but plans were in the works to build a sauna by the pond the next summer. Besides, we didn't get very many overnight guests in the winter anyway.

January 26, 1976
...Thanks so much for remembering Rebecca's birthday. We had a nice little party for her, just us...

The newspaper work is keeping me busy, now that school and town budgets are being worked on. But I enjoy it, and the extra money sure is nice.

That winter we also got a new car. Well, it was sort of new, a 1967 Renault with 44,000 miles on it. It sort of came in a kit. It sort of cost $200.

A woman in town had a brother who thought he was handy as a mechanic. The car needed a new gas tank. To replace the gas tank, (apparently) the engine had to be removed. The brother got as far as getting the engine and old gas tank out of the car, freaked, figured he had botched the whole thing, and left it. At least that is what she told Keith.

The car had been sitting in her garage with the engine and gas tank out for about two years when Keith heard about it. Other than the gaping holes where the engine and gas tank were supposed to be, it was in mint condition, still smelled like a new car inside. Keith struck a deal — he would get the car and all the parts, in exchange for a week's carpentry work and a cord of hardwood firewood.

After he filled that commitment, Keith spent about three days and $40 in car parts to put the vehicle back together. It purred like a kitten.

We still had the 1964 Volkswagen bug, the one with the VW van engine, but it had 140,000 miles on it, and one of the valves was going. That car had been good to us, carrying us many, many miles for very little money in gas and repairs. We also had the Jeep, but it was a gas hog.

Feb. 21, 1976
...We're not sure the sow is pregnant. It looks like she came into heat last week. Guess we'll just have to wait until the middle of April to see if anything happens...
It's about time to start maple sugaring again. The weather has been perfect all this past week, freezing nights and above freezing days. We got about a gallon last year, and that's just run out (we used it very sparingly), so it's time again.

About then we got another strange visitor — black and loud and sleek and pushy. The crow, or maybe it was a raven, flew into our clearing in the woods one day and perched on top of house. Then it moved down to the woodshed roof. Then it checked out the front porch.

We threw it some crumbs. It bowed and accepted our offering. To our surprise, it was still there the next day. When we were too slow to toss the tidbit, it came right up and ate it out of our hands. Then we discovered it would perch on an outstretched arm, occasionally on a shoulder. This was no ordinary animal. We thought it was magic.

The bird stuck around for a couple of weeks, delighting us daily with its audacity. And then, just as suddenly as it came, it disappeared.

March 8, 1976
...My belly has swelled up like a balloon the past two or three weeks. All of a sudden like...
Susie Coleman is pregnant too, due some time in May. And about a dozen other women around town that I know are due too. Sure is crazy. We're having our own miniature population explosion.
Rebecca is fine, keeps coming up with things that never cease to amaze me... Keith has been trying to explain to her about me having a baby, and she seems to understand more than I thought she would. Every now and then she'll pat my belly and say "Baby is growing?" or "Baby coming soon?"

That March we racked up more hospital bills.
Keith had started logging in our woods, felling trees to take to the sawmill for lumber. The third day in, while lifting a cedar log onto the stack, his back gave out. Unlike other back-wrenchings, this one didn't ease up after awhile. A couple of hours later he couldn't move for the pain, couldn't sit up, and couldn't walk to one of our cars.

We faced the inevitable, and called the ambulance. The crew had a nifty orthopedic stretcher that wrapped right around him without moving him on the bed.

Nothing showed on the x-rays. The doctor conjectured that a disk had slipped out of place, was crushed by the vertebrae, and then slipped back into place, albeit badly bruised. Keith was in traction for two days in the hospital. He grew two inches.

At home he mended ever so slowly, only able to stand or sit for brief periods. The inactivity was driving him crazy. Keith started worrying about bringing money into the house. So, I pushed the newspaper work harder than usual for a couple of weeks to relieve that pressure on him. Living the way we did, we didn't need much money, which sure helped.

April 2, 1976

...We did our income tax a while ago, and I thought you'd be interested to know (but not for general publication) that we had about $2,500 in taxable income all last year. I was amazed at the figure. Not so much that it was so low as much as how much we were able to do with that little. New car [the 1967 Renault], eating like kings, Keith with his I.O.O.F lodge every week, and a canoe trip or two, me gallivanting all over creation writing stories, absolutely no debts, and as much in savings at the end of the year as we started the year out with. I just find it hard to believe at times, because I don't feel that we scrimped that much. I guess there's a lot to be said for the simple life.

I will be starting a free 6-week course in chair rushing and chair caning at H.O.M.E. Co-Op in Orland. I'd like to know how to do it because chairs without seats are pretty cheap, used, around here, and it could come in very handy. A furniture-maker we know said the only guy he knows who does it, the one who canes his gorgeous hand-made chairs, is 82 and awfully slow (although he does a beautiful job). Keith has volunteered to babysit. I'd like to take a course in woodworking too, maybe this fall or next winter. There are a lot of little things I could fix or make around here if I knew how, and I hate to bother Keith when he's so busy on projects of his own...

I'm getting very big, bigger than I was last time at this point. It's starting to slow me down. This one is a heck of a lot more active too, I think. I'm predicting a boy, Keith says it's a girl...

April 19, 1976

Thank you very much for the anniversary gift. We put it to good use and had a real night on the town. Drove all the way to Bangor for a movie and a meal out. I felt like a kid on a date again. We might have looked the part too if I weren't so obviously big. We saw "One Flew Over the Cuckoo's Nest" because all our friends had been saying how great it was. I must say it was thought-provoking and well done, but very depressing. Put a bit of a damper on the evening. It wasn't what we had expected at all.

I know how Dad feels. I find it hard to believe it's been ten years already. I don't feel old enough for that. But I must admit we've packed an awful lot of living into the past ten years. It's been fun.

Haven't heard from Yankee Magazine yet on when that article will be in. I'll get you a copy when it comes out. The money they sent is already spent on flooring for this place.

Our sow never did anything [no baby pigs]. We took her to the auction last Thursday and got 39 cents a pound for her. She weighed 537 lbs., so after the auctioneer's cut, we got $200.

Finally got around to actually measuring the flow of water in our creek, and had my hopes for a water-powered electric turbine firmly dashed. The flow is about 8-10 cubic feet per minute, and the smallest turbine they make, for 500 watts, requires a minimum of 74 cf/m. Oh well. Maybe it's enough for a small water wheel....

On April 25, 1976, without advance warning, Andre the Seal changed his annual watery travel plans from Boston to Maine. Instead of heading for his pen in Rockland Harbor, as this wild seal had done for years, he showed up in a rowboat moored behind Hiram Blake Camp on the other side of Cape Rosier. Yes, IN the rowboat.

My editors at the ***Bangor Daily News*** told me in no uncertain terms that I was to get a picture of him, and get it to Bangor any way I could. I did as I was told, but I couldn't see what all the fuss was about — an attitude apparently shared by Governor Joseph Brennan, who would later get into hot water politically when he dared called Andre a summer visitor. Brennan issued a public apology for his impertinence.

Yes, this was the same Andre the Seal portrayed in Disney's 1994 movie, in which a sea lion, not a harbor seal, played Andre. One reviewer compared the casting of a sea lion to play a harbor seal as akin to having a sheep portray Moby Dick. I think it is closer to a whale portraying a dolphin, but her point about inaccuracy in Hollywood castings was well taken.

May 17, 1976

Susie Coleman had a girl last Friday, at home after about two hours labor. Eliot had his whole college class (he teaches a course) down for a do that night, and Susie started into labor while fixing supper. By the time they got finished eating, and Eliot had hustled them up to the campground around the fire and he got back to the house, she had had it. All by herself, with no one there. About a two-hour labor, and the baby weighed about 8 lbs., as measured by the fertilizer scale.

I got all this information second-hand from Hannah [not her real name], a woman working for Colemans, also pregnant, whom we've come to really like. She's not due until the end of November. I told you it seems to be a disease around here. She's my age, and the guy copped out on her when she found out she was pregnant. She decided that it was about time she had kids anyway if she was ever going to have any, so she's going through with it. I think she's together enough to do it. Anyway, I haven't seen Colemans' baby, and I don't know what they plan to name her.

Another pregnant friend is still going strong. I saw her this morning and she looked different somehow, so I think it will be soon, maybe tonight. I told her that and she just laughed. It's really a problem for her since she got pregnant right after a miscarriage without another period, so she really isn't sure when she's due.

I'm feeling pretty good, although it's aggravating to get tired all the time. There are just so many things I want to do that I don't have the energy for any more. Sure will be glad when the kid finally arrives.

May 22 is shaping up to being a big day. One of our goats is due, we get to move our mailbox up to the head of our drive from where it is now down by Nearings, and I go on a camping trip on an island with a bunch of women friends of mine. We're going to an island in the bay where some guy has some sheep that run wild most of the year. He's going to shear them next weekend, and these friends are planning on buying one of the fleeces and then dying it with natural dyes that they hope to find right on the island. They're really into spinning and dying. I've seen some of their stuff and it looks beautiful. It should be a lot of fun. I'm hoping to write an article on the whole outing for some well-paying magazine, whichever one will take it...

The garden is coming along fine and Keith is busy between that and all the carpentry jobs he has lined up, plus all the projects he would like to finish this summer. There's always so much to do around here, no chance of being bored. When people wonder what people did before television, I just laugh.

June 17, 1976

I'm sitting now in the audience waiting for the livestock auction to begin. A lot has been happening...

Somehow, when either Keith or some friends he was showing around didn't lock the gate right, our goats got out of their pasture and ate our apple trees. They completely stripped four of the trees down to the wood, and badly damaged six others. They were 4-year-old trees, just coming into blossom for the first time.

Keith loved those trees, and has never been overly fond of goats. He was ready to shoot every last one of them on the spot. I convinced him to sell them instead.

We let the word out, and right away sold two young nanny goats to a retired couple for $25 and $30. We got $50 each for three of our four milkers, bringing our running sales total to $205. But the last milker and four little nannies had no takers despite ads in the paper and signs posted in the feed store and all over.

Friends of ours were going to a livestock auction, and asked if we wanted to bring our goats. At that point it seemed like our only option.

It turned out better than I had anticipated. Our animals looked the best of the 18 goats there. We got $35 for Nicky, and a total of $73 for the four nannies. All went to different homes, and I got a good feeling that they'd be taken care of. We netted $108 at the auction, almost exactly what we had hoped to sell them for privately. That meant the whole herd sold for $313.

Then, classified ads in hand, I traveled all over the state looking for a family milk cow to replace the goats. I saw some pretty sad animals that some people wanted an awful lot of money for.

Finally, I visited Springdale Farm in the town of Waldo, where I found a beautiful, bred, registered Jersey heifer, a 4-H project, that farmer Colby Whitcomb was selling for $275. Her name was Jolly.

So we bought Jolly with the money we got from selling the goats.

June 17, 1976 (cont'd)

I liked the goats, but I was looking forward to a cow. I'm hoping the cow will pay for her keep in extra milk sales, and maybe butter sales if I get ambitious.

Rebecca was very good about all the exchange of livestock. By the way, we now have six turkeys and six ducks, about 3 weeks old...

We're all fine here. The garden is in, Keith is very busy with carpentry jobs, both at home and away, and I can never seem to find the time to write the stories I need or want to do. Keith has built a lovely staircase to the upstairs and has started to partition the upstairs off into rooms. It used to be such a hassle getting anything up or down on that ladder, this is a real luxury.

Keith didn't exactly make an outhouse, but he did make considerable improvements down there. We now have a box with a real toilet seat on it, over the hole. Not bad, actually. I've been getting on him a lot lately because we do have people coming here, and I get embarrassed when they ask us where our outhouse is.

Chapter 21 — More News and Letters

> Living around here sure makes one appreciate the little things in life.
> The outing on the island was quite an experience. In brief, we helped this young guy, Keith's age, round up what was left of his grandfather's sheep, seven on each of two islands, and shear them. Then, taking one fleece, we dyed the wool five colors from dyes we found on the island. Like pink from a lichen found on the rocks, and yellow from old man's beard, a fungus that hangs down from dead tree branches, things like that. It was all a big success, I got some nice shots, and I made some good friends in the process. We were out from Saturday morning to Wednesday afternoon.
> Eliot is trying to talk two of his summer helpers into baking bread this summer for his stand. They came down to talk to me, and I gave them the facts of life (like about $40 a week profit) and I think they were a bit dazed when they left. Don't know if I talked them out of it or not. Sure did bring back memories, though. I learned a lot doing it, but I'm glad it's over. I might even end up enjoying this summer, for a change.
> Our friend who had miscarried the previous summer finally had her baby Tuesday, only about six weeks after she first expected it. It was a boy. They haven't named him yet.
> Looks like we'll be getting a chance to test your theory on false labor. We went to the hospital in the wee hours of June 7 with what sure felt like the same signals I had had with Rebecca. And heeding the doctor's warning about this one probably happening quicker the second time around, we headed to Blue Hill when they felt nice and regular, about 5-10 minutes apart. Even had a good one on the last hill down to the hospital. Then, at the first sight of the hospital, nothing else happened worth mentioning. Sure was a let-down. I was all psyched up for it then, and for a few days afterward. It was really bad on Keith because he had worked a 14-hour day that day and had just gotten to sleep about an hour before I woke him up. Almost had a repeat last Sunday morning about 2 a.m. Keith told me to drink some wine, which we had heard would help in premature labor, and rolled over. I did, it worked fine, and I haven't had anything serious-feeling happen since. In fact, I think it'll be a while now.
> Oh yes, I forgot to tell you. My article in Yankee Magazine is scheduled for the September issue. But they decided they wanted color pictures for it, so Sunday I took some more shots of Mary Chase working her flax and sent them off. Hope they come out. The editor said it might mean another $100 or so if they do.

As that spring of 1976 came and went and summer approached, my journalistic skills were growing along with my belly. At many of the local government meetings I covered, I found myself trading weight gains and symptoms with Hugh Bowden, then a reporter and editor for the ***Weekly Packet*** in Blue Hill, whose wife Cathy was also about to contribute to the local population explosion.

I knew I had a very interesting life. It felt great to be so involved in my community, to have the personal and the professional merging at so many levels. Besides that, I had a loving husband (sure he was grumpy and moody at times, but nobody's perfect, certainly not me), a beautiful daughter, and a son on the way. Both Keith and I had interesting part-time jobs that used our individual talents, enough to provide for our needs. Our homestead, built with our own hands (with more than a little help from our friends), was making progress just about every day.

With a little variation on the Nearing theme, we were living the good life we had sought by moving to the Maine woods.

What more could I want from life?

Chapter 22
Heidi

With all the pregnant women on the Blue Hill Peninsula that bicentennial year, it looked like Helen's hope for a third generation was being fulfilled. Melissa, Heidi, and Becca would have many younger playmates within our back-to-the-land social circle.

I was already looking forward to the time when our five kids, Susie's and mine, would be old enough to casually pop in on each other, to live in each other's homes like I did when I was a little girl growing up on Youngstown's east side where the houses stood side by side on narrow city lots, and the back yards and sidewalks were our playgrounds.

So I wasn't entirely surprised one day late that spring of 1976 when I caught a glimpse of three-and-a-half-year-old Heidi in her bright yellow slicker, bopping along barefoot on the path through the woods between the Coleman campground and our clearing. I had been expecting it to start happening, just not quite this soon.

Dancing between the tree trunks to music only she could hear, Heidi's sprite-like form appeared like a specter, or like an Irish elf visible only to believers. She moved quickly, clearly on a mission.

Glancing at the napping Becca, I rushed out to intercept her.

"Hello Heidi."

"Hi." Head down, she was pressing on despite my interruption.

"Where are you going?"

"Helen's," she said firmly.

"Does Helen know you're coming?"

Heidi hesitated.

"You're going there all by yourself?"

She nodded confidently.

"Does your mother know where you are?"

She pondered the question. "Yes," she finally said quietly.

Right, I thought. Been there, done that.

*   *   *   *   *

"Hi, Olga. What'cha doing?" my grandmother said in her thick old-country accent to her grown daughter over the phone.

"Nothing in particular. Just fixing supper."

"Where's Jeanie?"

"She's outside playing in the sandbox."

"You sure?"

"Yes, I'm sure."

"Maybe you better go look," Grandma said into the phone, as I nuzzled my four-year-old arms and legs into my grandma's pillow-soft body. It had been a long, half-mile walk down the cracked sidewalks and the shortcut through the woods. I was exhausted but delighted to be in my grandma's warm kitchen reeking of Ukrainian cooking.

* * * * *

We had the only phone in the neighborhood. I couldn't call Susie, like my grandmother had called my mother, to let her know where her daughter was.

"Let's go find your mother," I said, taking Heidi's hand. "I'll bet she's looking for you."

Heidi was not sure she liked this change in her plans.

"Go see Helen," she insisted.

"Let's go find mama first," I said.

We turned and started retracing the path Heidi had come down. Not half way back we met her mother, frantic in her search. Her relief at seeing Heidi was palpable.

"I've been looking everywhere for you," Susie said to her wayward daughter.

"I go see Helen," Heidi explained simply, unperturbed by her mother's distress.

"I just turned around, and she was gone," Susie said to me.

"I know," I said. "Kids are like that." How well I knew.

"Thanks for stopping her."

"No problem," I said. "I'm sure you'll get a chance to return the favor." She will if my kids are anything like me, I thought to myself.

"Come on Heidi, let's go home," Susie said, still taking deep breaths, from running or in relief I couldn't tell. "We'll go see Helen some other time."

The woman I am calling Hannah, in her late twenties at that point, had the same kind of ethereal quality I saw in Heidi. Among all of us who were pregnant that year, Hannah glowed the most. Despite her tenuous circumstances, she had a calmness and serenity that I envied.

Hannah said she knew it the instant she got pregnant that fine spring day in a place far away from Cape Rosier. And she also knew immediately that she would not be marrying the father of her child. Those facts seemed to be not at all upsetting to her, at least as she would let on.

Only recently had she told me how difficult that time in her life had been, how, when the father of her child told her to get an abortion and never contact him again, she had started to made arrangements to put her baby up for adoption.

"I had nothing to offer this child," she said. "I had no hope."

To give her baby the best start possible, Hannah had decided to spend her pregnancy in the healthiest environment she could find. Somehow she had concluded that the Coleman farm, with its clean air, good water, healthy food, and its gardens in need of tending, was that special place. She would leave it up to destiny to see what came next.

"I will never forget," she said recently, "I was weeding in the Colemans' garden. And I suddenly knew that I was supposed to raise her and that help would be there."

As I recall, her folks in another state were not exactly pleased with her choices, but she made them nonetheless. She called her parents occasionally, collect, from our phone.

In fact, that phone let us in on a lot more of what was happening in our neighbors' lives than we normally would have found out. People knew they could use our phone any time they needed it, as long as they didn't abuse the privilege. The same grocery store rules applied — local or collect calls only. Most of the time they explained who they were calling, and why, as a way of assuring us that they were not unduly taking advantage of our hospitality.

That's how things stood when summer began in late June that year. And I was getting impatient. Susie had given birth to Clara, and other friends were adding to their family trees, while all I had to show for my huge belly was a bout of false labor.

Convinced that this baby's birth would be monumental, I looked forward to a July 4 delivery. Born on the Fourth of July. It had a nice ring to it.

But the bicentennial celebration came and went. In those weeks, a couple more women friends had increased their family size while decreasing their belt notches.

Another week went by.

And then another.

And then another.

I had expected this baby to be five weeks early, like my first one. I was already three weeks beyond what I thought was my delivery date. That made me eight weeks, or two months, overdue. By that reckoning, mine had to be the longest pregnancy on record.

What was he waiting for?

And then one sunny afternoon — it was July 24 and a Saturday — Susie and Hannah came out of their woods and walked up to me in the back pasture. They asked if they could use the phone.

"Sure," I said, pleased at the unexpected visit. "What's up?"

Ashen-faced, Susie looked at Hannah.

"You go," Hannah said to Susie. "I'll tell her."

Susie turned grimly away and strode quickly toward our house.

"Tell me what?" I turned to Hannah expectantly.

Hannah took me gently by the arm, not a normal gesture among strong, independent women. I looked at her, puzzled.

"Jean, Heidi has drowned."

Her words hit like a ton of bricks.

"No! What do you mean? No!"

"I'm sorry. It's true."

"How? Where? When?"

"In the little watering pond next to the farmstand."

Her grandmother had just arrived, she said, and of course wanted to see her grandkids. Everyone started looking for the girls. Melissa came running up, but no one remembered having seen Heidi for about 20 minutes. Melissa said she and Heidi had been playing by the pond, but she got bored and went off to do something else. Susie went over to the pond and found Heidi face down in the water.

"No! Oh my God no! Have they tried…"

"No, there's no way to save her. We've all been trying. I was in my tent when someone came and told me. I know how to do mouth-to-mouth resuscitation. I was one of the ones who tried to revive her. We tried for a long time. I could hear all the water inside of her. We finally gave up. Susie is calling the police. No, no one saw it. It must have happened quickly, since no one saw her struggle. There must have been two dozen people all over the place, working right there in the garden, but no one saw it happen."

I knew the pond was not very deep, but the sides were slippery clay. And she was such a little girl.

Oh my God. Poor Susie.

I ran to the house. Susie was on the phone. I hugged her anyway, and cried with her. What do you say to someone who has just lost a child? You just cry. You just cry and try to deal with the pain in your gut, the piercing hole in your emotions. Sweet little Heidi, the China doll. Susie, who loved her so very, very much.

I was overcome with my sadness. Susie seemed numb, in a shut-down shock.

After she got off the phone, Susie just left. I heard later she had gone into the woods, screaming Heidi's name.

I was told Eliot was wild in his grief. He took the only action he could — he went storming into his workshop and built a pine box for a casket.

Alone. Six boards. No need for hinges. No need to make it very big. She was such a little girl.

Two deputy sheriffs came in response to Susie's call.

The ambulance came, a routine dispatch on a drowning call.

The doctor came, Brad Brownlow, our family doctor, in his capacity as acting coroner. He pronounced Heidi dead.

The deputies insisted she be taken by the ambulance to the hospital.

Eliot said no, no hospital. What's the point? She's dead. We'll bury her here, in an old overgrown family cemetery, over there among the cedars.

The cops said you can't do that.

Eliot said I can do that and I will do that.

She has to be embalmed, they said.

She's not going to be touched by an undertaker. She was so pure, she's not going to get pumped full of chemicals now. You leave her alone, and leave us alone and get the hell out of here.

Bewildered, and not wanting to put his quandary out over the police radio, one deputy sheriff asked Eliot if he could use his phone.

No phone, Eliot says. Nearest phone is at the neighbors.'

Can you come with us there then? the cops asked.

"Can we use your phone?" the cops asked me.

One sat at our table with Eliot, by the kerosene lamp in the early dusk, while the other called.

"This fellow here wants to bury her on the farm," the deputy sheriff said into the phone. "Doesn't he need to take her to a funeral home?...Doesn't he at least need to take her to a regular cemetery? Doesn't she need to be embalmed? Aren't there laws about all this? I don't know, I've never had one like this before. They always done it like that, as far as I knew."

After several minutes of back and forth, with people at the other end of the line checking the rules and the laws, the officer put his hand over the mouthpiece of the phone and turned to Eliot.

"Well, Mr. Coleman, it seems you can do it the way you want. She doesn't need to be embalmed. And she can be buried in an already-established cemetery on your own property, which there is. The only thing you need is a permit to move a body."

"The cemetery is only 600 feet away. I'm only going to move her 600 feet."

"Well, it appears you can't do that without a permit."

"Okay, where do I get the goddam permit?"

"We're trying to find that out now, Mr. Coleman. They think a judge has to issue it, if it's not an undertaker who's doing the moving. We'll get it to you as soon as we can."

"Fine. While you're getting it, I've got a hole to dig."

I seem to recall that a glitch developed, and that Eliot had to interrupt his digging and go all the way to Ellsworth to sign the official permit. Others took over the grave-digging task.

I was told the ceremony was nice. It was held in the dark, about 10 p.m., about six hours after Heidi drowned. A simple pine box, a simple hole, and a gathering of people who loved her. Eliot was there. So was Keith. Hannah said she tried to sing a song.

"Everyone was in shock. Everyone felt so helpless," Hannah said. "At the same time, it was so much a freak accident, it made you wonder. It felt like it was such a meant-to-be thing."

Hannah said Susie wasn't at the funeral. I understood.

I was not there, either. Everyone told me to stay home. Because of my condition and all. I felt fine, physically, but my mind was so numb, I obeyed.

I sat curled up on the couch in the dark. Then I moved myself to the oversized rocking chair Keith had rescued from the torn-down lodge, and tried to calm myself with the rhythmic movement. Listening to the little noises my own baby Becca made asleep in her crib, I could make no sense of it all.

The safe homestead, the best place to raise kids, gone savage. It wasn't a charging bull, or a sharp cutter blade on a haying machine, the things you guard against. It was the little tiny pond, not even four feet deep in the middle. The pretty pond they used to water the baby plants when they needed some encouragement. The place to lie down flat next to big sister Melissa and watch polliwogs grow. A little tranquil pool of water — like my grandmother's lily pond.

Serenity gone killer.

This shouldn't have happened, my mind screamed.

Not to Heidi.

Not to us.

Not here.

There is no crime here in the woods. No bears left on the Cape, or other animals that could hurt us, things that would harm our babies. Our doors don't even have locks. We should escape death also.

After all, wasn't that really why we came, why we were out here? Weren't we out here to escape all that?

So, if this could happen to sweet Heidi, what in life is safe? What then could we count on?

Nothing?

Heidi Coleman, Heidi-Ho, Ho, Hodie — living on a beautiful Eden of a farm that was carved out of the wilderness by her folks, with an older sister she adored and a baby sister not quite two months old, a child being raised in love and freedom by parents trying so hard to protect her and her sisters against all the harshness the outside world had to offer — lively, sprite-like, adventuresome, unvaccinated Heidi, drowning at the age of 3½. It was beyond my comprehension.

Why would God do such a thing?

I slept fitfully that night. At three o'clock in the morning, I went into labor. I was surprised at this development. No one else was. I had been so busy grieving over Heidi that I had completely forgotten about my own over-ripe condition.

I gave birth to my son Dagan about 9 o'clock that morning in the Blue Hill Hospital. And once again, my regular doctor did not make the delivery. But this time it was not a phone mix-up, or a trip out of town. Unaware of my labor in those days before pagers, Dr. Brownlow was out at the Coleman farm, trying to help everyone there deal with their grief. As I cursed the stand-in doctor, a jerk of a man who insisted on forceps and refused to wait for my next expelling contraction, causing me to bruise internally and to rip terribly during my son's forced extraction, I at the same time could not begrudge Susie and Eliot the kind solace I knew Dr. Brownlow was at that very moment providing them in their anguish.

That Sunday afternoon, as I lay in the hospital bed, trying to get a handle on the mix of joy and pain in my heart, I suddenly realized I had neglected another duty. I called the newspaper, to make sure they knew Heidi had drowned.

Sorry not to have called earlier, I explained, but I was busy having my baby. You'll have to take it from here, I won't be filing the story. And, oh yeah, I'll be needing some time off.

This appeared on the front page of Monday's paper:

2 die in drownings

Separate drowning incidents took the lives of two persons in Maine Saturday, police officials said.

Heidi Coleman, 3, died Saturday in a shallow farm pond on her parents' Harborside farm. She was the daughter of Elliot and Susan Coleman. Hancock Sheriff Robert Williams was not available to provide details of the apparent accidental drowning.

A Waterboro man was the victim of an apparently overcrowded boat when the craft capsized off Woods Island.

A search held Saturday and Sunday failed to locate the body of Kenneth MacCorison, 32, who was in a 15-foot boat when it was swamped by water Saturday evening.

No follow-up news story appeared. And there was no obituary.

Shortly after Heidi's death, Susie penned a poem on construction paper, and decorated it with painted flowers. She gave a copy to Helen, who kept it close to her heart. Years later I was shown the poem, tacked firmly into the wooden wall in the inner corner of Helen's bedroom.

Susie has given me permission to reprint it.

In Memory of Heidi

Ho was a Sprite; She loved Life and Feared Little.
To All of Us Who Had the Privilege
Of Knowing her, She Taught Us
Many Things About The Little Secrets
of Living
Hodie Lived More Beautifully
in Three
Years than most live ever.
Ho longed "to reach the sky"
And in her own way she did
And Now Heidi's Delightful Refreshing
Spirit Lingers Everywhere
and in
Every Living Thing.
When the Sun is Shining
Ho is Smiling.
Sleep Well Ho
We Love You

Two weeks after Heidi's death, I found myself writing a news story about Scott Nearing's 93rd birthday, celebrating the fact that he had two books published in the previous five years, was in the process of building a new house, and was looking to the future. The irony was not lost on either of us.

Ten months after Heidi's death, the governor signed into law new legislation that permitted families to bury a relative without going through the expense of a professional funeral. The family could authorize a funeral director or some other person to obtain the necessary documents to transport and dispose of a dead human body.

I have wondered quietly, ever since that fateful weekend, if my son Dagan had indeed been waiting for something. With the odd juxtaposition of Heidi's death and Dagan's birth — her untimely exit from and his delayed entry into this place we call Earth — I have often contemplated the phenomenon Helen had never doubted — reincarnation. And in some strange way I have been comforted by the possibility.

Over the years, as we celebrated Dagan's birthday, I usually made a point of mentioning how Heidi had drowned on the farm next door the day before he was born. I think Dagan took my comments as Mom's strange way of dampening his festivities. I didn't specifically share my thoughts about reincarnation — until the day my lively, sprite-like, adventuresome young teenage son said his new snorkeling equipment that he had gotten for his birthday was really great, a lot of fun, and not only that, was helping him get over his fear of water.

"You have a fear of water?" I asked softly of this young man who had spent much of his life on the coastal waters and rivers of Maine, both in and out of canoes and kayaks.

"Sure do," he said matter-of-factly, "especially dark water with slippery, slimy bottoms."

"That figures," I said, as shivers went up my spine.

"Why does that figure?" he asked.

So I told him.

Chapter 23

And the World Came Tumbling After

After Heidi's death, nothing was quite the same.

I had learned the hard way that yet another one of my basic premises was wrong — you can try so hard to follow the greatest plan for living you can find or put together, and sometimes you can still get blindsided by something so awful that it will change you and those around you forever. Sometimes, no matter how much you might want to, you just can't go back to some other point in your life and pick up where you left off.

It wasn't so much a sense of fear that I was feeling, as it was the sad appreciation every day that everyone in our little family was alive and healthy.

As I went about my chores, I paused long enough to watch in wonderment as my children grew up before my eyes.

I noticed when my young daughter's face started to lose its baby fat and take on childhood contours.

We celebrated new teeth, new successful coordination of movements — walking, drawing, somersaults.

Holidays took on added meaning. They marked the successful progression of time.

With all that external tumult and internal turmoil, I yearned for a closer connection with my husband — at a time when so many of our friends seemed to be breaking up.

Eliot and Sue were again having troubles. So were Greg Summers and his girlfriend. One friend was on the verge of divorcing the husband who had refused to follow her to the Maine woods. Two other couples were reportedly having serious problems.

I wanted Keith and me to be the rock in the middle of the storm.

But Heidi's death seemed to have had a different effect on Keith than they did on me. He grew moodier, more distant. He spent more time in the woods, ostensibly hunting, or on the water in a canoe.

I suggested to Keith that we go canoeing as a family. Just a short trip even. Keith said the kids were too young, we would have to wait until next year. I suggested he and I go alone. He said there was no one to watch the kids. I said I wanted to go with him, just the two of us, we could find a sitter. He said he was too tired.

Meanwhile, other bad things were happening to people in our small community.

That year, fire swept through the office of *WoodenBoat* magazine in South Brooksville. Publisher Jon Wilson of North Brooksville had started the magazine in his primitive cabin in the woods a few years before, with the phone tacked to a post outside the family's home so as to not disturb the tranquility of their simple and quiet living situation.

Ultra-quaint, but true.

The magazine's needs soon outgrew that arrangement, so Jon moved the operation to a house overlooking one of the saltwater coves on the other side of town.

The crew was about to send off the layout sheets for the 16th edition when fire swept through the old building. Wilson said that miraculously, very little irreplaceable material was lost, thanks to the quick action of firefighters and other volunteers.

A disgruntled neighbor who apparently didn't like people "from away" was later charged with arson in the case.

In August Horsepower Farm in Penobscot, owned by Paul and Mollie Birdsall, was sprayed by a plane dusting a nearby wild blueberry field with the toxic pesticide Guthion.

I'll bet you thought "wild" blueberries meant pristine, untouched by sprayed pesticides or herbicides.

Think again.

Horsepower Farm was certified organic, and since that certification required a farm to be pesticide-free for three years, the pilot's mistake cost Birdsall three years of organic sales. The pilot was fined $1,200 by the state's Pesticide Control Board, and he lost his license to spray that fall — a time when not much spraying takes place anyhow. The pilot got his license back the following spring.

Then came another tragic death. On December 14, 1976, farmer Rob Hohner of North Brooksville was dragging some logs out of the woods with his tractor. As he tried to crest the steep hill with his heavy load, the tractor flipped over backwards on its big rear wheels, crushing him underneath. He was 28, a year younger than me.

I couldn't help but think of all the hung-up trees Keith had successfully dislodged, and how any one of them could just as easily have made me a widow like Rob's wife Pam.

And then, on Monday, January 17, 1977, those of us living in the northern two-thirds of Maine who had heard vague rumblings of discontent from the local Native Americans the past few years, awoke to discover we might not actually own the land beneath our own homes.

Non-Indians' eviction urged in state area

PORTLAND, Maine (AP) — The Department of Interior has recommended the eviction of 350,000 non-Indians living in the northern two-thirds of Maine. The suggestion is the heart of a preliminary report on the validity of land ownership claims made by two Indian tribes.

The draft report says Maine should give the Penobscot and Passamaquoddy Indians everything they've asked for — more than 12.5 million acres of land and at least $300 million in back rents and damages.

...One stumbling block brought out in the report is the need to identify each landowner in the disputed northern two-thirds of the state to determine the 18th century origin of all land titles.

...The lawsuit, first filed in 1972 on behalf of the two tribes, said tribal lands were seized in violation of the 1790 Indian Non-Intercourse Act. The Act forbids removal, transfer or taking of aboriginal Indian land without Congressional approval.

Chapter 24
In and Out of Focus

December 26, 1976

We had a truly wonderful Christmas this year, the best Keith and I can remember having. Rebecca got gobs and gobs of stuff, and the rest of us got things that we wanted. Thanks so much for all the stuff you sent, and for the stuff your check made possible.

We had candles on the tree that were incomparable to any Christmas lights I have ever seen. Thanks for the tree ornaments, too. They're lovely, engraved and all. Where did you get them? We got two stained-glass ones this year from a friend who does that for a living. Maybe someday we'll have a tree with only special ornaments on it.

We ate one of our own turkeys, and kept to our family (including Darryl) all day. Seemed around here to be the year for staying home for Christmas.

And to top it all off, Christmas night (last night) Jolly finally came through and had her calf, a little heifer. Mother and daughter are doing fine. I want to name her Holly Jolly Christmas (Holly for short), but I seem to be getting a lot of flak from the folks here. We're going to sell her since we won't be needing another cow for many years. Jolly is 3, and should be able to be milked for 12 or more years.

We missed seeing the calf born. I had such a strong feeling, checked Jolly three times before I went to bed. But the last time she was still chewing her cud and looking very comfortable, so I figured that I was just an old biddy with my intuition and let it go at that. This morning we found her with the calf, still a bit wet, but probably a couple of hours old.

I don't think I told you — Hannah had her baby Dec. 2, a beautiful 8-pound girl. Full head of hair. It was a 16-hour labor, not too bad, but longer than she expected, I'm afraid. She recuperated a lot faster than I did, however, looked great after two days. She's home with her folks in New York now for the holidays. She's living with Greg Summers and his new girlfriend, who live the next drive after Colemans. They have a very nice cozy cabin....

Dagan's sleeping habits are getting better, but ever so slowly. Keith has taken to calling him Dragon because of all the sleep he's lost to the fellow in the wee hours of the morning. Sometimes I can catch a nap in the middle of the day, but Keith doesn't have that option. I sure don't remember Rebecca being this noisy....

Well, it's almost eight o'clock and I'm dead tired. I've got my first real milking and calf-feeding to look forward to tomorrow morning. Got milk customers lined up starting on Tuesday. Have plans for making cheese and all sorts of goodies. As if I didn't have anything else to do with my time.

March 4, 1977

I guess 5 a.m. isn't such a bad time to write, if Dagan's up to keep me company anyhow.

We sold our calf last week, for $75, with no trouble, just put an ad in the paper. Bought three pigs about 10 weeks old, good size, plus a bag of pig food, for the money, with even a little left over. Pretty good trade-off.

We got our hot water system in last week too. Keith spent two days crawling under the house, running for parts and soldering pipes together and we now more or less have hot water on command. To make the gravity feed system work with that hot water tank, he had to sink the tank into the floor. Otherwise it was too high and wouldn't work. The water is still warm in the 25-gallon tank in the morning, and gets up to close to boiling pretty quickly. Sure makes it a heck of a lot easier to do the dishes. We can even take a bath now at the drop of a hat, instead of taking up the whole stove top with that big galvanized tub to heat water with. I was surprised at the difference it made, since we usually have a big pot of water heating on the stove anyhow. I know you think we're crazy, but we still get a lot of joy out of the little things.

I have a small article, couple of paragraphs and a picture, on a local furniture-maker coming out in the March Yankee Magazine. Not much, but it pays $25. It'll be under their Small Businesses and Crafts section. I have another tentative okay from Maine Magazine for the story I wrote on those people who do fireworks. They want it re-written a bit because they want it for their Business section and they need more figures on what it took to get started and how it's doing. I wrote it on the human interest side and didn't put much of that in....

I've sent off an application for Becca to go to nursery school next fall. She gets so little contact with kids her age. The school for 3-year-olds is two hours a day, twice a week. It only costs $5 per month, so that's no problem. It will be a problem to get her there, however. It's in Blue Hill, about 20 miles from here. I'm hoping I'll find someone else going there from around here so we can trade off.

Keith has been clearing out in back of the upper garden, on the other side of the chicken coop, for more pasture land. Getting firewood at the same time. It's looking good. We figured it out that winter is the busiest time for my reporting, because that's when the town meetings happen and a lot of other things seem to be going on. And winter is Keith's slack time since you can't do much outside carpentry work in the cold. In the summer it's just the opposite. Most of the school committees and planning boards don't even meet in the summer, and Keith never seems to stop moving then. So I guess it all evens out in the long run.

Darryl is doing pretty well on his land, felling trees for lumber and beams for his house. He has had a date or two with a local girl here...

March 27, 1977, Sunday

It looks like it's finally spring around here. It's raining full force outside, and the last of the snow is going quickly. We're expecting chicks from Sears next week. We ordered 25 Barred Rocks. Not that we don't like Rhode Island Reds, but we decided to color-code our chickens. When they're all the same color, we can't tell how old a certain chicken is, whether she's ready for the stew pot or not. So we decided to order a different color of chicken each year.

We also have some bees on order for delivery in May. They're a strain from Canada that is supposed to be hardy to minus-40 degrees in northern Canada. Most people who order bees get them from Georgia, and they just don't make it through these winters here. We lost most of ours that way. So we're giving it one more try.

Keith has started working again for pay. I'm still writing for the paper. Dagan is crawling up a storm, and is just starting to sleep through the night. And just starting to cut his first teeth. Rebecca is a charmer, gets sweeter every day. Doesn't like some of the rules we've laid down, about hanging up her coat and the like, but what kid does?

Well, it's time to milk the cow again...

Hello again [same letter] It's Monday after Easter.

Don't remember if I mentioned — Susie Coleman left again, a few weeks ago. Don't know what led up to it this time, but I understand it was rather sudden. She took Clara with her, left Melissa with Eliot. Someone said they saw a woman over there with him a couple of times lately, don't have the vaguest idea who it is. I've only seen her on the road, hanging all over Eliot, who looks like he loves it. She looks like a college kid.

Anyway, Susie was back for a visit yesterday, mostly to see Melissa. She's looking into two communes, in Tennessee and Colorado, where she'll hopefully be able to do her pottery. She looked great, but was understandably reluctant to talk about Eliot — mostly because Melissa was with her. I guess she'll take Melissa when she gets settled.

Keith is out checking clam flats. He's clam warden again this year.

We had kolachi for Easter breakfast and Ukrainian Easter bread with our own ham for lunch. Couldn't find any horseradish for the hard-boiled eggs.

Hannah is looking for a house to start a day-care center...

May 5, 1977
Happy Mother's Day!
Things have been really popping around here. I got free tickets to the Shriners Circus for last weekend from a school principal who had extras. We all went, for the first time ever. It was really great. Small time, but they had trained dogs, horses, bears, elephants (3), trapeze artists, jugglers, acrobats, the whole works. Rebecca is still talking about it. It makes a lot more sense to her now when a storybook of hers mentions the circus.

Maine Magazine is using my fireworks story in their July issue, but they've upgraded it into a full feature. They needed more stuff, so I got to visit my friends Dave and Liz Buell again. It was a good trip. They're really interesting people. (Said Dave Buell of his fireworks: "It's like painting on a black canvas at night. So what if it only last a few seconds? Lots of things in life are like that.") Wow! I'd like to invite them to the pig roast we're planning for this summer or fall.

The cherry trees are in blossom around here. The rhubarb is up, as is the asparagus. Peas are up, onions taking off. We seeded the ground above the pond to grass for hay.

Dagan has two teeth now, finally…

Have a happy Mother's Day. I'm thinking a lot about you lately, in motherly ways, now that I'm one too…

Okay, so I didn't always tell my mother everything that was going on, especially the unpleasant parts.

I have never kept a daily journal. But on occasion, when I am really upset or need to think things through, I take pen in hand. It really helps me to organize my thoughts. I thus have an eclectic collection of letters to myself, comments in the backs of working notebooks, vignettes in bound books of unlined paper, ruminations on random sheets of typing paper. This is one such entry.

Saturday, May 21, 1977
A nice pen, clean paper, a quiet spot. All necessary, because this isn't going to be easy.

It's a real crisis. At least for me it is. To Keith it's an annoyance, something I did that made a bad day for him. He says it's all my fault, that I overreacted all out of proportion to a simple statement, and blew up over nothing. Maybe he's right, but I think — somehow — that it's deeper than that.

Why did he get mad when I wanted to take a couple of pictures of him and the puppies? Am I overly sensitive lately? Am I expecting too much, of myself, of Keith, of our relationship?

…I've noticed lately that I'm not getting the love and affection I used to.

At least not the outward signs of it, the little courtesies, the "glad to see you" look when I come home. And I miss it. Lately Keith has been mostly ignoring me, tuning me out, not interested in what I do or think unless it inconveniences him — i.e., no butter. Maybe from that, I notice the discourtesies all the more.

...And when I try to do things on my own, for me alone, I'm shot down too. Disapproval. I'm not tending to my important duties — cooking, cleaning house, watching kids, helping him around the farm. And as for my newspaper work, after all it's just gossip (or so he says). Even though I do it well, it brings in much needed money, and I enjoy it, it's somehow frivolous, extraneous to my real work.

...I'm ruled by conflicting forces. I want to be independent and dependent at the same time. I can function quite well in the business world, but that is frowned upon in this household. So I am good at, and enjoy, something of very low esteem around here — but something of high esteem elsewhere. What a mess! On the other hand, that money from that "gossip" sure comes in handy, and if I can concentrate on that, I won't be nagging Keith. But if I concentrate on it too much, everything else, including Keith, gets out of focus.

Is Keith having as much trouble reconciling my roles as I am? He says he likes my money-earning, but I think he fears loss of his personal status as breadwinner in direct proportion to my paycheck. He resents my writing, even though he tries not to. To him it's superfluous, and very unseemly that it manages to pay money.

... I'm a security nut, born and raised. Security is a cow in the barn with a year's hay, no mortgage, and a happy family. Two out of three ain't bad.

Sunday afternoon, May 22

Things are better now, tempers have cooled. Keith is feeling better, after a good dope trip with Sarah. I wish I could find a release like that. Too much booze and I get morose. I've never had a good drunk. Maybe I should try the pipe next time it's passed around, even though I don't like smoke. I should give it a chance. (Keith would approve.) I need a way to relax at times, to give vent to built-up emotions....

And so it came to pass that the next time the pot pipe was passed around, I did not excuse myself from the circle or just pass it on to the next person.

I took a puff.

It was only the second time I tried to inhale. One drag on a cigarette in my youth was enough to keep me from becoming a tobacco smoker. I didn't like either the sensation or the taste. I know it helped immeasurably that my folks didn't smoke. But I also had discovered that the smell of stale tobacco smoke on the breath and clothing was nauseating. And more importantly to my penny-pinching mind, cigarettes cost too much. I couldn't see sending all that money up in smoke.

Despite repeated encouragement, I had refrained from joining the marijuana crowd at gatherings on Cape Rosier because I wasn't impressed by what I saw — reasonably intelligent people turning into babbling idiots who thought any stupid pronouncement or observation they made while under the influence was the height of brilliance. The form of recreation I enjoy most in life is a good conversation, and any hopes of that came to an end as soon as the pipe or joint was lit. I couldn't understand, then or now, why people would want to deliberately dull what senses they had. I think it takes a certain personality type. And clearly I didn't qualify.

Self-imposed stupidity, giddiness, fading off into quiet slumber, usually on whatever piece of furniture or floor they then happened to be perched — that was what I saw. But that was all I saw. I couldn't verify, through my empirical and detached observations, any dangerous effects of the drug that would prompt the government's hysterical condemnation.

Sure, it slowed down response time, just as alcohol did. It should be, and is, against the law to drive while either drunk or stoned. And in all likelihood, continued frequent use could result in long-term health affects, just like tobacco and alcohol.

But why tobacco and alcohol were legal, regulated and taxed, and marijuana filled up our jails and prisons and ruined people's lives and reputations, made no sense to me, then or now.

The other thing that struck me was the pacifying aspect of marijuana. I have seen several mean drunks, but I have never seen a mean pot-head. Whining pot-heads, yes, but not mean or violent.

Turns out, on that point at least, I wasn't the only one who noticed:

Marijuana used for tranquilizing

NEW YORK (AP) — Marijuana did not have the socially disruptive effects that alcohol use did in a group of adolescent delinquent boys, Stanford University researchers reported Tuesday.

Despite the fact that the two drugs were used with about the same frequency, alcohol use was greater in fights, difficulties with police and other authorities, trouble with family or friends and automobile accidents.

Marijuana was used by the youths for tranquilizing purposes to avoid difficulties and described by the youths as reducing "assaultiveness," while alcohol was used deliberately to "bolster courage." ...

— *Bangor Daily News* January 28, 1976

We weren't too worried about getting busted, down there in the woods. Heck, we were so far out in the boonies they wouldn't even come out to enforce the hunting laws. We were safe. (Although, when the military helicopters flew low overhead, I couldn't tell if Keith was nervous because of a flashback to his war experience, or for some other reason.)

I did refuse to allow Keith to grow pot in our regular gardens. I assume he had a patch out back, possibly not even on our property. I never asked, and he never told me. But supply never seemed to be a problem. Someone always had a cache. And everyone was willing to share. I never saw money change hands. (As a local legislator would say years later in explaining why prostitution was not a problem in his town: "Why pay for it if you can get it for nothing?")

But desperate times call for desperate measures. And I was getting desperate. I wanted my husband back. Maybe I was being an up-tight biddy. Maybe this was an experience we could share.

Members of the group nodded approvingly as I took my first toke. I coughed only slightly. They proceeded to grove out. I waited to see what would happen.

The experience did not live up to its advanced billing. Yes, I got a little fuzzy-headed, and perceptions became a bit distorted. But the smoke did not relax me or make me happy. I did not like that loss of control. As those around me became giggly, I got not only depressed, but downright morose. Just like alcohol's affect on me.

To my "never again" the next day, Keith said I just hadn't gotten enough of the stuff to have the right reaction. And with my sensitivity to smoke, maybe brownies would be better.

He whipped up a batch on the spot, adding extra greenery just to be sure.

I ate two brownies — and lost the next two days. I got so sick I thought I was going to die. Throwing up didn't help. I kept fading into and out of consciousness, to Keith's repeated weeping apologies.

"I'm sorry honey. I'm so sorry."

"I must have put in too much."

"I just wanted you to have a good high."

"I pushed you too far too fast. How are you feeling now?"

"This is all my fault. I'm so sorry, sweetie. You know I wouldn't ever do anything to hurt you."

In my more lucid moments I remember agreeing with Keith that he shouldn't take me to the hospital, even though that was where I belonged at that point. I needed my stomach pumped. But that would be walking into the lion's den. The doctor would probably have to report the overdose. And both of us would probably end up arrested. What would happen to the kids if we were in jail? Okay, the state of Maine had reduced marijuana possession to a misdemeanor that year, but that fact was not forefront in my foggy brain. And the shame would still be there. What about my job with the paper? Keith would surely lose his job as Clam Warden. And my mother — my mother would never understand.

Fear of public disgrace was the overriding factor, outweighing even what felt like the very real possibility of death.

I eventually came to.

Keith never again suggested I imbibe.

June 15, 1977
I'm stuck in a very dull meeting, so I'll see if I can write you a letter....

The garden looks great this year. The crows got all the corn when it rained for 10 days solid, but everything else is doing fine. Our sweet cherry tree had some beautiful blossoms this year, and it looks like we'll even get a few cherries, despite the goats eating the tree that was supposed to cross-pollinate with it.

We're trying to seed every bare piece of ground we have outside the garden to grass for the cow. It's slow, but it's coming. We've applied for pasture seeding funds through the extension office, for seeds, lime and manure, but we haven't heard yet. I'd like 2-3 acres in grass, and maybe two more in hay. I think we'd be all set then.

Keith is getting disillusioned with his Clam Warden job. He doesn't seem able to please anybody no matter how much time he puts into it. It's a thankless job. I think he'll be quitting it soon.

I think that's about all the news. The meeting is wrapping up anyway…

By now the cow had eaten down everything edible in our crude goat pasture, and Keith had resorted to cutting grass for the her every day in a field about two miles away. That took an awful lot of time, and it was clear the fresh fodder would not last the summer, or even until the newly sown grass in patches around our place grew into anything of substance.

Meanwhile, I was watching the established lush green grass growing up around the house and under the clothesline. I suggested to Keith that we should fence in that area and let the cow do a little mowing. He said he didn't have the time to do everything he had to do already, why was I adding another thing to that list?

So while he was gone one day, I set up a makeshift fence. I pounded a few stakes in the ground, not all of them straight. I nailed on a few plastic insulators. I ran a length of electric fence wire from the gate of the pasture, down the hill, around behind the clothesline poles, ending at the corners of the house. Since the dark green of the fir trees in the background made the gray steel wire practically invisible, I tied strips of bright orange surveyor's tape at intervals along the wire, so the cow could see her new border. It wasn't the prettiest sight to behold, but I figured it would do the job.

I attached the wire to the fence charger. Then I let her out.

Hesitant at first, she warily eyed the tape markers on the fence as I led her to the clothesline. Then she saw the grass. Head down, she plowed right in.

I stood there and smiled, knowing I was watching the transformation of chlorophyll and cellulose into milk. And I liked the idea that Jolly was performing double-duty — I wouldn't have to scythe the grass growing up around the house, or hand-trim the tufts around the many obstacles in the yard, like the posts holding up the clothesline. The cow was taking care of those details just fine.

When Keith came home and saw what I had done, he stormed into the house and refused to talk to me for three days.

Chapter 25

Shopping Around

July 30, 1977, Saturday

Thank you for Dagan's birthday present... We had a small party for him, just Keith's family and us. Had the last of our last-year's turkeys, out of the freezer. It was kind of weird, because we ate on a picnic table down by the pond, and while we're cutting into this 19-pound turkey, all the other turkeys for this year (six of them) were pecking around in the grass around the table.

This has been one hectic summer so far. I've been making yogurt and cottage cheese for sale along with the milk. Keith made a sign for the top of the driveway. We've been doing pretty well on the sales.

But we finally decided the other day that we're really not set up right to do a cow. To do it right, we would need a barn for the cow and the hay, and about an acre of good pasture, plus a decent hayfield. That's a lot of building, clearing, stump pulling, plowing, seeding, fertilizing and liming for one cow. And the land right here is not the best for a pasture no matter how much work we put into it. It's either too rocky or too wet. Also, if we didn't have to store winter hay in our upstairs, we could put a badly-needed bedroom or two up there.

All that, added to the fact that we can buy raw milk from Dick Chase, who has three milking Jerseys, made us decide that we're beating our heads against the wall for no real reason.

So we've put an ad in the paper to sell her. Only two calls so far, and no buyers yet. It's been a hard decision for me to make, because I've been milking cows or goats for four years now, but I think it's the right decision. I'll sure miss that cow, though. She's a good one, gentle, even-tempered, and does give good milk. We're asking $350 for her. We bought her for $275. She's re-bred to calve in January. Hope we can come up with someone who has the facilities to treat her right. But if we don't get more calls than we've had so far, looks like we might be keeping her for awhile. The place won't seem like a farm without a cow, though.

The gardens and the outside carpentry work have been keeping Keith pretty busy this summer. The garden is finally spurting ahead, after going nowhere in June. It'll still be close on the tomatoes and corn, but we've put 32 quarts of peas in the freezer so far, with two more rows of peas just coming in... A lot of summer people need houses repaired or fixed up. Then in the fall the pig butchering will start. Keith says it doesn't bother him like it used to.

Keith and I went out to dinner and a movie last week. Found a great Chinese restaurant in Bangor that's very reasonable (most meals were under $6), and absolutely delicious....

About the lights going out in New York — it seems hard for us to comprehend all the rioting and looting going on just because the electricity went off. What a precarious measure of civilization.

Eliot's holding a seminar, three in fact, this summer, where people pay him $125 to come for two weeks and hear him talk. I understand he's running into some trouble because some of his "students" aren't the dumb bunnies that are content to turn over his compost piles. They have chemistry and biology degrees, and Eliot just doesn't have the background (Spanish) to handle the questions they came to ask.

Nearings are into their new house, and it's beautiful. Seems a family, the Becks, will be moving into Nearings' old house next month, late. They have two kids, one five and one eight. That will be great for Rebecca, because that's not very far to walk, and she'll have someone almost her age to play with. Melissa doesn't come down very often, and right now she's with her mother in Colorado....

It's Sunday. We sold the cow last night to a farmer with more than 100 cows and 500 acres about 50 miles from here. I cried when she left, but she got a good home and company again. She came from a herd of 80. Suddenly today I discovered I have a lot of extra time, which I guess I usually spent worrying about the cow, or at least thinking about her, or cutting her grass, or making sure she wasn't tangled in the stake-out rope or gone through the electric fence. I told Hannah we'd sold the cow, and her first reaction was, "Wonderful. Now you're a free woman." It's true, and slowly dawning on me. In fact, we're talking about taking a week or so off this fall or winter, something we never even considered before this. I think it'll turn out all right.

I'm planning a "Spirit of '76" party next Sunday, for all the babies born last year. We missed a mother's party like that on Dagan's birthday because of Keith's family being here. I'm looking forward to it, and so are the few I've mentioned it to so far....

October 1, 1977

Some startling news. Susie Coleman is back, Eliot is gone, apparently more or less for good. Eliot is planning on taking a job as a manager of a 180-acre farm in western Massachusetts. Some guy he knows owns this place as a summer place, but if he can get it to be a producing farm, he can get a property tax break, and probably a break on his income taxes, especially if it doesn't make any money. Eliot will be managing it, plans to get some dairy cows, grow some vegetables to sell in Boston, and plans on making cheese out of the milk and selling the whey to a greenhouse grower in Boston who uses the stuff to grow plants hydroponically (with their roots in water instead of dirt). Sounds a bit bizarre, but that's Eliot. Right now he's on one of three European Farm Tours he's conducting this fall, before he goes to Massachusetts. Melissa is going with him, which surprised me. Seems she's tired of school here, and since it doesn't matter to Eliot or Sue if she misses school, she's going with Eliot. Sue will have Clara with her, she was a year old in May.

Susie looks better than I've ever seen her. She's into pottery now, and wants to do that here. Can't decide yet whether to do the whole vegetable stand bit yet. I don't think she's cut out for that big a job, but that's her decision.

I like the whole arrangement, because the biggest complaint we had about this area was all the hoards of people who have been crawling all over the place the past few years. First it was the Nearings, but that has calmed down a bit. But Eliot and his seminars and his apprentices and his apostles more than took up the slack. It'll be nice around here next summer. I hope.

The Becks, our new neighbors who moved into Nearings' old house, are very nice, but are very discouraged already. They're trying to go vegetarian and start homesteading at the same time, and couldn't figure out why they were so tired. I told them why, that we had done the same thing and found it was for the birds. If you're a veggie when you start homesteading, that's one thing. But to drastically reduce protein and at the same time burn up more calories is more than a body should have to contend with. They were a bit startled, but seemed to think I made some sense.

Also, Helen is starting in as Helen usually does, telling them one thing one minute, and changing it the next day, denying she ever said the first thing. They don't know how much she intends to charge them in rent or how much she wants them to pay for the house should they decide to buy it next summer — she keeps changing the amounts.

I told them there's a lot more to Helen and Scott Nearing than gardening in the country, and they said "Boy, is there ever!" I think they're kindred souls, and I think they could make it at homesteading, but not down there. We'll have to get to know them better, I think they're good people. They're in their mid-thirties I would say, and have two boys, ages 5 and 8.

Rebecca has been going to nursery school for two weeks now, in Blue Hill, two days a week for two hours each day. She seems to really like it, although the first couple of times she said there were too many kids (twelve). She doesn't say that anymore, so I think she's getting to know them better. Another mother and I trade off taking them in, so I only have to go once a week. I do my laundry and shopping while Rebecca's in school. She's learning some songs, which I catch her singing every now and then. I think that's great, because she doesn't get that from me. I just don't know that many little kid songs.

We had a pig roast a couple of weeks ago. Plans began last spring when a friend of ours went in with us on a pig. We killed it at about 85 pounds and put it, whole, in the freezer. Got it out, spitted it over a good fire, and invited about 50 people to dance, pig out and pot luck. Also had a make-shift sauna down by the pond. It was a really great party. Started about three in the afternoon, and everyone was gone by 9:30 or 10. Not bad, not too late...

I don't know if I wrote you, but I'm down on the **Bangor Daily News** of late. Starting in August, they decided to pay their correspondents (that's me) on a different wage scale. They upped what they pay per inch from 50 to 60 cents, but cut out paying for all expenses (postage, long distance phone calls, car mileage) and also cut out paying the minimum wage for sitting through long meetings like school committee meetings. It comes out to me getting about half what I was getting for the same amount of work.

So I haven't been doing much newspaper writing lately, mostly stuff I can get easily, by a local phone call or by mail, or by a short stop at the superintendent's office...

As a result, I've been looking into other ways to make some money, and I've hit on an idea or two, which I hope will work out.

On Monday I'm going to find out if I can rent space in Blue Hill, right in the center of town, and open a small store for fruit, fresh garden vegetables, cheese, nuts, and possibly some wooden kitchen utensils. I know, crazy, but just as I always wanted to have a bakery, I have also wanted to have a market like that. I had the bakery (more or less) when I did baking for the farmstands. I learned a lot, and got that out of my system. I think this has a lot more potential for profit, and there is not another store around anywhere here that offers what I would like to offer. I only intend to have it open June, July, August and September, to get the people who have a lot of money who live in Blue Hill or around here in the summer, and who do a lot of entertaining. A lot of the loose ends are pulling together already, but I won't know until Monday if I can get the place. The guy who owns the building told me to see him then...

Coincidentally, one of our former milk customers was over the other day visiting (one of those rich summer people) and I happened to mention my wild idea. It happens that she owned and ran a gourmet shop in Princeton, N.J. until just recently when she sold it. She was very enthusiastic, and went home and drew me up a list of at least 14 cheeses I might want to stock, how well they keep, and where I can get them — the suppliers she had. Wow! We also talked a bit about marking stuff up, and she gave me some good pointers.

The store could be a good outlet for surplus garden stuff, from our garden mostly, plus some of our friends. I was thinking of having it open Tuesday through Saturday, 10 a.m. to 5:30 p.m. Keith has been very cooperative about the whole thing. I'm obviously enthusiastic about it, and he doesn't have many carpentry jobs lined up for next year yet. So it looks like he would be fluid enough to be able to concentrate on making money from the garden and watching the kids. He has said often of late that he would like the luxury of just being able to work on this place instead of having to go out and make a living by fixing up other people's places. This would let him do it, from the looks of things. I don't know how it will work out, and it may fall flat on its face as early as this Monday, but I sure hope not. I'll keep you posted...

November 17, 1977, Thursday

Thank you for the birthday present. I had a very nice day. Keith made a three-layer birthday cake and decorated it himself. Went all out. When Keith hit 30 last year, he went into such a depression, it lasted for a week or more. Something about getting old. I feel so different it's almost comical. Somehow, I feel that 30 is a magic age, that I'm finally hitting my stride, and can now get on with all the things I wasn't old enough to do before. I have a feeling my letdown will come at 40...

Our tomatoes are going crazy. I canned my first tomatoes on Oct. 1. I now have about 100 quarts of tomatoes or tomato sauce, about a dozen half-pints of tomato paste, and a window-shelf full of about another 10 quarts ready to can. For some reason the tomatoes in the garden this year were mostly perfect specimens, not rotten around the stem like so many of them have been in years past. Green, but perfect. So we put them upstairs all over the floor in the room where we used to store hay for the cow. We'll have fresh tomatoes for a salad for Thanksgiving, and maybe for a week or two after that. I wish I knew what we did right this year that we weren't doing before. This is really great. I had given up on the idea of ever being sick of having tomatoes around, like I was when we got so many in Rhode Island.

Eliot is back from Europe, and it seems that after checking it out, that job on the dairy farm in Massachusetts doesn't look as lucrative as he imagined. So it's still up in the air what is going to happen, and who is going to be where. Melissa is going to school here. In answer to your question, many of Eliot's trips are funded from government or institutional sources. The Nearings financed one or two of his trips to Europe in past years.

The Becks will survive the winter, but they're not too happy with the situation. They've pretty much given up the idea of buying the Nearings' place, and think they'll look around for another place next spring. I told them that's a little late to start looking if they're planning on a garden and all, but I guess they'll just have to learn the hard way, like we all did up here. They're from Maryland, and he's a chemist. Other than that, I don't know much about their backgrounds.

...Now about the store. It's coming along slowly but positively. I'll be getting a lease on it soon, and plans are to open it either mid-May or June 1, and stay open through Christmas. I've gotten one of my friends agreeing to work there one or two days a week. I'm accumulating catalogs from wholesale cheese dealers and other suppliers, such as for coffee beans and nuts. I even took a business trip to Rhode Island and Boston a few weeks ago to check out some other stores, to talk to my friend Janie (who has a gift shop), and to see about suppliers for other stuff. It was very educational.

After looking at a number of stores, I decided I should call my store the Peasant Gourmet, peasant to bring it down to earth a little bit.

(I had long thought that peasant food was really the best food — simple recipes created throughout history by loving hands from fresh, home-grown or locally-grown ingredients. I envisioned my shop being the starting point for the best of Mom's traditional home cooking, for moms of any ethnicity.)

I'm hoping to keep start-up costs to under $3,000, including equipment and stuff for sale. It'll be interesting to see if I can do it. All the people I've mentioned the store to say that it can't lose in the Blue Hill area, and will probably far surpass my expectations. I certainly hope so.

I've got a supplier lined up for the fruits and produce that I can't buy locally from farmers here. ...I've also talked to some friends with big gardens, and they seem interested in supplying some stuff for the store. We'll grow as much as we can for it too, lettuce especially, and celery. We haven't decided what else yet. I was thinking of growing herb plants for sale, growing bean sprouts for Chinese cooking (they're so simple to do, cost practically nothing, and sell for a lot), and maybe making sauerkraut, molding butter into pretty designs if I can make a good butter mold, selling sourdough batter, things like that. That's all stuff I can do. I'll be buying a lot of food, and kitchen stuff too, specialty items that you can't buy anywhere else around here — stuff that you can probably find all over town in Youngstown, but that's so rare here.

I guess you can tell I'm a little excited over the whole thing...

December 7, 1977

...Keith finally bagged a deer, after weeks of trying — A nice 7-point buck. Delicious. We had steaks for supper tonight.

The pig is just about ready to slaughter too. Three more feed sacks of apples to go. I don't know if I mentioned to you, but the second pig has been bred (after much difficulty). She's due to farrow February 12. Although the freezer was out of meat in August, we've been doing pretty well with Keith's pig-killing. Most of the time the people don't want the pig's head, or the diaphragm (good stew meat). Two customers even gave us their leaf lard. Nice stuff. We used to just take jowl bacon from the heads, until we discovered how good tongues are. Now I've gotten pretty good at stripping off fat from the heads for lard, and about a pound or two of meat chunks. Sounds grizzly but I don't mind any more, and the meat's good, and free. If I'm really feeling thrifty, what's left is cooked for a couple of days, then fed to the chickens or dogs.

This is the year of the big pigs. Most of Keith's pig-killing this year has been on pigs over 300 lbs., one or two over 500. He's also done several sheep, and a few "beef critters," or steers. We got the heads and diaphragms on the steers, got tons of meat from them. It all would have gone to waste.

We also got some hides — sheep, steer and deer — curing around here. Keith is very intent about curing hides, but I've yet to see something done with them after all that work. They're cured and worked until they are soft, then just put away. Keith did make a dandy drum, hollowed out a cedar log and covered it with rawhide at both ends, like the Indians did. It's very nice.

We had a nice Thanksgiving, just us and Darryl and one big turkey...

We've just had a lulu of a snowstorm the past two days. Snow up to my knees and now wind blowing it all around. I understand school was held, but we haven't been out in two days. We were nice and warm with just the cookstove going, and it was 55 degrees in the house this morning with no fire most of the night. It was 25 degrees outside, and with a good wind. I was pleasantly surprised.

The newspaper finally decided what to do with its reporters like me. Starting next month, I'll be on a weekly salary of $56 plus car and phone expenses. For that I'm supposed to invest 15 hours of my time every week ($3.75 per hour), and they'll stop measuring the stories.

It'll be nice having a steady income of about $60 per week. I'll "give it a go" for awhile, see how it works out. No clock punching, as I understand it, just the honor system. I don't have to report to an office or anything. But I'll have to produce.

I'll try it at least until May when the store opens. That money will help out in buying things to sell in the store.

No, Keith isn't helping with the store, except for moral support and in doing the necessary carpentry work to get the place into a condition suitable to open. It's my project, and he's willing to let me do it, far enough to agree to stay home and watch the kids, which I think is a big commitment on his part. But then I only see this as a one or two-year project. Beyond that we'll just have to play it by ear.

Keith's looking forward to spending all his time working around here. There's so much that needs to be done, and lately he's been begrudging having to put off something because he had to go out and earn some money. So it'll be my turn for awhile. But he's made it quite clear he's not at all interested in the business end of the store, just as long as it makes us some money.

Chapter 26
Missed Demeanors

December 7, 1977
...Keith finally bagged a deer, after weeks of trying — A nice 7-point buck. Delicious. We had steaks for supper tonight.

That year Keith was more tenacious than I had ever seen him. He was determined to bag a deer. Just about every day during the November open season, he would go out in the late afternoon and climb into his tree stand in the woods across the road. And night after night, hours after the sun had set, he would come home, grumbling about the lack of sightings, or the missed shots.

When November came and went, he decided he wasn't going to let the closing of hunting season stop him. He had to get a deer. The nightly routine continued.

Knowing we had plenty of food already squirreled away, with more of it on the hoof in the back pasture, and well aware that we were not in any danger of starving or even missing a meal, I couldn't buy into his obsession. But it was no skin off my nose. I just went about my business.

One piece of that business was the result of a phone call I got — from an encyclopedia salesman. Even back then I usually gave the cold shoulder to unsolicited sales calls. But for some reason, I held on to this one.

He appealed to a mother's desire for well-educated offspring. I suspect he was using an old list of hospital births or a new list of nursery school attendees. Rather than hang up on him, I thought of my two babies, growing up without television and with minimal radio. Was I depriving them? Did they need more sensory input? Would a set of encyclopedias, like my folks had bought when we were kids, and which we learned a lot from when we were bored and started flipping through it, play to the curiosity of my own children?

Sure we were living on practically nothing, I thought to myself. But it's just a matter of priorities. And the kids' education was definitely a priority. Besides, I was still working for the newspaper, and had great plans for a shop in town next summer. We could swing it if we really wanted.

"How much?" I asked.

Well, we have different plans, he explained. Can we come out and talk to you about them?

"You don't want to come all the way out here," I said. "We live way out in the boonies. Just give me the information."

"Oh, we don't mind, not at all," he said in his innocence. "It'll be a nice drive. How does next Thursday afternoon sound?"

"Okay," I acquiesced, and gave him directions.

"It'll be easier if you come early afternoon, before dark," I said, thinking about the decided lack of streetlights in our part of town. As the NBC crew had learned, sunset in Maine in early December comes about 3:30 p.m.,

"Sure, sure," the eager salesman said. "See you then."

I hung up the phone and contemplated what I had just done. Keith would not be pleased. But damn it, this was my decision. If I decided to buy, I would use my money. How could he argue with his children's education? And besides, with luck the sales call would take place while Keith was still at work. I could compile all the information and make my decision before presenting it to him.

I kept putting off mentioning the pending rendezvous, particularly as, night after night, Keith came home packing a bad mood instead of a deer. No need to provoke him.

As that Thursday dawned, I realized the situation could get interesting. That sensation was heightened when, by mid-afternoon, Keith had come home from work, had changed into his hunting clothes, and had gone out after his elusive prey. No encyclopedia salesmen were to be seen.

Then, shortly before 5 p.m., I heard a distant shot from a rifle. It was pitch dark outside. About 15 minutes later, Keith came charging through the door, all excited and out of breath.

"I shot one! It was a good one! I know I got it because there's blood on the ground where I saw it last. But it ran off into the thicket. I need help to track it down."

I knew he didn't mean me. We were not about to leave two little kids alone in the house in the dark. I also knew that tracking any animal after dark was no easy task. But waiting for daylight to find a wounded animal could well mean a lot of spoiled meat, especially if the intestines had been punctured by the bullet. Not to mention an animal suffering longer than it should. Too bad it hadn't been an instant kill.

He got on the phone and called a couple of nearby friends. Advised them to bring strong flashlights. Told them where he would meet them.

And then he was gone again, slamming the door enthusiastically behind him.

I took a deep breath.

Not five minutes later there was a knock on the door.

Strange, I thought. Did one of Keith's buddies come here? I hadn't paid much attention to where he told them they were to meet. Where would I send him?

I opened the door and faced three people, two men and a woman, in full business attire. They all had worried expressions on their faces.

"Mrs. H...?"

"Yes?" I said. Had something happened to Keith in those five minutes?

Their relief was palpable.

"We finally found you! We had an appointment...?"

"Ah, the encyclopedia salesmen," I said, as my mind raced to the hunt in the woods. "Yes, come in. I had given up on you. I thought you would be here hours ago."

"Yes, well, we, uh, got a little turned around," one of them said. I nodded in understanding — of course, the roads in Brooksville, and how they all went around in circles, with other circular roads intersecting them like a series of Venn diagrams..

"Come in," I said. "Sit down and give me your spiel. But you'll have to be quick about it. I have to get dinner ready before my husband gets home."

"Sure, no problem," they said, as they sat on the canvas-reupholstered couch and spread out the information on the hand-made coffee table. They looked more than a little out of place in the small room lined with rough-sawn boards and lit with kerosene lamps. And they knew it.

They started in on their presentation. It took them a long time. It

The canvas-covered couch in the northwest corner of the cabin.

Chapter 26 — Missed Demeanors 243

became apparent that this offer was no great deal. I said so.

They added books every year, they said, to keep the information current.

That didn't make it any more affordable.

But they had payment plans.

Don't like payment plans.

But these are terrific, can be spread over many years.

"I like your product," I stood up, signaling that the interview was over. "But it doesn't look like it's appropriate for us right now. I'm sorry you came out all this way. Leave some of the information here, and I'll discuss it with my husband. But I really have to get started on dinner."

My heart sank as I heard voices coming down the drive.

"But we haven't told you about..." one of the salespeople persisted.

The door swung open and a very bloody Keith, rifle in hand, charged through it. All excited, he blurted out, "We got him..." and stopped short. He spun on his heel and looked at the three salespeople sitting on the couch. Their eyes all bugging out, they looked like three deer caught in headlights. You would have thought they had never before encountered an agitated and bloody man with a rifle in his hand.

"Who the hell are you?" he demanded.

"They're here to sell encyclopedias," I said as simply as I could.

Keith turned to me.

"I'd like to talk to you outside," he said through clenched teeth, ordering me out the only door to the house.

"What the hell are they doing here?" he whispered to me loudly on the outside step.

"They were supposed to be here before you got home from work."

"What do they know about what's going on here?" he asked. He was referring of course to the freshly-poached deer, but I knew that the salespeople didn't know that. I also knew that they could hear every word we were saying.

"Not a thing," I said. "We just talked about books."

"Get rid of them!" he hissed at me.

The instruction was not necessary. The salespeople could be seen through the crack in the almost-closed door, quickly gathering up their paperwork.

Before Keith and I could get back inside, the door was tentatively pushed open wider. We heard, "Um, we'll be going now. Nice meeting you...Both."

They hurried past us, they were in their car, and they were gone.

January 12, 1978, Thursday

[In answer to Mom's questions] Keith's deer weighed about 180 pounds, he says. He doesn't mount the heads, just keeps the antlers for a souvenir. It's more or less the thing to do around here. People usually tack them to their garages or woodsheds. Some people have quite a collection. One set a year can add up after awhile.

Chapter 27
Winter, Spring of 1978

December 28, 1977
Thank you for the great Christmas gifts. They warmed us inside and out. I got the kids some good snowmobile boots, with removable felt liners. They cost a mint, but they're very warm, and worth it if they're to go out at all this winter. Keith got some thermal underwear from you, which he badly needed. His others were all worn out. We got some holiday spirits with a good part of your check, and what was left went into the kids' bank accounts. The candy is being enjoyed by all. The tree ornaments are very nice, and nicely unbreakable. They were the only ones the kids were allowed to handle.

We went in for a lot of hand-made gifts this year. I knit Keith a heavy pair of wool socks. Darryl got a fancy needlepoint pin cushion from me. He said he could use one. For the kids, I took the check that Hina and Petie sent and bought some lumber to make the kids a table and chair set. It was my first attempt at furniture-making, and it came out a lot better than I expected it to. I also made a wooden butter-mold for a friend of ours, from a lump of firewood. It came out so well I think I'll make me one next.

Keith made baskets for both Darryl and me, out of "an ash tree that was waving around in the wind two days ago." They're nice, strong and sturdy — pretty too. Impressive for being his first attempt at making baskets. He also made a dandy rocking horse for the kids, strong enough to support himself, as he has demonstrated many times already.

Darryl made Keith a day backpack, to use when he goes cross-country skiing. Rebecca got a leather marble pouch from him. He gave me a dandy set of wood carving knives, something I've been thinking of getting for myself for some time. That's one of my new interests — wood carving. I've started to make a toy pig for the kids. I've got a lot to learn, but I'm having fun...

We had candles on the tree again this year — the only way to go as far as we're concerned. It was warm, into the 40s, all Christmas weekend, and all the snow melted. It's cold again now, frozen but no snow. If it stays cold like this long enough, we hope to get ice thick enough on the pond to cut into blocks for next summer's refrigeration. It's supposed to be 18 inches thick, ideally.

Keith has a new job for the next couple of months. He's building what are called "Maine Tanks" — composting toilets — for some woman on Deer Isle. She's the one who takes orders for the things. They're made out of concrete, usually poured into basements of new houses. She has four or five lined up to do. It's not the best weather for pouring cement, but I guess they manage with heaters and the like. They take a week or two each, depending on individual complications. He's done one so far, another one next week.

Keith built a new smokehouse a few weeks ago, and it's fired up now, filled with jowl bacons from the slaughtering he did this fall. He didn't kill as many pigs as last year. He killed one of our pigs about a week before Christmas. He wanted a fresh ham (unsmoked) for Christmas. It certainly was delicious. The other pig is bred, due Feb. 12, and seems to like the idea that all the food I bring her now she doesn't have to share with anyone.

We finally used up the last of the fresh tomatoes yesterday. They kept a long time. We planted some in October in the window. They're just starting to get some blossoms....

January 12, 1978, Thursday

Nice letter. Thank you. Guess I'll start at the top.

...I remember your pickled pigs feet. I love the smell of it, but unfortunately, I gag when I go to eat them. I don't know why. I made a batch once. Smelled delicious, but nobody ate it. So I never did it again. We do eat the tongue, from just about anything we can get our hands on. We enjoy that almost as much as fresh liver.

As for pig brains, if Keith does his job just right, there's not much left of the brains. He shoots them in the forehead, right between the eyes.

We went to a New Year's party over a friend's house. She and Keith collaborated on making a Mexican piñata, a paper-mache duck with all kinds of trinkets and hard candy inside... We had the kids over at a real pay-type babysitter. They loved it.

We saw "Close Encounters of the Third Kind" last week. I enjoyed it, but I didn't think it was very heavy, intense. Keith is still raving about it, though. I guess it hits different people different ways.

We had a lulu of a storm here Monday. Flood quality. Tore out just about every dock and wharf in town. The tides were high anyway because it was a new moon, and then six-foot waves on top of that. We didn't get much more than a downed tree or two (70 mph winds) on our property, but one of the two roads out of here was washed out, and the other one the water ate all the bank away right up to the asphalt. A friend of ours lost his 37-foot fishing boat — uninsured. Those things cost a fortune, but so do insurance fees. He's a commercial fisherman.

People say it's the worse storm in 30 years — or ever, depending on who you talk to. Some places, like the fishing pier at Stonington (we ate near there when you were here) were badly damaged, to the tune of $125,000 or so. Quite a blow. Electricity out all over the place. And here we were snug and warm. There are some advantages to living like this, at least once in awhile.

We're planning on cutting ice from the pond tomorrow. The ice house is all built, out of saplings, sort of log cabin style. It's 9 ft. by 12 ft., about 5 ft. high. Got two loads of sawdust with Darryl's truck and trailer. The sawdust is to put around the ice in the ice house for insulation. The ice house is on the far side of the pond, just into the woods under the trees to keep the sun off. Keith borrowed a rusty old ice saw, about six feet long, sharpened it up and it works amazingly well, better than the chainsaw. Guess they knew what they were doing. He has a rope strung from the ice house to the other side of the pond, and a pulley rigged to that huge set of ice tongs to get the blocks from the pond to the ice house. Makes it really easy. We'll just clamp onto a block of ice and walk it up to the ice house. We're going to have a crowd of people here to help us. The ice is about 14 inches thick. It would be better if it were 18, but we keep getting warm spells every couple of weeks. Another one is predicted for this weekend.

Supposedly 80 blocks a foot square are enough to last through a summer and into September. We're going to try it and see if it works. Keith is going to build an ice box for the kitchen. What a luxury that will be!

January 18 (same letter)

Ice cutting worked well. Could only fit 60 blocks in our ice house, but they look beautiful, clear.

February 24, 1978

Long time, no write again. Sorry, but I've been awful busy lately. I just spent three days in Boston trying to line up distributors for my store, and attending a wholesale gift show. ... My lease starts April 1, with opening day hopefully May 1. I don't know if I can get everything done by then. Whew!

Our sow had 9 piggies last week (Feb. 16). She rolled on one the first night, killing it, but the rest of them are doing just great. She seems to be a good mother.

Keith resigned as clam warden. It got to be quite a hassle, chasing all those people on the clam flats. Even with all his diplomacy (he has a way with people) he just couldn't seem to please anybody. Not that he didn't try either. But when you're in a car, and they're coming in by boat, they see you coming, take off in the boat, and there's not a thing you can do. But you get criticized for not nabbing them. The town won't provide him with a boat. So he resigned a few weeks ago. I was glad he did. It was certainly a disruptive force around here. And it's not really worth it financially. He got just over $1,000 for the year, including what they paid in car mileage. If you take out the mileage as an expense, he maybe got half that.

Keith is building our big table in his spare time. It's 4 feet wide, 6 feet long and about 5 inches thick. The wood has been seasoning for 3 years since he cut it off his dad's land. So far it looks pretty impressive, but he's got a long way to go. I'm going to make a sign for the shop out of a slab from further up the same tree.

We're having to haul water now starting today, from the pond. The water at the spring slowly freezes up to the point where we get down to a trickle. Happens every winter about now, just lasts until we get a day or two above freezing and some snow melts. Sure brings back my appreciation for running water.

I got my hair cut today, by a hairdresser. First time in about eight years. I just got fed up with what I could do with it. So I've got bangs now, and very short hair. I like it, but Keith says he doesn't, says it's so short it looks like a boy's haircut. I don't agree, but it'll grow. Maybe he'll like it in a few weeks. Sure does make me look different. It struck me at the hairdresser's, as I watched my hair being cut, how much I look like you now. It was like seeing you as I remember you looking when I was a kid.

The kids are growing every day...

March 26, 1978, Easter Sunday

Today was Easter, and I went all gung-ho this year for Tradition. I decorated a dozen eggs with Rebecca. Had to buy white eggs special. This is the only time of year around here that you can find white eggs, incidentally. Brown is the norm. The eggs came out okay as far as Rebecca was concerned, but the dyes just weren't bright enough for me. I finally wrote to that Ukrainian place for the dyes. I'll be prepared next year.

Today the kids hunted for the Easter eggs. I bought them some baskets at Woolworth's that they really liked, stuffed with marshmallow chicks, one solid milk chocolate bunny each, and some candy-coated almonds — just like I remember having as a kid.

I made Easter bread and pirohi yesterday, and I even found some horseradish and mixed it with beets for the eggs. Delicious. The pirohi was the best I ever made, really hit the spot for me. We had a whole leg of pork (front, I think) for dinner today. Just Darryl over, but the meat will go for sandwiches for a long time...

Keith is working with Fred Dyer, a local contractor here, for the time being. He finishes up the middle of April.

It's raining and snowing out right now. Still a lot of snow on the ground, but the ice in the ponds and lakes is getting weaker. We went ice-fishing a few weekends ago, had a lot of fun. Dagan forcefully claimed the first fish, a pickerel. Insisted on holding it for about five minutes, with his mittens on. That poor fish. They sure were good though. I will be glad when winter is finally over. It seems we've had more than our share of colds this winter, probably because Rebecca is in nursery school....

This an entry in a bound journal.

April 16, 1978

Today was our 12th anniversary. A most unusual day. We had nothing special planned, because Keith had come down with a cold.

Around 9:30 a.m. I happened to look out the back window and saw a fox chasing our chickens between the house and the garden fence. A beautiful animal, although the chickens were too busy to notice. He had grabbed one rooster, shaken it a few times and was holding it still in his mouth by the time Keith got out the door with a shotgun. When he saw Keith, the fox dropped the chicken and ran — just as a huge hawk swooped low (about 15 feet) over the scene. Keith fired once with what turned out to be birdshot, says he hit the fox with some pellets. A second shot with buckshot missed as the fox bounded into the woods, Keith in tennis shoes in pursuit.

He sic'ed the dogs on the trail. They immediately picked up the chase, but ran off after the fox well ahead of Keith.

Keith said a strong musk smell was noticeable, so it was a male fox. The first we've seen so close to the house. Rooster lost some feathers, but otherwise appears all right. He's the lower rooster on the pecking order. The hawk was not seen again.

A friend of ours came over half an hour later, dogs in tow. He found them at the Nearings, out of breath.

After the excitement, I worked on my store sign until noon. Very satisfying work, but very slow....

Went over Darryl's. He was killing his hens because he was getting too many eggs. Called me squeamish, but that's not it at all. It just doesn't seem right to kill them when they're doing just what they're supposed to be doing. It's like changing the rules in the middle of the game. There's a trust between animal and keeper, and I can't stop feeling that he's violating his trust with them. Although I can't explain it clearly, it doesn't set well with me. It just isn't right.

The scenery on the way home was extra sharp, beautiful. We live in a lovely country.

A full day, and quite a way to spend an anniversary.

I did not know then that there would be no 13th anniversary to celebrate.

Chapter 28
The Summer of 1978

Keith did a remarkable job converting a filthy blacksmith shop into a clean, sheet-rocked, painted, shelved, presentable gourmet shop in just a few weeks time. Sure some finishing touches were still left to be done when the shop opened the first week of May, but the customers didn't seem to mind. There weren't very many of them — customers, that is — anyhow, at first. But that is to be expected in late Spring on the coast of Maine. The seasonal influx of summer people and tourists starts intensely on Memorial Day weekend, and reaches full-bore about the Fourth of July.

I had by that time snagged Alice French, of Penobscot's "Muffin Shop" fame, to bake fresh bread for me. Another friend, Bobby Ann, came through with incredible baklava. The shop smelled wonderful every morning.

I discovered that drivers of refrigerated seafood trucks from Stonington, Maine, after dropping a load off at the docks in Boston, would normally return empty to Stonington. A few were willing to make some extra money by driving their empty rigs about three miles out of their way on their return trip, over to the produce market in Chelsea, Mass. Two or three times a week, I would arrange for a driver to pick up my ordered load of produce early in the morning, and drop it off at my shop that same afternoon on his way back to Stonington.

The arrangement worked like a charm. The produce was of better quality and fresher than any then available in grocery stores in either Blue Hill or in nearby Ellsworth.

Things were falling beautifully into place. Word was starting to get out about this great new place in town to buy good, peasant-quality (read: real, down-to-earth, like home-made or home-grown) food at reasonable prices. People were wildly enthusiastic. I was beginning to think that everything would work out even better than I had planned.

Meanwhile, I had been keeping up with my newspaper work.

The two jobs overlapped one Tuesday afternoon in May while I was busy pulling my new shop together. An editor in Bangor called me at the shop, and sent me to cover what turned out to be one of the strangest breaking news stories in my budding journalistic career.

I was told to get on down to the suspension bridge linking the island of Deer Isle to the mainland. It seemed the 2,400-foot span that carries

Maine Route 15 across Eggemoggin Reach between Sedgwick and Deer Isle had suddenly taken to undulating rhythmically up and down in six-foot waves, which proved very disconcerting to the people then driving over it. A state trooper took one look and closed down the bridge. An inspection by engineers from the Maine Department of Transportation was scheduled for 6 p.m.

That worked for me, since my shop closed at 5 p.m., and the bridge was less than a half-hour's drive away. I called Keith, who was home with the kids, and reached the site in time for the inspection.

It was eerie standing there with a handful of bureaucrats at the crest of this normally busy two-lane thoroughfare as this massive steel and concrete structure gracefully rippled in the breeze, by this time in waves "only" three feet from top to bottom and 20 to 50 feet in length.

Rumors had already started to fly that this bridge, which had been built in 1939, would succumb to the same forces that destroyed the Tacoma Narrows suspension bridge, also known as "Galloping Gertie," which undulated itself to death, collapsing into Puget Sound, Washington, four months after it was built in 1940.

The bridge inspectors assured everyone that, while the two bridges looked similar, they had been designed by different engineers and were built to different standards. What happened on the West Coast was not going to happen here.

Hope you're right, I thought. As I stood there, with this highly visible monument to stability, community, and life's connections literally shifting beneath my feet, I couldn't help but wonder if this would turn into my last assignment. Was this nuts, or what?

The engineers proclaimed that the waves were just a fluke, brought on by just the right breeze coming up Eggemoggin Reach at just the right angle blowing through the span's flexible cables, coupled with a more rapid than normal heating of the bridge because of the swift weather change. They called it "harmonic motion."

"The concrete was swaying and the cables were creaking in rhythm when the inspectors walked over it," I later wrote. "A NEWS reporter found walking was difficult, like that on a large boat in a storm, pitching back and forth. No rolling from side to side was apparent."

The DOT opened the bridge to limited traffic the next day, and then proceeded over the next several months to add more stabilizing cabling and wind monitors.

The inspections, monitors and extra bracing were a take-off of the Cold War mantra: verify, but truss.

Their tinkering worked. Now, a quarter-century later, that bridge is still standing — although some are again questioning its safety.

(In July 2003, the similar and equally stunning Waldo-Hancock Bridge, which carries Route 1 for 2,040 feet over the upper reaches of Penobscot Bay just outside Bucksport, was abruptly closed to trucks weighing more than 12 tons when maintenance workers discovered that a startling number of strands of the 72-year-old massive steel cables holding the bridge 130 feet up above the water were breaking. That weight limit diverted most construction vehicles and even heavier RVs to the next bridge upriver 20 miles away in Bangor, and local superintendents contemplated what to do about school buses come fall. Supplemental supporting cables are being rushed into place, but a brand-new bridge, estimated to cost between $57 and $87 million, is suddenly at the top of the DOT's agenda.)

It was about then — back there in May 1978 — that our neighbors the Becks moved out. This is what Helen had to say about them in a June 3 letter to her old friends Hank and Ada Mayer:

> The people we rented to in Sept. left last week. The winter was too much for them & they weren't up to the work or the place. They thought homesteading would be a lark. They did little more than ride their car around & watch TV, though they did some typing & secretarial work for SSI.

June 1978 came and went, and the shop was off and running. The Fourth of July parade marched right down Main Street past my shop. I took advantage of my ringside seat and interviewed the bugler, wrote a feature story about him for the newspaper. (Hey, why not?)

As predicted, the next few days saw the customer flow hitting full-stride, as the crest of the summer residents and tourists hit town. I was elated. I reveled at the prospect of soon bringing home enough bacon to provide Keith with the freedom to work full-time at home, improving our tiny estate.

And then, on July 9, 1978 — a Sunday, the only day off I had all week, and the same day some 100,000 hand-clapping, chanting backers of the women's Equal Rights Amendment were marching on Washington — Keith announced that we needed to talk.

"What about?"

"The stress. I can't take the stress anymore."

My mind raced.

For months I had been running in 15 different directions, trying to stock and staff a shop in between meeting my newspaper obligations. I

Chapter 28 — The Summer of 1978   253

was the one rising at 4:30 a.m., making my produce calls to Boston as quietly as I could so I wouldn't disturb anyone. Keith was the one at home with the kids, getting up when they did, working around the place just as he said he always wanted. He set his own schedule, did whatever he wanted to do. The kids were being great about the whole thing, not giving him any trouble at all.

And he's saying he couldn't take the stress anymore?

"What stress?" I asked.

"This double life. I just can't live this way any more."

"You have a double life?"

"Don't give me that. You know all about it. I told you. A long time ago."

"I don't have a clue what you're talking about."

"Yes you do. We had that long talk, way last year, more than a year ago, and I told you everything."

I was confused. The only such talk I could remember was the one where he had told me that a woman in our social circle, a woman I considered a friend, was like a soul-mate when it came to outdoorsy things like canoeing and hunting wild mushrooms.

"... And that we were having an affair," Keith interjected, very agitated.

"An affair..." I repeated numbly. I frowned and tried to think back.

And then, at that moment, the memory returned. Intact. It had been sitting there in my subconscious the whole time. Right there, right next to my rationale for dismissing the whole thing.

*   *   *   *   *

Back then, like now, Keith had come into the house and said he needed to talk to me. I was in the bedroom nursing Dagan. Keith began pacing in the small room, his tall shape repeatedly passing in front of the window at the end of the bed which overlooked the back garden. He was clearly very agitated.

"I don't know how to begin," he said.

"What is it? What's wrong?"

"It's [this friend]."

"What? Is something wrong?"

"No, she's fine. She's not hurt or anything like that. I mean what I have to say is about her."

"What about her?"

"It's just something I think you should know," Keith said, looking at the hand-hewn beams in the ceiling. "I just think you should know that we've grown very close. We have so many common interests. Like canoeing. And hunting. And mushrooming. And tanning hides and making drums and all that stuff that you don't care a bit about."

"Yes, well, with the kids and such taking up all my time, I think it's good for you to have someone to do those kind of things with," I said.

I knew I couldn't be everything to Keith, couldn't share his every interest. No spouse could. Clearly he didn't share all of mine. But we had the important stuff — two small children, a home we had built with our own hands. We also had a long history, he and I — shared experiences going back to high school and the Vietnam war. That was a whole lot of common interests, in my book. Real ones. I could forgive him some recreational time with someone else, someone who really dug what he dug in those arenas. So what if that someone was an uncloseted lesbian?

"And I've never been one to think that all your friends should be men…"

He turned and looked at me, with our son asleep at my breast.

"We're more than friends," he said.

"What do you mean?"

"I think she's my soul-mate."

Oh great, I thought to myself. That used to be a term he applied to me. What do I do about this development? Do I need to do anything?

"Well, it's good that you have someone you can relate to like that," I said.

"So you understand."

"What's to understand? You share a lot of the same interests, ones that I don't care a rip about. That's good, isn't it?"

"I guess so. But it's more than that."

"How so?"

"I don't know how to explain it."

He kept pacing as he groped for words. I watched him from the bed. The seconds passed into minutes.

"We have this thing going," he finally said.

"Define 'thing'."

"Well, I don't exactly know how to define it. It's both physical and mental."

"Define 'physical'."

"Well, you know…physical."

"No I don't know. What are you talking about?"

What could he be talking about? Lesbians do it with other women, don't they? This woman had many lesbian friends who visited her from out of state, usually showing up in pairs. I knew this because we often hosted meals that included all of them when they were in town. By and large they were interesting people. We talked openly about their relationships, current and former. One told me she was keeping in touch with an old girlfriend of Keith's canoeing partner, years after that relationship had gone sour.

"I don't exactly know how to explain it," Keith said.

"What's to explain?" I asked. "What are we talking about here?"

And then I asked the most implausible question I could think of.

"Are you telling me you are having an affair?"

He paused to ponder my question. It took him maybe half a minute to respond.

"Yes, I guess you could call it that."

He looked at me, waiting for me to react.

I looked at him, waiting for him to elaborate.

What did it mean for a macho guy like him to sort of admit to having an affair with someone of an alternate sexual orientation? Was he alluding to real sex or something else, something kinky I couldn't even imagine? Was that why he was being so hesitant? Did whatever he had going with her not fit the normal definition? What did he mean when he said "I guess you could call it that"? If I had called it something else, if I had come up with a different word or phrase, would he have latched onto that instead?

Why was he telling me this? What did he want from me? Was it over between them and he was just confessing his straying? It sure didn't sound like that. Was it over between us? Was he looking for a threesome? What?

I looked at our infant son asleep on my chest, and waited for the other shoe to drop.

After about a minute when neither of us spoke, Keith simply walked out of the room.

And he never mentioned the subject again — until that Sunday, July 9, 1978.

*   *   *   *   *

I was startled at his words, that Sunday in July.

But I was even more startled to be able to retrieve, intact, the complete conversation that we had had more than a year before, and which I had apparently successfully repressed all that time. The subconscious really does protect us from absorbing information we can't deal with, I thought to myself. I marveled at that automatic mechanism at the same time I struggled to absorb the resurfacing issue.

I knew in that instant that July day in 1978 that I would never again dismiss out of hand the possibility of a repressed memory being recovered. Because I just had. And I had immediate empathy with all those women who had been accused of ignoring evidence that was right before their eyes. "She had to know what was going on" was suddenly a silly thing to say. Of course she didn't, whoever she was. She couldn't. Her brain, protecting her, wouldn't let her.

Back then, so long ago, with two babies, practically no income, still reeling from Heidi's death, I had been in no condition, physically, mentally, emotionally or financially, to in any way deal with the situation Keith had alluded to. And with no further reinforcement coming from Keith in the ensuing days, weeks and months — after all, if it was really that important, Keith would have said SOMETHING more — the conversation simply faded from memory.

For some time our friends, mainly homesteaders and craftspeople, had been very busy breaking up and recoupling, like a strange game of musical chairs. Although I did not know it when we first moved to Harborside, it was a dance familiar to the elderly mentors of us all, Helen and Scott Nearing.

Scott was a married man with two children when he first started dating Helen in 1928. Helen's family was not at all pleased with the live-in arrangement that soon followed, and there is evidence that as the years passed Helen was not either. Scott never did get divorced from his first wife, Nellie Seeds. It was only after Nellie died in 1946 at the young age of 60 that, at Helen's insistence, she and Scott finally tied the knot.

Yet, all the while, I thought Keith and I would be different. For all our petty problems, we were solid.

Instead, I was about to learn that our particular situation was just another stanza, another chair, in that popular local game.

Fast-forward from that first "discussion" to July 1978, and Keith was finally adding some details, letting me know in no uncertain terms what he meant by an "affair." He made it quite clear that what he was talking about was real, regular, full-frontal, unprotected hetero-type sex.

"It's actually worse than I told you about back then," he blurted out, his face contorted. "I got her pregnant. It was when you were pregnant with Dagan."

Hoh boy. So much for my naïve assumptions that theirs was either a platonic or a somehow-peripheral physical relationship.

Dagan was about to turn two years old. So this had all started before Heidi had drowned?

I suddenly felt my brain split into layers. All at the same time, I was experiencing different levels of understanding about different pieces of

Chapter 28 — The Summer of 1978

this devastating puzzle. I was somehow able to comprehend Keith's words, formulate my thoughts, and witness my layering of those thoughts, simultaneously and almost as if from a distance. All this, while dealing with several different emotions that were welling up at the same time.

For instance, and strangely, I felt no animosity toward her. Obviously, his girlfriend had not had a baby when I wasn't looking. Under the circumstances, I found her decision understandable, if unbearably sad.

As for Keith, of course I knew right away that convincing a lesbian to have sex with him must have been the biggest ego boost going for my macho-man. (Bi-sexual? What is that?)

At yet another level, I began to have the usual reactions one would expect from a wronged wife, starting with an immediate sensation of intense humiliation. Wasn't I better looking than her? Certainly I was more even-tempered than her. How could he possibly prefer her over me?

But, more importantly, and overriding everything else, was my total and complete outrage. How could he do this to his family, to me and the children? He was the father of my children. How could he betray them like this? What was he possibly thinking? What kind of a man was he? How could I ever trust him again? What kind of a creep was I married to?

Then came the remembering of a personal detail which had once surfaced in casual conversation — and the realization that his girlfriend had one compelling attribute with which I could simply not compete. She had a trust fund, of unknown dimensions but apparently sizeable enough to keep her out of the local work force.

In that moment, as I combined that factor with the stunning revelation about the unintended pregnancy, deep in my heart I knew that my marriage was doomed.

Keith was still talking. Now he was telling me that all our friends had known about the affair since the beginning. And they all thought I knew too — because Keith told them I did. And apparently all those folks had been wondering all that time why I was being so calm and normal, and friendly toward his girlfriend.

By now the reason for all the stress that he couldn't handle any longer was perfectly clear. For almost two years, Keith had been expecting me to do what I always did — take a difficult situation into my own hands and do something about it.

But I hadn't, and he couldn't.

And now his girlfriend, who for more than two years had been fooling around with a married man with children, had grown tired of playing second fiddle and was finally demanding that he resolve the situation.

The only way to force the issue, Keith had apparently decided, was for him to provide me with more information, facts so powerful I could not ignore them. I would have to respond.

So he did. And I did, finally.

My brain was reeling with all this information, going in all directions at once. What to do? What to understand? How to react? How to survive?

I knew without a doubt that I was facing a divorce — the first one in my family.

But I was also keenly and immediately aware that the new information Keith had given me was the perfect way out. Now, with the unrepentant details of this affair hanging in the air, Keith had not only foreclosed any chance of reconciliation, he had handed me a socially-acceptable excuse to leave this marriage — a reason even my mother would understand.

By impregnating another woman — while his own wife was with child, no less — Keith had committed the ultimate societal taboo.

Keith said his girlfriend would be leaving, maybe temporarily, maybe permanently. She would be going on a five-month extended tour out West, taking her truck and camping out. That would give us, him and me, time to work things out, one way or the other.

That was the plan.

It was not an easy progression. As the days and then weeks passed, I tried desperately to function as a new shopkeeper, while trying to hold myself and the remnants of my family together. Keith sunk deeper and deeper into a sullen and then silent depression. Conversations were confined to only the essential details of living. The mood at home was grim.

Some of the shoulders I cried on were heaven-sent, and I am forever grateful. But the mantra of too many of the people I turned to for solace turned out to be: "I thought you knew."

Slowly, as I continued to mull things over, all kinds of little things — from stray comments to awkward situations — that had never made sense before suddenly fit together. And it became clear to me that his now-proclaimed girlfriend had not been the only other woman in Keith's life.

It no longer seemed strange to me that Keith would know when a different woman friend of ours came down with a case of genital herpes, or odd that he made a point of conveying that information to me.

I now had the answer to those questions about why Keith's truck had been in the driveway of a local woman's home in the middle of the day while her husband was off at work, was he doing a remodeling job there? ("I just stopped in to say hello," he had explained back then.)

And the woman in the nearby town of Sedgwick who had been making a pest of herself lately — I got the strong impression she had heard we were splitting up and had assumed that it was because of her.

After all this, I couldn't help but reassess situations in our lives going back many years. When Keith had worked on that fishing boat out of Point Judith, Rhode Island, had the boat really docked at 3 a.m., justifying a dawn return to the house? Or had the crew come in at dusk, gotten paid, and romped all night? Was it possible that was why the fishing income had been so meager and sporadic?

Just how long had my trust and faith been misplaced? Just who was this man I was married to, the one I had thought I knew so well?

I felt like I was back on the crest of the Deer Isle Bridge — surrounded by a sturdy but flexible social structure, standing there on familiar solid footing, while trying to catch my balance as inexplicable waves of revelation and depression washed over me, threatening to crumple my whole world in a heap under my feet.

It was time to jump off.

Chapter 29

First Divorce in the Family

Friday, October 13, 1978
Hello everyone,
Thought it was about time I wrote you to let you know what's been going on.

Keith and I have finally split up. I've moved into a small house in Harborside owned by friends of ours who live in New Jersey. The house is darling and cozy, and completely furnished down to the knives and forks. Two bedrooms, bathroom with shower, fully insulated, oil heat and the most beautiful wood-burning cookstove I've ever seen, plus a small apartment-size gas stove. And a washer and dryer. Just what I need right now. It's rented out in the summer, so I have to find something more permanent by mid-June, but that gives me some time. I moved in last Sunday.

I found out in the middle of the summer that Keith has been having an affair with a "friend" of ours, apparently for quite a while....

It certainly explained some frustrating situations I've been having to deal with. Also put our relationship — and its gaping weak spots — sharply into focus. I need much more in the way of a personal commitment than Keith is willing, or able, to give me.

We made half-hearted attempts at straightening things out the past two months — but only saw how very far we had to go. It finally got to the point where leaving would be such a relief for both of us.

I left because that place is Keith's place. I never felt it was my home, to do with as I wanted. Every time I tried, even little stuff like a flower garden, I got shot down, so I stopped trying, years ago. Just cleaned the place up as best I could. It's about time I had my own place.

Money will be a problem for a while, because the store has slowed down considerably from summer, to about one-third. But it's holding its own and I do pay myself something now. I'm back writing for the paper after taking the summer off, and that money helps a lot, part-time though it is.

The rent here is low, $75 per month plus all utilities. It's easily worth twice or three times that, but that's what they've charged the past two winters, so I don't feel I'm getting a hand-out from them.

The kids are fine, better now that the tension has died down. We've worked out a plan where Keith gets them for half a week and I get them for half a week. I've been taking them to the shop with me, which isn't the best arrangement in the world, but I can't afford a baby-sitter anymore or someone to work in the shop. Keith has been watching them when I have night meetings to cover for the paper. He's being very considerate — on a superficial level — since I left.

I'll be going back Sunday to try to clean out the rest of my stuff. I only took my clothes, some bedding, some clothes for the kids, and a little food — just what I could get by with. The shop is not nearly as hectic as when you came, and people seem very understanding of kid clutter.

I sometimes wonder how the shop would have done this summer — or even now — if I were able to concentrate on it, and not had to think about so many other unsettling things. Oh well, maybe next year. On the other hand, it was a blessing to have something important that I had to concentrate on. Took my mind off a lot of things.

People have been very supportive, and I try not to cry on too many shoulders. Many of my friends have been through similar messes, and are very helpful and understanding. That makes a big difference, because this sure hasn't been easy on the nerves.

Sorry for not letting you in on this sooner, but it's something I have had a very hard time bringing myself to put on paper. Especially when it has been in such a state of flux, changing every day. I can see things settling down now, and directions I need to go in. When I'm not depressed, the possibilities excite me. I never did the dating thing in high school, and it might be fun to give it a whirl. Trouble is a general lack of single men in the area. But I'm not going to be in any particular hurry.

I'd like to find a little house in Blue Hill, as much like this one I'm renting as I can, and fix it up to my tastes. I think I need that. I had thought of building but that seems overwhelming right now. But I need some alone time, to lick my wounds and get all my emotions straightened out. It'll take a while.

My phone is due to be put in on Monday, so it should be in by the time you get this, if you feel like calling. Might be best not to call at the store. Not a good thing to cry in front of customers, you know.

Well, it's late. I'd better get to bed, now that I've dropped my bomb.
Love to you all

I kept the shop open through the Christmas season. But it was clear I needed a more reliable, year-round income. About then I got a raise at the ***Bangor Daily News***, and hints at the possibility of a full-time job in a few months time.

To its credit, NBC News called in the fall of 1978, looking to do a "Where Are They Now?" follow-up to our Christmas Day 1973 national debut. I explained to the young producer that our marriage was in the midst of disintegrating. She apologized for intruding and conveyed the equivalent of "never mind."

In keeping with the "do-it-yourself" philosophy, we did our divorce "pro-se," agreeing to joint custody. Despite his abominable treatment of me, I really thought Keith should be given every opportunity to be a good, involved father.

We hired a local appraiser, who valued our 25 acres and cabin with no electricity or flush toilet at $22,000. Keith's girlfriend provided the money for Keith to buy out my half-interest. Our divorce was granted on Jan. 18, 1979 in Hancock County District Court. Oh, I also got the set of Noritake china, still in its shipping boxes, that Keith had bought for me in Vietnam on a military special.

That spring, as other seasonal businesses were coming out of their winter hibernation, I took out a newspaper ad and announced I would not be re-opening the Peasant Gourmet. Then I sold the shop equipment. I was pleased when new people signed a lease for the space, and opened the Blue Hill Gourmet, to rave reviews. It was an affirmation that at least my business instincts had been good.

In June, the ***Bangor Daily News*** hired me as a full-time reporter and began paying me professional wages. I went house-hunting.

The old farmhouse I bought from widow Evelyn Candage had four bedrooms and, more importantly, a roof that didn't leak. And it came with 10 acres of land, most of it relatively flat and suitable for cultivation. The farm was located a mile from the village of Blue Hill with its excellent elementary and regional high schools. It was also directly across the street from the Blue Hill Fairgrounds, on which every Labor Day weekend the immensely popular Blue Hill Fair had been held for more than 100 years. Most charming, it was a house I could afford.

The house did not, however, come with a full bathroom, just a toilet in a closet. The electrical wiring looked as though it had been installed by Thomas Edison himself. The house was uninsulated, and was heated by two wood stoves and a fuel oil pot-burner heater in the living room. Most of the sills were rotten, and the downstairs floors and windows needed to be replaced.

But it was all mine. I put $8,000 down and took out a $18,200 mortgage.

Strange as it may seem now, I never thought to question the validity of Keith's pronouncement about his girlfriend's unintended pregnancy. The first time I considered that possibility was a few years after our divorce, when Keith blindsided me, by inexplicably and without warning filing suit for full custody. His court motion was so nasty and twisted (and, the journalist side of my brain noted, inaccurate) that I realized I was dealing with a man who would say just about anything to get what he wanted.

But he didn't stop with the court filing. In the weeks and months that followed, Keith went looking for sympathy and support, proclaiming to everyone who would listen (including Helen) that we were in court because I was trying to take his kids away from him, instead of the other way around. (I refused to counter-sue for full custody, which was probably a mistake.) Later, when I got the social worker's report, I discovered that Keith told that state employee what he had been saying to others, that our marriage had ended because I insisted on pursuing a career.

Because the judge could find absolutely no reason to take my kids away from me (even the social worker wrote glowingly of me), eventually Keith's motion was denied, joint custody was retained, and the case was thrown out of court. But it took several court appearances, sworn testimony from friends on both sides who should not have been forced to take sides, phone conversations so bizarre that I bought a tape recorder and phone mike in self-defense, contentious counseling sessions to come up with a workable custody schedule, and a horrendous couple of years.

Chapter 30
And They Lived ... After

July 9, 1979
Just a note to let you know things are going great. As I was saying to Hugh Downs the other day —
He was out interviewing the Nearings for his show "20/20," and we got the tip from my old landlord in Harborside where the crew stopped for directions. He was very nice, much better looking than this picture when it came out in the paper. I'll be interested to see how their spot comes out in the show. I still say TV can't give the depth (or won't) that a lot of stories, like the Nearings, deserve to get, more than a skimming off the top...

December 9, 1979
...I got a nice surprise in my last paycheck. I'm now getting more than $300 a week — $304 to be exact.

The next summer, on June 25, 1980, Helen sold their old farmhouse with its stone-walled garden, hand-dug pond and about 22 acres of fields and woods to Stanley S. Joseph for $75,000, ten times what she had paid for the entire 140-acre farm 30 years before. Stan paid her $25,000 up front, and Helen took back a $50,000, interest-free mortgage. Stan would finish paying off the mortgage four years later, on May 20, 1984.

Notes in my private journal:

July 12, 1980
I have decided that I am a writer.
That may not seem like a revelation for someone who has worked more than eight years on two different newspapers. But it is, and it was a decision made somewhat reluctantly.
Coming off of seven years of homesteading, it's hard to relate writing with productivity. On the homestead, production was concrete. Accomplishments could be held, eaten, burned, climbed or slept in. Woodpiles and root cellars could be judged at a relatively quick glance.
But through all that, writing was still an obsession. It was, however, a frivolity. Although its income often put food in our mouths and gas in our cars, it was not a commodity, a tangible skill such as carpentry. It was ethereal. Keith called it gossip. You can't hold an idea in your hand.
So, thrust out on my own, the tendency was to test my skills against

those tangible commodities. I bought power tools, and hand tools. I tuned my car. I had the big garden plowed up.

The car continued to run, but the garden failed to beckon, and I came to the startling conclusion that I'm not particularly fond of vegetables. Onions and potatoes and carrots didn't compel me to weed them. Strawberries and raspberries would, but I never planted them. Cutting the grass is satisfying, but is a major production.

I want the house fixed so I will enjoy living in it. But the ShopSmith stands idle, with some of the attachments yet to be tried six months later. The fancy bathroom is at a standstill.

Knowing you can do something is different from wanting to. The difference is whether one has to, to get something done.

Getting a full-time, well-paying job changed that, although it took a full year to sink in.

I get paid well for writing. And the paper's editors think I'm doing well enough to keep me on the payroll, at least for the moment.

But the job is time-consuming, and the remaining hours, especially those spent with my kids, precious. Should I use those hours to weed a garden which I must force myself to enter — and lose that time with the children? They ask for my attention now. That won't always be the case, so I should — and I want to — give them that attention.

But something had to give. Kids, house and job could not all be successfully handled by this superwoman.

It finally occurred to me that I don't need all the money I'm making. I don't make that much by national standards, but I don't consume much by those standards either. I have some extra each month. I now have the means, and could enjoy, a house changed BY SOMEONE ELSE, but to my specifications.

Freed from the need to do everything myself led me to consider my skills, and what I could do well. Writing came up as the only thing I would want to do for a living. Other things I could do, but writing is my field. The other stuff I will dabble in as the urge arises, but writing is where I should concentrate my efforts....

I will eat the farmer's food and enjoy it, hoping the farmer likes farming. I will grow what I enjoy — flowers, tomatoes, maybe strawberries. I will buy clothing and furniture — probably used because they have more character — because I don't have the time to make everything. And I will relate to the carpenter, for his time and effort, and appreciate the results.

In doing so, I have in effect crossed the boundary from being a producer to being a consumer. I have turned my back on homesteading skills. I will only now pick and choose among them, the ones I care to pursue.

But I will not forget them. I still have wood to split, and I know how to milk a cow or a goat. If the need arises, I will be able to do the necessary work to survive. I am a survivor.

But it still seems so strange to be back away from the brink.

That fall of 1980, a mere 5½ years after my fateful discussion with then-Bureau Chief Maureen Williams, her successor, Chris Spruce, resigned.

And I became Hancock County Bureau Chief for the ***Bangor Daily News***.

Chapter 31
Going, going

About the same time, and unbeknownst to the outside world, Scott Nearing had already begun his long, final decline.

March 12, 1979
Dear Brett,
    It is obvious that Scott is failing — daily. He walks bent and very carefully. He took two bad tumbles on the ice this winter, and I watch his comings and goings to be sure he's alright. The morning of the day you came he woke up with slurred speech. Couldn't make himself understood for 10 or 15 minutes. He repeats his old stories, and dozes off very easily. This is all unlike his condition even a year ago.
    Naturally, I'm concerned. I'd thought he would stay 49 forever, and he did for a long time. Roger Baldwin, one of his old-time friends, said once: "when time will have tamed his fierce energies." Well, just that has happened. He's on the way out (at 96, why not) and he knows it and I know it. I want to make his last year or years as easy as I can...

It was in the summer of 1980 that ***Simple Food for the Good Life***, written by "that frugal housewife Helen Nearing," was published by Delacourte Press.

Helen had written the book reluctantly, after several years of prodding. Cookbooks sold well, the publishers said. But Helen did not enjoy cooking, and did not consider herself an expert in that field. Those of us who had sampled her carrot croakers tended to agree with her assessment. She finally acquiesced to their repeated requests, provided she could do it her way. They agreed. The book has been remarkably successful.

Feb. 2, 1981
Hank & Ada,
    ...Scott doesn't write letters (or books) anymore. He starts out, but then dozes & I don't disturb him. He'll jump up to fix fires and do outside work, but doesn't concentrate as he used to. And his foot balance is not so good, something for me to watch always.
    He didn't get to planting your walnuts though he intended to. Can it still be done in the Spring? Where? & how deep? Etc.
    Greetings, H

In May of 1981, I got a call from the big guys in Bangor. The newspaper's librarian had realized that we had a famous person among us, who was then pushing hard at 98, and we didn't have an obituary ready for when the inevitable happened.

I called Scott Nearing, and explained the situation — along with my awkwardness about asking for an obituary interview.

"Don't worry about it," he said. "Actually we were wondering when you would be getting around to it. The *New York Times* was here four years ago."

It was clear from the beginning that this interview was a joint project, with Helen interjecting, telling details as we went along. As a result, some parts of the interview were very disjointed, but I kept taking notes.

Then, about midway through the conversation, Scott suddenly said, "When you get all through with your questions, I want three or four minutes of your time."

Here are excerpts from my raw notes.

Scott Nearing

Born Aug. 6, 1883, Morris Run, Pa., in the northeast corner of Pennsylvania, a town of about 3,000 people then, much smaller now. It had been a coal and lumber producing center, but the coal was by now gone, and with the lumber cut off, the community was left without a foundation.

I lived there until I was about 14. Then I lived in Philadelphia for the next 20 years. Since that time I've lived all over the world.

My parents were Louis and Minnie (Zabriskie) Nearing. Zabriskie is Polish, Nearing is Dutch, from Vannearing.

Winfield Scott Nearing, my grandfather, was a superintendent for a coal mining company which owned the town, the houses, the stores, the schools, the people, everything.

I worked for $1.69 a day. My grandfather said he didn't want his grandson to get more than the workers. That was his generalization. I also learned the butcher's trade. In a slaughterhouse. Instead of buying the meat in Buffalo or Chicago, we imported cattle, killed them and cut them up.

I didn't go to school until I was 13 or 14. There were six of us children, I was the oldest. We had a governess. My mother undertook to educate that family. She undertook to educate her six chicks.

Helen: His family had high hopes for him. They put him in for West Point. But he lost the use of his right eye because someone hit him with a snowball with a rock in it. It burst a blood vessel in the retina, formed a clot over the retina. At the center of vision is a black circle, a black hole. That happened when he was 10 years old. The country lost a great general. Then they thought he'd be a lawyer.

Scott: But that was not reputable. But it was also not disreputable.
Helen: Then he was going to be a minister.
Scott: Then our minister turned fascist.
Helen: Scott was head of the Christian Endeavor Group. He taught Sunday School. When that happened he walked out and never went back. It's very hard to get him back into one at all. He's very down on orthodox religions.
Scott: I was in my mid-20s, early 20s.
Helen: Then he had a very fine teacher in the University of Pennsylvania, Simon Patten, a teacher so inspiring he went into economics. In 1908 Scott wrote an economics textbook. He got more from his royalties on the textbooks than his salary as a member of the faculty. They were high school books.
Scott: A textbook on economics is a very specific thing. It represents a point of view of a department more than the point of view of an individual. There were 14 people in the economics department. Ten worked under me. We had the whole of elementary economics, 500 students, split into small sections of 25-30 students per section, one lecture per week. The rest of the week we quizzed them on the topic of the week. It was particularized education.
Helen: Scott enjoyed teaching. That was his real love. It was their loss as well as his [when he was forced to leave].
Scott: Simon Patten was chairman of the department. I taught under his general direction. The school in which I taught was the Wharton School, founded by the president of Bethlehem Steel Corporation, who gave half a million dollars to have his point of view taught. Patten advised me not to discuss distribution of the total income into wages, profits and other forms of income.
Helen: So Scott immediately made distribution the main course of his investigation.
Scott: I wrote five books on the subject, year after year, after having been advised not to talk about it. After five years I got fired. In 1915. I was hired in 1906, fired in 1915.
Helen: They said, "Your services are hereby dispensed with."
Scott: A two-sentence letter from the president of the university, sent after the university was abandoned for the summer. There was a newspaper called the North **American**, published in Philadelphia. The publisher took my side in the controversy. He assigned one of his best reporters. He and I worked together for several months publicizing the case, which made quite a bit of noise. But, I never went back.

The board had 23 trustees. One of the leading trustees was asked by a **North American** reporter, "Why did you dismiss Nearing?"

He replied, "Do I have to give a reason when I throw out a stenographer?"

Everyone in the university is very aware of two types of people in administration. Mr. Limering Jones treated his professors like other trustees treated the stenographers. Other professors said, "I don't give a damn for Nearing or his ideas, but this is my fight. If they can fire him they can fire anybody."

Helen: The trustees stood firm. He never got his back pay.

Scott: I was reinstated without back pay 40 years later. In 1973, 58 years after I was dismissed, I was awarded an honorary Emeritus Professor of Economics.

Helen: They allowed it to happen but didn't approve it. The [university] president wanted to clear the air.

Scott: I then went to the University of Toledo, for two years. I spoke against the war, and they kicked me on out of there. In 1917. That was done by one vote. There were nine trustees at the University of Toledo. It was five against, four voted for me. The key [tenth] man absented himself from the meeting.

Helen: The nice thing is that Scott isn't bitter about any of it.

Scott: The world is set up that way. I've noticed that it is. No use losing sleep. That makes you sick. All that crowd is gone. I don't know anyone that's left.

Helen: Longfellow wrote — "if I should live to be the last leaf on the tree." He's the last leaf on the tree.

Scott: At one point in my life I was that simple-minded, but in my long experience I have lost that feeling.

Helen: There is a real generation gap between the first and second world wars. There were very few conscientious objectors to the Second World War. When the Korean War came, then the conscientious objectors came in by the dozens. There was a real gap when Scott's name was not known, and he was not active, Scott wrote very few lectures. There was a period of 10 years when we were absolutely on our own and really had to plug for a living, at gardening and sugaring. A Dutch friend left me enough money to buy the place next door, to buy the sugar bush [in Vermont]. We kept expanding. Now the gap is bridged, by the **Mother Earth News** and others.

There was a date when he turned into a vegetarian, a socialist, a pacifist, all at the same time. He thought it was all linked together.

Scott: That was 1917. I was 35.

Helen: That was one thing that we met on. If he hadn't been a vegetarian, I don't think I would have reacted as I did. We had that in common. I didn't hear him give a public talk for a couple of years. It was in Ridgewood, N. J., he was separated from his wife. My father and mother lived in Ridgewood. A high school teacher of mine took me around to meet him. When you're 17 or 18, a man 20 years older is pretty far off.

[A few years later, after she had gone to Europe and else where, she returned and saw Scott again.]

Helen: It was my father's instigation to get him to talk to the men's club. He [Scott] asked me what I had been doing all these years. He asked me to go for a ride, to see the autumn leaves. I broke a date to do it, I liked his voice on the telephone. I was then about 25. I went back again to Europe and saw my old fancy friends. I loved Holland, a very nice fancy rich Dutchman was in the offing. Scott wrote and said he was writing a book on war and could use my typing and research and such. I came home. Then we got an apartment downtown. It was three rooms, $20 a month, wood heat, at Avenue C and 15th Street, way down east. It was a snappy apartment house. We kept it for a year, while we were deciding whether to move permanently.

At that time nobody was living with a man without being married. It was really rough, for my parents, not for me. I felt I was just a toy in Europe, fun to have around. I saw through the frivolous life and enjoyed what I was doing. It was the end of fiddling though. There are a lot of good fiddlers in the world, a lot better than I was. I went on playing for quite awhile but never worked at it again. You paint one picture and then you paint another. You can't cling to them.

Scott: No, I'm not working on another book. I've got a couple of outlines and a manuscript or two, but nothing that's ready to publish. I waste too much time on things that once happened, and which are now indelible. These things that once happened, happened, period. There are two or three projects that are more or less matured, but they may never come to something. Or they may.

Helen: They're about social forces, how they affect mankind and the world. He sometimes spends up to eight years making an outline.

Scott: Every time you put out a book, it should be a work of art. A first-class job, the best that is possible under the circumstances. First-class is of supreme importance. Albert Hubbard made a fortune from this little private press. Everything was the best. His motto was "To do the best you can in the place you are and be kind." This is a good position. It is not mine at all.

[This statement was news to me. I thought had indeed that the motto was his. But then I realized I really connected it more with Helen.]

I don't know that I have a standard. Hubbard's is a typical liberal standard.

History does not repeat itself. History has never been the same twice. It's true of modern history, ancient history. Every individual epoch has its own characteristics. But all individuals more or less live sequentially, one life before another and after another. Life continues.

Helen: He's not going to have a tombstone or services, but if he had a tombstone, what we would put on it, if he had one? — indefatigable.

Scott: That's a good slogan. The trouble is, when you condense anything into a slogan, you're through unless you can come up with a better slogan. It's extremely dangerous to stop growing because at that point you begin to die. It's extremely dangerous to commit yourself to one idea. Be careful you're not caught in your own net.

We live from minute to minute, hour to hour, day to day, and at each point we are a little different. We are not the same twice on any two occasions. When you realize that, it becomes extremely important that the next minute be better than the last one. If you're going to change, change for the better, not the worse. No question you will change, the only question is the direction. If there is no change, this is the open door to death. Life is a progression. It is not a standing still. It is either a plus or a minus.

[Do you have any regrets?]

I have regrets every day. Something always comes up and it isn't quite what you wanted or it can be more than you are ready for. There are never two situations the same.

Helen: You said at the time you made your major decisions, you would act the same way, you told me then.

Scott: I prefer to say I stand by my decisions, I uphold them, I'm for them although I may not agree entirely with them now — in light of the fact that tomorrow is always different from today.

The Committee on Child Labor, where I worked for about 5 or 6 years. Would I work for them again? Of course. But it queered my career.

At Toledo, would I be against the war? Would I have written that pamphlet? Yes, but it would be a much better pamphlet against the war. If I could have made my opposition to war sharper, stronger, I would have.

[In his remarks to the jury at his 1918 trial, Scott repeatedly pointed out that despite their best efforts, the government prosecutors had not been able to find and present a single person who had been influenced to action by any one of his 40,000 anti-war pamphlets. Scott convinced the jurors that if they convicted him without proof of any impact, they would be convicting him for simply expressing his thoughts on paper.

It worked. In fact, it may have been the first time in our nation's history that the First Amendment was interpreted by a jury to protect this particular type of anti-government — and what some people consider highly offensive — speech.

The fact that he won his case in a lower court, however, means the precedent-setting decision did not make it to the Supreme Court, and thus into the history books.

I can only imagine, though, how much it must have pained Scott to repeatedly point out in that courtroom that there was not a shred of evidence that his writing had had any effect. So I was not surprised, some six decades later, to hear him say he wished he had written a better pamphlet.]

I hold to the same principles. Principle is merely a generalization. Day to day you have to modify your position a little bit to meet the situation.

Helen: At his 80th birthday celebration, they had a big affair in New York. I recited Kipling's "If" which suits him to a T. He was so embarrassed he got up and gave a bad talk. He never gives the same talk twice. The same points but he says them differently. One man [at the party] said Scott was a saint. Scott just cringed.

Scott: My reaction to the influx of adoration is, "it isn't so, what they say, they can't all be true." Or, "too bad they're not hoeing potatoes or something useful."

Helen: Do you ever see the **Mother Earth News**? We have a "Dear Abby" column. They ask us everything, from what do I wash my hair with, to do you believe in God?

Scott: It's all right to educate yourself.

Helen: But they shouldn't hang around, worshipping yourself [referring to Scott].

Scott: You've got it. *Je ne regret rien.*

Helen: It was very hard to get him to do an autobiography. We finally convinced him it's a history of an epoch. He made it very impersonal, a political autobiography. I got three lines. He didn't want to flaunt.

Scott: Can two billion people be wrong?

That comment of Scott's prompted Helen to bring out a copy of the March/April 1981 **Mother Earth News.** She showed me one of their "Dear Abby" columns.

> What is God? If you can tell us what you mean by the term, we can discuss the matter... If not, there's no way to get down to specifics. If you think of God as a heavenly Father, who can be nudged, or cajoled into granting benefits and excusing delinquencies...no, we do not believe. If you think of God as an arbitrary, autocratic ruler of the universe to be propitiated and worshipped...our answer, again, would be no. If "your" God is a tribal chief, a God of battle, and a leader of a chosen people... we do not believe in Him, or Her.
>
> However, if you see God as the unity of all things, including rocks, grass, beasts, clouds, stars and humans... if your God incorporates the above and the below, the plus and the minus, the killer and the

killed, the sinner and the saint, the creator and the destroyer... yes, we believe.

Letter, 5-10-81, in response. After reading your letter and after knowing a bit about the Bible, we still stick to what we wrote in Mother Earth #96. Whether two billion or 90 billion believe in a Jehovah God, if we don't, we don't. The **Bible** to us is one of many scriptures that show man the way. All religions have truth in them, and all can be accepted in part. But there is no religion higher than truth, and Truth is the whole magnificent universe. What is. We believe in that — and strive to lend a hand.

I asked Scott if their famous daily breakdown of four hours each at bread labor, avocational work and socializing still held.

Scott: It still stands, except the 4-4-4 are merely symbols. We're making maple syrup and there's a big sap run, which means you may have to work that day 12-14 hours. Whatever you adopt as a general format has to take into consideration exceptions that arise. There has to be a place for exceptions as well as the rules.

Helen said 170 copies of the 1977 Bullfrog Film had been sold so far. She also announced that German and Finnish editions of ***Living the Good Life*** would be coming out soon.

I wrote a feature-obituary, complete except for the time and circumstances of his death, and filed it with the paper's librarian.

*   *   *   *   *

July 13, 1981
Harborside, Maine
Dear Hank and Ada:

Perhaps you're right in not bothering to come to the SSI meeting....It was good of you to come as often as you did and obviously looked on it as a contribution to SSI which it certainly was. Now that gas is so high it becomes more and more of an expense for you.

We might bring up at the meeting this time that expenses could be paid for those who are furthest away and who wish to attend the meetings.

Yes, come later in the year if you can manage it. We're just having delivered this week six cords of six-foot maple and oak, which Scott will have to saw up and split and pile. By supplementing that with what we pick up on the beach etc. we'll be well set for the winter. (No easy supply of splendid wood such as we had in Vermont!)

Chapter 31 — Going, going

Considering that this is the first time we gardened in the space behind the house we have it good. The soil is poor and clayey but Scott has dug it three times and put in compost, hay, leaves and seaweed. We have super peas — 9 feet high. They're the best thing in the garden. Piles of lettuce; good carrot bed; a beet bed; kale and celery doing fairly well, and beans — but the brassicas very poor. We'll be getting corn and squash but can't fit much into our tiny garden. We've put in 4 rows of asparagus.

That's about it. Your garden must be huge and thriving, as ours used to be next door.

Stan, the new owner, is doing fairly well alone — his nice German girl went back to Europe and it looks as though she will not return. You don't know any nice hard-working girl looking for a husband?

Stan has so much stuff in his garden that he's got a sign up: VEGETABLES FOR SALE and he takes much of it to Blue Hill and sells it there. He's taking care of the place as well as a lone bachelor can.

The men need the women, don't they, Ada?

Piles of visitors drop in, as usual. Scott's nice to them all but he doesn't know one from another — even the local folks. Think his eyesight and hearing getting bad.

Love,
H&S

Undated, notation 1981 or 2 added
Dear Hank

Yes, Scott has slowed up considerably since last year in Acadia. He no longer could do as much work as he did then. And I'm not sure he could find the garden & tools for himself. He's very dependent on me, unless he's here on his home territory.

I took him to Vt. To [son] Bob's place last month & he got quite confused. Also last night people came for supper after hordes had been here all day. He was exhausted & asked who these people were (though he knew them). So I've got to watch out for everything all the time. I think I'd better keep him home. His brother Guy, 8 years younger, is & looks much older than Scott!

Fine if you could go to Cuba. Yes, we'd love some garlic. We use a clove a day — in soups & salad. And then I want to plant some.

Glorious Fall days. We do enjoy them.

Love,
H&S

[On stationery from the Pawling Health Manor, Hyde Park, New York]
Home, Jan. 10, 1982
Dear Hank & Ada:

We went to the above place (at their invitation) from Dec. 20 to Jan. 4 — & fasted for 10 days. It was enjoyable, a good vacation & cleansing, & a good start to the New Year.

I went on water only & Scott on juices & salads. We didn't want to risk more with him. Although I think when he decides it's time to die he'll just stop eating & I'll let him, of course.

He's still in good health & spirits but taking it more and more slowly. He carries in one piece of wood at a time & that gives him exercise. He also sleeps a lot. Has a good appetite.

I think this year he's getting ready to go on.

No, I'll need no help with the garden. It's so small & I can easily plant it myself. He builds compost & does the rougher work.

I hope you'll come to the SSI meeting though this summer. We may have to make decisions. The vast supply of his books is the main problem: how they can be distributed. Have a fine winter in Fla. We'll stay happily here.

Nearly every letter we get congratulates Scott on his appearance in the movie REDS. Have you seen it?

Love,
H&S

Aug. 4, 1982
[On a German postcard]
Dear Hank:

Just got home from Germany to find Scott even more diminished.

I'm still not clear as to if 2 or 3 of you are coming, & if tenting or should provide rooms at Vennos.

Let me know soon? Arriving here the 26th & staying 3 nights?
Love,
H.

In May 1983, author Mel Allen did a last interview with Scott.

He wrote this poignant piece for the August 1983 issue of ***Yankee Magazine*** (reprinted with permission).

Leaving the good life:
A reflective visit with Scott Nearing, who will be 100 years old this month
By Mel Allen

Helen and Scott Nearing, whose book, **Living the Good Life**, is the bible of the back-to-the-land movement, live on a windswept spit of land on Penobscot Bay in Hancock County, Maine, 20 miles from the nearest stores and banks, in Blue Hill. She is 79; he will be 100 on Aug. 6 (he was born the same year as Franz Kafka), and for 50 years they have had little use for towns or stores or banks.

They began homesteading in 1931 on a run-down, 65-acre Vermont farm at the foot of Stratton Mountain which they bought for $300 down and an $800 mortgage. Scott Nearing was nearly 50 and broke, living in New York City with Helen Knothe, a beautiful young violinist who later became his wife. In the stove in their East Side apartment they burned copies of his pamphlet, "The ABC's of Communism," for warmth. A leading Socialist, he had run for Congress and had sold out lecture halls debating Clarence Darrow. A professor of economics and sociology, he had been fired from three universities for taking stands against child labor and for his pacifism during World War I. His textbooks had been withdrawn and publishers refused his new work. The move to the country was for survival.

They had no electricity, and except for a battered pickup truck, no machinery. They fortified the soil with compost, heated with wood, and built a house of stone. They kept no farm animals and had no children. They ate only the vegetables they raised and the grains and fruits they bartered for. From their sugarbush, they boiled maple syrup for cash. But in 1952, feeling crowded out by Stratton Mountain ski developers, they moved to Maine, to another run-down farm on 140 acres of isolation. He was 70, she 49. They were starting over again.

One cold misty morning late last May, I visited "Forest Farm," now a garden spot that attracts several thousand people a year. Whenever I feel age descending and hopes receding, I think of Scott Nearing and I am cheered. I had seen him twice, in person, giving talks on gardening and the coming collapse of capitalism. His deeply tanned, wrinkled face atop a straight, sturdy body made me think, somehow, that he would scythe his meadow, chop his wood, and plant his garden forever. I did not have to buy his theories on Socialism to feel that he was a heroic man. But this was a melancholy drive down the Maine coast, for I had just received a letter from Helen Nearing that said that Scott was dying. "He's in no pain," she wrote, "just getting ready to leave a worn-out body."

There is a sign nailed to a pine tree at the end of the gravel driveway: "Visitors 3-5. Please help us to lead the good life." They are famous for their stone buildings, all done by hand with stones they gathered obsessively on walks through the fields, the woods, or along the shore. When I park I see a garage, a storage shed, an outhouse, the beautiful balconied house completed when Scott was 95, and a five-foot-tall wall surrounding the garden, all of stone, giving me the impression that I had dropped in at the estate of an English lord.

Instead it is Helen Nearing, with her white blouse torn at the shoulder, a faded red sweater and blue corduroys who greets me. Scott, her barber of 50 years, had not been able to cut her hair; a few strands stick out from her forehead like quills. She is weary, her face drawn, and when she sits down at the long wooden table in the kitchen to talk, her attention wanders, her ears cocked to the living room where Scott is sleeping. A fire burns in the cookstove. Herbs and onions hang from an oak beam and a breeze rustles chimes.

"I've never known him a day sick in bed," she says. "Never, never. We've never had a doctor. He was still working outside half a year ago. But one morning he just took to his bed and started to sleep. I think it was November; like he was hibernating. He was restless for a time, shouting out suddenly at night. Now he's contented. He doesn't complain. But sometimes he'll look at me wistfully and say, 'I wish I could carry the wood in for you.'"

She walks into the living room. The floor is stone, the walls paneled, and a massive wooden table sits before the picture window that looks out upon their cove. There is a woodstove in the corner, and on the other side of the room where bookshelves span the walls, Scott Nearing lies in a hospital bed with the sides up, like a crib, and beside the bed is a cot where Helen has slept the past several months. "This is my job now," she says quietly. "This is it."

He stirs at her approach. "What do you want, dear?" he says. His face is softer than I remembered, still tanned and weather-beaten but as peaceful as a baby's, and above his lip is a thin white mustache.

"Someone's come to see you," she says.

Blinking, he focuses on me. "Well, good," he says, "good."

I tell him I have found a whole batch of his early books and pamphlets in a secondhand bookstore.

"Thrown away?" he asks.

"No," Helen says quickly. "They've gone to a good person who will keep them."

"I'm going to have them reprinted," he says. He takes a deep breath and coughs. "Sure, sure," Helen says, comforting, and pulls a second blanket over him. He looks out the window to the calm, gray sea. In a moment he is asleep.

Chapter 31 — Going, going

They met when Helen was 24. She was independent and beautiful, a student of Eastern mysticism who had recently returned to the family home in Ridgeway, New Jersey, after studying violin abroad. At her father's request she invited Scott Nearing, then separated from his wife and living in Ridgeway, to speak at the Unitarian Church. Nearing liked her and took her for a drive. Like Helen, Scott had been born to a wealthy family. Raised in the coal-mining town of Morris Run, Pennsylvania, he was the grandson of Winfield Scott Nearing, the despotic ruler of the company town. Young Scott sided with the working class. He had a horror of riches and fancy living. When his first wife decorated their home with lace doilies and cut glass, he bought himself a wooden bowl and a wooden spoon and refused to eat from anything else.

"That first night he said, 'Do you believe in fairies?' " Helen tells me. "I thought, what kind of a guy is this? Of course I believe in fairies, and I told him so and he was very interested. I was going with four or five fellows at the time, but I was taken with his integrity, his purpose in life. Even those who disagreed with him responded to his warmth. And he was a vegetarian, as I was. I still tease him that if he hadn't been a vegetarian we wouldn't have hooked up."

We are in the kitchen and she laughs. "Can you imagine my parents? A Communist, a married man, and a man 21 years older. It turned their hair white!"

He told her to live poor for a while before she came with him, so she moved to a slum and found work in a Brooklyn candy factory. He told her to return to the glitter of Europe, to be sure she wanted his life. She did. When he asked her to return to the cold-water flat in New York City and help him research a book on war, she cut her long dark hair and took a boat home.

Soon she was a subsistence farmer in Vermont, where they evolved a system that would continue the rest of their lives. They worked four hours every day producing their food and shelter, four hours at their professions — his writing on social issues, her music — and spent four hours socializing. The latter was a little tricky in the hill towns of Vermont.

"Our ways amused the neighbors, baffled them, or annoyed them," Helen has written. "That we ate no meat was in itself strange, but during our 20 years in Vermont we never baked a pie."

There was little time for what Scott considered idle amusements. Once when an acquaintance invited him to play miniature golf, he replied, "When I lose my physical capacities, I will take up golf. When I lose my mental faculties, I will play miniature golf."

In 1946 Scott's wife died. "I told him 'I want your name,' " Helen says. "It's a bad name and I want it." In 1947 Scott and Helen were married. "And we've endured, haven't we?" she says. "And we're so different. His thinking is so pedantic, like he's always at a blackboard: 1,2,3,4, A,B,C,D. And he gets hooked up with me who sings, plays the fiddle and the organ, and yodels. And he doesn't even like music." She sighs, and stands up. "Let's see if he's awake," she says.

"Scotto, open your mouth," she says, propping up a pillow. "I'm giving you some rose hip juice."

"That's nice of you."

"Rose hip juice you made yourself. Picked them and pressed them."

He took a sip. Then another.

"Would you like some more?"

"Is it handy?" he asks.

"Yup. Right here."

Helen wipes his mouth and smooths his mustache. "He has a mustache now only because I'm too lazy to get in under his nose and shave it. He hates affectation. He heard Williams Jennings Bryan speak once, and he thought he was such an affected ass that he came home, shaved off his mustache, and gave away his dress suit. He hasn't had either since then."

We are speaking in the kitchen about families and the personal price one pays to be Scott Nearing. "People write to Scott," Helen says, "telling him he is a great man, an inspiration. But he had three sisters and two younger brothers who were ashamed of him. They thought he was a failure. We'd send them his books, and they'd come back unopened. He had two children. His son Bob is still friendly, but Scott severed relations with John in the '60s. He worked for Radio Free Europe, broadcasting propaganda to Europe. Scott said, 'You're working against the things I'm working for.' That was it. His son was John Scott Nearing, but then he dropped the Nearing.

"I asked Scott once if he would have lived his life differently. He said not in the big decisions, but in his personal relations. I think he meant he wishes he could have gotten along better with his son. But John died, so there's nothing to be done."

Past Scott's bed a door opens into a small, narrow room furnished with a desk, a typewriter, a bookcase. On the wall is a painting of Scott from a photograph by Lotte Jacobi. This is the Social Science Institute, the publisher of many of Scott's 50 social science books. Though **Living the Good Life** was a success, they never touched the royalties for living expenses. All the money went here, to the Institute to finance the research and publication of **Civilization and Beyond; USA Today; The Conscience of a Radical; Freedom, Promise and Menace.**

"I'd like someone to do a book of the early writings of Scott Nearing," Helen says. "Not just excerpts, but great chunks. There are things in there, important things that will never be read by anyone."

We step back into the living room. Scott is sleeping. His right hand rests on his forehead, as though he is deep in thought. She says softly, "I wonder where the real Scott Nearing is now."

We are eating lunch in the living room, sitting before the picture window on a bench made from a slab of driftwood dragged up from the cove. There is eggplant soup, an enormous ceramic bowl of popcorn, a bowl of steamed millet, peanuts, peanut butter, honey, apples, and bananas. Helen Nearing's motto of cooking is: "the most nourishing for the least effort."

"Scotto, we have soup and popcorn," she calls. She sits for a moment to crack some peanuts, then leaps to her feet to feed him handfuls of popcorn, returns to the table for more peanuts, then leaps up again to give him soup. I think of a mother bird feeding her nestlings, all that flying off and returning.

"Finish your soup," she tells me. "I'll give you Scott's Emulsion." Into my bowl she drops a couple of spoonfuls of peanut butter and a thick dropper of honey. "Work that down like cement," she says. She adds a scoop of the millet and some apple slices. "We eat this everyday." She laughs remembering a letter from a man who after reading **Living the Good Life** insisted on eating from a single bowl. "His wife divorced him. She said she wasn't going to eat like a dog."

A car drives up. It is a nurse to give Scott a bath.

"We were in the hospital for 12 days," Helen says. "I stayed with him in the room. When we got home, I thought I could take care of him, but I fell with him once. When I realized I couldn't, I just bawled because I thought I had to put Scott Nearing in a home. We went to a home for a while. I stayed with him and they were very nice to us. But this is where he belongs."

Since girlhood Helen had collected stones with bands of black or white around them. She called them "wishing stones" and felt that with them she had powers of divination. One day, knowing they must leave Vermont, she tied a wishing stone to a string, dangled it over a map of Maine, and closed her eyes. She imagined a saltwater farm, isolated enough so Scott could write in peace, run-down enough to be cheap. Over Penobscot Bay the stone circled in an every-tighter arc. That is where they found their present Forest Farm. And it was then that Pearl Buck, who had wanted to buy their Vermont farm, suggested they write a book about their homesteading adventure.

"It had never occurred to us," says Helen. "It was just how we lived." They co-authored **Living the Good Life**. It sold 3,000 copies in 1954, then went out of print. In 1970 Schocken Books reissued it to a new generation. It was compared to Walden, sold 170,000 copies, and made the Nearings celebrities as Scott approached 90. When the energy crisis hit in 1973, TV networks sent nattily dressed reporters to the farm. Scott would take them to his woodpile, hand them a saw, and put them to work. He'd smile into the camera. "No crisis here," he'd say.

We are upstairs on the balcony outside Scott and Helen's bedroom, so close to the sea you seem to touch it. "I sit up here," she says, "and wonder where I'll go when Scott goes. I think of Switzerland or Holland, where my mother is from. But then I ask myself, what could I get anywhere that I don't have here?

"I've remade my will so that the house will not go into the real estate market. I want it to be a homestead educational center. People could come and see where Scott Nearing lived."

"Not where Helen Nearing lived too?" I ask.

She laughed. "I'm just 'Helen and,'" she says. "When we sign books he signs his name and hands them to me and I write 'Helen and.' If I write my autobiography that will be the title. 'Helen and.'"

We walk into the guest room overlooking the garden. It is used by Nancy Richardson, a 32-year-old Pittsburgh woman who made a pilgrimage to the farm seven years ago, remained in the area, and now helps Helen care for the garden and for Scott. Like others in the house, the room is sparsely furnished. The walls are decorated with Japanese prints, a photograph of Helen's cat Pusso (killed by a fisher in October, and for which Helen mourns so much she cannot bear to look at it), and a painting of the stone house in Vermont which this one is modeled on.

"I learned detachment when we left Vermont," Helen says. "I thought if I ever had to leave anywhere again it won't be as hard as this. And when I went back a few years ago and saw that our house had become a ski chalet, well, I said, it's time to build its sister."

A bookshelf fills two walls of the room. "We've never had radio or television," she says. "I'd knit and he'd read to me or he'd shell beans and I'd read to him. If he tried one of his economics books I fell asleep. He liked Robert Louis Stevenson and anything by Tolstoy. I'd slip a science fiction in sometimes. Or stories about animals. Anything about animals."

She leans down and plucks a book from the bottom shelf. It's a biography, **Scott Nearing, Apostle of American Radicalism,** by Stephen J. Whitfield. She grimaces. "I don't like this at all," she says. She opens it. She has crossed out paragraphs with a marking pen. She reads the words partially hidden under her lines:

"This is not an intellectual portrait of Scott Nearing. I expect that his thought cannot bear the weight of intensive scrutiny." She shuts the book loudly. "I wouldn't let Scott read it. I said, 'Don't bother yourself with it.' "

In the corner of the room are two boxes stuffed with photographs, letters, notes. She says with satisfaction, "It's all here, a treasure trove. Someday I'll give them to a sympathetic biographer."

Stacked on a shelf are metal card files crammed with 5 x 7 index cards, their headings ranging from "The Future of Civilization" to "Composting." "He took notes on everything," she said. "He taught me his system. 'Don't put information in books,' he would say, 'where you can't get at it.' So I take notes, writing down pithy quotations."

Among her quotations is this one: "No meal is as good as when you have your feet under your own table." Beside that she has written, "Scott Nearing, an opinion, 1970."

We start downstairs. I see four words burned into a plank nailed to the wall: "Sunshine — birdsong — snowfall — trees." She looks in on Scott.

"Your eyelashes are growing into your eyes," she says. "Here, close your eyes," She snips quickly.

"Thank you very much," he says.

We go through a door into the woodshed. It can hold eight cords. A cord or so is left from the past winter. "He cut and stacked all that last year," she says. "Incredible, isn't it?"

A 50-foot-long stone storage shed stands beside the house. Inside, cardboard cartons filled with books are stacked four feet high. "Thoreau had a library of 600 Waldens. We have 6,000 Nearings." In a corner are boxes filled with letters from hopeful homesteaders. "The cruel thing was that more than anything he wanted to teach one class with the same students and watch them grow," she says. "And that was denied him. But he had more influence than if he'd been a college president, don't you think?"

In the next room are the tools that Scott loves — his axes, including a double-bitted axe he has had since 1900, bow saws, teeth sharp as razors, and wheelbarrows, as clean as if they were in a museum. "Scott has a favorite wheelbarrow," Helen says. "Whenever we were building with stone, that was the one he used to mix the cement." He never left a tool in a field. Even if he was only pausing for lunch, he'd wipe it clean with burlap sacking that hung from a peg in the toolshed. He once wrote, "Order in the woodshed, the woodlot, toolshed, yard and home are essential . . . care and artistry are worth the trouble."

We walk to the nearby farm where Helen and Scott lived for over 25 years before building their new stone house. A few years ago they sold it to Stan Joseph, after already selling many acres to other homesteaders. "We have only four acres left," Helen says, puffing slightly from the climb past boulders. "I wanted Scott to be relieved of the burden of cutting the grass and trimming the trees and weeding the garden." She stops and looks at me.

"But I never expected that none of the people who bought our land would stay our friends. We never see them. We were too organized, too methodical for them."

Soon the farm comes into view. A stone wall that took Helen and Scott 14 years to build surrounds the garden. Helen yodels, approaching the house, and we are welcomed inside by Stan Joseph's girlfriend. Helen has come to look at photos of Scott. There is one she would like copied. The two of them are walking down the road holding hands.

Stan Joseph comes in from the garden. He is a large man with a beard, a large hole in his checked, flannel shirt. There is an exchange of greetings. He points out a checkerboard hanging on the wall. "Look at that," he says. "I paid only a dollar for it at a flea market. I bet I can get $30 for it in the city."

"You know what you might like to give me is some mint," Helen ventures. "We have lost ours. I kept giving it away and now we have none left."

"Sure, Helen. We could work something out. What have you got to swap?"

We walk back to the house and at 1:30 the mailman comes. He has a package of blankets sent by a Hollywood producer who is interested in making a movie based on their lives. She scoffs: "Can you imagine?" But she is excited, walking into the house. "Our mailman has read some of Scott's books," she says. "He says he wants more real bad. He wants a list so he can check off the ones he wants."

It is time to leave and I go to Scott Nearing to say goodbye. I have a friend whose courage to build her own house came after reading **Living the Good Life**, and she had asked me to be certain I thanked him for her. So I did.

"You're welcome, I'm sure," he says. "I hope it turns out all right."

We shake hands and his grip is still firm.

"Will I see you again?" he asks.

I say I hope so. I say I would like to.

At the kitchen door Helen presses a dozen book lists into my hand. "Take them to bookstores. Tell them for God's sake to stock this man." She hands me a pamphlet of six pages with "SCOTT NEARING" at the top in bold letters. Beside it in smaller type, "August 6, 1883 - " with space for one last date and this statement:

Scott lived a long and purposeful life. He was dedicated to research and to serving. He searched for knowledge and the truth, while he dedicated himself to serve his fellows. From the ideas on death that appealed to him I have selected some which show the direction of his thought. He undoubtedly goes on researching and learning, and knows more now. This much, at least, we can share of his thoughts.

There would be no ceremony. His body would be cremated and the ashes spread on the garden.

"We planned everything," she says, "but I stupidly didn't expect it. We never talked about Scott going first. He was so vital, so strong. We were equals."

She stands on a knoll while I drive away. In other times she bade farewell to visitors with a ringing yodel, but as I look back she waves goodbye in silence before she turns back to the house. Later it struck me that Scott Nearing was giving Helen his final act of kindness, leaving the good life as he had lived it, slowly, patiently, one step at a time.

*   *   *   *   *

June 2 [1983]
Dear Hank & Ada:
This is to formally announce the date of the SSI meeting: August 6, 7 p.m. Come for dinner at 5. Will both of you be coming? & when? & how long would you like to stay? When you let me know I'll arrange a room.

We'll hope Scott will still be around. He's now confined to bed. Doesn't walk. We get him out in a wheelchair on sunny days (alas, too few). It's sad to see an erstwhile strong vigorous person reduced to this — but you saw it happen with your parents. I don't want to get so old. I'll fast.

Write soon?
H&S

On August 24, 1983, Scott Nearing died at home with Helen at his bedside. He had lived about three weeks beyond his 100th birthday. When notified of his death, I added those details to the beginning of Scott's prepared obituary.

Scott Nearing, 100, dies at farm
Economist, pacifist, was guru to back-to-the-land movement
By Jean Hay
NEWS Ellsworth Bureau

HARBORSIDE — Scott Nearing, patriarch of the back-to-the-land movement of the early 1970s, died Wednesday morning about 10:20 am in his home overlooking Penobscot Bay. Nearing, who had been in failing health for several months, turned 100 on Aug. 6. His wife, Helen, was at his bedside when he died.

Nearing, with his wife Helen, wrote **Living the Good Life**, a how-to book on living simply and sanely in a troubled world. The book was written in 1954, after the couple had spent 20 years on a Vermont homestead.

That book, like many others written by the Nearings, was first published privately by the couple.

During the 1970s when Nearing was in his late 80s, **Living the Good Life** was republished by Schocken Books along with a newly written autobiography, **The Making of a Radical**. Thousands of people, mostly young people in their teens and 20s, discovered the books and found their way over the back roads of Cape Rosier in mid-coastal Maine looking for inspiration from the couple. Some stayed for a few hours, others camped nearby for months.

Many sought simple reassurance that it was possible to live simply and well on a few acres of land. Many were unaware or only dimly aware of Nearing's stormy political past and how he had been fired from his last teaching job in 1917 — at the age of 35.

Born Aug. 6, 1883, in Morris Run, Pa...

...He studied economics, taught at the University of Pennsylvania and wrote textbooks until 1915, when he was fired for refusing to back down on his stance against child labor. He was 32. By that time he had married his first wife, had one son, and had adopted another son.

"The school in which I taught was the Wharton School, founded by the president of the Bethlehem Steel Corp who gave half a million dollars to have his point of view taught," Nearing said in an interview in 1981.

"They advised me not to discuss distribution of the total income into wages, profits and other forms of income. I wrote five books on the subject, year after year, after having been advised not to talk about it. After five years I got fired. That was in 1915."

Despite editorial support from several leading newspapers, Nearing was not reinstated. He moved to the University of Toledo, where he was fired in 1917 for his anti-war stance. The country was then fighting in World War I. Nearing never held another academic teaching job.

He decided he was a socialist, a pacifist, and a vegetarian. He moved to New York and in 1918 ran unsuccessfully for Congress on the Socialist ticket against Fiorello LaGuardia.

He wrote "The Great Madness," an anti-war book that led to his prosecution by the federal government for "attempting to cause insubordination and mutiny." Representing himself, he used the trial as a stage for spreading his ideas and was acquitted.

In time, Nearing became disgusted with socialism and joined the Communist Party. When he wrote a book disagreeing with the party line, the party expelled him.

Nearing lived on lecture fees and textbook royalties for a time, and then he and Helen Knothe, who was to become his second wife, moved from New York City to Vermont. They had decided it would be healthier to be poor in the country than in the city. In Vermont, they learned the ways of subsistence living and maple sugaring, topics which were to become the basis of two of their most popular books, **Living the Good Life** (1954) and **The Maple Sugar Book** (1950).

The Nearings moved from Stratton, Vt., to Harborside in the early 1950s. After two of their books were re-issued in the '70s, an influx of would-be homesteaders began to come to Harborside, a town with a year-round population of about 700.

The Nearings' formula for life included pacifism and vegetarianism and a structured day of four hours of what they called bread labor, four hours of work on a vocation, which in Scott's case was usually writing, and four hours of avocation or social interaction...

In 1973 Nearing was presented an Honorary Emeritus Professor of Economics degree from the University of Pennsylvania where he had been dismissed 58 years before. Nearing said the university wanted to clean up its mess with him as part of a major fund-raising drive they were about to launch. He noted that the board of trustees did not vote in favor of the award, but simply allowed it to happen...

In keeping with his wishes, no funeral services will be held for Nearing. He will be cremated and his ashes scattered over his home, Forest Farm, in Harborside.

"I am an old, old man. I think there is great importance to life, but I don't want to live longer than my ability to serve," Nearing said earlier this month in a UPI interview. "What good would life be without death? Death is as much a part of life as is birth."

Nearing is survived by his wife, the former Helen Knothe; a son, Robert of Troy, Pa.; and two granddaughters, Elka Schumann of Clover, Vt.; and Elena Whiteside of New Knoxville, Ohio.

— ***Bangor Daily News***, page one, Aug 25, 1983

The ***Boston Globe*** ran a long obituary, written by Edgar J. Driscoll Jr. It was very different from mine. Curiously, the account starts by saying that Scott was unsuccessful in his attempts to change 20th century society, and then proceeds to explain the profound impact Scott had had on so many people.

The New York Times also ran an obituary, quite a long one for that paper, based on the information its reporter had gleaned from that interview four years before mine. Here is what ran in ***The New York Times*** (reprinted with permission).

Scott Nearing, Environmentalist, Pacifist and Radical, Dies at 100
By Glenn Fowler

Scott Nearing, a prominent pacifist and radical in the early part of the century who later became an ardent environmentalist, died yesterday at the farm overlooking Penobscot Bay in Harborside, Me., where he lived with his wife, Helen. He was 100 years old.

Dr. Nearing, a leader of the "back to the land" movement after World War TWO, had been in failing health since early this summer. A family spokesman said he died in the simple stone house the couple built a few years ago on their 140-acre farm.

The Nearings wrote and lectured extensively on the virtues of the simple rural life and were favorites on college campuses. Among the better-known of his dozens of books were his autobiography, **The Making of a Radical**, published in 1972, and **Living the Good Life**, which he and his wife wrote in 1954.

Anti-War Crusader

Well into his 90's, Dr. Nearing, a tall, sparely built man, remained faithful to his doctrine of living off the land as completely as possible, felling trees and splitting logs for heat. But in his youth and his post-college years Scott Nearing was widely known not for his vegetarianism and natural living but as an outspoken radical and anti-war crusader.

He was born into a well-to-do family in Morris Run Pa., graduated from the University of Pennsylvania in 1905 and received a doctorate in economics there four years later. He taught at several colleges in the Philadelphia area, including the University's Wharton School of Economics, and at the same time became active in the movement to end child labor in Pennsylvania.

In 1915 he was dismissed from his professorship at Wharton for his outspoken opposition to capitalism. He then became dean of arts and sciences at the University of Toledo in Ohio. He also joined the Socialist Party and lectured at its Rand School in New York.

During that time he published an antiwar book, "The Great Madness," for which he was charged with sedition under the Espionage Act, but was acquitted. Later he was barred from entering Britain because of his denunciation of empire-building.

Always an individualist, he joined the Communist Party but was expelled in 1929 when he refused to change the manuscript for his book "Imperialism." It was three years later that he and Helen Knothe, a woman 21 years his junior who later became his second wife, decided to abandon urban living and move to rural Vermont. Ski resorts and other development

Chapter 31 — Going, going 289

led them to move to the Maine coast in 1952.

Defining himself a decade ago, Dr. Nearing said: "I have been a Socialist for a long time but I am not a Marxist. Just a tough U.S.A. radical."

During their years in New England the Nearings became passionate advocates of organic farming. Vegetarians, they did not eat meat, fish, eggs or most milk products, did not drink coffee, tea or alcohol, and forswore processed foods such as refined sugar and flour.

The Nearings developed a large following, particularly in the 1960s when many young people became disillusioned with conventional urban life. Dr. Nearing regarded himself as a teacher without a fixed schoolroom, traveling across the country to speak at forums and to student organizations, union meetings and clubs. Many of his followers visited him to celebrate his 100th birthday on Aug. 6.

A world traveler to study economic conditions, he visited China several times and regarded the Chinese form of Communism as far superior to that of Russia..

'Develop Way of Your Own'

He blended his radical economic views into his natural-living theories, advising young Americans in 1975 to "stop relying on the corner drugstore, the supermarket and the job market, stop relying on the U. S. way of life and begin to develop a way of your own."

Dr. Nearing's first wife was Nellie Seeds, who he married in 1908. She died in 1946.

In addition to Helen Nearing, whom he married in 1947, his survivors include a son from his first marriage, Robert Nearing of Troy, Pa., and by [sic] two granddaughters.

No funeral service is planned. Dr. Nearing's body will be cremated and the ashes scattered over his farm.

— **The New York Times** Thursday, August 25, 1983

Early that fall, right on schedule, ***Our Home Made of Stone***, a picture-book of their last house being built in Harborside, was published by Down East Books. Helen is the author of record.

Also that fall, Ellen LaConte, the woman who would become Helen's close friend and designated biographer, came into Helen's life.

Scott's last will and testament was signed and dated Oct. 17, 1982, the fall before he died, and was witnessed by neighbor Stanley S. Joseph of Brooksville and Susan G. Mills of Blue Hill, wife of attorney Barry Mills.

In it are three interesting paragraphs:

> To my comrades in the struggle for a kindlier and juster [sic] world, I send fraternal greetings. They serve a great cause. Many splendid triumphs lie ahead of them if they keep the faith, are eternally vigilant and work selflessly and without ceasing.
>
> To each of my children, grandchildren, great-grandchildren, nephews and nieces, I leave a fund of friendly advice which I have written out in my books. The contents are offered to them as the most important contribution I can make toward their growth and well-being.
>
> I intentionally make no other bequests to my son, Robert Nearing, or to my granddaughters, Elka Schumann and Elena Whiteside, daughters of my deceased son, John Scott Nearing. They will receive an inheritance under the will of my sister, Mary Nearing Spring, which passes to them at my death.

Reading that will, I realized that I too was a beneficiary of Scott's fund of friendly advice. But my inheritance from him wasn't found solely in his books. I had a good piece of it given to me personally, back in 1981, when we had concluded his obituary interview.

These were Scott's personal admonitions to me, writer to writer:

> You have to develop a pattern of life to be able to use situations rather than be used by them. If you just go around interviewing people, that is borderline. The essence of a good interviewer, that he or she knows the direction and keeps to it.
>
> You said you were going to write a book. If you succeed in getting into the book field, that is something you do.
>
> If you take the situation in hand instead of being a plaything of the situation:
>
> You must gather material.
>
> You have to classify the material so if you have to go back to it you can go back to it.
>
> The situation has to be yours to command instead of being commanded by the situation.
>
> In some form the material upon which you depend for your livelihood should be at your fingertips, in files, what have you, so people will come to you for information. This is so you will be the mistress of the situation instead of the victim. This means that your life becomes classified, segmented, so it can be broken up and put together again.
>
> This same thing can happen in your career as a journalist. Instead of being a victim of a situation, that you become a mistress of a situation. In other words, you take yourself seriously. At the same time

remember that anything can be overdone. Moderation in all things.

You become the master. You subordinate life in terms of your own objectives, instead of being pushed around by life. You play an increasingly important role in what happens to you, and to people near and dear to you.

"It's a real snug feeling to have written a book," Helen had summed up back then. "It's something to point to, to say, 'Look, I once did that, even if I can't do it any more.' "

And then, in a very personal observation, Helen added, "A person can be coddled by being a writer, but it can get to be too much."

Chapter 32
The In-Between Time

Helen and Scott's 4-4-4 plan, of four hours per day doing hands-on bread labor, four hours for intellectual head work, and four hours of socializing, was designed to provide the personal balance one needed for a full life.

Looking back, I realize that I too have maintained something close to that balance. Only my time frames for the head, hands, and heart (in my case, that meant politics) have been a little longer, with some overlap on the edges. Instead of four hours shifts, I do six-to-ten years.

The head and hands alternated first, the politics I would later add to the mix.

Starting fresh out of high school, it was six years of office work while Keith was in the Navy and afterwards that enabled us to move to the woods of Maine. I homesteaded in Harborside seven years. Toward the end of that period came my part-time work for the ***Bangor Daily News***.

I began full-time work for the ***BDN*** in 1979, the summer after I was divorced. By 1984, despite success, interesting work, a promotion and several raises, I knew it was time to start shifting gears, to get back to getting my hands dirty on a regular basis.

I had gotten back my taste for vegetables.

About then I met and joined forces with Dennis King, an organic farmer in Penobscot. A test-marketing of his surplus sweet corn in front of my Blue Hill farmhouse while the Blue Hill Fair raged across the road that Labor Day weekend in 1983 clarified the possibilities for us both. The corn disappeared in a heartbeat.

Location, location, location, the three things needed for a successful business. My farm was on a paved state-maintained and numbered road (Route 172), on the main route to the county seat for the entire Blue Hill peninsula. It was a mile from the heart of a village with a thriving and discriminating summer colony. It was also in an area that had no full-fledged well-stocked and staffed daily farmer's market.

The Spring of 1984 Dennis plowed up about an acre of ground behind my house. I bought a tiller and spent all my spare time planting, thinning and weeding, while Dennis tended his five acres of produce on his brother Ron's farm, as well as about 80 acres of pasture, grain and hayland.

He and I and a few farm apprentices built a small, 8 foot x 16 foot farmstand with fold-down sides, and set it in place next to my house. (MOFGA, the Maine Organic Farmers and Gardeners Association, has a great apprenticeship program, matching would-be organic farmers or gardeners with people willing to put them up and teach them how in exchange for work.)

Starting when the strawberries were ripe in late June, we opened Hay's Farmstand for business, five mornings a week, 9 am to noon, Tuesday through Saturday. After we closed up shop at noon, I went off to my day job.

The fledgling business was an immediate success, quite possibly in part because of what our customers didn't know.

Strange as it may seem now, at that point in time "organic" was equated with expensive rubbery carrots. So we made the marketing decision to not mention that our prime garden produce also had that little idiosyncrasy about it. We priced our harvest comparable to the grocery stores and the local Saturday morning farmers' market. With an insistence on quality — and with Dennis' flock of sheep and my herd of pigs (not to mention a hoard of hungry apprentices) to take care of all the imperfect culls — we soon developed a reputation for the best produce around. By the time the rumor had spread that our stuff was organic, our regular customers knew enough not to be scared off, although several asked in conspiratorial whispers if what they had heard was indeed true.

It took several years before we put "organic" on some signs. And we didn't get officially certified until we started selling carrots and other root crops wholesale out-of-state.

Even with such short hours, and only a few days each week, that first summer proved indisputably that the demand was there. But, even optimistically, a five-month season and an acre or two of cultivated ground could not be expected to replace the entire $25,000 income I then had from full-time, year-round employment at the ***Bangor Daily News***. At best, I could expect to clear about a third of that.

But that was OK, because I had a plan. As soon as the major repairs had been done on the house, I had started funneling two-thirds of my take-home pay from the ***Bangor Daily News*** into paying down my mortgage. Living that way for months and then years, I knew without a doubt that, once the mortgage was gone, I could afford to be a farmer.

In January 1985, six years into a 20-year mortgage, the farm was mine free and clear. On July 1, 1985, I quit my job at the ***Bangor Daily News*** and opened Hay's Farmstand for its second season.

The move was not just a good business plan. My kids were then 9 and 11. With my income coming from my own backyard, I could finally, once again, be a stay-at-home mom.

Meanwhile, Stan Joseph was adjusting as the new owner of the old Nearing homestead. He would write, years later, in his book ***Maine***

Farm: A Year of Country Life:

> In the first years, I came close to failing. There was far too much work for a single person, or maybe even two people, to do, and the house, barn, shed, and greenhouse all needed repairs.

I also knew that Stan couldn't possibly have realized when he bought the property from the Nearings in 1980 what a disruption their history would be on his life. The throngs who came to see the Nearings in their new stone house next door still wanted to see their old farm, now Stan's farm. They came up the drive uninvited, fully expecting Stan to be following exactly the industrious and deliberate Nearing recipe for the good life. But Stan had not bought the property with the intention of maintaining a memorial to Scott and Helen. He had his own, very different, style. The place was his, and he consumed it.

Stan's growing resentment of the unannounced intrusions was tempered the day in July 1982 when Lynn Karlin, yet another of those Nearing pilgrims, walked up that drive. Stan described the instant chemistry as a romantic cosmic event. Lynn, a successful freelance photographer for the likes of *New York Magazine, Country Living* and *House Beautiful*, moved in the next year. They were married in 1986.

Those years Helen was also reassessing what to do with her life.

Sept. 1, 1985
Forest Farm
Dear Ada and Hank:

> It's all right for you and the other members of SSI to sit in your comfortable homes and say: Carry on, Helen — but it's here and now and on my own steam I have to do it — and I'm running out of steam. This long trip of mine to Europe this winter is to get away from the push of busyness and get a proper perspective on the whole situation.
>
> Scott, Fred Blossom and I were the original instigators and directors of SSI. All others are only members. I am the sole director left. According to the constitution I (and the present President) can disband the organization and distribute the assets — which are only the book stock and the Good Life Fund. After all debts are paid what is remaining must go to some non-profit organization.
>
> I must say I'm thinking of doing it. It is a great burden and I would like to live my last few years more peacefully, as Scott did. He would not want me to be so burdened. In any case, I will keep the house open and the books moving as long as I live, even if not an organization to be responsible for. Social Science Institute was his idea, his

organization and his interest, with which I concurred but without him it is not mine; I am no social scientist as he was. I think he would agree: "Helen, let it go. Live your own life."

You asked what happened to the attorney who was going to "help." He now lives in Texas! And so it goes: the members scattered all over the place and not able to "help."

Yes, I have the sugarbush film but no machine to show it. No, two of the Good Life films are missing: borrowed by ? ? ?

The young couple from the University of Oregon will each get $50 a week to tend to orders here and keep house safe. The money will come out of the GLC fund; poor old SSI is in debt — to me!

I will write you from Europe this winter. In the meantime, in October I must go to Toronto and Vancouver for workshops.

How I wish Scott were still here !!!

Love,
Helen

In 1991, that gorgeous coffee-table book, **Maine Farm: A Year of Country Life**, with text by Stanley Joseph and photographs by Lynn Karlin, was published by Random House. Stunning photographs taken around the farm and around the neighborhood illustrated the rhythms and life on the Maine farm and small community known to so many visitors. The book not only tweaked deep memories for those of us who knew the place, but it also firmly established that the old homestead was now in the possession of a couple with a very different style.

Helen wrote the foreword in the book, and complimented the couple on what they had done to the place.

> Scott and I were square, simple-living, subsistence farmers on the land which they now own and occupy. They have a flair for the fantastic and the photographic. They heartily enjoy life together on the farm and keep it flourishing in food and flower products.
>
> Not that Scott and I didn't have a wonderful time building and working at it together. We did, but there was little frolicking in our lives. We were staid, systematic, and scheduled in comparison with Lynn and Stan...

Helen understood and accepted the transformation of the property, and was bestowing her blessing. Others, however, were not as forgiving. When the book came out and was reviewed in local papers, some critics were offended by the frivolity it displayed. Strangely, it wasn't so much the children dancing around the May pole or the communal sauna, as it was the white lounge chairs and beach umbrella set up on the edge of the pond that Scott (and others) had so painstakingly dug by hand. Somehow, in their minds, Stan and Lynn had defiled a memory.

Stan rebelled against the criticism, in minor and grand ways. The dramatic full-page color photograph of him holding a three-pronged wooden hay fork, taken by Cary Hazlegrove for the 1992 cookbook, ***Saltwater Seasonings: Good Food from Coastal Maine***, by Sarah and Jonathan Chase bears the caption:

Funny Farm proprietor Stanley Joseph at home on Cape Rosier.

Funny Farm. It was Stan calling it as he saw it.

But, as happened with so many other couples on Cape Rosier, things would turn sour on the old Nearing homestead. The couple was divorced in March 1993.

Meanwhile, despite Scott's death, people kept on coming to the new Forest Farm. Helen continued to be the gracious hostess, most winters migrating south or across the water to stay with friends.

Helen managed to pull herself together enough to write her own memoirs. ***Loving and Leaving the Good Life*** was published in 1992 by Chelsea Green. It came out to rave reviews.

In that book Helen gave us a remarkable window into her early life, particularly the mutual enchantment between her and the dashing young Indian Theosophist philosopher Jiddu Krishnamurti when she was still in her teens (Helen was born in 1904). After some heavy-duty globe-trotting, that relationship eventually cooled, and when Scott came along, Helen wrote, "I quit suitors and the high life" in Holland and joined him in New York.

Later in the book Helen repeated what she had said during my obituary interview with Scott — that a legacy from a former Dutch suitor had enabled her to buy the sugar bush in Vermont in 1934.

Helen also wrote at length about Scott's death, conveying the sense that it had been logical, deliberate, and in Scott Nearing fashion, well-done. She made it sound like the whole process had lasted about six weeks, no more than two months.

Helen did not mention any of the difficulties Mel Allen had written about in the ***Yankee Magazine*** article that came out the month Scott died. She didn't write, as she had in her letters to Hank and Ada, that Scott had been failing for years. She didn't talk about the probability that Scott had had a stroke the Fall of 1982, about the nursing home she felt compelled to place him in so she could get some rest, about the physical and emotional toll his diminishing capacities took on her.

Chapter 32 — The In-Between Time

Most difficult for many of us to understand, in her book Helen did not even mention longtime friend Nancy Richardson Berkowitz, who had stayed in the guest room and who was on hand almost daily for the last 10 months of Scott's life, helping Helen to move him, feed him, clean him, keep him comfortable as he faded away.

By 1991, Hay's Farmstand was well-established and was operating out of a 600 square foot post-and-beam, barn-like structure next to my farmhouse in Blue Hill. But despite the success of the business, the relationship between Dennis and me was on the rocks. Even though we had not married, it was not an easy parting. Lawyers were required to split up the business assets.

The summer of 1992, I tried to run the farmstand by myself. I could handle the work, the two-acres of garden and the quarter-acre of pick-your-own raspberries behind the house, but my heart wasn't in it. Unconsciously, my brain was getting ready to shift directions once again.

While I was in that impressionable state, Peter Robbins, a Sedgwick activist and one of the carpenters who had worked on my house, suggested that I attend a strategy session for a Green Party congressional candidate. He knew what button to push — he said the group needed better gender balance.

I went to that meeting, and found that new direction.

After hearing out Jonathan Carter, I decided to help him in his run for Congress in Maine's 2nd District, against incumbent Republican Olympia Snowe. Because of my journalism background, I volunteered myself as Carter's media coordinator.

The campaign was satisfyingly intense, and remarkably successful, considering the fact that for the most part it was half a dozen of us working our tails off, operating with no money in the campaign chest. Carter ended up with 8.8 percent of the vote, impressive for any first-time-out third-party candidate, and especially so for the Maine Green Party's first candidate for any office in the state.

Snowe was reelected by a five-point margin over her Democratic challenger Pat McGowan. The Democrats immediately labeled Carter the spoiler in the race.

(The case can be made that it was Ross Perot, not the fledgling Green Party, that did in McGowan's campaign. McGowan actually drew more votes in 1992 than in his first run against Olympia Snowe in 1990.

But Ross Perot's grass-roots organization, United We Stand America, drew to the polls a large influx of conservative people who didn't normally vote. As a result, Ross Perot came in second in Maine behind Bill

Clinton, actually beating out George H. W. Bush in a state where President 41 had a summer residence. Having cast a vote for Perot, it would appear from the election results that many of these new voters then proceeded to vote Republican on the rest of the ballot, giving Snowe the edge she would not have otherwise had.)

After that remarkable campaign experience, I decided to check around for a job with a paycheck, preferably one with a political connection, and landed in the office of Congressman Tom Andrews, a progressive Democrat from Portland in Maine's 1st District. My Green connections didn't faze him one bit. That job proved to be just what I needed. It was an inspiring look at politics from the inside.

By the summer of 1993, with no one, Democrat or Green, in the wings revving up for the next Congressional race in the 2nd District, I knew I wanted to personally take on Olympia Snowe. I had seen her politics up close and I was not impressed. With my congressional office work, government reporting and campaign experience, I knew the issues, and felt comfortable offering alternatives. I thought I could explain things to people and convince them to vote for me. I thought I knew what I was getting into.

Maine has only 1.25 million people, spread out over a lot of land. Maine's 2nd Congressional District is the largest district, area-wise, east of the Mississippi River. Yet the population is small enough that it is possible to feel that you know or have met most of them in one place or another. And it has not yet grown so sophisticated that it is impossible for a candidate to rise from the grassroots and go on to victory. Maine's history is sprinkled with many examples of that.

Still a registered Democrat despite my support of a Green, I announced my candidacy on Sept. 1, 1993 in Fort Knox State Park on the banks of the Penobscot River in the town of Prospect.

Helen had graciously agreed to introduce me, and did so with these words:

> I am not a political person
> Not a Republican, not a Democrat
> Or even a Feminist
> I might be called a Humanist
> I believe in human beings:
> Be they man, woman, or child
> I believe in human rights —
> And that
> Men should have as many as women.

Chapter 32 — The In-Between Time

> I believe in equal rights
> Equal opportunity
> Equal wages
> Equal partnership
>
> I think Jean Hay is an equal-righter
> She has been married and has
> two children — a girl and a boy:
> They are now grown and she is
> Free to work for the general welfare.
> She has farmed on the land
> She has done office work
> She has written for newspapers
> She is youthful and vital
> She is well-equipped to tackle
> The job of Congresswoman for Maine
> I intend to vote for her
> And hope you will too.

By January 1994 my Democratic primary campaign was picking up steam, even though I had also picked up two opponents. The campaign was definitely do-able. But then in March 1994, Senate Majority Leader George Mitchell changed my life, stunning the world by announcing he would not be running for re-election despite predictions that he would win in the biggest landslide Maine had ever seen. Suddenly, with his announcement, Maine had an open US Senate seat to fill that fall.

Olympia Snowe immediately jumped out of her (my) Congressional race and into the U.S. Senate race on the Republican side. My old boss Tom Andrews, under Mitchell's prodding, did likewise from the Democratic side.

At that point four more people entered the Democratic primary in the 2nd District. When the dust settled that June of 1994, the three of us who had started campaigning before George Mitchell jumped out all ended up at the bottom of the pack. We lost the Democratic primary to former state senator John Baldacci, who would go on to win Snowe's old seat. Snowe became the new U.S. Senator from Maine, and my old boss Tom Andrews was out of a job.

After licking my political wounds, I decided to hunker down while I figured out what life had in store for me next. With both my kids by then in college, I glommed together an income, working part-time as a reporter for the ***Weekly Packet*** in Blue Hill, freelancing for other papers across the state, and filling in part-time on the copy desk at the ***Bangor Daily News***.

Chapter 33

The Rest of Stan's Story

That was where things stood when I got the call about Stan's death.

I learned in that call that Ana, Stan's latest girlfriend, had just informed him that day that she had decided to leave the relationship, that she just couldn't take the isolation out there at the head of Cape Rosier. She then went shopping for food and supplies for her final departure. The nearest grocery store of any size was 20 miles away in Blue Hill, and the better-stocked supermarket and shopping center was 15 miles beyond that in Ellsworth. Going shopping was at best a half-day commitment, each trip underscoring the isolation she felt.

When she got back, she found first the note, then the car.

Stanley Stern Joseph of Harborside, Maine, known all over this part of Maine for his sheer enjoyment of life, at all hours of the day and night, had committed suicide. He had driven his car up the steep open field to the springhouse, the source of the water for the old four-room country farmhouse, hooked up a hose to the exhaust, and climbed in.

Only hours after they had found him, as the news was still spreading in the community, I called Helen. She told me that just a few weeks before, she and Stan had had a nice chat. She said she had again complimented him on what he had done to the place, making it his own. She said he accepted her kind remarks in the sincerity with which they had been given.

She had made her peace with him, and clearly she was grateful the conversation had taken place.

Her talk with Stan occurred shortly after she returned from a winter spent writing in Florida, in time to give a standing-room-only speech at an Earth Day festival in Bangor, where she announced that her newest book, **Light on Aging and Dying**, would be published that fall.

I brought myself back from my reverie, back to the May 3 memorial service on the farm, where multiple levels of sadness, anger, tears and laughter mingled with the buds and grass shoots that were inexorably getting ready to burst into spring despite the hundreds of feet trampling the grounds. I turned my attention once again to the people who were speaking into the microphone that had been set up under an apple tree.

White-haired Sara Christy, steel drummer extraordinare, was reciting a poem. The words had come to her in a flash, she said, and she had scribbled them down in pencil on a lined piece of paper:

Stan! You're not excused!
I want you to know that
You're not excused...

You can't leave the table
with your plate so full.
The bitterness of your last
offering remains on my tongue
And the warmth of you
At our final chat and your hug
At last open and real...
You were just getting started, my friend
And now who will water your babies?
Feed your Scrumpy? Light your Sauna?
So fire 'er up, and we'll toast you and roast you
and dance once more under your hats
As we curse and bless your outrageous soul

She spoke her words under the same tree on which one of the eulogizing participants, his back to the microphone and gathered throng, had a few minutes earlier proceeded to leisurely urinate, much to the chagrin of the rabbi standing 15 feet away, who was trying to figure out what to do when the man thankfully ran out of urine — at which point he zipped, turned to the crowd, and in a deep resonant voice, rendered a five-minute soliloquy on the mysteries of Stan, life and death. Two weeks later, in the local paper, a picture of that same man kneading a large wad of bread dough topped a feature story about a down-home, old-fashioned bakery he had just opened.

With his wintertime forays to exotic places, I always took Stan for a trust fund hippie. Yet he worked hard at his gardens, at raising and selling vegetables and flowers, at making and marketing dried floral wreaths. One of the many loves in his life reportedly left, years ago, saying she liked the good life, but didn't want to work quite that hard. At least that was her public reason.

Nancy Allen, a few years older than Stan and like him an organic farmer, with her hair finally growing back after breast cancer surgery and chemotherapy, looked back over the past year when she fought so hard to save her own life, and just shook her head at Stan's final flippancy.

One woman, in her grief, said she had to believe that the impulsive Stan she knew now feels he had made a terrible mistake, doing what he did.

That was contrasted an hour and a dozen eulogies later when a man said he believed that Stan, who so much had to be in control, had decided long ago how to take his own life when the time came. The only question was when that time would come.

The dozens, hundreds of people now at his farm, all those who had counted on Stan to show them how to live life to the fullest, were confused and angry. Since they aspired to be like Stan, wonderful Stan, exuberant Stan, full of life Stan, were they really just tripping down the path toward the same fate?

The yoga instructor recalled how Stan, in class, struggled to place the parts of his ungainly frame into the proper positions. But some of his limbs just wouldn't move as far as he wanted. The instructor then added that he understood Stan's pain, the one in his heart, not in his muscles, because he had lost his own wife this past winter, and had contemplated suicide himself.

Ana cried softly in the white wooden lawn chair, at one end of a short row of chairs that held Stan's mother, brother, and ex-wife Lynn. Coming from Schenectady, N.Y. for the service, Stan's mother was overwhelmed, not only by her son's incomprehensible deed, but by the love that was all around him in the hundreds who came to remember him — a love which was palpable, but apparently not enough to sustain him.

The rest of us were clustered behind those chairs, standing or sitting on the newly sprouting green grass on the hillside, just beyond the edge of one of Stan's freshly tilled gardens.

Ruth Robinson, writer, neighbor, and daughter-in-law to Carolyn Robinson, spoke of arguing with Stan. She said it happened about quarterly, when he would call up for some innocuous reason.

"He wanted to ask me how to order a new tire for his Garden Way cart, and I knew he already knew how to do that, so I knew he just wanted to get into it."

And she would come over and they would discuss politics and philosophy, and really go at it, and then she would go home for another few months. She lived about three miles away.

That was more my experience with Stan — intense, wanting to understand something, but it had to be done quickly. And then, when he had absorbed enough, boredom was written all over him, and he was on to something else.

As mourners drank in the day, unusually intense and warm for early May in Maine, everyone there who knew Greece compared the clarity of light and shadows around them to that found in Greece where Stan had spent many months and shot many breathtaking photographs.

Lying unspoken was the contrast of Stan's death with that of Scott

Chapter 33 — The Rest of Stan's Story

Nearing, who had died a dozen years before in the stone house just a few hundred feet away.

Scott was 20 years older than Stan would ever be when he started digging out that wet area behind the house, one wheelbarrow load at a time, turning it into the pond with an island in the middle, upon which Stan would later build his sauna.

Scott's passing had been done in slow motion, like a clock winding down for a last time, and no one objected. After all, at the age of 100, Scott had soundly beaten the demographics. Stan was only 52. And he was gone.

After she found Stan, Ana's first frantic call was to Keith, who was still living next door on those 25 acres we had bought from Helen and Scott so many years ago. He came over and administered CPR, working on Stan for 45 minutes until the ambulance arrived. It takes a long time for an ambulance to get to Harborside from Blue Hill.

I said to Keith at the service that it must have been hard for him to have done that, but that I was glad someone was there to try.

"It's impossible to bring someone back from carbon monoxide poisoning," he said stiffly, "but I didn't know that at the time or I wouldn't have started it on him."

Someone would comment later at the memorial service that Stan's body seemed small when it was found, in sharp contrast to that larger-than-life persona.

With people trying to make sense of it all and wondering where to go next, Helen quietly said that maybe the farm should be a place for study and learning and laughing, a memorial to the last two men who had lived there. She said it from her seat on the grass, the only words not recorded on tape.

After two hours in the bright sun, the rabbi asked if anyone else wished to speak. A woman in a strong voice shouted Stan's favorite cheer from the back of the crowd.

"Up your kilt!"

Nancy Richardson Berkowitz was upset with Helen for casting Scott's shadow onto Stan's memorial service, and told Helen so after the service.

I, on the other hand, was relieved and heartened by Helen's vision, and told Nancy so. Maybe, just maybe, that was what that farm was meant to be — a tribute to two very different men who insisted on living life by their own standards.

It was the only good thing I could possibly see coming out of the situation.

Eliot, who over the years seemed to be metamorphosing into Scott in both shape and mannerisms, laid out Stan's thriving spring seedlings inside the stone-walled garden for people to divide up and take home. Stan's dog Scrumpy, who had roamed comfortably among the crowd during the memorial service, was adopted by a family down the road. Stan's cremated ashes, contained in a beautiful hand-crafted cherry box, were buried next to the freshly fertilized apple tree under which the services had been conducted.

Stan understood fine craftsmanship. His paid obituary said Stan "was the only person who had been making an ancient basket boat called a coracle."

WoodenBoat founder Jon Wilson, who knew Stan through that mutual interest in fine hand-crafted boats, was also profoundly moved by the service. Jon was then contemplating starting another magazine, to be called *Hope*. The new magazine's public mission would be "to encourage understanding and a greater sense of possibilities; to help us glimpse the common bonds of our humanity without judgment, and to celebrate enduring human values, that they might find more currency in our culture."

That new magazine was indeed launched the next year. A feature on Stan, written by Jon, was in the premiere issue.

Stan seemed to live life so intently, and so joyfully, that we couldn't help but wonder what we had missed. What were the hints of a dark side that, if recognized, would have caused new colorful strips to be wound around the May pole this year, instead of it sporting the respectful flag at half-staff?

And then someone, standing by the buffet table, remembered that May Day was also a maritime signal of distress, and wondered if all these years Stan was trying to tell us something.

Years later, I would re-read the last paragraph Stan wrote in his book, in which he recalled a talk Scott Nearing had once given at the Common Ground Fair, a wonderful old-fashioned country fair put on every year by the Maine Organic Farmers and Gardeners Association.

> He talked about gardening and homesteading, and concluded by telling the audience, 'if you want to have a garden, just go out and do it. Just go out and do it. I've often heard those words as I think about taking on a new project or expanding the gardens. Despite any divergence from Scott's philosophy and practice Lynn and I have taken as we made the Maine farm ours, that too would be my best advice to anyone thinking about creating a new kind of life for themselves: 'Just go out and do it!'

So he did.
So he did.

Chapter 34

And the Time Came

September 1995. The Simpson trial — star football player O.J. Simpson charged with the murder of his ex-wife Nichole Brown Simpson and a friend Ronald Goldman — was in full swing in Los Angeles. Ultra-conservative columnist Cal Thomas was belittling First Lady Hillary Clinton's speech at the international Women's Conference in Beijing, China. Sen. Robert Packwood, an Oregon Republican, had decided to resign rather than face expulsion from the U.S. Senate for sexual and official misconduct.

Sept. 17 that year was a Sunday. It was also Day Nine of the investigation into the disappearance of Scott Croteau, 17, a Lewiston High School senior, football co-captain and straight-A student who had mysteriously vanished from his home the night before his team's opening home game. Croteau was described as "the All American kid" who "never gave anybody any trouble." Both the city and state police became involved. Search parties were launched. A National Guard helicopter was called in to use its infrared and thermal imaging equipment. U.S. Senator Olympia Snowe, a native of the Lewiston area, asked the FBI to join in the search.

I was working that Sunday at the *Bangor Daily News* as a copy editor. The shift on the copy desk began in mid-afternoon. I had not been scheduled to work. I had been called in that Sunday at the last minute to replace a rim editor who was out sick.

After I got settled in the newsroom, I called daughter Becca to cancel our plans for dinner. She said that was fine, that she could go visit her father instead. I said, "I thought he took the dogs to Lewiston today to help find that missing kid." For the past few years Keith had been raising and training search-and-rescue dogs, and was on call with the warden service.

She said, "They went, but the cops sent them home, because they found him."

"They found the kid? Alive or dead?"

"Dead, I think. Dad called and just said they were heading home. By the time they got there they didn't need the dogs anymore. If you want, I'll find out more tonight and give you a call."

"No, that's okay. Someone should be picking it up at this end, straight from the cops. But thanks for the tip. I'll keep an eye out for the story."

Lewiston is outside the *Bangor Daily News* circulation area, so any story we got would be coming over the Associated Press wire. I alerted the wire editor. No story. It was now 5 p.m. At 5:30 I asked her to check the wire for that story again. Nothing.

As is the case in many newsrooms, the best TV was in the Sports Department. The **BDN** had a large, color television mounted on a supporting column facing the Sports Desk. It was usually on and tuned to a sporting event.

The only TV on the news desk was a small 12-inch black and white set that had been purchased a dozen years before by retired editor Ken (not Kent) Ward, who had decided on his own to monitor the noon and 6 p.m. local news. Ken left the TV behind when he retired and it now sat perched on editor Rick Levasseur's desk. I had never seen it turned on.

With 6 p.m. fast approaching and still no wire story, I explained the situation to Rick and asked him if we could monitor the local Six O'clock News. If Scott Croteau had indeed been found, we might have to push a little to get the story out of the Associated Press and into our first edition.

Rick thought that was a good idea, and fiddled with the ancient box. The picture was fuzzy, but the audio was clear. And yes, indeed, it was the lead story. A body had been found in Lewiston, and authorities believed it was that of Scott Croteau. The news anchors moved onto another topic.

At that point the Sports guys, who had their TV tuned to another channel, called out that their broadcast had a reporter live on the scene in Lewiston. I rushed to that corner of the newsroom. The details were not pleasant. A body tentatively identified as Croteau's had been found about 3:40 p.m. in a wooded area behind a Rite Aid drugstore in Lewiston, hanging from a high tree limb about 500 yards from his home.

Authorities would eventually rule the death a suicide. But that determination would come days later. As I stood there in the clump of sports reporters, glued to the set as we watched the initial broadcast, Rick shouted out something very strange to my ears.

"Helen Nearing died? In a car crash? Did I hear that right?"

"What was that Rick?"

"Helen Nearing. I think they just said she died today in a car crash."

A chill went up my spine. Rick was on the phone, calling Stephany Boyd, a reporter in the Ellsworth bureau who was on call that Sunday. She phoned back a couple of minutes later with a confirmation from the State Police, and said she would file a story as soon as she could get it written.

All thoughts of the drama unfolding in Lewiston disappeared from my brain.

I offered Stephany my services as a resource, suggesting contacts. No one had done an obituary interview with Helen — after all she was only 91 and still vigorous, and we had waited until Scott was 97 to do his. Editor Wayne Riley went to check on what we had on Helen in the news library (also known as the morgue). I said we might be able to get some information on Helen from the 1983 obit I had done for Scott.

I offered to write a color piece to go with the news story. Wayne, knowing my connection to Helen and apparently concerned about my mental state, said it could wait a day if I needed to take the time. I said it couldn't. Part of my insistence that I write a story immediately was due to my journalistic instincts. I was a reporter, I had exclusive knowledge of the person in question, and I was in the perfect location to put that information to good use. The other part, I knew, was more personal — I had to focus on the thing I could do best, or I would go nuts. As luck would have it, the load on the copy desk turned out to be light that night. The rest of the rim crew said they would cover for me.

In a side office that had been vacated by a dayside reporter, I sat myself down at a blank computer screen, took several shaky deep breaths, and tried to compose my thoughts.

Helen's death was the lead story in Monday's paper. Stephany had done a good job. My color piece came at the end of the jump on page 2. The AP story on the discovery of Scott Croteau's body was in the lower right hand corner of Page One.

Here is what appeared about Helen:

Author Helen Nearing dies in car crash
Activist, 91, and late husband, Scott, inspired many to lead 'the good life'
By Stephany Boyd
Of the NEWS Staff

BROOKSVILLE — Revered as "founding mother" of the back-to-land movement, author and activist Helen Nearing died after a one-car accident near her Harborside home Sunday afternoon. She was 91.

Helen and Scott Nearing published the first of many books on "the good life" in 1953. The books became bibles for people wishing to live simpler lives, and inspired many to abandon jobs and city lifestyles in search of rural satisfactions and greater self-sufficiency.

Helen Nearing's most recent book, "Light on Aging and Dying," touts the benefits of death with dignity. Its author said in recent interviews that she would end her own life by starving, as her husband had, when the time was right.

Nearing was headed east on Route 176 in Brooksville around 1 p.m.

Sunday when the 1982 Subaru station wagon she was driving failed to negotiate a sharp curve, and struck a tree, said Dan Lawrence, a Maine State Police dispatcher. Nearing was taken by ambulance to Blue Hill Memorial Hospital, where she was pronounced dead. She was not wearing a seatbelt.

"We were really close, I talked to her every day," said Nancy Berkowitz of Blue Hill, who was among several people gathered at Helen's home Sunday evening for consolation, and to make preparations for a memorial service.

"I'm crushed," said Nearing's neighbor Eliot Coleman, a renowned author and gardener whose own work was inspired by the couple. "It was wonderful knowing her and having her as a neighbor, and it's going to be lonely without her."

"We know she's happy, and she was ready," said Nearing's friend Ellen LaConte of Belfast. "What we all have to deal with is how we will get along without her."

Daughter of a prominent New York businessman, and trained as a violinist, Helen Knothe met Scott Nearing when he was 45 and she was 24. After he was fired by the University of Pennsylvania and the University of Toledo because of his radical political views, the couple moved to Vermont, where they farmed, wrote and sold maple syrup from 1932 until the early 1950s.

Longing for greater isolation, they bought 140 acres in Harborside, where they built a farm from the ground up and lived together until Scott Nearing's death in 1983. He was 100.

During their 30 years on the farm, and even after Scott's death, countless disciples of the Nearings' way of life came to visit and learn. Many stayed in the area to build dreams of their own.

"People coming to see her was a little like people going to Ireland to kiss the Blarney Stone. She just represented something they wanted to see and touch," said Coleman, who once made the same pilgrimage himself, as had another neighbor, the late Stanley Joseph, who died last spring.

In his 1991 book **Maine Farm**, Joseph described visiting the Nearings in 1975 as a result of reading **Living the Good Life**, and how the book changed his life.

"The Nearings were practical people as well as philosophers, and in their book they explained how to garden organically, what could be done with all the food one grew, and how to live more in harmony with nature and the community. They didn't make it sound easy but they did show how to take more responsibility for what one did everyday," wrote Joseph.

Joseph eventually bought some of the Nearings' property, including the original house, and established his own Maine farm.

Coleman expressed surprise at the news of Nearing's death Sunday, describing her as a still vigorous "90-year-old teenager," who, to his knowledge had no trouble driving or doing anything else.

"There have been times when I've been sitting around here wanting to discuss an idea with someone, and the person who had the best mind to discuss the thing has been a 90-year-old woman," Coleman said.

In recent years, Nearing had spent much of her time making appearances to publicize her books, including **Loving and Leaving the Good Life**, published in 1992. As years passed, the organic farmer remained true to the vision she and Scott first espoused decades before.

When she addressed a standing-room-only crowd at an Earth Day event in Bangor last April, a single sentence summed up her philosophy: "Live simply and frugally with an eye to the needs of others to come."

A memorial service will be held at 2 p.m. Sunday, Oct. 1, at the Brooksville Community Center in South Brooksville, said LaConte.

— ***Bangor Daily News***, Sept. 18, 1995

My sidebar story was printed below the news story:

Writer was inspired by Nearings' example
By Jean Hay
Special to the NEWS
Commentary

It was a love story often lost in the details.

Helen Nearing gave up a budding career as a violinist in the 1930s to follow the great love of her life, self-described radical Scott Nearing, some 20 years her senior. From her perspective, she willingly was playing second fiddle to a man who stood on principle and chose a life of severe frugality and country living rather than bend his ideals to fit into a society he could not abide.

Theirs was a relationship that was beautiful to behold in its tenderness and caring, and an inspiration to thousands of people who followed their example of how to live the good life in Maine and other rural parts of New England. Some attribute their book **Living the Good Life**, often referred to as the bible of the back-to-the-land movement, with reversing the downward trend in Maine's population in the 1970s.

In 1983, Scott, at the age of 100, chose to die at home by refusing to eat. Helen supported him in that decision, and afterward carried on what she thought was his memory at the home they had shared in Harborside. She wrote a sequel to their earlier book, **Loving, and Leaving the Good Life**.

Before it went off to the publisher, Helen honored me with an advance draft of that book, and asked for my comments. What I told her seemed to startle her.

Chapter 34 — And the Time Came

I said that the book contained too much Scott and not enough her, that, although Scott's economics on how to live simply and sanely in a world gone mad made a lot of sense intellectually, it was her warmth and humanity which made me think going back to the land was not only possible but desirable. While Scott may have designed the system, Helen's touch was the one that put the "home" in homesteading. I could not accept the way she characterized herself in the book as a simple tagalong to Scott, because, of the two, she had the greater influence on my life.

From the look on her face, it seemed that no one — other than Scott — had ever talked to her like that before. She seemed close to tears.

I have been delighted in the years since then to witness others come up to her at gatherings where she spoke to standing-room-only crowds, and express the same sentiment. I suspect we collectively finally got through to her how much she was loved for herself, not for her secondhand connection to Scott.

I first met Helen and Scott in the week between Christmas and New Year's in 1971, when my former husband and I stopped by their Harborside home totally unannounced (they then had no phone) during a land-hunting foray. We found Scott out cutting firewood behind the home. We helped for a while and we were then fed lunch — vegetable soup kept hot on the woodburning stove, and a remarkably inedible cookie which even Helen called a carrot croaker. (In her frugality, she could not bring herself to toss out the pulp from juiced carrots, and mixed them up with some molasses and baked them in the ever-hot oven.)

The following month, we dropped them a note, asking if we could stop by again when we took a second look at a parcel of land in Stetson. Helen wrote back on a postcard to "come ahead, but don't sign anything until you come see us."

They sold us 25 acres of their farm for $2,000, the type of offer made to only three other couples. We eked out a homestead, built a house with timbers we felled, had two kids, and seven enlightening but non-electric years later got divorced.

In the 23 years since I first met them, I never once got a straight answer from either one as to why they made the offer to us, out of the thousands who were then coming annually to pay homage to this remarkable couple.

All I know is that their faith in us changed my life forever — and that I join thousands of others whose lives they touched in being forever grateful for their incredible example.

The next day I got a phone call at home. It was from Steve Bost of Bangor. I knew Steve from my political activities in 1992 and 1994. Steve had been the New England coordinator for United We Stand

America during Ross Perot's 1992 run for president. Steve was a recognized — and frequently quoted — political operative. I had talked with him a few times, and although we had some differences of opinion on a few national policy issues, he seemed like a nice guy, down to earth and a real straight arrow.

"I saw the article you wrote about Helen Nearing," I remember Steve saying. "I'm calling you because you're the only one I knew out of all the people mentioned in those two articles."

All that day I had been getting calls from people who had known Helen, people who wanted to share their shock, their grief, or their memories. I assumed Steve's call was to be one of those.

I was wrong.

"I just first want to make it very clear that this is not a political call, and I don't want to be part of any newspaper story. I just want you to convey some information to the appropriate people, and I trust you enough to think you would do it."

"Sure Steve. What's this all about?"

"I was in Brooksville yesterday with a friend, and I just happened to be driving behind Helen when she went around that corner. We rounded the curve just in time to see her car hit the tree."

I gasped. He continued.

"We stopped our car, and I ran to her car. I opened the passenger side door because she had hit the tree on the driver's side, and I crawled in."

Until that point I had visualized Helen failing to round that sharp corner, resulting in her hitting a tree straight ahead on the outside of the curve. But from Steve's description, it was clear she had successfully negotiated the curve, as she had thousands of times before, but that she hadn't straightened out the wheel after she was around the corner. The car kept going to the left, crossing the oncoming lane and hitting a tree on the opposite side of the road.

"She was curled up in a fetal position, no seatbelt on. There was hardly any blood, just what looked like a bump on her head. I felt for a pulse. It was pretty weak. I talked to her and asked her if she could hear me. Her eyes were closed, but she nodded her head slightly. She didn't seem to be in a lot of pain. Meanwhile, my friend was rummaging through the glove box for the registration. He's the one who told me who she was. Of course I had read all their books, but I had never met her before. It was quite a profound place to make her acquaintance.

"Someone from the house [where she crashed] had called the ambulance. Someone else stopped to help. We kept checking for a pulse, both at her wrist and at an ankle. It kept getting weaker and weaker. At one point I asked her again if she could hear me. She squeezed my hand.

Then the pulse got so weak that we couldn't feel it anymore, and we figured she was gone. By that time the ambulance arrived and they took her away.

"Jean, I just wanted you to convey to the people to whom it matters that Helen was not alone when she died, and that she seemed to be at peace in the end."

I was absolutely stunned by this information. I most assuredly would do as he asked. But there was one more thing I had to know.

Questions were already rampant about what had caused the crash. Was the road slick from a light rain falling on oily pavement that hadn't been washed by rain in several weeks? Had something medical or mechanical gone wrong with Helen or her car?

Steve said it had started to drizzle, but he didn't remember that stretch of road being slippery. But since I had raised the issue, he had thought it odd the way the car kept going around the curve. He had no way of knowing if it might have been a mechanical problem.

But when he crawled in the car and found Helen all curled up, with hardly any visible injuries but clearly in her last moments, he had wondered himself if something like a stroke at the very instant she was rounding that curve might have prevented her from straightening out the steering wheel.

We did not then discuss the other conjecture that was even then making the rounds — that Helen had deliberately caused her own death.

My own belief is that she did not.

Yes, Helen was old, and had been getting tired of the constant stream of visitors and the incessant demands on her time. Yes, she had decided to take a break to see a movie — albeit a political movie, "Strawberries and Chocolate," about how Cuba deals with its AIDs patients.

Yes, she had just signed the papers to transfer Forest Farm to Trust for Public Lands after her death.

Yes, her latest book, ***Light on Aging and Dying***, was just coming off the presses.

And yes, there were those of us who couldn't see Helen having the patience to starve herself to death the way she said Scott had, even though she always insisted she would.

But Helen was still vibrant, vigorous, mentally alert and stable. A rational person would not choose suicide by auto crash because of the very real possibility that it wouldn't be fatal. And being hospitalized or paralyzed would not be her style.

The location also didn't lend itself to a deliberate act. She didn't drive off a cliff or into a rock wall, she crashed into one of several medium-sized trees lined up along the road in front of someone's house. She had asked a friend to accompany her to the movies. (The friend had other plans.) The lifelong pacifist and vegetarian wouldn't have picked that particular spot, on a rising stretch of road with poor distance visibility, because of the possibility that she might hit another car as she crossed into the oncoming lane.

Whether it was road conditions, mechanical or physical malfunction, I strongly suspect Helen had only a second or two to see her fate coming. And I think that was enough time for her to prepare herself, before she hit that tree. I believe that she was ready, she was willing, and if that was to be her destiny on her way to her next life (she firmly believed in reincarnation), she was able to accept it.

I conveyed Steve's message to the appropriate people, as he had asked. They all expressed gratitude for the information.

For the private, unpublicized wake prior to her cremation, Helen's body was laid out in the living room of her house, just as she would have wanted. Home-grown and hand-picked flowers surrounded her corpse. A braided flower wreath graced her hair. Her feet were bare. Candles were burning.

David and I paid our respects, talked softly with the people who were there at the time, and left with our grief.

A friend who stayed told me later that shortly after we had gone, the Harborside postmaster showed up.

"She was quite intense and grim," my friend said. "I was touched. I didn't know she and Helen were that close."

Although the ***Bangor Daily News*** had printed the news report of her death on Monday, the day after her accident, Helen's column-length paid obituary did not run in that paper until Thursday, Sept. 21. It opened with these words:

> Helen Knothe Nearing died instantly when the car she was driving alone veered off the road near her home and struck a tree on Sunday afternoon, Sept. 17, 1995...

The ***Weekly Packet*** in Blue Hill, which covers Brooksville, had this story when its next edition came out that same Thursday. Notice that neither Steve Bost's account, nor this newspaper report, support the paid obituary's contention that Helen had died instantly at the scene of the crash.

Author, activist Helen Nearing killed in crash
Friends pay tribute; Harborside farm will be preserved
By James Straub

BROOKSVILLE — A single-vehicle accident in Brooksville Sunday, September 17, claimed the life of one of the area's most renowned residents.

Helen Nearing, author and activist who along with her late husband, Scott, inspired countless numbers of people to lead "the good life," died at Blue Hill Memorial Hospital shortly after the 1 p.m. accident on Route 176 in Brooksville. She was 91.

Nearing had left her Harborside farm Sunday to see a movie and was traveling east on Route 176 when the 1982 Subaru station wagon she was driving crossed the westbound land and struck a tree near the shoulder of the road. The accident occurred at a sharp left hand turn in the road.

State trooper Chris Coleman said there were no skid marks at the scene of the accident. "It's a mystery as to why she lost control of the car," he said.

According to the officer, witnesses who came to the accident scene seconds after it happened said there were no animals or other vehicles in the area that would have caused her to swerve. The Subaru was checked by a specially trained state trooper who found it to be free of defects. It was raining when the accident occurred, and Coleman said the wet road and sharp corner are considered factors in the accident.

He said his investigation is "far from over" and will include several interviews, but there is a "good possibility" that the specific cause of the accident will never be known.

Nearing was transported to the hospital by members of the Peninsula Ambulance Corps. Coleman said ambulance attendants had told him that she had a faint pulse at the scene and also when they arrived at the hospital. The cause of her death is listed as a broken cervical spine and head injuries.

Two long-time friends of Nearing, Diane Fitzgerald and Jeanne Gaudette, were with her when she died in the hospital. Fitzgerald said that after receiving permission from Nearing's sister, Alice Vaughan, to discontinue life support systems, the doctors allowed the two friends to be alone with Nearing.

"We stood and we meditated," Fitzgerald said. "We tried to help Helen with energy to pass over. We meditated with our hands around her head. She had a heartbeat for another five or ten minutes. She was very peaceful. Then there was a rush of cool air around her when her heart stopped beating."

Nearing's life and the news of her death touched a far-reaching contingent of people who had turned to the Nearings and their books for guidance in their own efforts to lead more simple lives.

"Scott and Helen Nearing are the reason that MOFGA exists," Russ Libby, executive director of the Maine Organic Farmers and Gardeners Association said Monday. Libby credited the Nearings as being the inspiration for hundreds of organic farmers who moved to Maine in the 1970s.

"I feel a deep sense of loss at Helen's passage," Libby said. "Yet, I'm grateful in some ways that it was an easy passage for her. She will be missed by many."

Both Helen and Scott had been featured speakers at the Common Ground Fair, an annual event sponsored by MOFGA. This year's Common Ground Fair will open on Friday, Sept. 22, in Union *[sic — it was actually held in Windsor]*. Helen Nearing was scheduled to speak at the fair at 1 p.m. Sunday, Sept. 24..

Libby said the time slot will now be dedicated to a remembrance of her life. Anyone wishing to share stories or memories of Helen will be welcome to participate.

As news of Nearing's death reached Augusta Monday morning, Libby said that several people gathered in his office and shared memories of the Nearings and their participation in Common Ground Fairs.

Libby said one person recounted the 1975 fair when literally hundreds of back-to-the-land Mainers waited in eager anticipation to hear words of wisdom from the keynote speakers, Helen and Scott Nearing.

When the time came, Scott got up and delivered this four-word speech: "Pay as you go."

The first of many books written by the Nearings, **Living the Good Life** was published in 1954. In 1952, they had moved from Vermont to Harborside, where they built a farm and continued to live a good life, simply and self-sufficiently off the land. Scott Nearing died in 1983 at the age of 100, having decided to end his life by starvation, in a process his widow described later in her book, **Loving and Leaving the Good Life**.

Helen Nearing's latest book, **Light on Aging and Dying**, was just released by Tilbury House publishers in Gardiner.

"That was a really big thing in her life, and it just got completed." Nancy Berkowitz, a close friend and companion of Nearings, said from Nearing's Forest Farm Tuesday morning. "She just got a book in the mail yesterday."

Berkowitz said that just last week Nearing had signed papers with the Trust for Public Land "That will keep the farm as it is forever." Eventually, the land will be managed through an organization to be known as the Good

Life Center. The Social Science Institute, an educational institution for organic and simple living started by the Nearings in the 1970s, will become part of the Good Life Center.

The farm now consists of four acres, a stone house, a walled garden with a sun-heated greenhouse, and a meditation yurt that overlooks Penobscot Bay.

A memorial service will be held at 2 p.m. Sunday, October 1, at the Brooksville Community Center in South Brooksville. "October 1 is World Vegetarian Day, which is very important to her [Nearing]," Berkowitz said.

Berkowitz said friends of Nearing are requesting that people attending the memorial service bring donations of non-perishable foods to be given to area food pantries for distribution to those who need assistance. A donation to the Good Life Center is requested in lieu of flowers. Send donations to The Good Life Center, Box 11, Harborside, 04642.

In addition to the special remembrance scheduled for the Common Ground Fair, an afternoon of Helen Nearing's favorite music will be aired on WERU [a local community-sponsored radio station] Saturday, September 23, from 3 to 5 p.m.

Volunteer programmer Alan Clemence, host of "You Never Can Tell," said this Saturday's show will feature exclusively music from Nearing's own collection of albums. Clemence said he talked to Berkowitz and Ellen LaConte to learn some of Nearing's favorite musical pieces.

Nearing had given up a budding career as a violinist when she met Scott, and she wrote of her favorite violin and musical pieces in **Loving and Leaving the Good Life**. Many of her folk music albums have favorite selections circled or underlined. "She actually left us a message of what she enjoyed," Clemence said.

Berkowitz had had a special relationship with Nearing over the past 18 years. For most of those years, she had spoken to Nearing on a daily basis and visited with her several times a week.

Although she feels a "profound amount of sadness" by the passing of her friend, Berkowitz knows she is not alone in her thoughts of Helen Nearing.

"There are hundreds of people who live in Maine because of the Nearings," she said. "The influence of their lives has touched so many people in such a deep way. Even people who never met them were influenced by them."

The *Weekly Packet*, for whom I frequently freelanced, also asked me to write a guest column for that week's paper. I took a very different tack than I had the previous Sunday in that quiet office off the *BDN* newsroom:

Guest Column
On Helen Nearing

Fifty years before the Vietnam War, Scott Nearing was defending himself in a federal court against an espionage charge for writing an anti-war pamphlet during World War I. Using a First Amendment defense, he was acquitted — but his publisher was convicted for printing his words.

Nearly a decade earlier, in 1911, he wrote a pamphlet against child labor at a time when that exploitation was considered a simple necessity to make a profit — the same excuse, incidentally, given by the South for the need to continue slavery.

Helen Knothe met Scott Nearing about the same time he wrote and published a book called Black America — in 1929, when other words were used to describe that portion of the population. Enchanted with a man who so strongly stood on principle, she left her budding career as a violinist to follow him.

The couple soon found that their strong views were simply unpalatable to the world of academia and high society for which they had been groomed. Teaching and lecturing jobs dried up. Realizing that economically their only choice was subsistence farming, they packed their belongings and headed for the hills of Vermont. Changing their views to conform with a society whose values they abhorred was simply not an option.

So first in Vermont, and then later in Maine, the Nearings worked their gardens, sawed and split their firewood, sold maple syrup and later blueberries for a cash crop, and wrote books and pamphlets.

They were a curious phenomenon in both states. It made no sense to many locals that the Nearings would refuse to climb the ladder of success in favor of a lifestyle many of them were trying desperately to leave behind.

But over time the Nearings gained the sometimes grudging respect of their neighbors. No question they were hard workers. No question they stood on principle and lived their beliefs.

And no question they valued the wisdom of the people who had been living by their wits for generations more than they valued the fancy-dancy hotshot ivory tower textbooks.

The Nearings wrote about that wisdom and their version of a simple but sane way of life in a book they called **Living the Good Life**. Self-published in 1954, it was an underground and poorly distributed book until Schocken reprinted it in 1970, and a whole generation of young people eager for stability devoured it.

In Maine, where it has often been said that the state's best export is its children, the outward population trend suddenly reversed. As if a special magnet had been secretly installed in the air-cooled engines, the Volkswagen vans were drawn from all across the country to the Nearing motherlode on the loop road around Harborside, and then, energized by the experience, would spin off into the hinterlands seeking real estate agents.

But this strange long-haired crowd, unlike so many waves that hit Maine in generations past, did not want to bring with it the society it had left behind. The ones who lasted more than a winter or two were found, for the most part, to be hard-working and gentle people. And suddenly the native subsistence farmers who had been disdained by the developers and considered quaint by the tourists, found themselves to be local gurus to the head-banded hippies seeking true knowledge — or at least useful information on how to shear a sheep.

Scott died 12 years ago at the age of 100, deliberately, by refusing to eat. He knew it was time.

Helen died Sunday with her sneakers on when she lost control of her car on a curve in the road made slick by the first rain in weeks. Her death came a week after she had signed papers to establish a teaching center on the Harborside farm. She was 91.

Consider what society would be like if Helen and Scott Nearing were not remarkable, but the norm. Think about a world where it was common for people to live their principles, to speak the truth as they saw it, to treat life — all life — with the reverence it deserves.

A pipe dream? Only if we think it is.

One thing I am sure of is that this planet is a far better place for Helen and Scott Nearing having lived their lives according to this, their favorite and oft-repeated mantra:

"Do the best that you can in the place that you are, and be kind."

The Sept. 21 edition of *Maine Times* had this story by deputy editor Betta Stothart:

Helen Nearing's parting gifts: a book and a future for Forest Farm

All day Monday, friends and neighbors of Helen Nearing came to her stone house on Cape Rosier to say farewell to the woman whose life had become an example of frugal and responsible living. According to her wishes, Nearing's body was laid out in her living room for a day-long wake. On Tuesday, Nearing, who believed in reincarnation, was taken to Auburn for cremation. Her ashes will be returned to Harborside and scattered with the ashes of her former husband, Scott Nearing.

Helen Nearing, who, with Scott, co-authored the best-selling book **Living the Good Life**, was killed Sunday when her yellow Subaru station wagon failed to negotiate a turn near her Cape Rosier home and struck a tree, killing her instantly. She was 91.

Nearing had announced many times that, when the time was right, she would choose to leave this world deliberately, as did her husband, who at the age of 100 stopped eating. Yet friends say the events preceding Sunday's accident seemed strangely to suggest that her departure would come sooner.

On Thursday, she signed papers establishing stewardship for Forest Farm and The Good Life Center. And on Monday, the day after her death, her latest book, *Light on Aging and Dying*, was delivered, printed and bound, to her home.

Nearing chose the Boston-based Trust for Public Lands, an organization devoted to preserving land and significant places, to act as the steward of her handmade stone house, organic gardens, and all the papers she wrote with Scott Nearing. The Trust for Public Lands is also the protector of Walden Woods, site of Henry David Thoreau's famed cabin.

Peter Forbes, regional director for the Trust, said Monday that three years of discussion led to Thursday's signing. "To have that document signed and to lose her within a week is really profound. I think we all feel really alone, but I think she knew," said Forbes, who was also a friend.

According to Forbes, The Good life Center will likely have an appointed board of directors which will be charged with maintaining a set of programs designed to enable people to continue the experiences embodied in the lives of Helen and Scott Nearing.

Forbes said one idea is to conduct an annual competition in which the winner would be allowed to spend a year at Forest Farm, gardening, maintaining the land, and continuing the homesteading tradition defined by its creators.

Forbes said the Nearing's first Maine home, which was owned by Stanley Joseph, may also become part of The Good Life Center. Joseph, who died last spring, left the property to his brother.

Nearing's final book, *Light on Aging and Dying*, was scheduled to be the subject of a fall book tour. Instead, discussion groups and memorials may be held in her honor.

Rob Groves, a neighbor who answered the phone at Helen's house Monday, said she left behind a garden overflowing with ripe tomatoes, flowering kale, strawberries, beans, squash and parsnips. Two compost piles had just been turned for the last time, and were "almost as neat as Scott ever kept them" said Groves.

On Oct. 1, National Vegetarian Day, a memorial service will be held for Nearing at the Brooksville Community Center. According to her wishes, donations can be sent to The Good Life Center or to HOME (Homemakers Organized for More Employment), a community farm in Orland that helps provide shelter and aid for the poor.

The weekly ***Ellsworth American***, brought to local prominence by owner and former ***Washington Post*** editor James Russell Wiggins, in its Sept. 21 ran a report by Shirley Chase. It read in part:

Helen Nearing dies in crash

...Their method of living involved great strength of purpose and commitment, as it involved both of them in hard physical labor; and it put emphasis on a greater than average sense of responsibility for one's self and for the community. The Nearings inspired countless others to become actively involved politically.

Many others followed their example, moving to Maine, settling down to farm, doing for themselves in the Nearings' back-to-earth manner. Many believe the book was a powerfully motivating factor in starting the great migration to Maine beginning in the 1960s.

It might surprise some to know that Helen Nearing, while continuing her violin studies in Europe in the 1920s, was introduced to Krishnamurti and his brother Nityananda, which led her to accompany them to India where she became acquainted with Raja Yoga, meditation, and Eastern music making. In her words, "I returned to the United States after years abroad, with my head in the clouds and with no knowledge of what had been going on in the world. I had hardly done a stroke of work in my life and had lived generally as a parasite. I was a complete political ignoramus."

Meeting Scott Nearing changed all that. Scott Nearing was a radical socialist, one who "parted company with Western civilization." When he met Helen, he felt that she should learn how the "other half" lived. He convinced her to get in touch with reality, to take a job in a factory to get a "real-life education." She started with "candy packing at $22 a week and living in a $7-a-week hall bedroom in Brooklyn." For $20 a month they lived in a three-room cold-water unheated flat in New York City on 14th Street. This led them to decide to be "poor in the country [rather] than poor in the city." The couple then moved to Vermont, and later to Harborside.

Up to her death, Nearing was accepting up to 10 to 12 visitors a day — those who came to enjoy her unique personality, her keen intelligence, and the warmth she radiated. And they came to visit the farm and buildings that the Nearings had built with their own hands from the ground up.

Maine Times, for which I had also freelanced, asked me to do a "Back of the Book" essay on Helen. I told them I was overexposed on the issue, that they should ask someone else. They insisted.

This is what ran Sept. 28:

Lessons learned from Helen and Scott

Editors note: Helen Nearing died Sept. 17

HARBORSIDE — From day one, Helen and Scott Nearing insisted that we call them by their first names. At the time, when I was in my 20s and they were 50 and 70 years ahead of me, I thought the request odd, not to mention in direct violation of how I had been taught, growing up in Ohio, to show respect for my elders. On the other hand, it would be disrespectful not to address them as they wished, so I did.

Only looking back many years later did I realize what a powerful message that simple request had sent to me. Not only were they treating me as an equal, but I instantly became a contemporary, during the Vietnam War era, of a man who had been tried under the Espionage Act for writing anti-war pamphlets in World War I.

I often felt I was living in a time warp during the seven years we were Helen and Scott's nearest neighbors on Cape Rosier. Part of that, of course, was self-induced. Following the example laid out in **Living the Good Life**, we had deliberately moved from a comfortable suburban lifestyle, with all the modern appliances, to a homestead without electricity or running water on the 25 acres of land the Nearings had sold to us. I did not grow up hauling water and cooking homegrown food on a woodburning cookstove, but my mother did, and now my two kids have those kinds of stories to tell.

Once Helen and Scott got me used to being treated as an equal despite my youth and inexperience, I was ready for their next major lesson — to be open to possibility by always challenging my assumptions. Two events, where I was not the only one to get that message, stand out.

The first was at one of the discussion groups the Nearings moderated every Monday night in their cavernous living room. With windows on three sides, a huge stone fireplace, and the interior wall entirely taken up with just part of their large collection of books, the room could comfortably hold two or three dozen people.

I was sitting on a bench next to one of the visitors who came by the hundreds and thousands every summer and stayed anywhere from an hour to a season. We were leaning against the bookshelves, which I had recently helped Helen rearrange, when the subject of flying saucers came up.

"Anyone who believes in flying saucers is stupid," the pilgrim next to me said with conviction.

There was an awkward pause in the room, Helen smiled her "I see you're sure of that" smile, and then the next person brought up another subject. I gently poked the young man in the ribs, and pointed to the bookshelf behind us. About eight inches of space on one shelf was taken up with Helen's books on UFOs and other extraterrestrial phenomena. He blanched, then quietly tried to fit unobtrusively through the cracks in the wooden floor.

The second event happened in the winter of 1975, shortly after we learned that Central Maine Power Company had bought an option to 400 acres of land across the road from the Nearings. Proposing to site a nuclear power plant across the street from that particular pair did not strike us rabid environmentalists as the smartest public-relations move CMP could make. And, to say the least, it didn't sit well with those of us who would be living up the road within spitting distance of the sucker.

Helen, civic minded as she was, sweetly asked CMP to send out someone who could detail the company's plans to the property's abutters. CMP was happy to comply.

"Let's hear what the man has to say," Helen said, matter-of-factly introducing the speaker to at least a dozen of us, in denim and plaid, in braids or beards (or both), politely seated in her toasty-warm, wood-heated kitchen. Clearly, we were not to jump to conclusions until we had heard him out.

Their heavy kitchen table, made from a single slab of wood at least 4 inches thick and 6 feet long, had been pushed up against the far wall. The young man stood in front of that table, smiled at our eager faces, explained his mission, and said cheerfully:

"Well, you all use electricity...."

We looked at each other, looked at him, smiled back, and collectively shook our heads in the negative. The electric line on Cape Rosier at that point ended at the Nearings — it had been extended to the farm just before Helen and Scott bought the property — and we all lived beyond the last pole.

The panic on the CMP rep's face was for all the world like that of an explorer who had stumbled across a flesh-eating cult — and who suddenly realized we were all between him and the door. Not to worry; he was in a room full of vegetarians. But it was nice to see that healthy color in his office-whitened cheeks.

Strangely enough, CMP let the option lapse on that 400 acres. There was a problem with getting rights-of-way to bring the power out to the nearest grid. Or something.

When we accepted their offer to sell us a part of their farm, I thought it would be great to have Helen and Scott as neighbors, because we could run to them for advice on gardening and homesteading. And I knew we would need that advice.

I'm sure I share a sentiment with many thousands of people when I say that, in dealing with the Nearings, we got more than we bargained for.

Yes, they taught us how to build compost and grow carrots. But more importantly, they showed us what it looks like up close and personal to treat everything and everyone on Earth with respect and love, to live a life grounded on one's principles, and to find delight in the unanticipated.

On Sept. 29, 1995, I wrote this letter to Steve Bost:

> I want to thank you for calling me the day after Helen died. I did pass on your experiences to those closest to her, and they really appreciated your thoughtfulness, and for being there in Helen's last conscious moments.
>
> I thought you might want to see what ran in her hometown paper, the Weekly Packet (copy enclosed). As far as I'm concerned, there is no contradiction between your experience losing her pulse in the car, and the final declaration of death after a temporary revival by CPR. Diane Fitzgerald told me that Helen had a pulse, but was not breathing on her own by the time Diane got to the hospital — within minutes of Helen's arrival by ambulance.
>
> I thought the diagnosis of a broken neck to be interesting, especially since you told me she nodded her head and squeezed your hand. The only thing I can conjecture is that her neck may have been cracked in the accident, and got further jostled in the attempts to revive her.
>
> As you can see, the way the trooper described the scene, he was implying what you said you suspect — that something internal may have happened to Helen before the crash. No autopsy was done, so we'll never know for sure.
>
> Through a series of strange incidents, several of them involving Helen and Scott, I have grown to sincerely believe that nothing in this life is coincidental. So it must have been important, in some sort of cosmic way, for you to be with Helen in that car. I know it was important for Diane and Jeanne to be with her when she finally and officially died in the hospital. I'm still trying to figure out if I fit into this scenario as any more than a messenger. If not, that's fine with me...
>
> Since I haven't gotten anything from you, I am assuming you did not put something together for me to read at her memorial Sunday. That's fine. It sounds like there may not be a place to do that during the proceedings anyway.
>
> You looked tired in the article on your latest venture. [Ross Perot had just announced a petition drive to get Perot's new Independence Party officially recognized in all 50 states, and Steve had less than three months to collect 26,565 signatures in Maine.] It's been a long couple of weeks, hasn't it?
>
> Thank you again for calling. It meant a lot to me.

Helen's scheduled speaking time at the Common Ground Fair, just a week after her death, turned into an impromptu memorial service, with

Chapter 34 — And the Time Came

dozens of people coming up to the mike to share their thoughts and feelings with hundreds of people in the stands.

The official memorial service Oct. 1 in the Brooksville Community Center and gymnasium, the site of many Brooksville Town Meetings the Nearings had attended, was packed to the gills. I and my friend David, who had accompanied me to Stan's memorial service just a few months before, got there early to help with the parking. David had also decided on his own tribute — he printed up Scott and Helen's favorite sayings in large type, pasted then on the back of my old campaign posters, mounted them on stakes, and pounded them into the ground like Burma Shave signs on the side of the road leading to the Community Center where Helen and Scott had attended so many annual town meetings.

As people walked to and from the service, they could read:

Helen Nearing
1904-1995

And Be Kind

Where You Are

In The Place

That You Can

Do the Best

GO

YOU

AS

and

PAY

Scott Nearing
1883-1983

Helen's will, filed in Hancock County Probate Court, reiterated her bequest of Forest Farm to Trust for Public Lands, along with her library, and her and Scott's published works and copyrights. She requested that TPL sign a conservation easement with Blue Hill Heritage Trust to protect the property "in perpetuity from inappropriate use or development."

She then bequeathed $15,000 "to my good and loyal friend Nancy [Richardson] Berkowitz," along with $5,000 each to her children "toward college, though that's not a command."

The rest of her estate, including bank accounts, stocks, bonds, and proceeds of insurance policies, she bequeathed to "my friend Ellen LaConte." Probate records did not indicate the size of that bequest.

Helen left no endowment to Trust for Public Lands for the support of Forest Farm. She and Peter Forbes at TPL had anticipated three years of Helen's active participation in fund-raising efforts to establish such an endowment.

Helen had signed her last will and testament on August 15, 1995, a month before her death.

I took this photo of Helen in May 1992

Chapter 35
Good Life Economics 101

Living as a homesteader on Cape Rosier in the 1970s was an incredible experience for me. It was there that I learned life's deep lessons — how to be responsible for myself at the most basic level, as well as how interconnected we are to all the other lives on this earth, both human and non-human.

On the homestead, those lessons are more than philosophical. It is one thing to know on an intellectual level that milk comes from cows and goats. It is quite another to present a good meal to a friendly animal, then pull up a stool, lean a shoulder into her side, reach underneath, and with a firm grasp, accept a warm, white, healthy liquid in exchange for her contented munches at the other end.

Many how-to books in the 1960s and 1970s, by the Nearings and several others, offered good solid information on a lot of different topics. The magic about the Nearings was that after they pushed our buttons, they egged us on to action.

After all, here was a couple who had tried to work within the system, but when they followed their beliefs they found themselves outcasts in their own society. Many of my generation could relate to that. For Scott it was academic and political rejection; for Helen it was her family's mortification when she took up with a married man.

(To a question of why she had no children, Helen in ***Loving and Leaving the Good Life*** wrote:

> It was bad enough at the time — 50 years ago — to live, unmarried, with a man; to have had illegitimate little Scotties and Scottinas around would have killed my devoted parents. They had had enough to bear as it was with my unconventional behavior.

I asked her once how she had managed that, in those days before birth control pills and devices. She looked uncomfortable for a few seconds, then would only say, "There are ways."

Only years later, reading her letters to Scott, would I learn that she had once miscarried and had been advised by her doctors to never get pregnant again.)

The Nearings opted to drop out, another sentiment that proved popular in the '60s and '70s. But rather than suggest mind-altering drugs or violence to deal with a reality we could not abide, the Nearings professed that we could get the freedom and independence we wanted through good planning (using our brains) and hard work (using our muscles). And, best of all, they insisted that it was possible to do all this on a part-time basis, thus feeding our suspicion that the 40-hour work week was all a capitalistic plot to enslave the masses, us included.

But mine was also a generation raised on the mantra: "If it sounds too good to be true, it probably is." The slight suspicion that this whole back-to-the-land scheme was actually a bunch of hogwash, I believe, is what drove the masses to visit Harborside. We needed to see for ourselves that the place actually existed in more than someone's imagination. We needed to touch the stones in the wall surrounding the garden, witness the lush, weed-free greenery inside those walls, confirm with our own eyes that Helen and Scott were indeed alive and living well.

And if, while we were there, we were able to help them out with a little wood-splitting or some rock-hauling or compost-building, well, it was the least we could do to make up for the interruption we had caused in their lives.

By the time Keith and I had begun our homesteading journey, we had swallowed whole the Good Life theory of economics.

To our credit, I think, we did manage to pull off the financial end of it. We came into the Maine woods with enough money saved up from our jobs in conventional society to buy our meager 25 acres at the going rate for land and to build a house using our own trees, scavenged windows, and a load of rough green lumber. Devouring all those how-to books, we did grow most of our food, lived with little in the way of modern conveniences or garish clutter, bought hardly anything, spent as little time as possible on renting out our brains and muscles for cash money, and managed to live warmly and well-fed on a level of income far below the national poverty level.

What we didn't do was do all that on four hours a day. There were simply too many time-consuming tasks involving exhausting physical work. Once we got done what had to be done, we didn't have much time or energy for anything else. It didn't take long for progress to be counted in smaller and smaller increments — unless we had visitors and put them to work.

But, we reasoned, it wasn't the fault of The Plan that we had chosen to raise animals, and to make our own cheese and culture our own yogurt. It wasn't Helen's fault that I defied her example and wasted my time baking bread and pies. And when kids entered the picture, we expected that all thoughts of limiting homesteading work schedules would go out the south-facing windows. They did.

Their plan surely would have worked the way they said if only we had

Chapter 35 — Good Life Economics 101

done it the way the Nearings said they did it.

I didn't know then that — farm animals and kids notwithstanding — there was no way in hell Keith and I could have homesteaded the way the Nearings actually did it.

When it came time to create the Board of Stewards for the new Good Life Center, I was glad to add my name to the list of about 70 people who would oversee the continuing operation of Forest Farm and the Nearings' writings.

Looking over the list, I recognized only a quarter of the names. Many of them lived out of state. Helen and Scott's impact had indeed been far-reaching.

Yet, despite my continuing support of their homesteading philosophy, there came a time when I needed to confront those things about the Nearings that had always nagged at me.

The little inconsistencies, dietary and otherwise, I could ignore. Some of their firm pronouncements ("When enough bread labor has been performed to secure the year's living, we will stop earning until the next crop season") I had long ago dismissed as not only short-sighted, but downright irresponsible.

But what bothered me most was that several points in Scott's economic formula just didn't add up. Since Scott was the trained economist, I attribute the Good Life economic remarks to him.

For instance, the Nearings started their Vermont tale by stating that they bought a 65-acre rundown farm from the Widow Ellonen for $300 down and an $800 loan. I always thought it was odd that the Federal Loan Bank in 1933, in the middle of the Great Depression, would allow a mortgage amounting to more than a full year's wages to be assumed by a man of 50 with no job, no income, and no farming experience.

Yet ***Living the Good Life*** goes on to tell us that the first spring they were in Vermont, Scott and Helen decided to buy the "large tract of cut-over land on Pinnacle Mountain, adjoining our place and lying back from the town road." Scott explains in great detail why the tract of John Tibbets' land cost only $3 an acre, but doesn't say how many acres were involved. Was a "large tract" several hundred acres? Where did the money come from to buy it?

Then they turned around and bought the sugar bush next door from the Widow Hoard. How much did that cost? How did they pay for it? A bigger mortgage? Strangely, economist Scott Nearing doesn't say.

In the very next chapter, "Our Design for Living," Point #3 insists on:

> No bank loans. No slavery to interest on mortgages, notes and I.O.U's.

"The money lenders are able to enjoy comfort and luxury, without doing any productive labor," the Nearings state, and they were agin it.

So, what happened to their $800 mortgage? What was going on here?

When it came time to write this book, I knew I needed to do a little detective work. I found and followed the clues left lying around in their books. I gave new importance to Helen's off-hand remark when I was interviewing Scott — a statement she later repeated in ***Loving and Leaving the Good Life*** — as to how they came to own the sugar bush in Vermont. I poured over deeds, probate documents, personal letters spanning several decades donated to the University of Vermont by their lifelong friends Hank and Ada Mayer. I talked to Helen's biographer, Ellen LaConte.

A week spent in the Nearings' old stomping ground in Vermont proved very productive, after David and I got the geography straightened out. The Nearing and Knothe land holdings jumped back and forth across three town lines, Jamaica, Winhall and Stratton, with the deeds in each municipality neatly recorded in each of those town halls.

A chance meeting — if you believe in coincidences — with Greg Joly in the Jamaica Vermont Town Hall resulted in a delightful afternoon and a very helpful guided windshield tour of all the old Nearing properties in Vermont. Greg, also a member of the far-reaching Good Life Center's Board of Stewards, was in the town office on school board business, saw our Maine car with my name on an old political bumper sticker, and made the connection.

The same week we were in Vermont, George Breen, who had bought a portion of the Vermont Forest Farm from the Nearings in the early 1950s, was making a visit to The Good Life Center in Harborside. While there, he donated some documents he had in a file, including a bill of sale between Helen and Mercy Hoard.

Putting all this research together, here's what we found:

Ellonen property

Scott Nearing bought the Ellonen farm on Dec. 6, 1932. The deed describes the property as having 75 acres in Winhall and 10 in Stratton — not the 65 acres they mention in their book. Scott put $300 down and assumed the remaining $800 on the mortgage the Ellonens already had on the property. That 35-year mortgage had begun its life on Feb. 21, 1923, as a $900 mortgage at 5 ½ percent interest. In nearly 10 years, the principle had been reduced by only $100.

Just over a year later, on Dec. 28, 1933, that mortgage was discharged as paid in full.

The following month, on Jan. 15, 1934, Scott Nearing of Ridgewood,

NJ, transferred 10 acres of this land in Winhall to Helen Knothe of Patterson, NJ.

Tibbets property

On Jan. 2, 1933, less than a month after Scott bought the Ellonen farm, Helen Knothe bought 57 acres of land in Jamaica from John C. Tibbets. That same day, Tibbets sold Scott Nearing two adjoining parcels, a 50-acre piece and a 400-acre piece. Total acreage: 507.

In *Making of a Radical*, Scott tells us of "a rather large forest tract, bought for $2,200, and a moderate-sized farm bought at the same time for $2,500." No mortgages were recorded on any of these Tibbets woodlot parcels.

Linscott property

On Dec. 12, 1933, two weeks before he paid off the Ellonen property, Scott bought two parcels of land in Winhall, totaling 215 acres, from Charles and Linda Linscott. Scott makes no mention of the Linscott properties in *Living the Good Life*, but this may be the "moderate-sized farm" he mentioned in *Making of a Radical*. No price is given in the deeds, but the Linscotts had an outstanding mortgage of $547.54.

Once again, there are no mortgages listed for Scott on either of these properties.

Hoard property

On Dec. 5, 1934, Mercy Hoard and Helen Knothe signed a sales agreement to 75 acres in Winhall, for a price of $1,600. It was hand-written on stationery of L. P. Martin & Son, Vermont Real Estate, Newfane, Vt. Helen made a $60 down payment, with the balance to be paid within 30 days. Mercy Hoard reserved the right to sugar the property during the 1935 spring tapping season, and was to vacate the property by May 1935. On Dec. 21, 1934, the deed is signed and recorded.

No mortgage is recorded in Helen's name. A week after the deed transfer was recorded, Mercy Hoard's three-year-old mortgage is discharged as paid in full.

Four months later, on April 12, 1935, Mercy A. Hoard sold another 35 acres in Winhall to Scott Nearing. No price is mentioned. No mortgage is recorded.

Sarah Clayton sandpit

On Aug 25, 1933, Sarah M. Clayton sold a 13-acre sandpit to Scott Nearing for $135. On June 20, 1934, Scott transferred three acres of this property to Helen.

In the 28 months between December 1932 and April 1935, Helen Knothe and Scott Nearing had gone on a land-buying binge that netted them 930 acres of land in three towns. To put that in perspective, a square mile contains 640 acres. They were land barons even by Vermont standards.

Just adding up the figures we have for most of the properties, we get $7,535. That was a lot of money to drop into a rural community at the height of the Great Depression. Where did all that money come from?

During Scott's obituary interview, and again in ***Loving and Leaving the Good Life***, Helen mentioned a legacy from a former Dutch suitor, without identifying him. But she told Ellen LaConte about him. His name was J.J. "Koos" Van Der Leeuw. His family was in the cocoa importing and manufacturing business in Amsterdam. The family was a major contributor to the Theosophical Society. Helen had met Koos on her travels with Krishnamurti. For a short time she had worked for Koos as a secretary. And yes, he had asked Helen to marry him.

LaConte said Koos, a private pilot, died in a plane crash shortly after Helen returned to these shores at Scott's behest. LaConte said she believes the legacy was in the neighborhood of $30,000 to $40,000.

In a letter to Hank and Ada Mayer, Helen stated that when she and Scott first moved to Vermont, a day's wages amounted to $2.50. That means in the early to mid-1930s the annual pay for someone working full-time five days a week in Vermont was about $600. A six-day-a-week worker earned $750 a year. That is assuming that year-round, full-time work could be found.

Even after paying for all that land, Scott and Helen had plenty left over from that legacy alone to get them through several years without having to lift a finger.

But that one-time legacy was not their only source of unearned income. And this is where things start to get a little strange.

Among the documents filed in the registry of deeds are two agreements with Floyd Hurd, dated four days apart and identical except one is with Scott and the other is with Helen.

Jamaica, Vermont, April 6, 1935

Agreement between Helen Knothe and Floyd Hurd concerning the Hoard Place sugar lot.

Floyd Hurd will sugar the Hoard sugar lot, providing the labor, the wood, the evaporator, the gathering and storage tanks, and 1,000 buckets with covers and spouts.

Chapter 35 — Good Life Economics 101

> Helen Knothe will provide the sugar lot, the sugar house, 1,000 buckets with covers and spouts, two small storage tanks for use on the sugar lot, and the pipe needed to connect them with the sugar house. All buckets and covers provided by both parties shall be galvanized.
> Floyd Hurd to take two-thirds and Helen Knothe one-third of the syrup. This agreement shall be binding on both parties until the end of the sugar season in the spring of 1938.
> Recorded in the Winhall Town Clerk's Office, May 4, 1935.

Scott's agreement was signed April 10, 1935, and recorded the same day as Helen's.

Incidentally, Charles Linscott, from whom the Nearings bought 215 acres in 1933, was the brother of Zoe Hurd, Floyd's wife.

Two things about these sugaring agreements jumped out at me. The first is the time frame. In one chapter in *Living the Good Life*, Scott says he and Helen sugared with Floyd Hurd from 1933 to 1940. In another chapter, the first sugar they had to sell was in 1934. A third reference was to the above written agreement, dated 1935.

Helen and Scott didn't buy the Hoard property until the winter of 1934-35, and didn't sign the sugaring agreement until after the sugaring season in 1935 had ended. It would appear that the first year Scott and Helen had any syrup to sell was in the Spring of 1936.

Whatever the starting year actually was, this is what Scott wrote in *Living the Good Life*:

> That first year, without raising a finger, we got one-quarter of the syrup crop for the use of the tools and the bush and some fuel. In a syrup season lasting from four to eight weeks, owning only the maple trees, the sugar house and some poor tools, and doing none of the work, we got enough syrup to pay our taxes and insurance, to provide us with all the syrup we could use through the year, plenty to give away to our friends and to sell.

The important thing to note here is not that Scott got the percentage wrong, but that he signed on to this agreement at all.

This is the same man, remember, who blasted the money lenders for being:

> able to enjoy comfort and luxury, without doing any productive labor.

The sugar bush Floyd Hurd worked had been bought with someone else's (Koos') money. Yet this man with such strongly held, and publicly proclaimed, communistic and socialistic beliefs apparently did not hesitate to accept between a quarter and a third of the take, based solely upon the fact that he and Helen owned the means of production — the sugar bush, the sugar house, and some of the equipment.

> That summer, however, we discovered that maple syrup in Vermont is better than cash.

Why did they have to wait until summer to make this discovery? For the simple reason that rural Vermonters did not buy maple syrup. Those not in the syrup business could make enough for family consumption by tapping a few trees in the back woodlot and boiling the sap down on top of the wood stove that is going hot and heavy that time of year anyway. On a small scale, this process added much-needed humidity to the home's dry winter air. Any extra syrup made this way would be passed on to friends or end up as Christmas presents. Maple syrup was the zucchini of the Vermont woods.

Real Vermont maple syrup may be a legitimate agricultural commodity, but on the open market it is also a luxury item. It wasn't until the dreaded "summer people" and tourists showed up, bringing their disposable incomes with them, that Helen and Scott realized what they had.

Yet Scott did not write kindly about the summer community.

> Summer people do more than upset Vermont's economy. By living on their places during the summer and closing them for the balance of the year, they turn sections of the State into ghost towns. Neighborhoods, to be meaningful, must have continuity. Part-time towns are parasitic dead towns...
>
> If this process goes far enough, Vermont will develop a suburban or vacationland economy, built on the dollars of those who make their income elsewhere and spend part of it during a few weeks or months of the Vermont summer. Such an economy is predominately parasitic in terms of production, although income and expense accounts may be in balance. Carried to its logical conclusion, it would make Vermonters sell their labor-power to summer residents, mowing their lawns and doing their laundry, thus greatly reducing their own economic self-dependence. Such an economy may attract more cheap dollars to the state, but it will hardly produce self-reliant men.

Clearly Scott considered lawn-mowing, laundry and other service work to be demeaning. This is the same man who, when he was on a lecture tour, had his shoes professionally shined. But never mind that — taking care of oneself was good; taking care of other people for pay was bad.

Yet the contemptible summer folks and the detestable tourists who

Chapter 35 — Good Life Economics 101

brought home a cute and pricey jug or jar of maple syrup as a momento were the only ones who had the money and the desire to buy what Helen and Scott had to sell. Upon this contradictory base Helen and Scott built their Vermont self-sufficiency.

But they didn't just let the customers come to them. Despite their anti-capitalist stances, Helen and Scott were both excellent marketers. It didn't take them long to decide that retail was the way to go. Lifelong friend Hank Mayer sold both syrup and maple sugar candy for them in the Midwest. Several shops in Vermont carried their product in small glass "Carrie Nation" jars that Helen had a factory make especially for her. Stores in New York clamored for all they could get.

On July 24, 1941, the *New York Herald* ran this story:

Maple Sugar Candy
Tells Stories in Pictures
NY Violinist in Search of Vermont
Summer Home Finds a Business Instead
By Clementine Paddleford

Maple sugar picture boxes come to Fifth Avenue from a forest farm in the heart of the Vermont hills. The candy pieces are in amusing forms heretofore unused by the maple-sweet packers. Cleverly these are arranged to tell stories in pictures. Choose for the child "Little Man in the Woods,"...Tadpoles of the family love "Pigs in Clover," three pink pigs with clover clumps everywhere. "Three Rabbits Out Late" is a grouping for the older youngsters and the whimsical-minded grownups.... "Little Red Schoolhouse" would have pleased Hansel and Gretel with its maple-sugar walls, roof and candy door...

MUSICAL FARMER — Designer of these maple scenes is a New York violinist who has gone rural and for keeps. It was four years ago that Helen Knothe traveled to Jamaica, Vt., in March to look for a summer place. The first thaw had come. Farmers were harvesting their principal crop, the maple sap. Helen dug in and helped. The whole colorful procedure of maple sugaring fascinated the young musician for its basic principles were no different, she discovered, than those practiced in some remote past by the Indian squaw...Two weeks of sugaring and the violinist had changed her life plans. She would be a sugar farmer and no dilly-dallying. She bought a hundred acres of maple woods. She did and still does her own clearing. She makes her own sugar roads through the "bush." She cleans the tanks and sap gatherer, the pails, more than one thousand buckets in all. She oversees the boiling of the sap into syrup. She makes her own sugar and sells her own crop. She refuses to do what neighbor farmers do, sell syrup to big companies who blend to public tastes. More money, she reasoned, to build her own market and pack her own syrup and her own maple sweets.

...This year Helen has but 500 gallons of syrup — just half a crop. The weather this spring wasn't right for sap rising. Syrup is stored in gallon glass containers and repacked as needed or evaporated into sugar. The candy Helen makes is the old-fashioned granulated sugar crystallized while hot, as the pioneers did. Better flavor, she thinks, than those fancy soft creams that have come into vogue in recent days.

Candy beats syrup sales. Folks love those unusual shapes and the picture package. Something else that sells the sugar and is Helen's innovation — maple candy colored pink, yellow, rose and green. Now several of the larger sugar makers have borrowed her idea. She wishes that they would take their eyes off her kitchen in the hills.

Accompanying the story is a photo with the caption:
> Helen Knothe, down from Vermont, sets up a maple tree display of her handicraft sweets.

Near the end of ***Living the Good Life***, in summarizing the self-sufficiency of their Vermont experience, the Nearings proclaimed among other things that:

> We bought no candy....

Of course they didn't buy candy. They sold it.

And then there is the curious way Helen and Scott say in ***Living the Good Life*** that they priced their maple syrup:

> We kept careful cost figures, but we never used them to determine whether we should or should not make syrup. We tapped our trees as each sap season came along. Our figures showed us what the syrup had cost. When the season was over and the syrup on hand, we wrote to various correspondents in California or Florida, told them what our syrup had cost, and exchanged our product for equal value of their citrus, walnuts, olive oil or raisins. As a result of these transactions, we laid in a supply of items at no cash outlay, which we could not ourselves produce. Our livelihood base was broadened as a result of our efforts in the sugar bush and the sap house...

How this exchange looked from the other end is a bit murky. Did their friends grow what they exchanged with Helen and Scott and use the same accounting system as the Nearings to determine value? Or did they just buy locally and ship it out? Or, in a scenario that I think is equally possible, did their friends in warmer climates simply subsidize the Nearings by agreeing to these food exchanges, possibly at inflated prices for syrup?

...We also sold our syrup and sugar on the open market. In selling anything, we tried to determine exact costs and set our prices not in terms of what the traffic would bear but in terms of the costs — figuring in our own time at going day wages.

Now I happen to think that is quite a statement for a economist to make. Was he really disavowing the free market concept of supply and demand? Under their accounting system, was their syrup more — or less — expensive than others? Did they figure out that they would have to sell their syrup at retail, with all the extra work that involved, in order to recover their production costs, including that of their own labor?

Economist Scott Nearing does not say.

Five years after they bought their first piece of Vermont property, the Nearings started selling off their holdings.

The first, three acres of the sandpit property, Helen sold to Fred Richmond on May 14, 1937. This was probably the parcel with their experimental log cabin, which they say in *Living the Good Life* that they sold for $600.

On July 17, 1940, Scott Nearing of Jamaica transferred five acres of that sandpit lot to Helen Knothe of Winhall. (Curiously, many of the deeds between Helen and Scott in these years list different towns of residence. They seemed to alternate. One deed has Scott a resident of Jamaica and Helen of Winhall, while on the next deed it might be the opposite.) The next month, on Aug. 21, 1940, Helen sold that five acres, including its dwelling and a springhouse, to Ben Chew Tilghman Jr. of Philadelphia. Their book puts the sale price at $2,000.

Next came 50 acres of the Ellonen property, including the house, a barn and bathhouse, which they sold to Paul A. and Adele Rapp Costello of Long Island, NY. According to a Sept. 26, 1942 agreement, the price was $1,900. Accepting a $500 down payment, the Nearings took back a $1,400 mortgage, payable monthly "together with interest" until the Costellos could secure a bank mortgage, but no later than Jan. 1, 1944. The actual deed transferring the property was signed Nov. 30, 1943, the same day the Costellos got a $950 mortgage with the Vermont Savings Bank.

On July 2, 1943, three years after he had bought the sandpit property with the stone house, Ben Tilghman transferred the property back to Helen. No financial details were recorded in the deed.

The following year, 1944, old friends Hank and Ada Mayer were getting serious about moving to Vermont, and expressed interest in the sandpit property with the stone house. Helen became very concerned.

Jamaica, Vt. March 24 [1944]
Dear Hank & Ada,

I feel prompted to send you a letter. I don't know if Scott will approve. I'll get his OK before sending it.

It's about your coming here.

It's a great pity, Hank, you couldn't come here for all or part of sugaring. It's not so much that we needed or didn't need the help. It would have given you a slant on the job, & the winter here. Both have been long drawn out. It's been cold so long & so late that we're just about getting into the swing of sugaring & it's already late in March (We started tapping out 23rd Feb.)

And if you'd been here, Hank, we could have talked over a lot of things before you finally move your family here.

You know the advantages of living here I trust, so we won't go into that. Let's look at the other side of the ledger before you take the fatal plunge.

Here are things as they've been going over in my mind the last month or two.

The stone cabin was built for a summer place; never conceived of it to be used year round. Ski weekends might have been possible. After all one can put up with cold or inconveniences for a short time, & food can be brought in.

A stove in the kitchen will keep bathroom & kitchen snug. (And I trust, but don't know about, water pipes in & out.) Heatilator in living room has not to my knowledge ever really heated up main room. It's big, & long, & high, & hard to heat. The bedroom would just have to be kept closed & cold. That's alright for 1 or 2 persons. I had a NY apt. for years where the bedroom was the "icebox." But with more of you, & children — not so good.

One of the schoolteachers up here lived in the house for one winter but gave up all idea of heating big rooms & moved cot & all into kitchen & was very snug!

There's no place to store food for any length of time or in cold weather. There's a small outdoor root cellar but things would freeze there in winter, & it's too small for a family.

People up here still live as they used to in the old days — barrels of flour, tubs of this, bushels of that, 1000 quarts of canned stuff. You just can't go to the store for what you want when you want. First, the distance. Second, in winter, the roads may not be open.

Another storage problem is clothes. There just ain't no attic (only a place to put light boxes) & while a few cupboards could be put in they'd be far from adequate for a family.

Whereas you could camp along in the room space for a few summer months, when it really came to living in it, all winter & all year, you'd find yourselves horribly cramped for just room space for 4 people.

There's no garage for a car & that would be bad in winter. If you did manage to put one up this summer (with [wartime] material restrictions, etc.) if by the house it would be terrific hill for car to climb in winter & if put by side of road you'd always have to clamber up to house in probably deep snow.

To build yourselves a house in the near future looks highly improbable. In any case you couldn't get it done by next winter, which is my main concern for you.

I wish you'd come and looked the place over years before when you first got the idea. Then there were places for sale in the valley much better adapted for you all. Large house (any could have been "fixed up" sufficiently), big cellars, gardens, etc. Now I don't know of a "farm" up here for sale & it would be so much better for you. There's only Hans Salo's up at the foot of the hill by the schoolhouse, & that fills all specifications except it's a mile from us.

Couldn't you try this? Not tear up your roots there completely. Come for the summer with a minimum of household goods. Live in your house, feel it out, look around, & if it's to be for good, in that or any other house up here, one or both of you could go back & wind up your affairs. But in the meantime let it pend?

Maybe I'm butting in more than I should but these things have come up recently in my mind & must out. Hank might have come & worked this preliminary business with us himself. As it is, why don't you all come, in the summer?

There's another thing. Hank will presumably want & expect to earn his living up here. Of course he can sugar with us & that'll bring in some cash, but does he know what else he will do here for ready money? Hire out in some gang to lumber? If there were timber on his own place he could cut cord wood to sell, or have cows or chickens, but not on the few acres of the cabin site!

It all seemed so nice when you were here. It was summer & the birds were peeping, etc. Now it's cold winter & the snow drifting against the windows & these grim thoughts appear & reappear. Think them over, will you?

Of course we want you in the valley. That's taken for granted. Now, can it be done & is it practicable? It's for you to decide.

Love, Helen

Jamaica, Vt. April 5 [1944]
Dear Hank,

Thanks for your letter. I'm glad I didn't put you off the Valley (not that I tried. I was only being realistic & watching out for your interests so you'd know more what you're getting into.)

About sugaring. Of course we expected & want your help. Cooperatively (on a share basis if possible) or on a "hire" basis, which we don't like so well. As for other earn-your-living work. We've already got as much as we can tackle paying out every week for Vernet & Charlie. As long as we can afford it & as long as they will we'd like to keep them on. I know we couldn't swing a third man, & even Charlie is only possible on account of the high price of timber & wood right now. Come low prices Charlie'll probably have to go & with correspondingly low wages Vernet possibly too, to find something more remunerative. When we came here wages were $2.50 a day & they might well go back to that. There's no possible guarantee of such these days.

The first time I see Mary Salo (we're up to our ears in sugaring & rarely get off the place) I'll ask her about farm. Report has it they want $3,000. Jack Lightfoot's place opposite might be for sale sometime, probably at $4,000! Ten years ago all these places were near $2,000.

No time for more now. But please write your further reactions.

Love to you both, Helen

By the time World War Two was over, Helen and Scott had subdivided and sold off three parcels of land with houses (two of which they had built and the third they had added onto). At that point they still owned about 90 percent of their original spread — the large Tibbets tract, the Linscott property, the Hoard property, and a few acres from the Ellonen property.

Scott says in ***Living the Good Life***:

> As things turned out, we never got into the timber business, nor did we make use of the Tibbets tract. After paying taxes on it for about

18 years, we found that it carried an estimated two and a half million board feet of merchantable timber and the lumber barons were after it. The great increase in lumber prices due to the war of 1941-45 had made the Tibbets tract worth more than 10 times the amount we paid for it in 1933. Since this increment was due, not to any efforts of ours, but to the growth of the United States in population and wealth, and particularly to participation in war, we made up our minds that we would not profit in any way from the butchering of the trees....

This all sounds very egalitarian and high-minded. But was it true? Did they really never get into the timber business? How else can Helen's note to Hank in 1944 — that she and Scott were able to keep two men on the homestead's weekly payroll (!) only because of "the high price of lumber and wood right now" — be explained? What else could those two men be doing relative to that high price, if not cutting down trees and hauling them off to be turned into lumber or wood pulp for paper?

How much did Helen and Scott net from their employment of these men? Did Helen and Scott only try to break even on the stumpage, as a humanitarian way of providing much-needed local employment? Was the price of lumber so high that, once they did a little logging, the men could be assigned to do other necessary work on their property?

Or, by employing those two men, were the Nearings looking to recover the original purchase price of the woodlot? If selling off some of the wood allowed them to recover the purchase price of the land, is that why Scott felt he could give the property away?

....So we deeded the entire Tibbets tract to the town of Winhall in 1951.

Whatever the motivation, the facts are clear. Helen and Scott on Jan. 2, 1951 did indeed deed over 550 acres of land in Jamaica — 60 percent of their original 930 acres — to the town of Winhall for a municipal forest. Five hundred of those acres were from the original Tibbets tracts, and were by then in Scott's name alone, while the other 50 included 32 acres of the original Hoard property and the remaining portion of the Ellonen property that Scott and Helen still owned.

Oddly, what the Nearings don't explain in their book is why the town of Winhall got a municipal forest located in the town of Jamaica. The simple answer is that they offered it to Jamaica first, and got turned down. That rejection was an indication of the level of suspicion and distrust that had built up between the Nearings and their neighbors during their tenure in Vermont.

While not mentioning the Jamaica controversy, Helen in *Loving and Leaving the Good Life* does say that even in neighboring Winhall the gift was viewed with suspicion.

> The town grudgingly accepted it, judging it was some sort of tax dodge. They could not conceive it was given out of the goodness of his heart...My half of the property, when sold, enabled me to buy the place in Maine.

We talked with Winhall selectmen Ted Freedman during our September 1998 research trip to Vermont. He said that the town has awarded only two logging contracts on that property in the past five decades. Once was right after the town acquired the tract, the other about 25 years later. Other than that, the mountaintop was being used only by a local trapper who had permission to set a line of traps. The town official said the property was probably due for another log harvest sometime soon.

The selectmen also pointed out that ownership of the tract was not without its costs. Under Vermont law, municipal forests are not exempt from property taxes. In 1997, the town of Winhall paid the town of Jamaica $2,200 in property taxes.

In August 2003, the town of Jamaica sent the town of Winhall a bill for $3,460.74 for the 2003 property taxes on what it listed as 509 acres of land. Town valuation of that tract was placed at $136,400.

It would appear that now, every year, the town of Winhall is paying the town of Jamaica about the same or more in property taxes than Scott and Helen originally paid to buy the acreage 70 years ago.

On Oct. 19, 1951, Helen K. Nearing bought 140 acres of land in Harborside, Maine, from Mary W. Stackhouse who, Helen wrote, "had found it too lonely for one woman to live way out on the point of Cape Rosier." She had owned the property about six years. Property transfer tax stamps tell us the farm cost Helen about $7,500. No mortgage is recorded. "There was a bubbling spring on the edge of the woods that ran by gravity into the kitchen," the authors reported

On Jan. 4, 1952, Helen Knothe Nearing sold 65 acres of the Hoard land with its stone house and other buildings in Winhall, Vt. to George B. and Jacqueline Breen, for $15,000. The Breens had just sold their home in Hartford, Conn. for $18,000. Helen says in *Loving and Leaving the Good Life* that she and Scott sugared one last time, in the spring of 1952, before moving on to Maine.

This is what Helen had to say about the Breens, in *Loving*...

> We sold the place to an apparently likely couple who later became real-estate developers, benefiting from the proximity of Stratton Mountain, the largest ski area in the East at the time. Our forest farm and sugar bush became cluttered with cottages and seasonal folk. Our experience was typical for rural Vermont in the past four decades.

In *Making of a Radical* Scott says the Breens eventually sold "the buildings and part of the farm for $90,000." That was six times what the Breens had paid Helen for it.

Indeed, both Nearing sugarhouses have been converted to human housing. Nearing's beautiful stone house on the last 12 acres is now owned (and has been stunningly restored, remodeled and expanded) by Darlene and Ernest Palola. And on the hill behind the stone house is Forest Farm Estates, filled with 30- and 40-year-old chalet-style houses.

But the implication that the Breens had broken some sort of trust, in my opinion, was not fair to the Breens. Apparently in an attempt to stave off the inevitable, the Nearings had added a clause in their sales agreement with George — if he sold off any part of the farm within five years, he would have to split the profits with the Nearings.

It doesn't look like Breen watched that deadline very carefully. He sugared that bush for 13 years before he created Forest Farm Estates, during which time he was a major player in two Vermont sugaring organizations. In fact, George Breen may have been the first one to experiment with using rubber tubing as a way to collect sap in a sugarbush, a development which revolutionized the industry.

And, remember, when Helen sold Stan Joseph that 22 acres, stone-walled garden and old house in 1980, she sold it for 10 times what she had paid Mary Stackhouse for the entire 140 acres, including that same house, in 1952.

Greg Joly recently found among Helen's papers a clipping of an article headlined "Life in a Guru's Wake," dated Aug. 30, 1983, written by Jackie Breen. We tried to pin down which newspaper had run it, but none we asked claimed it. We also could not locate Jackie Breen. We would like to think the author and newspaper would approve of our reprinting the story here.

Life in a Guru's Wake
By Jackie Breen

It was "The Maple Sugar Book," written by Scott and Helen Nearing, that took me and my young family to Vermont in the early '50s, on invitation of the authors. We were to learn that, indeed, many hundreds of people like ourselves had made the trek to that remote mountain valley in the lap of Stratton where the Nearings created "the good life" for themselves on their hillside maple farm.

We bought their Forest Farms, as the place was called, in 1952, and the Nearings moved to a new challenge on Penobscot Bay in Maine. Scott died there last week at the age of 100. He was almost 70 years old when they left Vermont with a few buckets of his precious compost and, if he had had his way, very little else. I remember watching them pack their things, ceiling high in the car, and was not at all surprised to hear later that Scott pulled up to the closest dump that day and, while Helen protested in tears, flung everything over the bank and drove off.

There was much for them to teach us, a suburban family, that spring of '52, starting with the skills of maple sugaring, maple candy-making and packaging, but mostly Scott and Helen were determined to "hook" us into good nutrition. My first contribution to their vegetarian table was a disaster which I later called my "apple pie sacrilege" — white flour, refined sugar, butter, "dead" apples. I faced Scott timidly across the long plank table in their kitchen, the pie between us, and just waited as he put the first forkfull into his mouth.

"I'm afraid to say that you are a good cook," he said. "Now, if you ate these apples raw, you'd all be better off."

The Adelle Davis nutrition books came after that, I met my first bean sprout in the Nearing kitchen and learned to compost "anything" that had a name.

The farm had all, but not modern conveniences. Just to flush the toilet, one carried a pail of water from the pump in the kitchen, through the living room and hall (on different levels) to the opposite end of the farmhouse. Always, the water slopped. There was no gracious way to do it. After two years, we broke down and modernized.

We tried to refrigerate with our very cold spring water, gravity fed through coils in a box and it worked beautifully. Only the floor under the box rotted out from condensation in a short time. The refrigerator came back into our lives after that.

How many times over these 31 years have I heard the same question — why did they leave? Especially perplexed were the many who had visited their Forest Farms. It was a splendid place and complete. The organic gardens, three of them, could not be improved upon, the nine buildings were all in top condition, the tool shed supplied with everything to maintain order on the place, wood sheds full, a cleared maple sugar bush with four miles of sap collecting pipes on the forest floor.

I felt sure in my early years farming there that it was the numerous people from all over the world, who dropped by mostly without notice, that drove them away. Sometimes during the summer months, a dozen or more groups or families per week came to Forest Farms. They wanted to meet the Nearings, study organic gardening, see the farm, discuss politics, learn to build with stone, to survive on little — whatever. Some stayed for days, even weeks. I came to realize that these "visitors" were really "students" and an important part of Scott's life, for he was a bone-deep teacher, and the farm was one of his favorite classrooms.

The answer to the question, "Why leave?" I believe, is that, creative as the Nearings were, and as healthy as they were, they needed the new challenge to feel fully alive so they went on.

On Jan. 12, 1954, Helen and Scott sold the entire Linscott property in Vermont, all 215 acres of it, to author and longtime friend Pearl Buck, whose married name was Pearl S. Walsh. With that, the Nearing/Knothe land ties to Vermont were severed.

Behind the Blueberry Curtain

In Maine, after a few disappointing years trying to sell vegetables, Scott decided they would plant hybrid high-bush blueberries for a cash crop. It was another high-value, luxury commodity. (As hard as it may be for people in Maine and Vermont to believe, millions of people in this country have gone their entire lives without once tasting real maple syrup or fresh blueberries.)

But blueberry bushes are slow-growing plants. After setting out 228 two-year-old blueberry plants early in their Maine experience, they record in ***Continuing the Good Life*** that:

> "in 1957 we picked 5 ½ quarts; in 1958, 60 quarts; in 1960, 120 quarts. In a word, it was seven years before we had blueberries for sale. Thereafter the pick rose steadily to 655 quarts in 1965, 1034 quarts in 1970; and 1296 quarts in 1971, which was our banner year. Since then we pick around 800 quarts.

At $3 (plus or minus 50 cents) a quart, even at the peak of production, the Nearings' blueberry sales would have at best brought in about what Keith and I were then living on. So, in theory, a homesteader could function on blueberries as a cash crop — if they could get past the first seven start-up years.

But theory did not match reality when it came to the Nearings' blueberries.

A one-page detailed accounting of the blueberry project's planting and production costs, found in the Nearing papers years later by Greg Joly, showed that 20 years after the blueberries were planted, the Nearings still had not recouped their investment in plants, upkeep costs and equipment expenses. From 1952 to 1971, planting, upkeep and equipment expenses totaled $18,445.95, while berry income (including blueberries, strawberries and raspberries) totaled $11,616.20, for a net loss of $6,829.75.

What is not recorded on the one-page account sheet is how many of the boxes picked were actually sold. For instance, their best income year was 1971, Helen's "banner year," when sales of blueberries and some of the 156 raspberry boxes picked brought in $610.95. Doing the math, it would appear they sold about one out of every six blueberry quarts picked. Some of the rest were taken home by the pickers who picked on shares (no labor costs are mentioned in Scott's accounting). Many were fed to workers and guests, some were given away, still more were frozen (and later sprinkled liberally on bowls of ice cream).

The bottom line on the berry venture is that the Nearings had no blueberry income until 1960. And two decades after planting the bushes, they still had not recovered start-up and maintenance costs. But even if the expenses are totally disregarded, at the peak of production the Nearings simply did not make a living on the sale of their berries. In good years, according to their berry income figures, sales may have covered their property taxes.

So if their "cash crop" did not cover their living expenses, what did the Nearings do for money?

They had bought the Maine farm for half of what the Breens had paid for the Vermont property, so there was a cushion there.

And they may have had some money left from the settlement of the estate of Scott's father in 1940.

According to Scott's son Robert, Scott's father Lewis made his fortune from the wholesale liquor business and by running the company store at the mine owned by Scott's grandfather W. S. Nearing. Interviewed in the fall of 2002, Robert Nearing said all of Lewis Nearing's children, including Scott, split the proceeds from the sale of the family's estate and holdings.

"I'm sure it was one million bucks in 1940," Robert said. "Scott kept his share to write a book." He remembered his Aunt Dorothy commenting that Scott's "writing a book was the last thing Papa would want" to have happen with his money.

"When they wanted to make a trip, the subject of money never came up, only the timing," Robert Nearing noted. "They argued only about their love life, but not about money."

Also, a few years before Helen and Scott left Vermont, three other sources of income converged for Scott. In ***Making of a Radical*** Scott explained that in September 1950 he became eligible for

> a minimal monthly Social Security check based on my work with Federated Press in the 1920s and 1930s.

Some are surprised that Scott would have accepted a government check from a government he clearly despised. After all, when President Harry S Truman dropped the atomic bomb on Hiroshima on Aug. 6, 1945, Scott's 62nd birthday, he wrote President Truman a note, saying "Your government is no longer mine."

But I do not see any contradiction here. Since Scott was a socialist at heart, the concept of a national income security plan for retired people, which we know as Social Security, was certainly compatible with Scott's professed beliefs. Social Security — and the First Amendment which kept him out of jail in 1919 — were probably the only pieces of the U.S. federal government that Scott saw any benefit in.

According to Social Security records, he did not get a lot of money. Although computer records don't go back to his first check, Scott's monthly benefit in 1962 was $40, grew to $70.40 in 1972, and was at a high of $182.90 when he died in 1983. (Although he turned 65 in 1948, he earned credits toward his Social Security as late as 1967-69, when he had a regular World Events column in ***Monthly Review***.)

But Scott also mentioned two other revenue sources which, unlike Social Security, do not seem at all in keeping with his anti-bank, anti-capitalist philosophies. Those were:

> a modest annuity from paid-up insurance policies, and a like amount from a trust fund left by my sister Mary [which] keep me on the black side of the ledger.

This is how Scott explained the insurance annuity:

> I hit on a scheme that has paid off handsomely over the years. I estimated that my maximum earning period would probably be in the years before I was forty. Income would be greatly reduced after forty, if, as seemed likely, society's axe fell on me for speaking out. So I worked out an insurance policy on which I would pay premiums from age 25 to 45, pay nothing from 45 to 65, and be paid an annuity from

65 to the end of my life. Should I die in the years from 25 to 65, the policy provided full coverage for my family. I took this proposition to several insurance companies. They accepted it. Since then, this 'double contingent endowment' policy has been widely sold.

Notice that Scott had worked out this "scheme" when he was 25, in 1908.

In 1972 in ***Making of a Radical*** Scott gave those annuities from several insurance companies credit for giving him the freedom to do what he saw as his life's work:

I have been able to live for the last 20 years modestly on the insurance checks which these policies have provided. Meanwhile I could devote most of my time, and the greater part of my energy, to educational work. I did not have to cater to special interests or fear what consequences might arise from my words or actions. Orally and in writing I could help to build them into the life of the local and the larger communities.

Yes, it is so much easier to be philosophical, dogmatic, eccentric, or even radical, when you don't have to worry about where your next dollar is coming from.

After laying out those three sources of income — Social Security, insurance annuities, his sister Mary's trust fund — Scott wrote in 1972:

In place of my last regular academic job, which I lost more than 50 years ago, I have built as solid an economic base from which to carry on my educational work as one can hope to establish in a society founded on private capitalist monopoly and international piracy.

That's quite a statement, considering he had just explained how the bulk of his economic base was structured on the very private capitalist monopolies and international piracy he deplored. The income that gave Scott the freedom to write and proselytize the last half of his life came either directly from those awful banks that he detested so much, or from investments in Corporate America, multi-nationals, or the highly successful military-industrial complex.

Although they budgeted carefully, did grow a lot of their food, worked hard and didn't spend much money, it was banks, stocks, annuities, monetary gifts, inheritances, and unearned income from other people's labor that kept Scott and Helen going for most of their frugal homesteading lives, as far back as the early sugaring days in Vermont.

"Helen told me Scott died without a penny in his pocket," Robert Nearing said. "I believe that. He was smart enough to put it into this place," referring to Forest Farm and Social Science Institute. "He told me he wouldn't leave me a nickel, so I expected that. Although, the $1,000 insurance policy went to me."

The other side of the ledger

And that's just Scott's side of the ledger. We know very little about Helen's contribution to their financial stability, beyond the fact that its very foundation came from the land purchases her unexpected inheritance allowed in Vermont. Her family also owned a successful clothing store in New Jersey. Her father died in the 1940s (warranting a *New York Times* obit), her mother in the 1950s, after Helen and Scott moved to Maine. Presumably there was an inheritance.

Helen began receiving Social Security in January 1968, based on her own earnings, not on her status as a dependent wife. What earnings? In one letter to the Mayers, Helen mentioned that Social Science Institute paid her $50 a week to do the paperwork and book orders. Social Security records show credits earned, all from self-employment, in the Maine years 1955-64, 1969-72, 1977, 1979-83, 1986-87, 1991-92, and 1994. The records do not show the type of self-employment she claimed, but those years seem to coincide with the writing and publishing of several of their books.

Helen's first monthly Social Security check of $52.90 in 1968 grew to monthly payments of $795.10 by the time she died 27 years later.

For the five years from 1986-1990, Helen also received what Social Security records describe as a pension from Penn Mutual Life Insurance Company of Horsham, PA. The Social Security official I talked to said the pension was not large, did not impact the Social Security payouts, and might possibly have been a widow's pension.

In *Loving...*, Helen stated,

> We have separate economies and bank accounts, and handle our financial affairs independently of each other. On occasion we borrow and lend to each other, and have joint family accounts which I keep and present for settlement a couple of times a year.

One day, well after Scott had died, I decided to broach the subject which had long been a matter of heated debate among those of us who had tried to function within the confines of their stated economic bounds. I asked Helen the question.

And she admitted to me that "of course" both she and Scott "had money" from sources other than their cash crops and books. She was reluctant to elaborate.

Non-profit realities

But what about the income they had from their books and lecture fees? Scott repeatedly dismissed that income as if it were all self-contained.

In *Continuing the Good Life* he wrote:

> Our supply of printed matter, postage and stationery comes to us via our Social Science Institute, to which organization we hand over all royalties and lecture fees. Our travel expenses are paid by those who ask us to talk.

And, indeed, at the annual meetings of the Social Science Institute (a non-profit organization which therefore has to have a board of directors and an annual meeting) the accounting showed that to be the case.

I attended a couple of those meetings, which were scheduled for August at Forest Farm to allow board members (all old friends) to combine business with Scott's birthday celebration. The annual report detailed income in the neighborhood of $18,000 to $20,000 in the years I attended, with expenses for postage, shipping, newspaper and magazine subscriptions, printing of Scott's less-popular writings, "research," buckets of peanut butter and other food for the visitors and itinerant workers who helped with farm and building projects, all carefully documented. These figures did not include on-the-road expenses paid by lecture hosts. A few years later, I heard the board gave Eliot grant money to buy a tractor for his farm. As on any good non-profit accounting sheet, the income and expenses matched perfectly.

In my early days in Maine, when I acted as their secretary, or transcribed manuscripts for presentation to publishers, my name was on that annual accounting. But so was Helen's. And when that happened, when Social Science Institute paid Helen Nearing for her accounting and secretarial services, the line between bread labor and avocational pursuits blurred.

A book and royalty income of $18,000 in the waning days of the popularity of *Living the Good Life* was a heck of a lot of cash at a time when Keith and I were living on about $3,000 a year. And the impact of that income was far from self-contained. Those legitimate business expenses added greatly to the "good" in the Nearings' good life.

In *Making of a Radical*, Scott makes that point:

> How did we manage, on a subsistence basis, to finance our travels at home and abroad? Beginning in 1913, with the unlimited mileage allowance provided for me by the Ladies Home Journal in connection with some articles on progressive education, I have never lacked travel money. Numerous trips to Europe, to Latin America, and to Asia were paid for by lecture fees which I received on my return and by my writings. The sale of books and pamphlets at meetings held in North America has often added to travel funds. An important travel assistance has been the generous provision of room and board by friendly hosts and hostesses all over the world.

Their normal routine was to spend three to five months every winter on the road. Every other year, they would spend those winters traveling abroad.

Because Keith and I didn't write and sell books, we couldn't afford the magazine and newspaper subscriptions (all legitimate business expenses) like those that filled the Nearing mailbox — although I did get a free newspaper when I worked for the ***Bangor Daily News***.

Because we didn't give lectures to people who paid our travel expenses, we didn't get to see as much of the world as the Nearings did — although my relatives were generous with gas money if we visited them.

We didn't have a tax-free "research" account to cover phone bills, postage, car expenses or trips to non-lecture locations all over the world. The people who stayed with us and helped us with our building projects were fed what came out of our own garden and food we bought with our meager "working out" income — and we were thankful for the help.

It's not that it is impossible to live the homesteading part of the good life the way the Nearings recommended. We did it, and so did hundreds of other young idealists.

But by now I knew why our version of "the good life" didn't match the pictures in the book.

Living the Good Life indisputably changed my life, and I think for the better. It came along just at the right point, presenting the perfect solution for a husband who, by his own admission, did not fit into traditional society. Their book provided the assurances I needed that a different way was not only possible for us, but desirable. Like most people, I took from the book what my soul said I needed, and pretty much ignored the rest — at least for the time being.

Even though I was in my 20s when we moved to Harborside, I finished growing up under the Nearing wing. I learned that the simple life may be uncluttered, but it is indeed not simple, that life itself only grows more complex the older one gets.

I learned that these riveting writers and gardeners were not only not perfect, but that each had a very colorful past. The more I have learned about their earlier lives, the more fascinated I have become.

It was reassuring to me that one did not have to have lived a perfect early life to get to the point late in life, as they apparently did, of being able to live in harmony and peace with oneself and with others. That alone gives me hope.

For the Nearings, homesteading was a means to an end. For us and hundreds like us, homesteading was an end in itself. That different focus colored many of our choices and perceptions, as we tried to integrate the Nearing teachings into our daily lives.

Long ago, I realized that other "followers" of the Nearings might want to learn some of the realities behind the Nearing philosophies, and to have an active discussion about the inconsistencies in their many profound messages.

That's one of the reasons I wrote this book — because, unlike the good doctor who refused to confirm that she gave the Nearings monthly B-12 shots in their later years, I do have sympathy for people who believe everything they read in a book, and then go out and try to live their lives by it.

> How Many a Man Has Dated
> A New Era In His Life From
> The Reading Of A Book.
> — Henry David Thoreau

Afterword

Research for this book turned up some other tidbits that might be of interest to Nearing friends and followers.

For instance, the book we ordered from Book of the Month Club in 1971 was *Living the Good Life: How to Live Sanely and Simply in a Troubled World*, published by Schocken Books. It was a hardcover edition, second printing.

But the book published by Social Science Institute in 1954 had a this title: *Living the Good Life: Being a plain practical account of a 20-year project in a self-subsistent homestead in Vermont together with remarks on how to live sanely and simply in a troubled world.*

Whew!

Also, the inviting Afterword in our 1970 edition, the welcoming phrasing that I felt made it OK for Keith and me to simply drop in on the Nearings when we were in the neighborhood, had disappeared by the 9th printing in 1972.

Our hardcover edition had these three paragraphs:

> ...Flocks of young people have visited our Vermont and Maine homesteads. Many of them have been impressed by our way of life and have decided to try out homesteading for themselves.
>
> In the 1930's homesteading in the United States attracted a trickle of interest. Today the trickle has become a steady stream.
>
> We welcome the trend and assure our fellow homesteaders that audacity, courage, persistence, careful planning and plenty of good, hard work will bring abundant and satisfying rewards in this field as they have in so many other aspects of human experiment and experience.
>
> Helen and Scott Nearing
>
> Harborside, Maine
> April 1970

In the 1972 paperback copy that I picked up many years later, those paragraphs are gone from the Afterword, replaced with:

> ...Countless people, young and old, have visited our Vermont and Maine homesteads. Many of them have been impressed by our way of life and have decided to try out homesteading on their own account. A sight of the place and us at work seems to add to what

they have learned from the book, so we are happy to share our experience with them on the spot.

It is easy to add a bit of water to the soup to stretch it for a crowd or mix up some oats and oil and raisins for extra horse-chow when unexpected visitors drop in, but putting up people is another thing, In Maine we no longer have a guest house or space to lodge visitors, but we are glad to meet and talk with those who are earnestly seeking, who write to us in advance and come to Forest Farm at times convenient to them and to us. On any other basis numerous visitors would disrupt the daily routines of our good life.

Helen and Scott Nearing

Harborside, Maine
April 1970

I cannot fathom how our land-hunting trip to Stetson — as well as the entire course of my life — would have been different if our working copy of *Living the Good Life* had contained those later words.

Now for some updates:

On Cape Rosier, the 412 acres across from the Nearings that Central Maine Power had coveted has become an expensive subdivision sprouting several million-dollar homes. With all that new property tax money, the town has improved and repaved the road past the Nearings' old homestead, all the way to the north entrance to the subdivision. It also repaved the road less traveled — the left turn at the Grange fork in the road — through Cliffordville all the way out to the south entrance of that same subdivision. The dirt road in between, running past my old homestead and the Coleman farm, has been nicely graded and ditched.

No power plant was ever built on the uninhabited 900-acre Sears Island. After a cargo port was rejected for environmental reasons, in 1997 the state quietly bought the island from the railroad that owned it. It is said the last and largest uninhabited island in Penobscot Bay may be turned into a state park.

Also in 1997, Maine Yankee, the state's only nuclear power plant, located in Wiscassett, was prematurely and permanently shut down for safety reasons, 11 years before its license to operate was due to expire.

In the late 1970s, President Jimmy Carter signed the precedent-setting Indian Land Claims Settlement, clearing all those deeds and titles to two-thirds of the land in the state of Maine. Since claims on the $8 million settlement were based on proven Native American lineage, it suddenly became a good thing to be a Penobscot or Passamaquoddy Indian. People who had hidden or ignored their ancestors were newly proud of their heritage. It was a positive and empowering turn of events, both financially and psychologically.

A few years ago, after a couple of decades of health departments across the country forbidding restaurants from using wooden cutting boards because of the assumption that loosely grained wood would harbor germs, someone finally did a test. It turned out that the government-approved plastic boards were loaded with creepy-crawlies that hung in there despite thorough cleanings, while the ordinary wooden cutting boards seemed to have an innate antiseptic quality that killed germs naturally.

Three cheers for those wooden bowls in the Nearings' kitchen.

Also, it turns out that vegetarians can come pretty close to duplicating the protein found in meat by combining a legume and a grain in the same meal. Like beans and rice. Or split pea soup and crusty whole-grain bread. Hmm. How about wheat grass and alfalfa sprouts?

Maybe Tuck wasn't so crazy after all.

After initially warming to the idea of rejoining the two properties for a learning center, Stan Joseph's brother Jay decided to keep the old Nearing/Joseph homestead in his family, at least for the time being. Like many homes in the area, it gets limited seasonal use. The house itself has seen some modifications and improvements, and the fields have been kept neatly trimmed. But the famous wall built by Helen and Scott to protect their quarter-acre garden has been breached on two sides, and the last time I saw it, the fertile ground inside those walls sported a tangle of head-high weeds. The walls are falling down because the cement between the rocks is beginning to crumble. Scott was miserly in his cement mix, adding as little dry cement as possible to the beach sand and water, presumably to save money. Helen, on the other hand, used a rich mix for her pointing, smoothing off the top of the walls and filling in the spaces around the rocks on the wall faces with her small trowel. On some sections of what is still standing, it is clear that Helen's efforts are the only thing holding the remaining structure together.

In the summer of 2003, as this book was being finalized, Adele Costello, a widow in her 80s, put her 1820 farmhouse along with 26 acres in Bondville, Vermont, up for sale for $475,000. This is the core of the parcel that Helen and Scott bought in 1932 for "$300 down and an $800 mortgage" The Nearings had added a stone room with a fireplace, and sold 50 acres and the house to Adele and her husband Paul in 1943 for $1,900. Beautifully maintained over the 60 years it has been in the Costello family, the house was included in the Stratton Foundation Nearing Symposium house tour in June 2002. Adele, a gracious host during that tour, can no longer drive, and, according to Greg Joly, is moving to Alaska (yes, I know, where they don't have roads, but also where her daughter lives).

In March 1998, Carolyn Worthington Robinson, died of leukemia at the age of 83. Her obituary stated that she "literally wrote the book on homestead farming and practiced what she preached at Undercliff Farm on Cape Rosier." That book, ***Have-More Plan: A Little Land — A Lot of Living,*** written with her ex-husband Ed and first published in 1945, sold more than 700,000 copies, triple the number of copies of ***Living the Good Life***.

On October 30, 1999, Dorothy "Dottie" Cousins Gray, that down-to-earth native Mainer with a heart of gold who knew what was going on deep in the woods six miles from her farm, died after a brief illness. A member of the Cape Rosier Grange for 53 years, she was 67. I miss her.

Herbert L. Hutchinson Jr. died Aug. 29, 2001, at an Ellsworth nursing home. He was 81, which meant he was 56 when I first encountered him at that Brooksville Fire Department meeting in 1975. A fisherman most of his life, Herbie had served as a volunteer fireman in Brooksville for 40 years.

In mid-December 1999, Harborside Postmaster Dorothy Crockett abruptly resigned, giving the standard two-week notice. At the same time, she summarily evicted the U.S. Post Office from the annex of her home, under the terms of her decades-old lease.
The Harborside Post Office thus simply disappeared as of Dec. 31, 1999. All the Harborside mail is now channeled through the newly-built Brooksville post office just off Cape Rosier. New mailboxes have sprouted in front of homes within walking distance of Dottie's house.
On Jan. 1, 2002, two years and a day after her sudden retirement, Dorothy Rinehart Crockett died in a nursing home in Ellsworth. She was 91.

The Good Life Center is now an official non-profit organization. In September 1998, the Board of Directors received title to the Harborside real estate, including the stone house, garage, walled garden and about four acres of land overlooking Orr Cove, from Trust for Public Lands, whom Helen had chosen to oversee the formation of the new non-profit organization. A residential internship has been set up, and so far eleven people (including five couples) have lived at Forest Farm, tending the gardens, and greeting the visitors who still show up in droves.

The house for the most part remains the way the Nearings left it. The composting toilet is functioning well. The refrigerator and freezer are still out of sight in the basement, alongside the newly-added washing machine, bought to accommodate the resident stewards (two so far) who have had babies during their stays at Forest Farm

Since Helen left no endowment with the property, fund-raising to cover basic expenses, repairs and improvements is a continuing process. Book sales provide a substantial part of the operating budget. Donations and bequests are welcomed and encouraged.

Some of the major projects undertaken include work on the leaking metal roof and the crumbling stone chimney, both of which were beautifully redone in 2002. A small energy-efficient biodiesel heater has been installed in the new office set up in Scott's former workshop at one end of the stone garage. Plans for solar panels are in the works.

I have been a member of the Board of Stewards of the Good Life Center since its inception. A few years ago, at one of the semi-annual meetings of that group, held at Forest Farm in Harborside, the subject of Scott's first wife came up.

Scott's granddaughter Elka Schumann told us that the story of Nellie Seeds Nearing and her house full of doilies was another fabrication of Helen's. Elka was only a girl when Nellie died, but she said she never saw a single doily in her grandmother's spare, neat, almost Spartan house.

Ellen LaConte, the woman Helen designated as her biographer and to whom Helen left the bulk of her financial assets, has been busy doing what Helen wanted her to do — writing the truth about Helen as Helen told her and as Ellen saw it.

Ellen's first book, ***On Light Alone, a Guru meditation on the Good Death of Helen Nearing***, was published by Loose Leaf Press exactly a year after Helen's death.

She followed that the next year with the chapbook ***Free Radical: A Reconsideration of the Good Death of Scott Nearing***. In it, Ellen explained very delicately and humanely that Helen's public version of Scott's death was a myth. Helen had told Ellen the truth, almost as if in confidence — that Scott had been failing for some time, had probably had a stroke 10 months before, that it was all Helen and young friend Nancy Richardson Berkowitz could do to keep him clean, fed and comfortable. When Nancy left for a few weeks, Helen did not have the strength to hold up Scott as she tried to move him, and fell with him. She was forced to face the fact that she needed help. A short stay in a nursing home was followed by a schedule of nurses and aides from Four-Town Nursing Service coming out to the house on a daily basis.

All of those details, of course, had been brought out in Mel Allen's article for *Yankee Magazine* published the month Scott died. But in the years after Scott's death, Helen had glossed over them, polished the hard and difficult details down so completely that they literally disappeared from her recounting, from her talks, from her book. (And yes, some of us have been guilty of reinforcing those gilded stories.)

But over the years Helen had heard from people who had not read Mel Allen's piece, and who had tried unsuccessfully to duplicate Helen's recounting of Scott's path toward a straightforward, clean, slow, deliberate suicide. And they wanted to know what they had done wrong, why it had been so hard, why Scott could do it and they couldn't. Unable to tell them herself, Helen was counting on Ellen to set them straight after she died.

In her chapbook, Ellen forgave Helen, understanding that Helen needed to maintain the myth of Scott as the giant of a man, to whom she had devoted her entire life. His death had to match his life, even if some of the details had to be bent in the telling.

But when the chapbook came out, Ellen started getting nasty letters. It seems that many people do not want to hear the truth about their heroes.

When *The Sun* magazine published extensive excerpts of Ellen's 26-page chapbook in its August 1998 issue, several people responded, praising Ellen for her information, and for her courage in setting the record straight.

However, Keith was among those who wrote a letter to the editor blasting Ellen for her temerity.

> Helen and Scott are gone. Writing revisions to the story of Scott's death serves no purpose. By writing of lies and myths at this time, LaConte has gone well over the line of propriety. Has she no shame?

When I read that letter to the editor, I had to smile. It serves no purpose to correct lies and myths? It is improper, even shameful, to tell the truth? No, it wasn't homesteading that had ended our marriage two decades before.

As for me — in 1996 I sold my Blue Hill farm to Scott Howell and Sarah Bushman. They still farm the property, have fixed up and added onto the old farmhouse, and run Organic Harvest in the old Hay's Farmstand building.

That same year, and despite my poor showing in the Democratic Congressional primary two years before, when it looked like no candidate who shared my views was willing to challenge Sen. William S. Cohen, I again threw my hat into the political ring. As Yogi Berra would say, it was déjà vu all over again. Cohen unexpectedly announced his retirement, and I suddenly found myself in a five-way Democratic primary, which was won by former Maine Governor Joseph Brennan (the same fellow who had apologized to Andre the Seal for calling him a "summer visitor").

My first two books were the direct result of those two runs for federal office.

The first book, **Proud to Be a Card-Carrying, Flag-Waving Patriotic American Liberal**, we published in September 1996. It is a compilation of 50 columns, speeches and essays that I wrote over the course of 15 years. It is dedicated

To Helen, who died as she had lived — going full blast.

In 2002, our newly-formed BrightBerry Press published my second book, *A Tale of Dirty Tricks So Bizarre: Susan Collins v. Public Record*. It is a behind-the-scenes look at how far Collins and the **Bangor Daily News** were willing to go to defeat Joe Brennan in that 1996 U.S. Senate race.

It occurred to me only later that, not only had I followed in Scott's homesteading footsteps, but my political campaigns had also closely paralleled his. He and I had both run for Congress, and then for a statewide office (his was for Governor of New Jersey in 1928). We both spoke our minds as clearly as we could to small but eager audiences, and we both lost our races — although he did considerably better than I.

David Bright and I are now married, and I am thankful every day that I too was able to find my soulmate. For many years after my divorce I had no hope that that would ever happen. And I am well aware that I would not be as happy as I am today were it not for what transpired on Cape Rosier — the good beginning and the bad ending — in the 1970s. Life holds many surprises, ironies, and twists of fate.

In May 1999, David and I bought a 30-acre farm in the hills of Dixmont, Maine. Part of an old dairy farm, the remodeled 1830 farmhouse came complete with two bathrooms, a dishwasher and a three-meter satellite TVdish. We aren't exactly homesteading, but we have planted three acres of raspberries and highbush blueberries on some of that pasture land, shooting for a productive, certified organic pick-your-own operation when the plants mature in a few years.

Meanwhile, we are reveling in the beauty of old elms and maples, magnificent trees unlike any of those which struggled to grow, but could not thrive, on the thin acid soil in Harborside. Thick stone walls, rusty barbed wire fences (which we are doggedly trying to extract) and old rock-lined wells abound. Our pastures have deep rich soil and generations of history. Two ponds irrigate our fields and gardens. We have watched fox confront Canada geese in our back field, wild turkeys scavenge in our harvested gardens, deer nibble the grass and bushes, a coyote set up a stake-out at the edge of the woods.

Like Cape Rosier, this farm and the hills that surround it emit a strong energy field that interrupts my thoughts. But here it is oh, so very different. The Harborside energy I feel as powerful and intense and one that says "Pay Attention!" The one here feels strongly centered, and says to me, "watch the birds," "look at that," "take care of me." "be at peace."

From the day the Nearings offered to sell us some of their land nearly three decades ago, I have felt a growing responsibility to tell this story. Helen's push, urging me to get it down and get it right, has intensified in the years since her death. Sometimes I have sensed it in the form of gentle help with writer's block. Other times she has been less than subtle.

Who but Helen could so seamlessly coordinate Greg Joly's trip to the Jamaica Town Hall on school board business with our showing up unannounced in that remote Vermont building looking for Nearing deeds? Or put that B-12 prescription slip in such an unlikely place? Or compel George Breen to take important missing documents to Forest Farm just when I needed them?

But now the memoir is done, and, right on schedule, I am feeling the pull to get back to the natural cycle of planting, tending to, picking, and politicking.

And so, here ends the accounting of my years living next door to the good life during the 1970s, and the reverberations from that experience in the two decades that followed.

It is what it is.

Read it any way you want.

Some of you might even get it.

Meanwhile,

I'm off and running on something else.

List of Family Photos

The photos in this book, unless otherwise indicated, came out my family photo album. I took most of the photos in which I'm not the subject. Family members or friends took the rest. None are professional quality, but are included to add a dimension to this story it otherwise would not have.

The old Nearing homestead as it appeared in the early 1950s. (from the Nearing archives)..5
Wooden bowls on a rack in the kitchen of Forest Farm. 20
That's me at 20 months of age, standing in front of my grandmother's vine-covered milkhouse. I'm blocking the view of my sister, Barbara. (Photo by Olga A. Hay, June 20, 1949)...25
That's me squaring a log with a hewing axe 35
The wooden bridge over our creek. Photo was taken from the cabin-side of the creek, looking toward the town road...42
I'm on the left, giving Scott and a friend a tour of our construction site. Helen is bending over, checking out our cement form work. 44
A close-up of the movable forms used to build the concrete walls. Notice the size of the rocks we used. 48
The sills are on, and the wooden ceiling in the root cellar is in place. 50
The post and bean frame of our cabin was coming together nicely. 74
Our experienced Glenwood cook stove...79
The first Harborside Hilton. (chicken coop) 84
Feeding baby Muffin. 87
I'm resting in the rocking chair from the Lodge. Note the bags of animal feed stacked to the ceiling, and the pumpkins under the bed. 108
The hand-cranked grain mill (as seen on TV) 114
Ashley stove...116
The southwest corner of the cabin with its large sun-catching windows....126
With dog Brandy standing guard, the baby goats use the couch to test their climbing skills. Month-old Becca is more interested in other things. 129
The Blake family grave marker. 143
An Aladdin kerosene lamp illuminates the tools of a homesteading time/date management system..160
The garage/workshop at the new Forest Farm, seen from the garden......200
The rear of the stone house. The greenhouse is on the right....................201
The canvas-covered couch in the northwest corner of the cabin...............242
I took this photo of Helen in May 1992. 326

Index

Alden, Robin, 36
Allen, Mel, 276, , 277, 296, 357, 358
Allen, Nancy, 301
Ames, George, 155
amulet, 1
Ana, Stan's last girlfriend, 3, 300, 302, 303
Andre, the seal, 206, 359
Andrews, Tom, 298, 299
Arnold, John H., (CMP rep), 175
ashram, 55, 56
B-12, vitamin, 193-196, 352, 360
Baldacci, John, 299
Barbara, Jean's sister, 25, 162
Barrows, Nat, 36
Beatty, Warren, 161
beehives, bees, 22, 27, 31, 86, 89, 90, 92, 100, 182, 195, 225
Berkowitz, Nancy Richardson, 282, 297, 303, 309, 316-318, 325, 357
Birdsall, Mollie & Paul, 221
Blake family, 143-155
Blake, Hiram, campground, 206
Blavatsky, Helena Petrovna, xi
Blue Hill Farm Inn, 105
blueberry, 19, 91, 94, 97-98, 108, 186, 189, 221, 345-346
Bodnar, Ted, 26
Bost, Steve, 311-314, 324
Boston Globe, The, newspaper, *vi*, 287
Boston Land Company, 155
Bowden, Hugh, 209
Brandy, the dog, 30, 81, 90, 98
Breen, George, 330, 342-344, 360
Breen, Jackie, *vi,* 330, 342-344

Brennan, Gov. Joseph, 206, 358-359
Bright, David, *vii*, 2-4, 314, 325, 330, 352, 359
Brownlow, Dr. Bradley, 94, 119, 121, 123-124, 215, 217
Brubaker, Brett, 198, 199, 200, 201, 267
Buell, Dave & Liz, 226
Bullfrog Films, 198, 199, 274
Buck, Pearl, 281, 345
Bush, Herbert H. W., President, 298
Bushman, Sarah, 358
canning lids, 91, 156, 157, 186
carrot croaker, 20, 163, 267, 311
Carter, Jimmy, 354
Carter, Jonathan, 297
Cassandra, Keith's sister, 90, 93, 108, 135-136, 157, 182
Catholic, 10, 54-55
Central Maine Power Company, 161-166, 174-175, 323, 354
chamber pot, 28-29
Chase, Dick, 67-68, 74, 100, 232
Chase, Jonathan, 296
Chase, Mary, 67, 173, 209
Chase, Sarah, 296
Christy, Sara, 300
CIA, 45-46, 61-62
Clark, Frances, 147
Clayton, Sarah, sandpit, 331
Clifford, Ferd, 155
Clinton, William, President, 298
Clinton, Hillary, First Lady, 306
Colson family, 145, 146, 150, 153, 154
Commercial Fisheries News, 36
Common Ground Fair, 304, 316-

317, 325
Condon, Richard, 145
Cook, Dr. Richard A., 194, 195
Costello, Adele and Paul, 337, 355
Crockett, Dorothy (Dottie), 47, 63, 314, 356
Croteau, Scott, 306-308
Damrosch, Barbara, 4
Darryl, Keith's brother, 24, 77, 85, 101, 108, 157-158, 223, 225, 238, 245, 247-249
Davis, Adele, 99, 120, 344
Dietrich, Dr. Mary, 195-196, 352
diphtheria, 138, 147, 148, 149, 150, 152, 153
doilies, 279, 357
Downs, Hugh, 264
Dyer, Fred, 137, 158, 180, 198, 199, 200, 248, 294, 337
Ellonen farm, 329-331, 337, 340-341
Ellsworth American newspaper, 144, 174, 321
Farr, Lura, 62
Farr, Phil, 62, 63, 170
FBI, 46, 61- 63, 306
Ferguson, the chicken, 81-82, 84
Fitzgerald, Diane, 315, 324
Forbes, Peter, 320, 326
Freedman, Ted, 342
French, Alice, 250
Garden Primer, 4
Gary, volunteer worker, 48-49, 52, 54-55, 58-60
Gaudette, Jeanne, 195, 315
Grandma, Jean's, 26-27, 91, 183, 212
Grandpa, Jean's, 26-28
Grandparents, Keith's, 9-10
Gray, Dorothy (Dottie), 43, 115, 121, 156, 160, 356

Gray, Otis, 154
Great Madness, pamphlet, 47, 286, 288
Grindle, Louise, Town Clerk, 144, 145, 147, 149, 168, 170
guru, 55, 56, 57, 285, 319, 343, 357
Hall, Susie, 36, 108
Hannah, 206, 212-214, 216, 223, 225, 233
Hazlegrove, Cary, photo by, 296
Hay, Olga, v, 73, 123, 211
Hay, Joseph C. Jr., 8, 27
Hoard, Mercy, farm, 329-333, 340-342
Hoey, Tom, 4
Hohner, Rob, 221
Holbrook Island Sanctuary, 154
Holocaust, 54
Horseshoe Market, 105
Howard, Jessie, 47
Howard, Tracy, 15, 43-44, 60, 92
Howell, Scott, 358
Hubbard, Albert, 271
Hudak, David, 172, 173
hunting, hunters, 13, 24-25, 97, 103, 104, 105, 107, 186, 220, 229, 240, 241,242, 253, 254, 311
Hurd, Floyd, 332-333
Hurlburt, Dr. Roger, 193-195
Hutchinson, Herbie, 169, 177, 356
icebox, ice tongs, 25, 26, 247, 338
Idora, 51-55, 58-60, 74
insurance, medical, 73, 85-86, 110
insurance policies, annuities, 189, 246, 325, 333, 347-349
Island Ad-Vantages newspaper, 144

Index

Jewish, 45, 54, 55, 60
Joey, Jean's brother, 85
Johnson, Doris Blake, 149, 150, 152
Jolly, the cow, 208, 223, 231
Joly, Greg, vii, 196, 330, 343, 345, 356, 360
Joseph, Stan, 1-4, 264, 275, 283, 284, 289, 293-296, 300-304, 309, 320, 325, 343, 355
Juno, the goat, 96, 128-130, 133
Karlin, Lynn, 4, 294-296, 302, 304
King, Dennis, 292-293, 297
Kraamer-Ferguson, E. M., architect, 198
Krishnamurti, 296, 321, 332
LaConte, Ellen, 289, 309, 317, 325, 330, 332, 357-358
LaGuardia, Fiorello, 47, 286
Lamaze natural childbirth, 95, 101, 118-119, 122
leghold traps, 97, 189
Levasseur, Rick, 307
Libby, Catherine, 149, 151
Libby, Russell, 316
Lightfoot family, 191, 340
Linscott, Charles & Linda property, 331, 333, 340, 345
mackerel, holy & otherwise, 4, 93, 137, 158
Maine Farm, A Year of Country Life, 4, 293-295, 309
Maine Magazine, 224, 226
Maine Organic Farmers and Gardeners Association (MOFGA), 171, 292, 304, 316
Maine Times, 319, 322
Mansfield, Jayne, 10
massage, foot, 64-67
Mayer, Hank & Ada, 252, 267, 274-276, 285, 294, 296, 330, 332, 335, 337-341
McCloskey, Robert, author, 145
McGowan, Patrick, 197
milkhouse, 25, 26, 27, 183
Mitchell, George, 299
MOFGA, 171, 292, 304, 316
Mom, *see* Hay, Olga
Mother Earth News, 270, 273
Muffin, the goat, 87-89, 90, 93, 96, 156, 250
Murray, Dr., 121-122
NBC-TV News, 111-114, 241, 261
Nearing, Nellie Seeds, 256, 289
Nearing, Robert, Scott's son, 275, 280, 287, 289, 290, 346, 348
Nearing, John Scott, Scott's son, 280
New York Herald, vi, 335
New York Times, 99, 102, 268, 287, 289, 349
Nicky, the goat, 96, 129-133, 208
Oliver, Ernest & Helen, 176
Organic Gardening magazine, 24, 109
Paddleford, Clementine, vi, 335
Palola, Darlene & Ernest, 196, 343
Pease, Mrs., from Rhode Island, 19, 114
Penobscot Bay Press, vi
Perot, Ross, 297-298, 324
placenta, 72, 73, 120, 123, 128, 183
postmaster, *see also* Crockett, Dorothy, 47, 60-62, 314
Providence Journal, 6, 12, 19, 23, 73, 89, 167
Puss-O, Helen's cat, 45, 189, 282
Reds, the movie, 161, 276
Reed, John, 161

Richardson Berkowitz, Nancy, 282, 297, 303, 309, 316-318, 325, 357
Richmond, Fred, 337
Riley, Wayne, 308
Robbins, Peter, 297
Robinson, Carolyn, 124-125, 133, 302, 356
Robinson, Ruth, 302
roto-tiller, 91, 116, 292
Saltwater Seasonings: Good Food from Coastal Maine, 296
Sasha, the goat, 90, 93, 96
sauna, 2, 67-69, 74, 173, 203, 235, 295, 301, 303
Schlosser, Frank, 173
Schumann, Elka, Scott's granddaughter, 287, 290, 357
Scott, John (Nearing), Scott's son, 280
Sears, Roebuck, 85-86, 88, 127, 225
Sears Island, Searsport, 163, 166, 174-176, 354
Self-Sufficient House, 197
Simpson, O. J., trial, 306
Smith, Perry, 105
Snowe, Olympia, 297-299, 306
Spirit Cove, 2
Spring, Mary Nearing, Scott's sister, 290
Springdale Farm, 208
Stackhouse, Mary W., 342-343
Stetson, Maine, 6, 14, 22, 311, 354
Stratton Foundation, 356
Stratton Mountain, Vermont, 6, 277, 287, 330, 342-343
Summers, Greg, 133-136, 172, 220, 223
Sun, magazine, 358
Tani, John, and his cabin, 30-31, 45, 64, 88, 98, 132, 136
Thoreau, Henry David, 283, 320, 352
Tibbets, John, woodlot, 329, 331
Tilghman, Ben, 337
traps, 97, 189, 342
Trowbridge, Dr. Nelson, 193-196
Trust for Public Lands, 313, 317, 320, 325, 326, 356
Tuck, 38-40, 355
Tyson, Forrest, 198, 199
United We Stand America, 297, 311
vaccine, vaccination, 138, 140, 141, 217
Van Der Leeuw, J. J. Koos, 332, 333
Varnum, Margaret Lord, 147
Venno, Lucy, 149, 153, 276
Vietnam, 9, 10, 11, 12, 17, 19, 37, 43, 50, 167, 183, 254, 262, 318, 323
Walking John, 189
Wall Street Journal, 99
Walsh, Pearl S., 345
Ward, Ken, 307
Ward, Kent, 170-171
Weekly Packet, 210, 299, 315, 318, 325
Wharton School of Economics, 46, 269, 287, 289
Whitcomb, Colby, 208
Whiteside, Elena, Scott's granddaughter, 289, 291
Whitfield, Stephen J., 283
Williams, Maureen, 168, 170, 266
Wilson, Jon, 221, 304
WoodenBoat magazine, 221, 304
Yankee Magazine, 173, 206, 209, 224, 277, 296, 354, 357

The Good Life Center
372 Harborside Road
Harborside, Maine 04642

Forest Farm
the last homestead of Helen and Scott Nearing
on Penobscot Bay in Harborside, Maine,
is open for visitors throughout the year.
Tour the Nearings' organic gardens
and their last hand-built stone home.

Hours **July and August** are 1-5 p.m. daily
Closed Wednesday.

September through June *Usually* open Thursday through Monday
1-5 p.m. *(Please call ahead to confirm --207-326-8211)*
Closed Tuesday and Wednesday.

Admission is free. But consider when you see the donation bowl that Helen and Scott did not leave the **Good Life Center** an endowment. At this time, it relies totally on donations and book sales to support the work of **The Good Life Center**. (We gently suggest $5 per person.)

Please check the Good Life Center website:

www.goodlife.org

for more information including
a list of available books, with prices
schedule for summertime Monday Night Meetings
applications for resident stewardship,
internships, etc.

e-mail: info@goodlife.org

Mission Statement

The mission of *The Good Life Center* is to perpetuate the philosophies and lifeways exemplified by Helen and Scott Nearing, two of America's most inspirational practitioners of simple, frugal and purposeful living.

Building on the Nearing legacy, *The Good Life Center* encourages and supports individual and collective efforts to live sustainably into the future. Guided by the principles of kindness, respect and compassion in relationships with natural and human communities, *The Good Life Center* promotes active participation in the advancement of social justice, creative integration of the life of the mind, body and spirit, and deliberate choice in living responsibly and harmoniously in an increasingly complicated world.

Proud to Be a Card-Carrying, Flag-Waving, Patriotic American Liberal

Direct from the grass roots to you, read what Jean Hay has to say...

...on liberalism: "Hate to tell you, folks, but taking your definition of a liberal from Rush Limbaugh is akin to taking your definition of a Jew from Hitler, either before or after he, as Marge Schott explained, 'went too far.'"

...on abortion rights: "I do not see my America in the Republican drive to declare the wombs of American women to be government property."

...on the military: "People who do not respect people of other genders or sexual orientation should not be issued weapons and taught how to kill."

...on career women having babies while single: "I have known such women, and I can find no fault with their decision -- or their children. ... I think it makes some men nervous when some women decide they can do without them."

...on violence: "Real men know how to control themselves."

also: "Do we really now live in a country where the neighbors can consider someone perfectly normal, except for the fact that he's killed a couple of people?"

...on the flag-burning amendment: "Better the flag than the federal building. The flag can take it."

...on seizing the opportunity: "When God hands you an apple, you bite."

$10

50 columns, essays, political speeches
184 pages plus 11-page appendix on National Economic Security Plan

Library of Congress Catalog Card Number 96-94746
ISBN 0-9657759-0-9

A Tale of Dirty Tricks So Bizarre: Susan Collins v. Public Record

Read how Maine's Republican Senate Candidate Susan Collins and the *Bangor Daily News* teamed up in the 1996 U.S. Senate race to create a scandal where none existed, all over someone who dared to look at her public record.

Read excerpts from sworn testimony at the 1999 libel trial against the *BDN* and political reporter/columnist John Day.

Read how, two years into Collins' first term as U. S. Senator, John Day and Collins' campaign manager Robert Tyrer, under oath, both pointed the finger at Susan Collins as the source of the information and named Susan Collins as the instigator of the public records "scandal."

Did the journalistic ploy work? The *Bangor Daily News* thought so. And the 1996 voting records support that view.

This is an insider's look at one U.S. Senate race, written by a woman who was a candidate for that office in Maine's Democratic primary that same year.

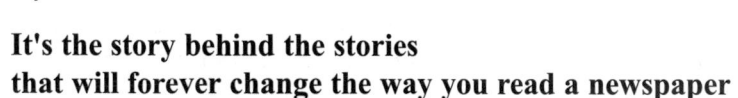

**It's the story behind the stories
that will forever change the way you read a newspaper**

128 pages
including scans of critical public records
that have since been destroyed

$10

Published in July 2002 by
BrightBerry Press
4262 Kennebec Road, Dixmont, Maine 04932

ISBN 0-9720924-0-4

Order Jean's books directly from the Publisher

Meanwhile, Next Door to the Good Life
360 pages
24 family photos
$20

A Tale of Dirty Tricks So Bizarre: Susan Collins v. Public Record
128 pages
$10

Proud to Be a Card-Carrying, Flag-Waving, Patriotic American Liberal
50 columns, essays & speeches
184 pages & appendix
$10

Please enclose $4 for Priority Mail for one book, plus $1 for each additional book to the same address. ($10 for shipping outside the U.S.) Maine residents add 5% sales tax

Send Check, Money Order or VISA/MasterCard numbers including expiration date, plus "ship-to" address, e-mail & phone number to:

BrightBerry Press
4262 Kennebec Road
Dixmont, ME USA 04932

www.brightberrypress.com
Phone 207-234-4225